CRIME, PRISONS, AND JAILS

ISSN 1938-890X

CRIME, PRISONS, AND JAILS

Kim Masters Evans

INFORMATION PLUS® REFERENCE SERIES
Formerly Published by Information Plus, Wylie, Texas

GALE
CENGAGE Learning·

Farmington Hills, Mich • San Francisco • New York • Waterville, Maine
Meriden, Conn • Mason, Ohio • Chicago

Crime, Prisons, and Jails

Kim Masters Evans

Kepos Media, Inc.: Steven Long and Janice Jorgensen, Series Editors

Project Editor: Laura Avery

Rights Acquisition and Management: Ashley Maynard, Carissa Poweleit

Composition: Evi Abou-El-Seoud, Mary Beth Trimper

Manufacturing: Rita Wimberley

Product Design: Kristine Julien

Cover photograph: © txking/Shutterstock.com.

While every effort has been made to ensure the reliability of the information presented in this publication, Gale, a Cengage Company, does not guarantee the accuracy of the data contained herein. Gale accepts no payment for listing; and inclusion in the publication of any organization, agency, institution, publication, service, or individual does not imply endorsement of the editors or publisher. Errors brought to the attention of the publisher and verified to the satisfaction of the publisher will be corrected in future editions.

Gale
27500 Drake Rd.
Farmington Hills, MI 48331-3535

ISBN-13: 978-0-7876-5103-9 (set)
ISBN-13: 978-1-4103-2558-7

ISSN 1938-890X

This title is also available as an e-book.
ISBN-13: 978-1-4103-3268-4 (set)
Contact your Gale sales representative for ordering information.

Printed in the United States of America
1 2 3 4 5   21 20 19 18 17

OCT   2017

TABLE OF CONTENTS

about probationers and parolees. Also featured are reform initiatives designed to reduce recidivism.

Juveniles commit and are arrested for crimes ranging from murder to curfew violations. This chapter supplies statistics on arrests of juveniles and their outcomes in the juvenile justice system. Changing approaches to juvenile delinquency are traced. Trends in confining juveniles as adults are reported and the characteristics of juveniles in residential placement are profiled.

PREFACE

Crime, Prisons, and Jails is part of the *Information Plus Reference Series*. The purpose of each volume of the series is to present the latest facts on a topic of pressing concern in modern American life. These topics include the most controversial and studied social issues of the 21st century: abortion, capital punishment, care of senior citizens, education, the environment, health care, immigration, national security, social welfare, water, women, youth, and many more. Although this series is written especially for high school and undergraduate students, it is an excellent resource for anyone in need of factual information on current affairs.

By presenting the facts, it is the intention of Gale, a Cengage Company, to provide its readers with everything they need to reach an informed opinion on current issues. To that end, there is a particular emphasis in this series on the presentation of scientific studies, surveys, and statistics. These data are generally presented in the form of tables, charts, and other graphics placed within the text of each book. Every graphic is directly referred to and carefully explained in the text. The source of each graphic is presented within the graphic itself. The data used in these graphics are drawn from the most reputable and reliable sources, such as from the various branches of the U.S. government and from private organizations and associations. Every effort has been made to secure the most recent information available. Readers should bear in mind that many major studies take years to conduct and that additional years often pass before the data from these studies are made available to the public. Therefore, in many cases the most recent information available in 2017 is dated from 2014 or 2015. Older statistics are sometimes presented as well if they are landmark studies or of particular interest and no more-recent information exists.

Although statistics are a major focus of the *Information Plus Reference Series*, they are by no means its only content. Each book also presents the widely held positions and important ideas that shape how the book's subject is discussed in the United States. These positions are explained in detail and, where possible, in the words of their proponents. Some of the other material to be found in these books includes historical background, descriptions of major events related to the subject, relevant laws and court cases, and examples of how these issues play out in American life. Some books also feature primary documents or have pro and con debate sections that provide the words and opinions of prominent Americans on both sides of a controversial topic. All material is presented in an evenhanded and unbiased manner; readers will never be encouraged to accept one view of an issue over another.

HOW TO USE THIS BOOK

In general, crime has been on the decline in the 21st century. Some crimes, however, are increasing in number among different segments of the population. For example, violent crime has decreased since the 1990s, whereas identity theft has increased. Besides exploring crime in the United States, this volume examines the U.S. penal system as well as its inmates. Prisons and jails are an important and controversial part of the effort to control crime in the United States. Much public funding is spent on the construction of new prisons and jails and on the maintenance of old facilities, but many people question the effectiveness of prisons and jails as a deterrent to crime. Who is locked up in U.S. prisons, what crimes have they committed, and how effective is the prison system? These and other basic questions are discussed in this volume.

Crime, Prisons, and Jails consists of 10 chapters and three appendixes. Each chapter is devoted to a particular aspect of crime, prisons, and jails in the United States. For a summary of the information that is covered in each chapter, please see the synopses that are provided in the

Table of Contents. Chapters generally begin with an overview of the basic facts and background information on the chapter's topic, then proceed to examine subtopics of particular interest. For example, Chapter 1, An Overview of Crime, describes the evolution of the criminal code and its moral basis. The legal system categorizes crimes as to their seriousness, a process that affects the severity of the punishments that are meted out for them by the justice system. Classes of crimes involving killing, nonlethal bodily harm, sex, theft, and alcohol or drug use are briefly summarized. Hate crimes, terrorism, crimes committed by immigrants, and cybercrime are also covered, because these topics are of particular interest in the early 21st century. Annual expenditures at various levels of the criminal justice system are reviewed, and polling results are presented to illustrate the state of public opinion about crime. The chapter ends with a discussion of criminal notoriety, the curious fascination that some infamous criminals have aroused throughout U.S. history. Readers can find their way through a chapter by looking for the section and subsection headings, which are clearly set off from the text. They can also refer to the book's extensive Index, if they already know what they are looking for.

Statistical Information

The tables and figures featured throughout *Crime, Prisons, and Jails* will be of particular use to readers in learning about this topic. These tables and figures represent an extensive collection of the most recent and valuable statistics on prisons and jails, as well as related issues—for example, graphics cover the number of people in jail or prison in the United States, the characteristics of those on probation, and the amount of money the government spends on the criminal justice system. Gale, a Cengage Company, believes that making this information available to readers is the most important way to fulfill the goal of this book: to help readers understand the issues and controversies surrounding crime, prisons, and jails in the United States and to reach their own conclusions.

Each table or figure has a unique identifier appearing above it for ease of identification and reference. Titles for the tables and figures explain their purpose. At the end of each table or figure, the original source of the data is provided.

To help readers understand these often complicated statistics, all tables and figures are explained in the text. References in the text direct readers to the relevant statistics. Furthermore, the contents of all tables and figures are fully indexed. Please see the opening section of the Index at the back of this volume for a description of how to find tables and figures within it.

Appendixes

Besides the main body text and images, *Crime, Prisons, and Jails* has three appendixes. The first is the Important Names and Addresses directory. Here, readers will find contact information for a number of government and private organizations that can provide further information on aspects of crime and the U.S. prison and jail systems. The second appendix is the Resources section, which can also assist readers in conducting their own research. In this section, the author and editors of *Crime, Prisons, and Jails* describe some of the sources that were most useful during the compilation of this book. The final appendix is the detailed Index. It has been greatly expanded from previous editions and should make it even easier to find specific topics in this book.

COMMENTS AND SUGGESTIONS

The editors of the *Information Plus Reference Series* welcome your feedback on *Crime, Prisons, and Jails*. Please direct all correspondence to:

Editors
Information Plus Reference Series
27500 Drake Rd.
Farmington Hills, MI 48331-3535

CHAPTER 1
AN OVERVIEW OF CRIME

CATEGORIZING CRIME
Morality and Mental State

The criminal codes for western societies evolved from the Judeo-Christian bible. This is evident in the criminal justice system of the early American colonies, which was deeply influenced by the Christian church. People could be prosecuted for witchcraft, gossiping, and blasphemy (insulting or showing contempt for God or anyone or anything considered sacred). Numerous sexual activities outside of those approved by the church were defined as crimes. So-called "blue laws" dictated what people could and could not do on Sundays; for example, church attendance was mandatory in some communities. Working, traveling, engaging in commerce or recreation, and many other activities were forbidden on Sundays, and violators faced severe penalties, including execution. Over time, U.S. legal codes evolved to reflect greater separation between the church and the state. Behaviors that had been deemed criminal because they violated church dictates slowly became decriminalized. Nevertheless, some "blue laws" lingered into the 21st century, for example, those regarding alcohol sales on Sundays.

The Latin term *mala in se* means "morally wrong" or "inherently wrong." *Mala in se* crimes are those condemned universally as wrong or evil because the criminal action is inherently bad. Crimes such as murder and stealing have been considered wrong since ancient times. They remain morally unacceptable in the 21st century. Other behaviors, however, have been alternatively accepted and rejected as crimes based on changing public attitudes. Slavery was once considered a legal practice in the United States. Eventually, it became so morally repugnant to enough people that it was deemed a crime. American attitudes about the criminality of alcohol and drug usage and certain sexual activities have varied over time, as will be explained later in this chapter.

Some minor crimes are considered *mala prohibita*, which translates from Latin as "wrongs prohibited." These are behaviors that are not inherently bad in themselves but are prohibited by government policy. Many traffic laws are *mala prohibita*. For example, speeding is criminal not because it is morally wrong but because it is deemed criminal by government authorities.

An important element in how crimes are categorized and punished is called *mens rea*, which translates from Latin as "guilty mind," or more commonly, "criminal intent." The U.S. justice system seeks to determine the mental state of a perpetrator at the time the criminal act was committed and to assign punishment accordingly. Intentional criminal acts that are planned in advance are considered much more serious than unintentional criminal acts or crimes committed in the "heat of passion."

Punishment Categories

Governments' decisions about how to punish certain crimes are based, in part, on the moral beliefs of the society in which the crimes occur. Although *mala in se* behaviors are universally condemned as wrong, punishments for these crimes can vary significantly between societies and between governments. During the colonial period in U.S. history, the death penalty was commonly meted out for crimes such as horse stealing and robbery. Over time, societal morals demanded less harsh punishments for these crimes. The evolution in U.S. attitudes about appropriate punishments for criminal behavior is discussed in more detail in Chapter 7.

Under U.S. law, crimes are divided into three broad categories: felonies, misdemeanors, and infractions. Felonies are considered the most serious crimes and are punished the most severely. The word *felony* is believed to be derived from a Latin word meaning "evil doer." Crimes that inflict death or serious injury or the threat of death or serious injury are considered felonies. Many property crimes that involve large economic losses to the victim are also classified as felonies. In general, people convicted of felonies are punished with prison terms at least a year in length and are sometimes assessed a fine of many thousands of dollars. Convicted felons may also lose some of their constitutional rights, such as the right to vote in elections. In some states the loss of rights only applies while a felon is incarcerated; in other states rights can be lost permanently. The most serious felony is the intentional murder of another human being. This crime is considered so heinous that capital punishment (execution) is sometimes the penalty for committing murder.

Misdemeanors are less serious crimes than felonies. They involve less personal harm and lower economic losses than felonies. These "lesser" crimes are typically punished with jail sentences of less than one year and fines of up to a few thousand dollars. People convicted of misdemeanors do not typically lose any of their constitutional rights once their sentences are served.

States divide felonies and misdemeanors into levels or classes to indicate their relative seriousness. For example, Virginia law (2017, http://law.lis.virginia.gov/vacode/title 18.2/chapter1/section18.2-9/) specifies six classes of felonies and four classes of misdemeanors. In both categories Class 1 crimes are the most serious and punished the most severely. Other states use a letter system in which Class A felonies or misdemeanors are considered the most serious in their category.

Finally, the least serious crimes are called infractions (or petty offenses). These include minor traffic and parking violations and violations of local ordinances. The punishment for an infraction is usually only a fine of up to a few hundred dollars.

DEFINING THE TYPES OF CRIMES

Crimes are defined and punished differently by different jurisdictions within the United States. In general, the punishments become more severe with increasing seriousness of the crime. Sorting out all the various and complicated legal definitions for particular crimes can be challenging. This section will present some general and widely used definitions for the most common crimes.

Killing Crimes

Killing crimes are defined and punished at various levels, depending on the mental state of the killer and the circumstances under which the killing took place. Criminal intent (or lack thereof) plays a major role in how these crimes are categorized. The categorization is important because it profoundly affects the sentence that can be imposed.

Killing with criminal intent is typically called murder. There are various degrees (or levels) of murder in

criminal law. First-degree murder is the most serious charge and means the killer planned the crime and deliberately carried it out. First-degree murder is often described as deliberate killing with "malice aforethought." Malice is the desire or intent to cause great harm. Aforethought means "previously in mind." In other words, murder committed with aforethought is premeditated (considered and thought through before being committed).

Second-degree murder is a lesser charge that is applied to a killing that may or may not be intentional but is not premeditated. A person who gets into a fistfight and ultimately kills his or her opponent might be charged with second-degree murder. This crime might also be called manslaughter. There are two levels of manslaughter: voluntary manslaughter and involuntary manslaughter. In general, voluntary manslaughter is considered a more serious crime than involuntary manslaughter and incurs more severe penalties.

Voluntary manslaughter is a killing believed to be intentional but not premeditated. It occurs on a sudden impulse, as in the fistfight example. Involuntary manslaughter is an unintentional killing that occurs as a consequence of reckless behavior or extreme negligence. The reckless behavior is typically some minor unlawful action that is not ordinarily expected to result in a death. An example is a driver who runs a red light and inadvertently strikes and kills a pedestrian crossing the street. Ordinarily, running a red light is a minor crime. The accidental taking of life elevates the crime to the level of manslaughter. Involuntary manslaughter involving extreme negligence may also be called criminally negligent homicide. Involuntary manslaughter involving recklessness, rather than negligence, is often called nonnegligent homicide.

An accidental killing that occurs as a result of a felony is a much more serious crime in the eyes of the law. Some states define a crime called felony murder. It can be charged against any willing participant in a serious felony (such as a bank robbery) if a person is inadvertently killed as a result of the felonious act. These laws apply even to criminals who are not actually in the victim's presence at the time of the accidental death (e.g., getaway drivers at bank robberies). As a result, these laws are highly controversial.

Some homicides are not considered criminal. These include killings performed in self-defense and accidental killings that occur during noncriminal actions. Intent and circumstances are the primary elements that influence whether criminal charges are filed and the extent of any resulting punishments.

Bodily Harm Crimes

Bodily harm crimes are crimes that are intended to cause or do cause personal injury to another person. The primary example is assault, which is an attempted or completed attack on a victim by a perpetrator who intends to inflict or recklessly inflicts bodily harm.

AGGRAVATED AND SIMPLE ASSAULT. In general, there are two levels of assault: aggravated assault and simple assault. Aggravated assault charges are typically filed if the attacker uses a deadly weapon and/or intends to inflict or does inflict serious injury to the victim. Aggravated assault can also result from reckless behavior. Simple assault is a lesser crime that does not include the more serious circumstances or consequences to the victim. Simple assault can also be charged when a person's extreme negligence causes bodily harm to another person. Some state laws define a crime called assault and battery that includes both threat (assault) and bodily attack (battery).

In most jurisdictions the penalties for assault (or assault and battery) are more severe when the victim is a public official, such as a law enforcement officer, firefighter, social worker, judge, or schoolteacher, who is attacked while on duty.

Sex Crimes

Sexually based offenses involve some type of sexual activity that is deemed illegal. Changing moral views over time have slowly led to decriminalization of some activities that were once outlawed. In 2003 in *Lawrence v. Texas* (539 U.S. 558), the U.S. Supreme Court struck down as unconstitutional a Texas law that prohibited people of the same sex from engaging in sexual conduct. The ruling invalidated similar laws across the country. According to Deborah L. Rhode, in "Why Is Adultery Still a Crime?" (LATimes.com, May 2, 2016), as of 2016, 21 U.S. states still had laws criminalizing adultery (consensual sexual acts by married people with partners other than their spouse). In light of the *Lawrence v. Texas* ruling, the adultery laws would likely not survive court challenges and are rarely enforced; nevertheless, they remain on the books. Rhode notes that the criminal code serves as a kind of moral guide even if some laws are almost never applied. Laws against fornication (consensual sexual acts between unmarried people) lingered in some states as of April 2017, including Idaho (https://legislature.idaho.gov/statutesrules/idstat/title18/t18ch66/sect18-6603/), Massachusetts (http://www.mass.gov/courts/case-legal-res/law-lib/laws-by-subj/about/sex.html), and Virginia (http://law.lis.virginia.gov/vacode/title18.2/chapter8/section18.2-344/). In 2005 the Supreme Court of Virginia found the state's fornication law to be unconstitutional. Nevertheless, the unenforceable law remained on the books as of April 2017 because it had not been revoked by the Virginia legislature.

The most serious sexual offenses are those in which force or the threat of force is used by the perpetrator and those in which the victims are children. Rape, or sexual assault as it is called in some states, is a crime that has different definitions depending on the jurisdiction.

In addition, state laws typically classify rapes at different felony levels depending on the circumstances of the crime. For example, Indiana law (2017, http://iga.in.gov/static-documents/9/a/6/7/9a6777b4/TITLE35_AR42_ch4.pdf) classifies rape as a Level 1 felony if the rape includes the threat or use of deadly force, the perpetrator has a deadly weapon (such as a firearm), the victim is seriously injured during the attack, or the victim is unknowingly drugged by the perpetrator. Otherwise, rape is a Level 3 felony in Indiana.

Use (or threat) of force and lack of consent are common elements that define rape when the victim is an adult with full mental and physical capacities. Statutory rape is a separately defined crime in which the victim is either younger than a legally set age of consent or the victim is an adult with a debilitating mental or physical condition. In these cases a crime occurs even if the victim consents to the sexual activity and no force or threat of force is used.

Many other offenses besides rape may be considered sexually based crimes under the law. Typical examples include offenses related to prostitution or pornography. Depending on the circumstances, these crimes might be deemed felonies or less serious misdemeanors.

Theft Crimes

Theft crimes cover a broad spectrum of offenses. The most serious theft crime is called robbery. An important distinction between robbery and other theft crimes is that robbery involves an element of personal force and harm or the threat of personal force and harm to the victim. Thus, robberies are typically face-to-face crimes in which the victim is personally menaced by the perpetrator. This can occur on the street (e.g., a mugging or carjacking) or in a business or residence (e.g., a bank robbery or home invasion). Because of the danger to the victims posed by these personal encounters, the penalties for robbery are typically more severe than the penalties for other theft crimes.

Burglary is a theft crime that includes unlawful entry, such as into a house. Burglary is sometimes also known as breaking and entering, although the actual act of "breaking in" is not always required. In general, any entry made without the owner's permission (e.g., through an unlocked door) may legally be considered burglary.

Theft (or larceny) is a broad category that includes many different offenses. For example, California's penal code Section 484(a) (2017, http://law.onecle.com/california/penal/484.html) defines theft as:

> Every person who shall feloniously steal, take, carry, lead, or drive away the personal property of another, or who shall fraudulently appropriate property which has been entrusted to him or her, or who shall knowingly and designedly, by any false or fraudulent representation or pretense, defraud any other person of money,

labor or real or personal property, or who causes or procures others to report falsely of his or her wealth or mercantile character and by thus imposing upon any person, obtains credit and thereby fraudulently gets or obtains possession of money, or property or obtains the labor or service of another, is guilty of theft.

Many other theft-type offenses are also defined by law. Examples include forgery, counterfeiting, fraud, identity theft, confidence games, writing bad checks, and embezzlement. In all these cases, the intent of the perpetrator is to obtain something of value through illegal means.

Theft crimes are generally classified into levels or degrees of seriousness based on the particular circumstances of the crime. These classifications often take into account the economic losses to the victim. In other words, a large-value theft is treated more severely than a low-value theft. Consequently, a large-value theft is likely to trigger a harsher sentence than a low-value theft.

WHITE-COLLAR CRIMES. White-collar crimes are a subset of theft crimes. They differ from crimes such as burglary and robbery in that white-collar crimes are typically conducted without the threat or use of violence and without physical labor (e.g., breaking into a building) on the part of the perpetrator. Examples include fraud, counterfeiting, and embezzlement. White-collar crimes are discussed in detail in Chapter 5.

Alcohol and Drug Crimes

Alcohol and drugs are substances that can impair judgment and inflame passions. People under the influence of these substances may engage in reckless or violent behavior that seriously harms others. Societal concerns about alcohol and drug use have varied dramatically throughout U.S. history.

ALCOHOL CRIMES. During the late 1800s and early 1900s a Progressive movement swept the nation in which many people believed that laws could "socially engineer" Americans out of immoral and destructive behaviors—such as drinking alcohol. Some states passed laws that were intended to restrict its consumption. By 1918 alcohol was considered such a menace to the public good that its manufacture and sale were outlawed by Congress via the 18th Amendment to the U.S. Constitution. Prohibition, as it was called, proved to be unworkable and was abandoned at the federal level in 1933. Nevertheless, states and local jurisdictions have passed laws that criminalize certain alcohol-related actions, particularly public drunkenness and driving under the influence of alcohol.

DRUG CRIMES. The history of drug criminalization has also been checkered. Drugs such as cocaine and heroin were once common ingredients in popular products that Americans bought and consumed. Over time, growing awareness about the physical, psychological, and social harms associated with the use of these drugs spurred laws against them. Modern drug laws are complex and sometimes controversial as Americans continue to debate how best to control human behaviors that are considered undesirable to the public good. A detailed discussion of drug crimes is presented in Chapter 4.

Hate Crimes

Hate crimes are criminal offenses that are motivated by the offender's personal prejudice or bias against the victim. The first federal legislation against hate crimes was passed in 1969. Since that time additional laws have expanded the types of offenses that are considered hate crimes. Chapter 2 presents hate crime statistics and discusses the legislation and constitutional issues associated with hate crimes.

CYBERCRIME

The digital age has provided new means and modes of communicating and new avenues for criminal behavior. Chapter 5 describes various financial crimes committed via electronic media, such as e-mail fraud and website scams. Digital devices and platforms are also utilized in other types of crime that involve sexual misconduct, bullying, threats, harassment, and stalking. In some cases the activities may not rise to the level of criminality. For example, sexting is the act of sending someone sexually explicit messages or images via cell phones. Sexting between consensual adults may not be illegal (depending on the jurisdiction), but could violate laws, particularly child pornography laws, if any minors are involved. Sexually explicit images can also be used by perpetrators who wish to embarrass, harass, manipulate, or extort victims. Revenge porn is a type of nonconsensual pornography in which sexually explicit images of people are electronically posted or distributed (e.g., on a website) without their consent to embarrass or harass them.

Cyberbullying is a general term that encompasses many types of abusive behavior accomplished through digital means. The Centers for Disease Control and Prevention (CDC) calls it "electronic aggression." In "Technology and Youth: Protecting Your Child from Electronic Aggression" (July 2008, https://www.cdc.gov/violenceprevention/pdf/ea-tipsheet-a.pdf), the CDC provides some specific examples:

- Disclosing someone else's personal information in a public area (e.g., website) in order to cause embarrassment

- Posting rumors or lies about someone in a public area (e.g., discussion board)

- Distributing embarrassing pictures of someone by posting them in a public area (e.g., website) or sending them via e-mail

- Assuming another person's electronic identity to post or send messages about others with the intent of causing the other person harm

- Sending mean, embarrassing, or threatening text messages, instant messages, or e-mails

Although cyberbullying is often discussed in terms of the victims being minors, many adults are also victimized. Bruce Drake of the Pew Research Center presents in "The Darkest Side of Online Harassment: Menacing Behavior" (June 1, 2015, http://www.pewresearch.org/fact-tank/2015/06/01/the-darkest-side-of-online-harassment-menacing-behavior/) survey results from 2014 in which 40% of adult Internet users said they had been harassed online. Although being "called offensive names" was the most commonly cited behavior, more menacing actions also took place, including physical threats, sustained harassment, stalking, and sexual harassment. Drake notes that approximately 5% of the people who had been victimized reported the incident to a law enforcement agency.

In some cases, cyber misconduct runs afoul of long-standing laws against extortion, pornography, stalking, or unlawful surveillance. Many jurisdictions have rushed to pass new laws that specifically prohibit the most egregious types of electronic harassment. For example, in 2014 a new law went into effect in Georgia (http://law.justia.com/codes/georgia/2014/title-16/chapter-11/article-3/part-3/section-16-11-90) that prohibits nude or sexually explicit electronic transmissions (even those including adults) "when the transmission or post is harassment or causes financial loss to the depicted person and serves no legitimate purpose to the depicted person." Although a first offense is treated as a misdemeanor, subsequent violations are considered felonies. The Cyberbullying Research Center (http://cyberbullying.org/), a private organization, provides an online clearinghouse of information about laws related to cyberbullying, sexting, and other cyber activities that may be criminal.

Threatening or harassing words transmitted electronically have proven difficult for lawmakers to criminalize because of constitutional concerns. The First Amendment of the U.S. Constitution protects the right to freedom of expression (i.e., freedom of speech). Threats are not considered protected speech; however, there is a very high bar for legally classifying statements as threats. In 2015 the U.S. Supreme Court ruled in *Elonis v. United States* (No. 13-983) in favor of Anthony Douglas Elonis, who had been convicted of making online threats against various people. According to U.S. Courts, in "Facts and Case Summary—Elonis v. U.S." (2017, http://www.uscourts.gov/educational-resources/educational-activities/facts-and-case-summary-elonis-v-us), Elonis was arrested in 2010 for violating a federal antithreat law by posting threatening comments on Facebook about his former wife, co-workers, a kindergarten class, the local police, and a Federal Bureau of Investigation (FBI) agent. He was sentenced to nearly four years in prison and lost his appeals. The Supreme Court, however, overturned Elonis's conviction, finding that there was no proof that the defendant "meant what he said in a literal sense." Elonis's lawyers argued that "he was an aspiring rap artist and that his comments were merely a form of artistic expression." In June 2016 the North Carolina Supreme Court struck down that state's cyberbullying law after finding it unconstitutional.

TERRORISM

Terrorism is difficult to define legally. In fact, there are many different definitions under federal and state laws. For example, in 22 USC Section 2656f(d)(2) (2017, http://www.law.cornell.edu/uscode/text/22/2656f), which focuses on foreign relations, the federal government defines terrorism as "premeditated, politically motivated violence perpetrated against noncombatant targets by subnational groups or clandestine agents."

Generally, the term *terrorism* is associated with violent actions that are perpetrated by people with a certain mind-set against other people. The perpetrators of terrorist acts typically justify their behavior as appropriate because it is waged against people they consider to be enemies for various political, social, and/or religious reasons. Thus, terrorism is the ultimate hate crime and is motivated by bias.

Much modern terrorism is international in nature, meaning that it involves perpetrators and victims of different nationalities. The scope of international terrorism places it squarely under the jurisdiction of federal authorities. Some horrifying acts of international terrorism have taken place, including the September 11, 2001 (9/11), attacks on the United States. Such acts are criminal under U.S. law, and the perpetrators can be tried and convicted of criminal offenses. However, capturing and trying foreign nationals can be difficult, particularly when they are in countries unfriendly to the United States. In some cases, the U.S. armed forces may become involved, as they did in the war in Afghanistan (2001–2014), to capture alleged terrorists for prosecution under U.S. law. Terrorism cases involving foreign nationals have been prosecuted through military tribunals, or more commonly, through federal courts. For example, in 2014 Sulaiman Abu Ghaith (1965–) was sentenced to life in prison for aiding the terrorist group al Qaeda and conspiring to kill Americans. The article "Sulaiman Abu Ghaith Sentenced to Life in Prison" (BBC.com, September 23, 2014) notes that Abu Ghaith was a Kuwaiti clergyman and the son-in-law of Osama bin Laden (1957?–2011), the mastermind behind the 9/11 attacks.

Domestic Terrorism

Terrorism is domestic when the perpetrators and the victims are citizens or residents of the same country, such as a terrorist attack that is carried out on U.S. soil by U.S. citizens or residents. The perpetrators can be charged with a variety of crimes, such as murder, assault, arson, and so on. Also, federal and state laws specifically define certain terrorism-related crimes. For example, the Michigan

Anti-terrorism Act (https://www.legislature.mi.gov/(S(0hrehh 45aygcqkzbeiyflp3m))/documents/mcl/pdf/mcl-328-1931-LXXXIII-A.pdf) defines terrorism as a willful and deliberate act that is also a violent felony under state law, an act considered dangerous to human life, and "an act that is intended to intimidate or coerce a civilian population or influence or affect the conduct of government or a unit of government through intimidation or coercion." As a result, domestic terrorists can face charges for "regular" crimes and/or crimes specified under antiterrorism laws.

The main distinction between acts of domestic terrorism and other domestic crimes hinges on motive. It can be difficult to determine whether a particular crime is committed for sociopolitical reasons, personal reasons (e.g., revenge), or a mixture of these motives. For example, in October 2002 two men dubbed "the Beltway snipers" terrorized people in the District of Columbia area with a killing spree that left 10 people dead and three wounded. One of the perpetrators, John Allen Muhammad (1960–2009), was described in the media as committing the killings for a mixture of personal and sociopolitical reasons. He reportedly hoped to extract revenge on his former wife as well as extort money from the government to fund a terrorist training camp. Muhammad was ultimately convicted of a number of crimes, including murder and terrorism-related charges, and was executed in 2009.

It should be noted that "making terroristic threats" or "terroristic threatening" is considered a crime under federal and state statutes. These threats do not necessarily involve acts of terrorism as the latter is defined. For example, Texas law (http://www.statutes.legis.state.tx.us/Docs/PE/htm/PE.22.htm) states that a person commits a terroristic threat by threatening to commit violence against any person or property for a variety of reasons, including to "place any person in fear of imminent serious bodily injury." Thus, "terroristic threats" do not have to meet the definition of terrorism that hinges on bias or sociopolitical motivations. Therefore, a person could be charged with making terroristic threats for threatening someone over a personal matter.

Types of Domestic Terrorism

The Global Terrorism Database (http://www.start.umd.edu/gtd) is a project of the U.S. Department of Homeland Security's (DHS) National Consortium for the Study of Terrorism and Responses to Terrorism at the University of Maryland. The database contains information from 1970 through 2015 about more than 150,000 terrorist cases worldwide. Information about perpetrators is provided as known; however, many perpetrators remain unidentified. A search of the database for incidents within the United States as of January 2015 returned 2,693 incidents.

Terrorism cases involving jihadists (people who use the cover of the Islamic religion to carry out violence against those who they believe stand in the way of Muslims) elicit intense media and public attention. U.S. citizens or residents who conduct such attacks are called "homegrown" jihadists. In October 2015 Jerome P. Bjelopera of the Congressional Research Service testified before a congressional committee. In *Terror Inmates: Countering Violent Extremism in Prison and Beyond* (October 28, 2015, http://docs.house.gov/meetings/HM/HM05/20151028/104102/HHRG-114-HM05-Wstate-BjeloperaJ-20151028.pdf), Bjelopera notes, "Since 9/11, more than 250 people have been convicted for their involvement in homegrown violent jihadist plots."

Based on information contained in the Global Terrorism Database, many of the 2,693 terrorist attacks that have happened within the United States since 1970 are believed to have been conducted by ecoterrorist groups. These are extremist groups that support environmentalism, animal rights, or similar causes, but use criminal violence to promote their ideas and attack their perceived enemies. For example, radical animal rights activists are believed to be behind bombs that exploded outside the homes of two University of California, Santa Cruz, biomedical researchers in August 2008. One person was wounded in the attacks. The scientists were allegedly targeted because they use animals in their research (research that the university claims is being conducted using the highest humane standards). The remaining incidents of U.S. domestic terrorism in the database that are not examples of homegrown jihadism are attributed to perpetrators with a variety of political, religious, and social biases, such as white supremacists and antiabortion activists.

Six domestic terrorist incidents that have occurred in recent decades are of particular note:

OKLAHOMA CITY BOMBING. On April 19, 1995, a 2-ton (1.8-t) truck bomb exploded outside the Alfred P. Murrah Federal Building in Oklahoma City, Oklahoma, killing 168 people and injuring more than 800. The attack was perpetrated by Timothy McVeigh (1968–2001), a 27-year-old military veteran with ties to antigovernment militia groups. McVeigh was executed by lethal injection in June 2001. Terry L. Nichols (1955–), an accomplice who helped McVeigh plan the attack and construct the bomb, was sentenced to life in prison without the possibility of parole.

OLYMPIC PARK BOMBING. On July 27, 1996, during the Olympic Games in Atlanta, Georgia, a nail-packed pipe bomb exploded in a large common area. One person was killed and more than 100 people were injured. Authorities had no leads at the time, but similar explosive devices were later used in bomb attacks on a nightclub that was favored by homosexuals and two abortion clinics.

These incidents led investigators to Eric Robert Rudolph (1967–), a Christian extremist whose views combined antigovernment political sentiments with antihomosexual bigotry and opposition to abortion. Rudolph eluded capture for five years before he surrendered to authorities in May 2003. Confessing to the Olympic bombing, he said he was motivated by antigovernment and antisocialist beliefs. He was sentenced to life in prison without the possibility of parole.

ANTHRAX ATTACKS. On September 25, 2001, a letter containing a white powdery substance was handled by an assistant to the NBC News anchor Tom Brokaw (1940–). After complaining of a rash, the assistant consulted a physician and tested positive for exposure to the anthrax bacterium (*Bacillus anthracis*), an infectious agent that, if inhaled into the lungs, can lead to death. Over the next two months envelopes testing positive for anthrax were received by various U.S. news organizations and by government offices, including the offices of the U.S. Senate majority leader Tom Daschle (1947–; D-SD) and the New York governor George Pataki (1945–). As a result of exposure to anthrax that was sent via the U.S. mail system, five people died, including two postal workers who handled letters carrying the anthrax spores. Hundreds more who were exposed were placed on antibiotics as a preventive measure.

The FBI eventually traced the source of the anthrax to the U.S. Army Medical Research Institute of Infectious Diseases, a bioweapons laboratory at Fort Detrick, Maryland. At first, authorities focused on a civilian researcher at that facility who was later cleared of the attacks. In August 2008 Bruce Ivins (1946–2008), another researcher at the same laboratory, committed suicide before he could be arrested and charged with the crime. The FBI has expressed confidence that Ivins was the perpetrator of the 2001 anthrax attacks. Nevertheless, because he will never stand trial, some doubts remain about the strength of the government's case against Ivins.

BOSTON MARATHON BOMBING. On April 15, 2013, two bombs exploded near the finish line of the Boston Marathon, killing three people and injuring more than 200 others. The perpetrators were two brothers: Tamerlan Tsarnaev (1986–2013), who was killed during the subsequent manhunt, and Dzhokhar Tsarnaev (1993–), who was captured by police. Their family has ties to Chechnya, a Russian republic that has been roiled by violent clashes between Islamist groups and government forces. In "Boston Suspects Are Seen as Self-Taught and Fueled by Web" (NYTimes.com, April 24, 2013), Michael Cooper, Michael S. Schmidt, and Eric Schmitt indicate that authorities believe the brothers "were motivated by extremist Islamic beliefs but were not acting with known terrorist groups." In 2015 Dzhokhar Tsarnaev, a naturalized U.S. citizen, was given the death penalty after being convicted of the attack. As of April 2017, his sentence was being appealed and had not yet been carried out.

SAN BERNARDINO OFFICE PARTY SHOOTING. On December 2, 2015, a married couple—Syed Rizwan Farook (1987–2015) and Tashfeen Malik (1986–2015)—opened fired at a holiday party that was attended by Farook's coworkers at the Inland Regional Center in San Bernardino, California. Fourteen victims died during the attack. Farook and Malik were killed during a shootout with the police after fleeing the scene. Jennifer Medina et al. indicate in "San Bernardino Suspects Left Trail of Clues, but No Clear Motive" (NYTimes.com, December 3, 2015) that Farook was born in the United States to Pakistani parents. Malik had a conditional "green card," meaning that she had applied for permanent residency in the United States and had received preliminary approval for that status. Authorities believe the two were sympathetic to Islamic radical groups.

ORLANDO NIGHTCLUB SHOOTING. On June 12, 2016, Omar Mateen (1986–2016) opened fire inside the Pulse nightclub in Orlando, Florida, leaving 49 dead and dozens wounded before he was killed by police. According to Ralph Ellis et al., in "Orlando Shooting: 49 Killed, Shooter Pledged ISIS Allegiance" (CNN.com, June 13, 2016), Mateen was born in the United States to Afghani parents. He reportedly called 911 during the rampage and pledged his support for the terrorist group Islamic State of Iraq and the Levant (also known as the Islamic State of Iraq and Syria). In January 2017 Noor Salman (1986–), Mateen's widow, was arrested by the FBI and charged with aiding and abetting her husband before the attack and with obstruction of justice. At her arraignment hearing in April 2017, Salman entered a plea of not guilty; her trial was expected to begin later that year.

IMMIGRANTS AND CRIME

Crimes committed by immigrants to the United States became the focus of much public and political attention in the months leading up to the 2016 presidential election. The Republican candidate Donald Trump (1946–) focused heavily on the issue during his campaign. He famously pledged to build a wall along the nation's southern border and to deport illegal immigrants who are afoul of the law.

Federal laws dictate which foreign nationals (i.e., aliens) can enter the United States and the obligations they must meet. Any person who fails to abide by these laws is considered an illegal immigrant. This category includes aliens who sneak into the country and those who enter legally but later violate immigration rules, such as by staying in the United States after their visa has expired. (A U.S. visa is a federally issued "permission slip" that allows a foreign national to enter the United States for a specific purpose and stay for an extended period, typically more than 90 days.) In *Interior Immigration Enforcement: Criminal Alien Programs* (September 8, 2016, https://fas.org/sgp/crs/homesec/R44627.pdf), William A. Kandel of the Congressional Research Service notes that "unlawful presence in the United States itself is a civil violation, not a criminal offense." Kandel continues: "Unlawful presence is only a criminal offense when an alien is found in the United States after having been formally removed or after departing the country while a removal order was outstanding."

The DHS refers to illegal immigrants as "unauthorized immigrants." As of April 2017, the agency's most recent estimate of the size of this population was published in 2013. Bryan Baker and Nancy Rytina of the DHS indicate in *Estimates of the Unauthorized Immigrant Population Residing in the United States: January 2012* (March 2013, https://www.dhs.gov/sites/default/files/publications/Unauthorized%20Immigrant%20Population%20Estimates%20in%20the%20US%20January%202012_0.pdf) that around 11.4 million unauthorized immigrants were believed to be in the United States as of January 2012.

Criminal Aliens

Aliens, whether in the country legally or illegally, are called "criminal aliens" if they commit any "regular" (nonimmigration-related) offense under federal, state, or local laws. Examples include murder, assault, theft, and driving under the influence of alcohol or other drugs.

In *Fiscal Year 2016 ICE Enforcement and Removal Operations Report* (December 2016, https://www.ice.gov/sites/default/files/documents/Report/2016/removal-stats-2016.pdf), the U.S. Immigration and Customs Enforcement (ICE) notes that it shares responsibility for enforcing immigration law with the U.S. Customs and Border Protection and the U.S. Citizenship and Immigration Services. According to ICE, it removed more than 3.1 million aliens between fiscal years (FYs) 2008 and 2016. (The federal fiscal year begins October 1 and ends September 30; thus, FY 2016 extended from October 1, 2015, to September 30, 2016.) As shown in Figure 1.1, more than half (58%) of the removals in FY 2016 were of convicted criminal aliens. The remaining removals were of noncriminal immigration law violators. Figure 1.2 provides a breakdown by location of the alien convicted criminals who were removed as a percentage of total removals. In FY 2016 nearly all (92%) of the aliens apprehended and removed from the interior region of the United States were convicted criminals, compared with 45% of the aliens apprehended and removed from the border regions (including ports of entry).

FIGURE 1.1

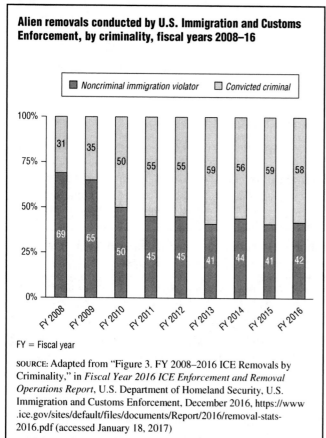

Alien removals conducted by U.S. Immigration and Customs Enforcement, by criminality, fiscal years 2008–16

FY = Fiscal year

SOURCE: Adapted from "Figure 3. FY 2008–2016 ICE Removals by Criminality," in *Fiscal Year 2016 ICE Enforcement and Removal Operations Report*, U.S. Department of Homeland Security, U.S. Immigration and Customs Enforcement, December 2016, https://www.ice.gov/sites/default/files/documents/Report/2016/removal-stats-2016.pdf (accessed January 18, 2017)

FIGURE 1.2

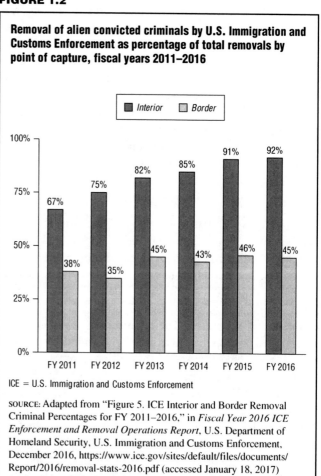

Removal of alien convicted criminals by U.S. Immigration and Customs Enforcement as percentage of total removals by point of capture, fiscal years 2011–2016

ICE = U.S. Immigration and Customs Enforcement

SOURCE: Adapted from "Figure 5. ICE Interior and Border Removal Criminal Percentages for FY 2011–2016," in *Fiscal Year 2016 ICE Enforcement and Removal Operations Report*, U.S. Department of Homeland Security, U.S. Immigration and Customs Enforcement, December 2016, https://www.ice.gov/sites/default/files/documents/Report/2016/removal-stats-2016.pdf (accessed January 18, 2017)

TABLE 1.1

Noncitizen prisoners under the jurisdiction of state or federal correctional authorities, yearend 2015

Jurisdiction	Total
U.S. total[a, b]	65,107
Federal[b, c]	21,479
State[a]	43,628
Alabama	169
Alaska[d, e]	/
Arizona	4,570
Arkansas	287
California	/
Colorado[f]	1,458
Connecticut[d]	485
Delaware[d]	317
Florida	7,193
Georgia	2,395
Hawaii[d, g]	84
Idaho	233
Illinois	1,681
Indiana	586
Iowa	186
Kansas	330
Kentucky	145
Louisiana	128
Maine	46
Maryland	620
Massachusetts[g]	619
Michigan	555
Minnesota	472
Mississippi	23
Missouri[f, g]	474
Montana	18
Nebraska	235
Nevada[h]	/
New Hampshire	133
New Jersey	1,270
New Mexico	156
New York[f]	4,132
North Carolina	1,351
North Dakota	23
Ohio	477
Oklahoma[f]	0
Oregon[h]	/
Pennsylvania	1,089
Rhode Island[d]	52
South Carolina	461
South Dakota	86
Tennessee[f]	264
Texas	8,448
Utah	349
Vermont[d, h]	18
Virginia	696
Washington	769
West Virginia	18
Wisconsin	472
Wyoming	55

The Bureau of Justice Statistics (BJS) is an office within the U.S. Department of Justice. The BJS estimates that at yearend 2015 there were 65,107 noncitizen prisoners under the jurisdiction of state and federal correctional authorities. (See Table 1.1.) This total includes all convicted noncitizen prisoners regardless of their immigration status (i.e., legal or illegal). Note that data were not available for 2015 from Alaska, California, Nevada, and Oregon. The omission of California is particularly important because it is a border state and may contain a relatively large number of imprisoned noncitizens. In addition, Table 1.1 does not include noncitizen inmates held

TABLE 1.1

Noncitizen prisoners under the jurisdiction of state or federal correctional authorities, yearend 2015 [CONTINUED]

/Not reported.

Unless otherwise noted, noncitizens are identified by individual jurisdictions as persons with current citizenship of a country other than the United states as of December 31, 2015.

[a]Total U.S. and state counts of noncitizen prisoners for 2015 will be lower than expected due to the exclusion of California data. California was unable to report the number of noncitizen prisoners in 2015.

[b]The Federal Bureau of Prisons holds prisoners age 17 or younger in private contract facilities; 64 such prisoners were housed in contract facilities in 2015.

[c]Federal counts include only those persons held in Bureau of Prisons facilites and do not include persons held in detention facilities specific to U.S. Citizenship and Immigration Services, U.S. Immigration and Customs Enforcement, or U.S.Customs and Border Protection.

[d]Prisons and jails form one integrated system. Data include total jail and prison populations.

[e]Alaska has not submitted 2015 data to National Prisoner Statistics (NPS) for noncitizens or persons age 17 or younger since 2012.

[f]Non-U.S. citizens are defined as foreign-born.

[g]Citizenship based on prisoner self-report.

[h]State did not submit 2015 NPS data for noncitizens or persons age 17 or younger. Data are from 2014.

Note: Jurisdiction refers to the legal authority of state or federal correctional officials over a prisoner, regardless of where the prisoner is held. The definition of non-U.S. citizen varies across jurisdictions. Interpret data with caution.

SOURCE: Adapted from E. Ann Carson and Elizabeth Anderson, "Appendix Table 9. Noncitizen Prisoners and Prisoners Age 17 or Younger under the Jurisdiction of State or Federal Correctional Authorities, by Sex, December 31, 2015," in *Prisoners in 2015*, U.S.Department of Justice, Bureau of Justice Statistics, December 2016, https://www.bjs.gov/index.cfm?ty= pbdetail&iid=5869 (accessed January 21, 2017)

in thousands of local jails around the country. Kandel states, "In 2013, ICE published estimates indicating that approximately 900,000 aliens were arrested for crimes every year; that approximately 550,000 criminal aliens convicted of crimes exited law enforcement custody every year; and that 1.9 million removable criminal aliens currently resided in the United States."

GOVERNMENT JURISDICTION AND SPENDING

As noted throughout this chapter, criminal legislation and law enforcement are carried out by federal, state, and local governments. Sometimes government entities have overlapping responsibilities. State and local governments have always played a central role in controlling crime. They operate police and law enforcement agencies, court systems, and correctional facilities, such as prisons and jails. The federal government enforces laws that fall within its jurisdiction. Examples include mail fraud, bank robbery, gun laws, counterfeiting, forgery, espionage, immigration violations, child pornography, drug trafficking, and money laundering. The federal government also operates the federal court system and has its own prisons for people convicted of federal crimes. In addition, the federal government provides funding for some state and local crime-control programs.

Table 1.2 shows criminal justice system expenditures by federal, state, and local governments in FY 2012. It

TABLE 1.2

Government expenditures on criminal justice, by level of government, fiscal year 2012

[Amount (thousands of dollars)]

Activity	All governments*	Federal government	State governments	Local governments
Total justice system	265,160,340	56,267,000	86,266,232	132,500,445
Direct expenditure	265,160,340	51,941,000	80,929,314	132,290,026
Intergovernmental expenditure	—	4,326,000	5,336,918	210,419
Police protection	126,434,125	31,395,000	14,815,502	84,053,185
Direct expenditure	126,434,125	28,977,000	13,411,966	84,045,159
Intergovernmental expenditure	—	2,418,000	1,403,536	8,026
Judicial and legal	57,935,169	15,894,000	22,770,081	22,049,483
Direct expenditure	57,935,169	14,670,000	21,256,019	22,009,150
Intergovernmental expenditure	—	1,224,000	1,514,062	40,333
Corrections	80,791,046	8,978,000	48,680,649	26,397,777
Direct expenditure	80,791,046	8,294,000	46,261,329	26,235,717
Intergovernmental expenditure	—	684,000	2,419,320	162,060

*The total lines for each criminal justice activity, and for the total justice system, exclude duplicative intergovernmental amounts. This was done to avoid the artificial inflation that would result if an intergovernmental expenditure of a government were tabulated and then counted again when the recipient government(s) expended the amount. The intergovernmental expenditure lines are not totaled for the same reason.
Notes: Local government data are estimates subject to sampling variability.
Federal Government data are for the fiscal period beginning October 1, 2011 and ending September 30, 2012.

SOURCE: Adapted from Tracey Kyckelhahn, "Table 1. Percent Distribution of Expenditure for the Justice System by Type of Government, Fiscal 2012 (Preliminary)," in *Justice Expenditure and Employment Extracts, 2012—Preliminary*, U.S. Department of Justice, Bureau of Justice Statistics, February 26, 2015, https://www.bjs.gov/index.cfm?ty=pbdetail&iid=5239 (accessed January 18, 2017)

includes both direct expenditures and intergovernmental expenditures. The latter are amounts transferred between levels of government. For example, in FY 2012 the federal government transferred $4.3 billion to state and local governments to fund justice system activities.

Overall, the federal government spent $56.3 billion on the nation's justice system in FY 2012. (See Table 1.2.) Most of the money ($51.9 billion) was for direct expenditures. The breakdown of the federal total by activity was $31.4 billion for police protection, $15.9 billion for judicial and legal activities, and $9 billion for corrections. State governments spent $86.3 billion on their justice systems in FY 2012. Most of the money ($80.9 billion) was for direct expenditures. The breakdown of the state total by activity was $14.8 billion for police protection, $22.8 billion for judicial and legal activities, and $48.7 billion for corrections. Local governments spent $132.5 billion on their justice systems in FY 2012. Nearly all the money ($132.3 billion) was for direct expenditures. The breakdown of the local total by activity was $84.1 billion for police protection, $22 billion for judicial and legal activities, and $26.4 billion for corrections.

Figure 1.3 categorizes direct justice system expenditures by government level. For the justice system as a whole, local governments accounted for about half (49.9%) of the total direct expenditures, state governments accounted for 30.5% of the total, and the federal government accounted for 19.6% of the total. As shown in Figure 1.3, local governments paid the largest share (66.5%) of the direct expenditures for police protection,

FIGURE 1.3

Direct government expenditures on criminal justice, by level of government, fiscal year 2012

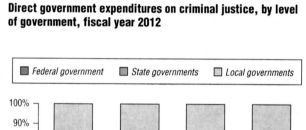

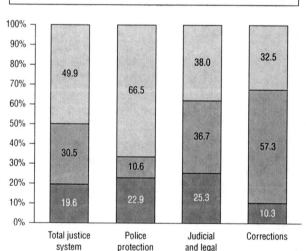

SOURCE: Adapted from Tracey Kyckelhahn, "Table 1. Percent Distribution of Expenditure for the Justice System by Type of Government, Fiscal 2012 (Preliminary)," in *Justice Expenditure and Employment Extracts, 2012—Preliminary*, U.S. Department of Justice, Bureau of Justice Statistics, February 26, 2015, https://www.bjs.gov/index.cfm?ty=pbdetail&iid=5239 (accessed January 18, 2017)

whereas state governments paid the largest share (57.3%) of the direct expenditures for corrections. In regards to judicial and legal activities, local governments bore

FIGURE 1.4

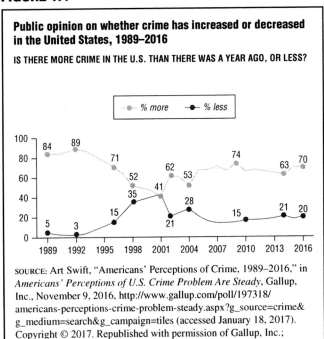

Public opinion on whether crime has increased or decreased in the United States, 1989–2016

IS THERE MORE CRIME IN THE U.S. THAN THERE WAS A YEAR AGO, OR LESS?

SOURCE: Art Swift, "Americans' Perceptions of Crime, 1989–2016," in *Americans' Perceptions of U.S. Crime Problem Are Steady*, Gallup, Inc., November 9, 2016, http://www.gallup.com/poll/197318/americans-perceptions-crime-problem-steady.aspx?g_source=crime&g_medium=search&g_campaign=tiles (accessed January 18, 2017). Copyright © 2017. Republished with permission of Gallup, Inc.; permission conveyed through Copyright Clearance Center, Inc.

FIGURE 1.5

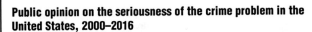

Public opinion on the seriousness of the crime problem in the United States, 2000–2016

OVERALL, HOW WOULD YOU DESCRIBE THE PROBLEM OF CRIME—IS IT EXTREMELY SERIOUS, VERY SERIOUS, MODERATELY SERIOUS, NOT TOO SERIOUS, OR NOT SERIOUS AT ALL?

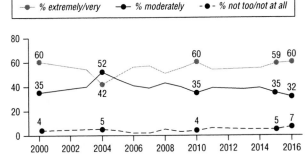

SOURCE: Art Swift, "Perceived Seriousness of U.S. Crime Problem," in *Americans' Perceptions of U.S. Crime Problem Are Steady*, Gallup, Inc., November 9, 2016, http://www.gallup.com/poll/197318/americans-perceptions-crime-problem-steady.aspx?g_source=crime&g_medium=search&g_campaign=tiles (accessed January 18, 2017). Copyright © 2017. Republished with permission of Gallup, Inc.; permission conveyed through Copyright Clearance Center, Inc.

slightly more of the direct expenditures (38%) than did state governments (36.7%).

PUBLIC OPINION ABOUT CRIME

Gallup, Inc., conducts annual polls asking Americans about their opinion on crime in the United States. As shown in Figure 1.4, more than two-thirds (70%) of respondents told Gallup in October 2016 that they believed crime had increased over the previous year. This value has risen dramatically since 2001, when 41% of those asked said crime had increased from the previous year. Older polling results, however, show much more pessimism about the nation's crime rate. In 1992, 89% of respondents said they believed crime had increased since the previous year.

As is explained in Chapter 2, the nation's violent crime rate was high during the early 1990s and then declined sharply over subsequent decades. During this period, however, public opinion polls reveal that Americans remained strongly convinced that national crime was increasing each year. This is illustrated in Figure 1.4. Pew also regularly questions the public about crime. In "Voters' Perceptions of Crime Continue to Conflict with Reality" (November 16, 2016, http://www.pewresearch.org/fact-tank/2016/11/16/voters-perceptions-of-crime-continue-to-conflict-with-reality/), John Gramlich of Pew notes that polls show that more than half of those asked between 2002 and 2015 said there was more crime in the country than a year ago. Analysts are puzzled by this disconnect between the data and the perceptions of the American public. One popular theory is that the 24-hour news cycle and intense

media coverage of criminal acts convince Americans that crime is more rampant than the data suggest.

Gallup pollsters have quizzed Americans about the seriousness of the nation's crime problem as a whole and in their local area. In 2016 six out of 10 (60%) of those asked said they were extremely worried about the crime problem in the United States. (See Figure 1.5.) Another 32% said crime is moderately serious nationwide, and 7% said it is either not too serious or not serious at all. This breakdown of opinions has been relatively consistent since 2000. The primary exception was in 2004, when a higher percentage perceived crime as moderately serious (52%) than extremely or very serious (42%).

Since 1972 Gallup pollsters have asked Americans whether there is more crime or less crime in their local area when compared with the previous year. (See Figure 1.6.) Through the mid-1990s the percentage of respondents saying there was more crime in their area was generally much higher than the percentage saying there was less crime in their area. Since that time the difference between the two factions has narrowed considerably. In 2016, 45% of those asked said crime had increased over the past year in their area, compared with 33% who said it had decreased. Another 20% thought it had remained at the same level.

CRIMINAL NOTORIETY

Criminal acts, especially those involving *mala in se* offenses, violate society's moral beliefs about appropriate

FIGURE 1.6

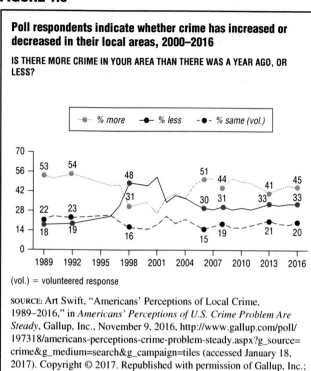

Poll respondents indicate whether crime has increased or decreased in their local areas, 2000–2016

IS THERE MORE CRIME IN YOUR AREA THAN THERE WAS A YEAR AGO, OR LESS?

(vol.) = volunteered response

SOURCE: Art Swift, "Americans' Perceptions of Local Crime, 1989–2016," in *Americans' Perceptions of U.S. Crime Problem Are Steady*, Gallup, Inc., November 9, 2016, http://www.gallup.com/poll/197318/americans-perceptions-crime-problem-steady.aspx?g_source=crime&g_medium=search&g_campaign=tiles (accessed January 18, 2017). Copyright © 2017. Republished with permission of Gallup, Inc.; permission conveyed through Copyright Clearance Center, Inc.

behavior. Nevertheless, there is a curious fascination in the United States with certain criminals who have become infamous (i.e., famous for bad deeds).

Some perpetrators gained notoriety because of the eras in which they lived. Billy the Kid (William H. Bonney, 1859?–1881), Butch Cassidy (Robert Leroy Parker, 1866–1937?), and the Sundance Kid (Harry Alonzo Longabaugh, 1863–1909?) are well-known outlaws of the Old West. Their criminal acts have been romanticized (depicted in an idealized and rather favorable manner) to highlight the adventuresome aspects of their exploits, rather than their victims. Some gangsters and bootleggers who operated criminal enterprises during Prohibition (1920–1933) became celebrities. Al Capone (1899–1947) headed a notorious mob of Chicago gangsters blamed for numerous killings, including the St. Valentine's Day massacre of February 14, 1929, which left seven people dead. The wealthy and sociable Capone reveled in the publicity he received. Laurence Bergreen describes in *Capone: The Man and the Era* (2014) Capone as having an image of "grisly glamour."

The Great Depression (1929–1939) also featured outlaws who captured the public imagination. John Dillinger (1903–1934), Pretty Boy Floyd (Charles Arthur Floyd, 1904–1934), Baby Face Nelson (Lester J. Gillis, 1908–1934), and Bonnie and Clyde (Bonnie Parker, 1910–1934, and Clyde Barrow, 1909–1934) are infamous criminals of the era. They are primarily remembered as bank robbers, although they committed other violent acts, including murders.

Murderers who kill multiple victims (especially strangers) are relatively rare in U.S. criminal history, but they garner much public attention. In *Serial Murder: Multidisciplinary Perspectives for Investigators* (2008, https://www.fbi.gov/file-repository/stats-services-publications-serial-murder-serial-murder-july-2008-pdf), the FBI defines serial killers as perpetrators who kill at least two victims in separate events at different times. Serial killing holds a particular fascination in American society. The FBI notes, "There is a macabre interest in the topic that far exceeds its scope and has generated countless articles, books, and movies." Scott A. Bonn explains in *Why We Love Serial Killers: The Curious Appeal of the World's Most Savage Murderers* (2014) that "serial killers tantalize, terrify, and entertain the public." Infamous examples include Ted Bundy (1946–1989), who raped and murdered dozens of girls and women, and John Wayne Gacy (1942–1994), who raped and murdered dozens of teenage boys and young men. Both killers were captured and executed for their crimes. Charles Manson (1934–) was found guilty in 1971 of ordering his cult members to gruesomely kill seven people. He was originally given the death penalty, but his sentence was changed to life in prison after California abolished capital punishment. Over the decades Manson has been the subject of much media attention and has received "fan" mail from devotees.

CHAPTER 2
CRIME TRENDS

The U.S. Department of Justice (DOJ) is the primary government source for national crime statistics, particularly data collected consistently over time. As is noted in Chapter 1, criminal offenses are enforced by state or federal authorities depending on the crime. The DOJ's Bureau of Justice Statistics (BJS) compiles data on cases that are handled by the federal justice system, and the Federal Bureau of Investigation (FBI) compiles data related to crimes reported to local law enforcement agencies and prosecuted at the state level. The latter data set is far larger than the federal data set because most crimes fall under state or local jurisdiction.

In *Federal Justice Statistics, 2011–2012* (January 2015, https://www.bjs.gov/content/pub/pdf/fjs1112.pdf), Mark Motivans of the BJS presents data related to the federal justice system. Figure 2.1 shows the number of suspects and defendants (people charged with crimes) whose cases were processed at the federal level between fiscal years (FYs) 1994 and 2012. (The federal fiscal year begins October 1 and ends September 30; thus, FY 2012 lasted from October 1, 2011, to September 30, 2012.) In FY 2012 more than 172,000 people were arrested by federal authorities. As shown in Figure 2.1, federal cases overwhelmingly involve drug and immigration offenses. Drug crimes are discussed in detail in Chapter 4. Therefore, the remainder of this chapter will focus on statistics related to crimes that fall under state or local jurisdiction.

The FBI's Uniform Crime Reporting (UCR) Program gathers crime data from law enforcement agencies throughout the country and publishes selected data annually in *Crime in the United States*. As of April 2017, the most recent edition, *Crime in the United States, 2015* (https://ucr.fbi.gov/crime-in-the-u.s/2015/crime-in-the-u.s.-2015), was published in September 2016. According to the FBI, in "FBI Releases 2015 Crime Statistics" (September 26, 2016, https://ucr.fbi.gov/crime-in-the-u.s/2015/crime-in-the-u.s.-2015/resource-pages/2015-cius-summary_final.pdf), 16,643 of the 18,439

city, county, university and college, state, tribal, and federal agencies eligible to participate in the UCR Program submitted data in 2015. Not every agency, however, contributed data for every crime that was tracked by the UCR Program. In other words, the tables and figures in *Crime in the United States, 2015* provide crime statistics on only those crimes that were reported to the UCR Program and do not reflect the total number of crimes that were committed or processed by local agencies.

The FBI compiles two main sets of crime statistics: crimes reported to agencies and crimes cleared by agencies. Reported crimes do not necessarily result in arrests or convictions. Cleared offenses are of two types. The first type of cleared offenses consists of crimes for which agencies report that at least one person has been arrested, charged, and turned over to the court for prosecution. This does not necessarily mean the person arrested was guilty or convicted of the crime. The second type of cleared offenses includes those cleared by "extraordinary means," that is, offenses for which there can be no arrest. Such cases include, for example, a murder-suicide, when the perpetrator is known to be deceased.

The FBI collects data for dozens of specifically defined crimes. Some of these crimes are categorized as violent crimes or property crimes. In *Crime in the United States, 2015*, the FBI defines violent crimes as those that "involve force or threat of force." These crimes include murder and nonnegligent manslaughter, forcible rape, robbery, and aggravated assault. The FBI classifies four types of crimes as property crimes: burglary, larceny-theft, motor vehicle theft, and arson. The FBI explains that "the object of the theft-type offenses is the taking of money or property, but there is no force or threat of force against the victims."

REPORTED CRIMES

Table 2.1 lists the number of certain crimes that were reported yearly by law enforcement agencies between

FIGURE 2.1

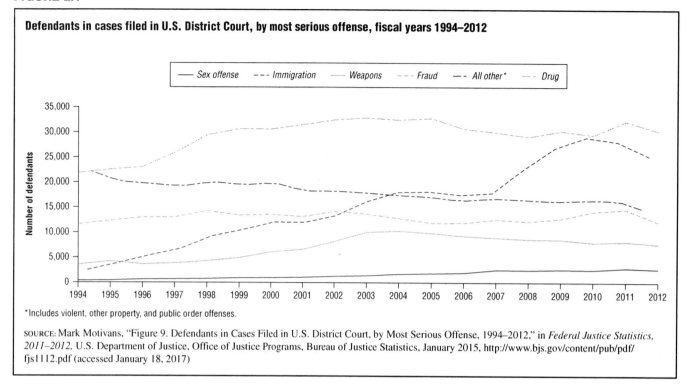

Defendants in cases filed in U.S. District Court, by most serious offense, fiscal years 1994–2012

*Includes violent, other property, and public order offenses.

SOURCE: Mark Motivans, "Figure 9. Defendants in Cases Filed in U.S. District Court, by Most Serious Offense, 1994–2012," in *Federal Justice Statistics, 2011–2012*, U.S. Department of Justice, Office of Justice Programs, Bureau of Justice Statistics, January 2015, http://www.bjs.gov/content/pub/pdf/fjs1112.pdf (accessed January 18, 2017)

1996 and 2015 and the rates of these crimes per 100,000 inhabitants. In 2015 nearly 1.2 million violent crimes were reported, down from almost 1.7 million in 1996. The overall rate for violent crime in 2015 was 372.6 per 100,000 inhabitants. This value was down considerably from a rate of 636.6 per 100,000 inhabitants in 1996, but up slightly from a rate of 361.6 per 100,000 inhabitants in 2014.

Murder and Nonnegligent Manslaughter

According to the FBI, in *Crime in the United States, 2015*, murder and nonnegligent manslaughter is "the willful (nonnegligent) killing of one human being by another." The murder statistics do not include suicides, accidents, or justifiable homicides by either citizens or law enforcement officers.

The total number of reported murders and nonnegligent manslaughters in 2015 was 15,696 for a rate of 4.9 per 100,000 inhabitants. (See Table 2.1.) During the 1990s the murder rate was much higher; in 1996 it stood at 7.4 murders per 100,000 inhabitants. The rate began a sustained decline and dipped below 5 murders per 100,000 inhabitants for the first time in 2010. It should be noted that Table 2.1 does not include the thousands of people who were killed as a result of the September 11, 2001, terrorist attacks against the United States.

The FBI collects detailed homicide data in the UCR Program's Supplementary Homicide Report (SHR). SHR data include the age, sex, and race of the offenders and victims, the relationship between the offenders and

victims, the circumstances surrounding the murders, and the types of weapons used in the murders. Note that not all these statistics are reported by all agencies for every reported murder, offender, and victim.

MURDER OFFENDERS AND VICTIMS. Table 2.2 includes SHR data for 15,326 murder offenders. Because offender data are based on reported crimes rather than on actual arrests, SHR tables classify the age, sex, and race of some offenders as "unknown." SHR categorizations for 2015 murder offenders by sex are:

- Male offenders—9,553 (62.3% of the total)

- Female offenders—1,180 (7.7%)

- Unknown—4,593 (30%)

SHR categorizations for 2015 murder offenders by race are (note that the percentages do not sum to 100% because of rounding):

- White offenders—4,636 (30.2% of the total)

- African American offenders—5,620 (36.7%)

- Other races—283 (1.8%)

- Unknown—4,787 (31.2%)

The ages of 5,203 murder offenders are listed as unknown. (See Table 2.2.) Offenders for which ages are known fall mostly within the range of 17 to 34 years old.

SHR data for 13,455 murder victims in 2015 are shown in Table 2.3. The vast majority (10,608, or 78.8% of the total) were male, whereas 2,818 (20.9%)

TABLE 2.1

Violent crimes and property crimes by volume and rate per 100,000 inhabitants, 1996–2015

Year	Population[a]	Violent crime[b]	Violent crime rate	Murder and nonnegligent manslaughter	Murder and nonnegligent manslaughter rate	Rape (revised definition)[c]	Rape (revised definition) rate[c]	Rape (legacy definition)[d]	Rape (legacy definition) rate[d]	Robbery	Robbery rate	Aggravated assault	Aggravated assault rate	Property crime	Property crime rate	Burglary	Burglary rate	Larceny-theft	Larceny-theft rate	Motor vehicle theft	Motor vehicle theft rate
1996	265,228,572	1,688,540	636.6	19,645	7.4			96,252	36.3	535,594	201.9	1,037,049	391.0	11,805,323	4,451.0	2,506,400	945.0	7,904,685	2,980.3	1,394,238	525.7
1997	267,783,607	1,636,096	611.0	18,208	6.8			96,153	35.9	498,534	186.2	1,023,201	382.1	11,558,475	4,316.3	2,460,526	918.8	7,743,760	2,891.8	1,354,189	505.7
1998	270,248,003	1,533,887	567.6	16,974	6.3			93,144	34.5	447,186	165.5	976,583	361.4	10,951,827	4,052.5	2,332,735	863.2	7,376,311	2,729.5	1,242,781	459.9
1999	272,690,813	1,426,044	523.0	15,522	5.7			89,411	32.8	409,371	150.1	911,740	334.3	10,208,334	3,743.6	2,100,739	770.4	6,955,520	2,550.7	1,152,075	422.5
2000	281,421,906	1,425,486	506.5	15,586	5.5			90,178	32.0	408,016	145.0	911,706	324.0	10,182,584	3,618.3	2,050,992	728.8	6,971,590	2,477.3	1,160,002	412.2
2001[e]	285,317,559	1,439,480	504.5	16,037	5.6			90,863	31.8	423,557	148.5	909,023	318.6	10,437,189	3,658.1	2,116,531	741.8	7,092,267	2,485.7	1,228,391	430.5
2002	287,973,924	1,423,677	494.4	16,229	5.6			95,235	33.1	420,806	146.1	891,407	309.5	10,455,277	3,630.6	2,151,252	747.0	7,057,379	2,450.7	1,246,646	432.9
2003	290,788,976	1,383,676	475.8	16,528	5.7			93,883	32.3	414,235	142.5	859,030	295.4	10,442,862	3,591.2	2,154,834	741.0	7,026,802	2,416.5	1,261,226	433.7
2004	293,656,842	1,360,088	463.2	16,148	5.5			95,089	32.4	401,470	136.7	847,381	288.6	10,319,386	3,514.1	2,144,446	730.3	6,937,089	2,362.3	1,237,851	421.5
2005	296,507,061	1,390,745	469.0	16,740	5.6			94,347	31.8	417,438	140.8	862,220	290.8	10,174,754	3,431.5	2,155,448	726.9	6,783,447	2,287.8	1,235,859	416.8
2006	299,398,484	1,435,123	479.3	17,309	5.8			94,472	31.6	449,246	150.0	874,096	292.0	10,019,601	3,346.6	2,194,993	733.1	6,626,363	2,213.2	1,198,245	400.2
2007	301,621,157	1,422,970	471.8	17,128	5.7			92,160	30.6	447,324	148.3	866,358	287.2	9,882,212	3,276.4	2,190,198	726.1	6,591,542	2,185.4	1,100,472	364.9
2008	304,059,724	1,394,461	458.6	16,465	5.4			90,750	29.8	443,563	145.9	843,683	277.5	9,774,152	3,214.6	2,228,887	733.0	6,586,206	2,166.1	959,059	315.4
2009	307,006,550	1,325,896	431.9	15,399	5.0			89,241	29.1	408,742	133.1	812,514	264.7	9,337,060	3,041.3	2,203,313	717.7	6,338,095	2,064.5	795,652	259.2
2010	309,330,219	1,251,248	404.5	14,722	4.8			85,593	27.7	369,089	119.3	781,844	252.8	9,112,625	2,945.9	2,168,459	701.0	6,204,601	2,005.8	739,565	239.1
2011	311,587,816	1,206,005	387.1	14,661	4.7			84,175	27.0	354,746	113.9	752,423	241.5	9,052,743	2,905.4	2,185,140	701.3	6,151,095	1,974.1	716,508	230.0
2012	313,873,685	1,217,057	387.8	14,856	4.7			85,141	27.1	355,051	113.1	762,009	242.8	9,001,992	2,868.0	2,109,932	672.2	6,168,874	1,965.4	723,186	230.4
2013	316,497,531	1,168,298	369.1	14,319	4.5	113,695	35.9	82,109	25.9	345,093	109.0	726,777	229.6	8,651,892	2,733.6	1,932,139	610.5	6,019,465	1,901.9	700,288	221.3
2014[f]	318,907,401	1,153,022	361.6	14,164	4.4	118,027	37.0	84,864	26.6	322,905	101.3	731,089	229.2	8,209,010	2,574.1	1,713,153	537.2	5,809,054	1,821.5	686,803	215.4
2015	321,418,820	1,197,704	372.6	15,696	4.9	124,047	38.6	90,185	28.1	327,374	101.9	764,449	237.8	7,993,631	2,487.0	1,579,527	491.4	5,706,346	1,775.4	707,758	220.2

[a]Populations are U.S. Census Bureau provisional estimates as of July 1 for each year except 2000 and 2010, which are decennial census counts.
[b]The violent crime figures include the offenses of murder, rape (legacy definition), robbery, and aggravated assault.
[c]The figures shown in this column for the offense of rape were estimated using the revised Uniform Crime Reporting (UCR) definition of rape.
[d]The figures shown in this column for the offense of rape were estimated using the legacy UCR definition of rape.
[e]The murder and nonnegligent homicides that occurred as a result of the events of September 11, 2001, are not included in this table.
[f]The crime figures have been adjusted.
Note: Although arson data are included in the trend and clearance tables, sufficient data are not available to estimate totals for this offense. Therefore, no arson data are published in this table.

SOURCE: "Table 1. Crime in the United States by Volume and Rate per 100,000 Inhabitants, 1996–2015," in *Crime in the United States, 2015*," U.S. Department of Justice, Federal Bureau of Investigation, September 26, 2016, https://ucr.fbi.gov/crime-in-the-u.s/2015/crime-in-the-u.s.-2015/tables/table-1 (accessed January 18, 2017)

TABLE 2.2

Murder offenders where age, sex, race, and ethnicity are known, 2015

Age	Total	Sex			Race				Ethnicity[a]		
		Male	Female	Unknown	White	Black or African American	Other[b]	Unknown	Hispanic or Latino	Not Hispanic or Latino	Unknown
Total	**15,326**	**9,553**	**1,180**	**4,593**	**4,636**	**5,620**	**283**	**4,787**	**1,312**	**4,598**	**4,408**
Percent distribution[c]	100.0	62.3	7.7	30.0	30.2	36.7	1.8	31.2	12.7	44.6	42.7
Under 18[d]	667	616	51	0	236	412	14	5	104	269	91
Under 22[d]	2,648	2,403	239	6	916	1,638	69	25	404	1,108	322
18 and over[d]	9,456	8,327	1,109	20	4,324	4,755	268	109	1,183	4,125	1,169
Infant (under 1)	0	0	0	0	0	0	0	0	0	0	0
1 to 4	1	1	0	0	0	1	0	0	0	0	0
5 to 8	2	1	1	0	1	1	0	0	0	0	1
9 to 12	9	8	1	0	4	5	0	0	2	2	2
13 to 16	341	320	21	0	119	210	9	3	54	147	44
17 to 19	1,263	1,143	119	1	442	784	28	9	193	527	156
20 to 24	2,448	2,180	262	6	844	1,513	66	25	330	1,030	273
25 to 29	1,814	1,607	204	3	739	997	52	26	214	756	244
30 to 34	1,251	1,082	165	4	610	584	40	17	175	509	173
35 to 39	840	733	107	0	449	368	17	6	104	382	115
40 to 44	594	506	88	0	350	223	17	4	79	269	69
45 to 49	449	384	63	2	251	175	20	3	47	200	56
50 to 54	453	390	60	3	295	128	16	14	46	225	46
55 to 59	278	248	29	1	174	94	9	1	23	148	30
60 to 64	149	136	13	0	103	41	1	4	5	74	23
65 to 69	88	77	11	0	60	27	0	1	7	44	12
70 to 74	52	42	10	0	37	10	4	1	3	32	7
75 and over	91	85	6	0	82	6	3	0	5	49	9
Unknown	5,203	610	20	4,573	76	453	1	4,673	25	204	3,148

[a]Not all agencies provide ethnicity data; therefore, the race and ethnicity totals will not equal.
[b]Includes American Indian or Alaska Native, Asian, and Native Hawaiian or other Pacific Islander.
[c]Because of rounding, the percentages may not add to 100.0.
[d]Does not include unknown ages.

SOURCE: "Expanded Homicide Data Table 3. Murder Offenders by Age, Sex, Race, and Ethnicity, 2015," in *Crime in the United States, 2015*, U.S. Department of Justice, Federal Bureau of Investigation, September 26, 2016, https://ucr.fbi.gov/crime-in-the-u.s/2015/crime-in-the-u.s.-2015/tables/expanded_homicide_data_table_3_murder_offenders_by_age_sex_and_race_2015.xls (accessed January 18, 2017)

were female. The remaining 29 victims (0.2%) were of unknown sex. (Note that the percentages do not sum to 100% because of rounding.) Whites accounted for 5,854 (43.5%) of the victims, and African Americans accounted for 7,039 (52.3%) of the victims. Another 366 victims (2.7%) were of other races, and 196 victims (1.5%) were of unknown race.

The vast majority of murder victims (12,228, or 90.9% of the total) were aged 18 years and older. (See Table 2.3.) Only 1,093 victims (8.1% of the total) were under the age of 18 years. Ages were reported as unknown for 134 victims (1%). Overall, people between the ages of 20 and 39 years accounted for the largest numbers of murder victims in 2015.

MURDER CIRCUMSTANCES. Table 2.4 describes the circumstances for 13,455 of the total murders reported in 2015. The circumstances of 5,366 murders, or 39.9% of the total covered by the SHR, were unknown. Of the reported murders, 2,014 (15%) were known to be associated with felonies, mostly robberies and narcotic drug law violations. Another 117 (0.9%) of the reported murders were suspected of involving felonies. Nearly half (5,958, or 44.3%) of the reported murders occurred because of other circumstances, mainly arguments and brawls between people.

As shown in Table 2.4, the relationship between the murder offender and victim was unknown in 6,432 (47.8%) of the murders. Of the 7,023 murders in which the relationship could be ascertained, 1,375 murders (10.2%) were committed by strangers (people unknown to the victims). The three most common relationships were those in which the victim was the offender's:

- Acquaintance—2,801
- Wife—509
- Girlfriend—496

Overall, 1,721 of the victims were murdered by family members.

MURDER WEAPONS. Table 2.5 shows the weapons used in 13,455 of the murders committed in 2015, as reported in the SHR. Nearly three-fourths (9,616, or 71.5%) of the murders involved firearms. Knives or other cutting instruments were used in 1,544 (11.5%) of the murders, and personal weapons (hands, fists, feet, etc.) were used in 623 (4.6%).

TABLE 2.3

Murder victims where age, sex, race, and ethnicity are known, 2015

Age	Total	Sex			Race				Ethnicity		
		Male	Female	Unknown	White	Black or African American	Other[a]	Unknown	Hispanic or Latino	Not Hispanic or Latino	Unknown
Total	13,455	10,608	2,818	29	5,854	7,039	366	196	2,028	7,971	2,224
Percent distribution[b]	100.0	78.8	20.9	0.2	43.5	52.3	2.7	1.5	16.6	65.2	18.2
Under 18[c]	1,093	761	329	3	504	544	26	19	193	611	189
Under 22[c]	2,624	2,135	487	2	954	1,598	44	28	488	1,484	443
18 and over[c]	12,228	9,773	2,448	7	5,296	6,451	339	142	1,823	7,305	1,974
Infant (under 1)	168	104	63	1	89	65	8	6	24	104	28
1 to 4	260	153	106	1	130	117	6	7	32	160	58
5 to 8	91	49	42	0	58	30	1	2	12	57	16
9 to 12	56	35	20	1	30	22	3	1	9	30	6
13 to 16	282	218	64	0	110	167	4	1	62	141	49
17 to 19	996	870	126	0	325	647	16	8	191	546	159
20 to 24	2,431	2,102	329	0	764	1,596	45	26	414	1,398	368
25 to 29	2,071	1,733	338	0	717	1,290	48	16	321	1,201	331
30 to 34	1,647	1,340	307	0	650	927	49	21	266	974	254
35 to 39	1,263	1,021	241	1	539	666	45	13	200	728	223
40 to 44	925	701	222	2	467	428	23	7	150	545	158
45 to 49	781	586	194	1	399	330	33	19	118	485	115
50 to 54	737	568	169	0	428	282	17	10	84	468	120
55 to 59	580	425	154	1	363	183	27	7	57	389	102
60 to 64	360	250	109	1	226	114	12	8	36	231	54
65 to 69	235	168	67	0	166	59	6	4	14	168	41
70 to 74	159	93	65	1	113	33	9	4	11	100	33
75 and over	279	118	161	0	226	39	13	1	15	191	48
Unknown	134	74	41	19	54	44	1	35	12	55	61

[a]Includes American Indian or Alaska Native, Asian, and Native Hawaiian or other Pacific Islander.
[b]Because of rounding, the percentages may not add to 100.0.
[c]Does not include unknown ages.

SOURCE: "Expanded Homicide Data Table 2. Murder Victims by Age, Sex, Race, and Ethnicity, 2015," in *Crime in the United States, 2015*, U.S. Department of Justice, Federal Bureau of Investigation, September 26, 2016, https://ucr.fbi.gov/crime-in-the-u.s/2015/crime-in-the-u.s.-2015/tables/expanded_homicide_data_table_2_murder_victims_by_age_sex_and_race_2015.xls (accessed January 18, 2017)

Rape

Rape is a crime of violence in which the victim may suffer serious physical injury and long-term psychological pain. According to the FBI, in *Crime in the United States, 2015*, until 2013 the UCR Program categorized rape using what it called its "legacy" definition: "the carnal knowledge of a female forcibly and against her will." In 2013 the FBI revised its definition of rape for the UCR Program. Under the new definition, rape includes "penetration, no matter how slight, of the vagina or anus with any body part or object, or oral penetration by a sex organ of another person, without the consent of the victim. Attempts or assaults to commit rape are also included in the statistics presented here; however, statutory rape and incest are excluded." Statutory rape is an offense in which the victim cannot legally consent to sexual intercourse because the victim is either too young or is mentally or physically incapacitated in some way.

Rape is a very intimate crime, and rape victims may be unwilling, afraid, or ashamed to discuss it. As a result, many rapes are likely not reported to law enforcement authorities. In 2015, 90,185 rapes (legacy definition) were reported to law enforcement agencies for a rate of 28.1 rapes per 100,000 inhabitants. (See Table 2.1.) The legacy rape rate has declined dramatically since 1996, when it was 36.3 rapes per 100,000 inhabitants. In 2015, 124,047 rapes (new definition) were reported to law enforcement agencies for a rate of 38.6 rapes per 100,000 inhabitants.

Table 2.6 provides additional information about selected offenses as reported by 14,851 agencies in 2015. The data show 86,252 completed rapes (new definition) and 4,207 attempted rapes (new definition).

Robbery

According to the FBI, in *Crime in the United States, 2015*, robbery is defined as "the taking or attempting to take anything of value from the care, custody, or control of a person or persons by force or threat of force or violence and/or by putting the victim in fear." The robbery count in 2015 was 327,374 for a rate of 101.9 per 100,000 inhabitants. (See Table 2.1.) This is down significantly from 1996, when the rate was 201.9 per 100,000 inhabitants.

In *Crime in the United States, 2015*, the FBI lists the locations of 284,772 robberies that were reported in 2015. The largest portion (39.8%) occurred on the street or highway, while 19.1% occurred at miscellaneous locations,

TABLE 2.4

Murder victims where relationship to offender and circumstances are known, 2015

Circumstances	Total murder victims	Husband	Wife	Mother	Father	Son	Daughter	Brother	Sister	Other family	Acquaintance	Friend	Boyfriend	Girlfriend	Neighbor	Employee	Employer	Stranger	Unknown
Total	13,455	113	509	125	131	255	162	108	32	286	2,801	365	152	496	95	8	10	1,375	6,432
Felony type total:	2,014	3	37	8	12	28	18	7	9	36	533	68	9	34	18	5	1	388	800
Rape	12	0	0	0	0	1	0	0	0	0	6	0	0	2	1	0	0	0	2
Robbery	595	0	0	0	0	0	0	0	0	3	128	20	1	0	2	3	1	211	225
Burglary	102	0	0	1	1	1	0	0	0	7	30	1	0	2	4	1	0	24	31
Larceny-theft	16	0	0	0	0	0	0	0	0	0	6	2	0	1	0	0	0	5	2
Motor vehicle theft	41	0	0	0	1	0	0	0	0	4	11	0	0	3	0	0	0	13	9
Arson	19	0	2	0	0	1	0	0	1	1	2	0	0	0	0	0	0	6	6
Prostitution and commercialized vice	6	0	0	0	0	0	0	0	0	0	1	0	0	0	0	0	0	1	3
Other sex offenses	15	0	1	0	0	0	0	0	0	0	5	0	1	1	1	0	0	3	3
Narcotic drug laws	468	0	0	0	0	1	1	0	0	4	174	22	1	4	0	0	0	28	234
Gambling	5	0	0	0	0	0	0	0	0	0	5	0	0	0	0	0	0	0	0
Other-not specified	735	3	34	7	10	24	17	7	8	17	165	23	6	21	10	1	0	97	285
Suspected felony type	117	4	7	1	0	7	3	0	1	4	19	2	0	6	0	0	0	8	55
Other than felony type total:	5,958	84	367	80	92	171	110	88	19	176	1,714	229	120	355	59	2	7	588	1,697
Romantic triangle	106	3	14	2	0	0	0	0	0	1	52	4	3	9	0	0	0	8	10
Child killed by babysitter	36	0	0	0	0	0	0	0	0	3	30	1	0	0	1	0	0	0	1
Brawl due to influence of alcohol	112	0	2	0	2	1	1	11	0	4	37	8	1	1	4	1	0	20	19
Brawl due to influence of narcotics	75	0	2	2	1	5	2	1	0	1	28	8	1	3	0	0	0	7	14
Argument over money or property	184	2	5	3	2	4	0	4	1	10	100	9	3	3	5	0	0	11	22
Other arguments	2,941	64	242	45	64	35	20	62	5	100	940	150	97	276	34	1	4	281	521
Gangland killings	188	1	0	0	0	1	0	0	0	1	36	6	0	0	0	0	0	28	115
Juvenile gang killings	604	0	0	0	0	0	0	0	0	0	105	3	0	0	0	0	0	56	440
Institutional killings	24	0	1	0	0	0	0	0	0	0	18	0	0	0	0	0	0	3	2
Sniper attack	5	0	1	0	0	0	0	0	0	0	1	0	0	0	0	0	0	0	3
Other-not specified	1,683	14	100	28	23	125	87	10	13	56	367	40	15	63	15	0	3	174	550
Unknown	5,366	22	98	36	27	49	31	13	3	70	535	66	23	101	18	1	2	391	3,880

Note: The relationship categories of husband and wife include both common-law and ex-spouses. The categories of mother, father, sister, brother, son, and daughter include stepparents, stepchildren, and stepsiblings. The category of acquaintance includes homosexual relationships and the composite category of other known to victim.

SOURCE: "Expanded Homicide Data Table 10. Murder Circumstances by Relationship, 2015," in *Crime in the United States, 2015*, U.S. Department of Justice, Federal Bureau of Investigation, September 26, 2016, https://ucr.fbi.gov/crime-in-the-u.s/2015/crime-in-the-u.s.-2015/tables/expanded_homicide_data_table_10_murder_circumstances_by_relationship_2015.xls (accessed January 18, 2017)

TABLE 2.5

Murder victims where murder weapon and circumstances are known, 2015

Circumstances	Total murder victims	Total firearms	Handguns	Rifles	Shotguns	Other guns or type not stated	Knives or cutting instruments	Blunt objects (clubs, hammers, etc.)	Personal weapons (hands, fists, feet, etc.)	Poison	Pushed or thrown out window	Explosives	Fire	Narcotics	Drowning	Strangulation	Asphyxiation	Other
Total	13,455	9,616	6,447	252	269	2,648	1,544	437	623	7	1	1	82	70	14	96	120	844
Felony type total:	2,014	1,458	1,042	36	40	340	178	84	72	1	0	0	34	40	2	16	14	115
Rape	12	2	2	0	0	0	1	2	4	0	0	0	0	0	0	1	0	2
Robbery	595	467	366	5	15	81	42	27	26	0	0	0	0	0	0	7	5	21
Burglary	102	66	33	7	4	22	13	8	2	0	0	0	3	0	0	0	2	8
Larceny-theft	16	12	8	0	0	4	1	0	1	0	0	0	0	0	0	0	1	1
Motor vehicle theft	41	19	9	1	1	8	10	2	2	0	0	0	0	0	0	0	1	7
Arson	19	0	0	0	0	0	0	0	0	0	0	0	14	0	0	0	0	4
Prostitution and commercialized vice	6	3	3	0	0	0	1	1	0	0	0	0	0	0	0	0	0	1
Other sex offenses	15	6	5	0	1	0	1	1	2	0	0	0	0	0	0	2	0	3
Narcotic drug laws	468	389	306	7	2	74	19	7	4	1	0	0	0	35	0	0	0	13
Gambling	5	4	3	0	0	1	1	0	0	0	0	0	0	0	0	0	0	0
Other-not specified	735	490	307	16	17	150	88	36	31	0	0	0	17	5	2	6	5	55
Suspected felony type	117	84	56	1	4	23	9	3	2	0	0	0	0	0	0	2	4	13
Other than felony type total:	5,958	3,941	2,884	140	162	755	913	203	410	4	0	0	11	20	9	47	72	328
Romantic triangle	106	76	54	3	7	12	19	4	4	0	0	0	0	0	0	1	1	1
Child killed by babysitter	36	1	0	0	0	1	0	4	19	0	0	0	0	0	1	0	1	10
Brawl due to influence of alcohol	112	41	27	2	2	10	31	9	14	0	0	0	1	0	0	0	1	15
Brawl due to influence of narcotics	75	41	26	2	1	12	8	1	6	0	0	0	0	9	0	0	1	9
Argument over money or property	184	127	95	10	5	17	31	12	3	0	0	0	0	0	0	5	1	5
Other arguments	2,941	1,822	1,325	50	99	348	633	111	186	2	0	0	7	1	5	29	29	116
Gangland killings	188	175	146	5	0	24	8	1	1	0	0	0	1	0	0	0	1	1
Juvenile gang killings	604	578	465	6	3	104	20	1	2	0	0	0	0	0	0	2	0	3
Institutional killings	24	1	0	0	0	1	2	2	13	0	0	0	0	0	0	0	3	1
Sniper attack	5	4	1	2	1	0	2	1	0	0	0	0	0	0	0	0	0	0
Other-not specified	1,683	1,075	745	60	44	226	161	57	162	2	1	0	2	10	3	10	34	167
Unknown	5,366	4,133	2,465	75	63	1,530	444	147	139	2	1	1	37	10	3	31	30	388

SOURCE: "Expanded Homicide Data Table 11. Murder Circumstances by Weapon, 2015," in *Crime in the United States, 2015*, U.S. Department of Justice, Federal Bureau of Investigation, September 26, 2016, https://ucr.fbi.gov/crime-in-the-u.s/2015/crime-in-the-u.s.-2015/tables/expanded_homicide_data_table_11_murder_circumstances_by_weapon_2015.xls (accessed January 18, 2017)

TABLE 2.6

Details about selected offenses, 2014–15

| Population group | Rape (revised definition)[a] | | Rape (legacy definition)[b] | | Robbery | | | | Aggravated assault | | | |
	Rape	Assault to rape-attempts	Rape by force	Assault to rape-attempts	Firearm	Knife or cutting instrument	Other weapon	Strong-arm	Firearm	Knife or cutting instrument	Other weapon	Hands, fists, feet, etc.
Total all agencies:												
2014	81,046	4,218	6,712	403	119,583	23,486	26,181	126,903	151,957	126,457	215,342	179,850
2015	86,252	4,207	7,158	428	123,358	23,759	27,397	127,053	170,941	127,189	220,012	183,451
Percent change	+6.4	−0.3	+6.6	+6.2	+3.2	+1.2	+4.6	+0.1	+12.5	+0.6	+2.2	+2.0

| Population group | Burglary | | | Motor vehicle theft | | | Arson | | | Number of agencies | 2015 estimated population |
	Forcible entry	Unlawful entry	Attempted forcible entry	Autos	Trucks and buses	Other vehicles	Structure	Mobile	Other		
Total all agencies:											
2014	912,987	553,566	100,764	473,809	94,806	68,148	18,229	9,475	12,207	14,851	293,138,011
2015	838,673	512,605	96,012	494,782	96,507	68,255	17,502	9,353	11,414		
Percent change	−8.1	−7.4	−4.7	+4.4	+1.8	+0.2	−4.0	−1.3	−6.5		

[a] The figures shown in this column for the offense of rape were reported using the revised Uniform Crime Reporting (UCR) definition of rape.

[b] The figures shown in this column for the offense of rape were reported using the legacy UCR definition of rape.

Note: No agencies over 1,000,000 in population submitted rape data using the legacy UCR definition in 2015; therefore, the UCR Program could not provide a 2-year comparison for this agency group size.

SOURCE: Adapted from "Table 15. Crime Trends: Additional Information about Selected Offenses by Population Group, 2014–2015," in *Crime in the United States, 2015,* U.S. Department of Justice, Federal Bureau of Investigation, September 26, 2016, https://ucr.fbi.gov/crime-in-the-u.s/2015/crime-in-the-u.s.-2015/tables/table-15 (accessed January 18, 2017)

16.5% occurred at residences, and 14.4% occurred at commercial houses (nonresidential structures that are used for businesses other than gas stations, banks, or convenience stores). Robberies at convenience stores accounted for 5.7% of the total, whereas gas or service stations accounted for 2.7% and banks for 1.7% of the total. (Note that the percentages do not sum to 100% because of rounding.)

WEAPONS INVOLVED IN ROBBERIES. Table 2.6 provides additional information about 301,567 robberies reported by 14,851 law enforcement agencies in 2015. More than half (174,514, or 57.9%) involved a weapon, such as firearm (123,358), knife or other cutting instrument (23,759), or some other type of weapon (27,397). The other 42.1% (127,053) of the robberies were strong-arm robberies in which the offenders used bodily force to rob their victims.

Aggravated Assault

Aggravated assault is defined by the FBI in *Crime in the United States, 2015* as "an unlawful attack by one person upon another for the purpose of inflicting severe or aggravated bodily injury." The agency further notes that aggravated assault typically involves "the use of a weapon or by other means likely to produce death or great bodily harm." Attempted aggravated assaults that involve weapons or the threat to use weapons are included in this category. However, an aggravated assault that occurs during a robbery is categorized as a robbery.

In 2015, 764,449 aggravated assaults were reported to law enforcement agencies nationwide for a rate of 237.8 aggravated assaults per 100,000 inhabitants. (See Table 2.1.) The rate has declined substantially since 1996, when it stood at 391 aggravated assaults per 100,000 inhabitants.

WEAPONS INVOLVED IN AGGRAVATED ASSAULTS. Table 2.6 provides additional information about 701,593 of the aggravated assaults that occurred in 2015 as reported by 14,851 law enforcement agencies. Nearly three-quarters (518,142, or 73.9%) of the assaults involved weapons. Perpetrators used their hands, fists, feet, and so on in the remaining 183,451 assaults for 26.1% of the total. Overall, firearms were involved in 170,941 (24.4%) of the aggravated assaults.

Violent Crime and Property Crime

As noted earlier, the FBI includes four crimes in the category of violent crime: forcible rape, murder and nonnegligent manslaughter, aggravated assault, and robbery. A crime that includes more than one of these violent acts is counted only once, under the most serious offense committed. According to the FBI, in *Crime in the United States, 2015*, the hierarchy is murder and nonnegligent homicide, forcible rape, robbery, and aggravated assault. Thus, a forcible rape in which the victim is also robbed

FIGURE 2.2

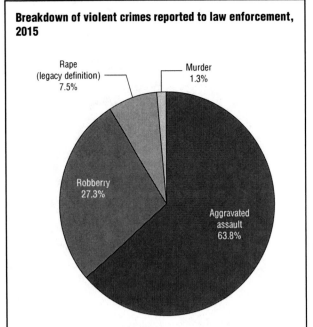

Breakdown of violent crimes reported to law enforcement, 2015

SOURCE: "2015 Violent Crimes," in *Latest Crime Statistics Released,* U.S. Department of Justice, Federal Bureau of Investigation, September 26, 2016, https://www.fbi.gov/news/stories/latest-crime-statistics-released (accessed January 18, 2017)

would be counted as a forcible rape, not as a forcible rape and a robbery. In 2015 nearly 1.2 million violent crimes were reported by law enforcement agencies. (See Table 2.1.) As shown in Figure 2.2, the breakdown of reported violent crimes by percentage was (note that the percentages do not sum to 100% because of rounding):

- Murder and nonnegligent homicide—1.3% of reported violent crimes

- Forcible rape (legacy definition)—7.5% of reported violent crimes

- Robbery—27.3% of reported violent crimes

- Aggravated assault—63.8% of reported violent crimes

The FBI includes four crimes in the category of property crime: larceny-theft, burglary, arson, and motor vehicle theft. In 2015 nearly 8 million of these property crimes were reported for a rate of 2,487 per 100,000 inhabitants. (See Table 2.1.) According to the FBI, the hierarchy for property crimes is burglary, larceny-theft, and motor vehicle theft. The property crime hierarchy lies below the violent crime hierarchy, meaning that a violent crime that includes one or more property crimes is counted only under the appropriate violent crime. Arson is not included in the hierarchy. It is always counted separately, even when it occurs in conjunction with another violent or property crime. As shown in Figure 2.3, the breakdown of reported property crimes in 2015 by percentage was (note that the percentages do not sum to 100% because of rounding):

FIGURE 2.3

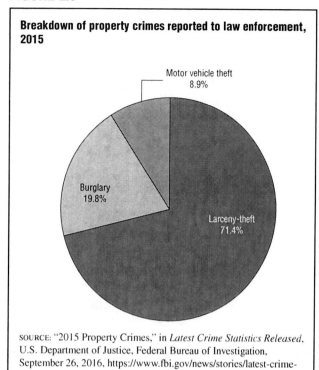

Breakdown of property crimes reported to law enforcement, 2015

Motor vehicle theft
8.9%

Burglary
19.8%

Larceny-theft
71.4%

SOURCE: "2015 Property Crimes," in *Latest Crime Statistics Released*, U.S. Department of Justice, Federal Bureau of Investigation, September 26, 2016, https://www.fbi.gov/news/stories/latest-crime-statistics-released (accessed January 18, 2017)

- Motor vehicle theft—8.9% of reported property crimes
- Burglary—19.8% of reported property crimes
- Larceny-theft—71.4% of reported violent crimes

The following four sections describe the statistics for individual property crimes.

Burglary

According to the FBI, in *Crime in the United States, 2015*, burglary is defined as "the unlawful entry of a structure to commit a felony or theft." Unlawful entry includes both forcible and nonforcible entry (e.g., entering a home through an unlocked door without the owner's permission). The FBI's definition of structure includes houses, apartments, offices, barns, stables, and so on, but does not include automobiles. Attempted forcible entries are included in the burglary category.

Nearly 1.6 million burglaries were reported in 2015 for a rate of 491.4 per 100,000 inhabitants. (See Table 2.1.) This rate is down from 1996, when it was 945 burglaries per 100,000 inhabitants. Table 2.6 provides additional information about 1.4 million of the robberies reported to 14,851 law enforcement agencies in 2015. Overall, 838,673 (57.9%) of the robberies involved forcible entry, while 512,605 (35.4%) involved nonforcible but unlawful entries. The remaining 96,012 (6.6%) offenses were attempted burglaries. (Note that the percentages do not sum to 100% because of rounding.)

A separate data set by the FBI covering nearly 1.4 million burglaries in 2015 (https://ucr.fbi.gov/crime-in-the-u.s/2015/crime-in-the-u.s.-2015/tables/table-23/table_23_offense_analysis_number_and_percent_change_2014-2015.xls/output.xls) indicates that the vast majority (999,446) of these burglaries occurred at residences. The rest were at nonresidences, such as stores or offices.

Larceny-Theft

Larceny-theft is defined by the FBI in *Crime in the United States, 2015* as "the unlawful taking, carrying, leading, or riding away of property from the possession or constructive possession of another." Larceny-theft does not involve the use of force, violence, or fraud. Examples of fraud-based crimes are embezzlement, forgery, and passing bad checks. Larceny-theft does include offenses such as shoplifting, pocket picking, purse snatching, stealing items from motor vehicles, and stealing bicycles. Attempted larceny-thefts are also included.

In 2015 law enforcement agencies reported 5.7 million larceny-thefts for a rate of 1,775.4 per 100,000 inhabitants. (See Table 2.1.) This rate was down substantially from 1996, when it was 2,980.3 per 100,000 inhabitants. According to the FBI, the total value of property lost by victims to larceny-theft in 2015 was approximately $5.3 billion.

Table 2.7 provides details about just over 5 million of the larceny-thefts that occurred in 2015 based on information from 14,420 law enforcement agencies. Thefts from motor vehicles (excluding accessories) accounted for 1.2 million of the offenses. This was the largest category among the specifically identified larceny-theft crimes. It accounted for 24% of the total. Shoplifting crimes (1.1 million) and thefts from buildings (582,055) made up 22.3% and 11.6%, respectively, of the total.

According to the FBI, the average loss to victims due to larceny-thefts in 2015 was $929 per offense. A breakdown by average value is shown in Table 2.7:

- Value over $200—2.3 million offenses or 45.7% of the total
- Value of $50 to $200—1.1 million offenses or 22.3% of the total
- Value less than $50—1.6 million offenses or 32% of the total

Motor Vehicle Theft

In *Crime in the United States, 2015*, the FBI defines motor vehicle theft as "the theft or attempted theft of a motor vehicle." Included in the definition of motor vehicles are cars, trucks, sport-utility vehicles, buses, motorcycles and motor scooters, snowmobiles, and all-terrain vehicles. Other types of motorized vehicles (e.g., boats, tractors, and construction equipment) are not included.

TABLE 2.7

Details about larceny-theft crimes, 2014–15

[14,420 agencies; 2015 estimated population 283,415,007]

Classification	Number of offenses 2015	Percent change from 2014	Percent distribution*	Average value
Larceny-theft (except motor vehicle theft):				
Total	5,014,269	−2.1	100.0	929
Larceny-theft by type:				
Pocket-picking	27,341	+2.8	0.5	652
Purse-snatching	20,276	−2.2	0.4	563
Shoplifting	1,118,390	+1.3	22.3	262
From motor vehicles (except accessories)	1,203,497	+3.7	24.0	782
Motor vehicle accessories	349,954	−1.7	7.0	573
Bicycles	180,123	−0.2	3.6	444
From buildings	582,055	−7.4	11.6	1,394
From coin-operated machines	11,407	−4.5	0.2	497
All others	1,521,226	−7.0	30.3	1,512
Larceny-theft by value:				
Over $200	2,289,505	−3.3	45.7	1,969
$50 to $200	1,119,662	−3.0	22.3	106
Under $50	1,605,102	+0.1	32.0	20

*Because of rounding, the percentages may not add to 100.0.

SOURCE: "Table 23. Offense Analysis: Number and Percent Change, 2014–2015," in *Crime in the United States, 2015*, U.S. Department of Justice, Federal Bureau of Investigation September 26, 2016, https://ucr.fbi.gov/crime-in-the.u.s/2015/crime-in-the-u.s.-2015/tables/table-23 (accessed January 18, 2017)

In 2015, 707,758 cases of motor vehicle theft were reported in the United States for a rate of 220.2 motor vehicle thefts per 100,000 inhabitants. (See Table 2.1.) This rate was down considerably from 1996, when the rate was 525.7 motor vehicle thefts per 100,000 inhabitants. Table 2.6 provides additional details about 659,544 of the motor vehicle thefts based on information from 14,851 law enforcement agencies in 2015. The vast majority (494,782, or 75%) of the thefts were of automobiles. Another 96,507 (14.6%) of the thefts were of trucks and buses, and 68,255 (10.3%) were of other types of vehicles. (Note that the percentages do not sum to 100% because of rounding.) According to the FBI, the total value of stolen motor vehicles in 2015 was more than $4.9 billion.

Arson

Arson, as defined by the FBI in *Crime in the United States, 2015*, is "any willful or malicious burning or attempting to burn, with or without intent to defraud, a dwelling house, public building, motor vehicle or aircraft, personal property of another, etc." Arson statistics only include fires determined to have been set on purpose; those that have been classified as suspicious or of unknown origin are excluded.

The FBI notes that statistics for arson crimes are incomplete because of limited reporting by law enforcement agencies. As reported in *Crime in the United States, 2015*, those agencies that did supply full- or partial-year arson statistics to the FBI reported 41,376 arsons in 2015. Table 2.6 provides detailed information about 38,269 of the arsons. Nearly half (17,502, or 45.7%) involved buildings, such as residences or other structures. Another 9,353 (24.4%) involved mobile property, such as cars, and 11,414 (29.8%) of the arsons involved other types of property, such as crops or fences. (Note that the percentages do not sum to 100% because of rounding.)

GUNS AND CRIME

As noted earlier and shown in Table 2.5, the FBI reports that firearms were used in 9,616 (71.5%) of 13,455 murders reported in 2015. Likewise, Table 2.6 shows that firearms were used in 123,358 robberies (40.9% of the total) and in 170,941 aggravated assaults (24.4% of the total). The number of these crimes declined dramatically between 1996 and 2015. Thus, crime-related firearm use likewise decreased sharply. Nevertheless, highly publicized mass murders committed with firearms (particularly in schools) since the late 1990s have raised concerns about gun availability.

Gun Control

Laws that regulate gun ownership by certain groups of people date back to the country's founding. Worries about firearms in the hands of criminals have spurred legislative prohibitions targeting known felons (people who have been convicted of felony crimes). In addition, the state and federal governments have historically enacted restrictions on certain types of firearms, for example, the "tommy" submachine guns favored by gangsters during the 1930s. In 1968 President Lyndon Johnson (1908–1973) signed into law the Gun Control

FIGURE 2.4

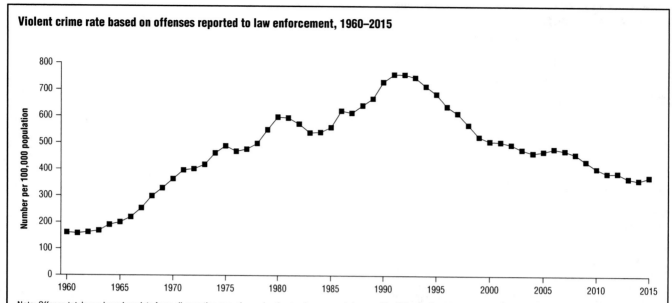

Violent crime rate based on offenses reported to law enforcement, 1960–2015

Note: Offense totals are based on data from all reporting agencies and estimates for unreported areas. The 168 murder and nonnegligent homicides that occurred as a result of the bombing of the Alfred P. Murrah Federal Building in Oklahoma City in 1995 are included in the national estimate. The murder and nonnegligent homicides that occurred as a result of the events of September 11, 2001, are not included in the national estimates. Arson data are not included.

SOURCE: Adapted from "Violent Crime Rate," in *Uniform Crime Reporting Statistics*, U.S. Department of Justice, Federal Bureau of Investigation, undated, https://www.ucrdatatool.gov/Search/Crime/State/TrendsInOneVar.cfm (accessed January 18, 2017) and "Table 1. Crime in the United States by Volume and Rate per 100,000 Inhabitants, 1996–2015," in *Crime in the United States, 2015*, U.S. Department of Justice, Federal Bureau of Investigation, September 26, 2016, https://ucr.fbi.gov/crime-in-the-u.s/2015/crime-in-the-u.s.-2015/tables/table-1 (accessed January 18, 2017)

Act of 1968, noting, "Today we begin to disarm the criminal and the careless and the insane." Despite these strong words, violent crime escalated greatly over the following decades. As shown in Figure 2.4, the violent crime rate increased from about 160 reported offenses per 100,000 population in 1960 to nearly 760 reported offenses per 100,000 population during the early 1990s.

In 1993 Congress passed the Brady Handgun Violence Prevention Act (Brady Act). In "About NICS" (2017, https://www.fbi.gov/services/cjis/nics/about-nics), the FBI notes that the Brady Act strengthened federal firearms regulations and established the National Instant Criminal Background Check System (NICS). Licensed federal firearms dealers in some states use the NICS to confirm that potential purchasers can legally buy firearms. Provisions of federal law prohibit certain people from possessing or receiving a firearm. For example, the FBI indicates that prohibited people include those convicted of a crime punishable by imprisonment for a year or more. Note that state laws can include additional prohibitive measures.

The NICS began operating in 1998. According to the FBI, in "National Instant Criminal Background Check System" (2017, https://www.fbi.gov/services/cjis/nics/ nics), more than 230 million transactions had been processed through the system. The agency notes that nearly 1.3 million transactions were denied by the NICS during that period. Figure 2.5 provides a breakdown of the denial

causes. The vast majority of the denials were based on the criminal histories of the potential purchasers.

HATE CRIMES

As is noted in Chapter 1, hate crimes are crimes that are motivated by the offender's personal prejudice or bias against the victim. There is no single, comprehensive legal definition for the term *hate crime*; however, the FBI defines it in *Hate Crime Statistics, 2015: Methodology* (Fall 2016, https://ucr.fbi.gov/hate-crime/2015/resource-pages/methodology_final.pdf) as "criminal offenses that were motivated, in whole or in part, by the offender's bias against a race, gender, gender identity, religion, disability, sexual orientation, or ethnicity, and were committed against persons, property, or society."

In 1990 Congress passed the Hate Crime Statistics Act, which required the U.S. attorney general to "acquire data ... about crimes that manifest evidence of prejudice based on race, religion, disability, sexual orientation, or ethnicity" and to publish a summary of the data. The Hate Crime Statistics Act was amended by the Violent Crime and Law Enforcement Act of 1994 to include bias-motivated acts against disabled people. Further amendments in the Church Arson Prevention Act of 1996 directed the FBI to track bias-related church arsons as a permanent part of its duties. According to the agency, in "FBI Releases 2013 Hate Crime Statistics" (December 8, 2014, https://www.fbi.gov/news/pressrel/press-releases/

FIGURE 2.5

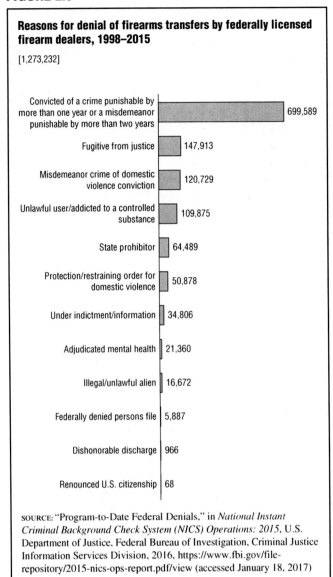

Reasons for denial of firearms transfers by federally licensed firearm dealers, 1998–2015

[1,273,232]

Reason	Count
Convicted of a crime punishable by more than one year or a misdemeanor punishable by more than two years	699,589
Fugitive from justice	147,913
Misdemeanor crime of domestic violence conviction	120,729
Unlawful user/addicted to a controlled substance	109,875
State prohibitor	64,489
Protection/restraining order for domestic violence	50,878
Under indictment/information	34,806
Adjudicated mental health	21,360
Illegal/unlawful alien	16,672
Federally denied persons file	5,887
Dishonorable discharge	966
Renounced U.S. citizenship	68

SOURCE: "Program-to-Date Federal Denials," in *National Instant Criminal Background Check System (NICS) Operations: 2015*, U.S. Department of Justice, Federal Bureau of Investigation, Criminal Justice Information Services Division, 2016, https://www.fbi.gov/file-repository/2015-nics-ops-report.pdf/view (accessed January 18, 2017)

fbi-releases-2013-hate-crime-statistics), the Matthew Shepard and James Byrd Jr. Hate Crime Prevention Act of 2009 added the bias categories of gender and gender identity (transgender and gender nonconforming) to the hate crime monitoring program. The gender-identity category covers people who self-identify and/or behave as being of a different gender than their birth gender.

The Constitutionality of Hate Crime Legislation

The constitutionality of hate crime legislation has been challenged on the grounds that these laws punish free thought. In 1992 the U.S. Supreme Court, in *R.A.V. v. City of St. Paul* (505 U.S. 377), found a Minnesota law outlawing certain "fighting words" to be unconstitutional. In this case, the defendant had burned a cross "inside the fenced yard of a black family." A law limiting pure speech or symbolic speech can only be upheld if it meets the "clear and present danger" standard of *Brandenburg v. Ohio* (395 U.S. 444 [1969]). This standard means that speech may only be outlawed if it incites or produces "imminent lawless action."

However, in *Wisconsin v. Mitchell* (508 U.S. 476 [1993]), the Supreme Court upheld laws that impose harsher prison sentences and greater fines for criminals who are motivated by bigotry. The court found that statutes such as the Wisconsin law in question to be constitutional because, unlike the Minnesota law, they do not criminalize protected speech. Instead, they allow for stiffer penalties to be imposed on people convicted of crimes when they are found to be motivated by hateful biases.

Hate Crime Statistics

Data on hate crimes are likely incomplete because many incidents may not be reported or cannot be verified as hate crimes. Some victims may not report hate crimes because of fear that the criminal justice system is biased against the group to which the victim belongs and that law enforcement authorities will not be responsive. Attacks against gays and lesbians may not be reported because the victims do not want to reveal their sexual orientation to others. In addition, proving that an offender acted from bias can be a long, tedious process, requiring much investigation. Until a law enforcement investigator can find enough evidence in a particular case to be sure the offender's actions came, at least in part, from bias, the crime is not counted as a hate crime.

In *Hate Crime Statistics, 2015* (Fall 2016, https://ucr.fbi.gov/hate-crime/2015), the FBI notes that in 2015, 14,997 law enforcement agencies reported 5,850 hate crime incidents involving 6,885 offenses. Nearly all (5,818) incidents were due to a single bias on behalf of the offender (note that the percentages do not sum to 100% because of rounding):

- Race/ethnicity/ancestry bias—56.9%
- Religious bias—21.4%
- Sexual-orientation bias—18.1%
- Gender-identity bias—2%
- Disability bias—1.3%
- Gender bias—0.4%

The remaining 32 incidents were multiple-bias hate crimes that involved 52 victims.

In total, 4,482 of the hate crime offenses in 2015 were considered crimes against people, 2,338 were deemed crimes against property, and 65 were classified as crimes against society (e.g., prostitution, gambling, or drug violations). The FBI notes that 41.3% of the hate crimes against people involved intimidation, whereas 37.8% involved simple assault and 19.7% involved aggravated assault.

Eighteen murders and 13 rapes (legacy and revised definitions) were also reported as hate crimes.

CRIME TRENDS

As shown in Table 2.1, between 1996 and 2015 both the number of crimes reported each year and the crime rate decreased for all the crimes that are monitored by the DOJ under the UCR Program. Older UCR data are available from the agency's UCR Data Tool (https://www .bjs.gov/ucrdata/index.cfm), an online database. The BJS notes in "Frequently Asked Questions" (January 26, 2017, https://www.bjs.gov/ucrdata/faq.cfm) that the database only includes data from law enforcement agencies of cities with populations of at least 10,000 people and counties with populations of at least 25,000 people. Thus, the data differ slightly from those presented in the FBI's annual *Crime in the United States* reports.

Violent Crime Trends

Figure 2.4 shows that the violent crime rate climbed dramatically during the latter decades of the 20th century, from about 160 reported offenses per 100,000 population during the early 1960s to nearly 760 reported offenses per 100,000 population during the early 1990s. The rate then tumbled to 362 reported offenses per 100,000 population in 2014. It rose slightly to 373 reported offenses per 100,000 population in 2015.

Figure 2.6 shows the murder and nonnegligent manslaughter rate per 100,000 population between 1960 and 2015. The rate peaked at 10.2 offenses per 100,000 population in 1980 and remained at or above 7.9 offenses per 100,000 population into the 1990s. In 1994 the rate began to decline. It dropped to 4.4 offenses per 100,000 population in 2014 and then rose to 4.9 offenses per 100,000 population in 2015.

Figure 2.7 shows the forcible rape (legacy definition) rate per 100,000 population between 1960 and 2015. The rate peaked at 42.8 forcible rapes per 100,000 population in 1992 and then began a general decline. In 2013 it dropped to 25.9 forcible rapes per 100,000 population, before beginning to rise again. In 2015 the rate was 28.1 forcible rapes per 100,000 population.

Figure 2.8 shows the robbery rate per 100,000 population between 1960 and 2015. The rate was above 200 robberies per 100,000 population much of the time from the mid-1970s onward, peaking at 272.7 offenses per 100,000 population in 1991. A sharp decline followed. In 2014 the rate was 101.3 robberies per 100,000 population. It increased slightly to 101.9 robberies per 100,000 population in 2015.

Figure 2.9 shows the aggravated assault rate per 100,000 population between 1960 and 2015. During the early 1960s the rate was less than 100 aggravated assaults per 100,000 population. The rate skyrocketed over the following decades, reaching 441.9 offenses per 100,000 population in 1992. The rate then began a dramatic decrease, dropping to 229.2 aggravated assaults per 100,000 population in 2014. It rose to 237.8 aggravated assaults per 100,000 population in 2015.

FIGURE 2.6

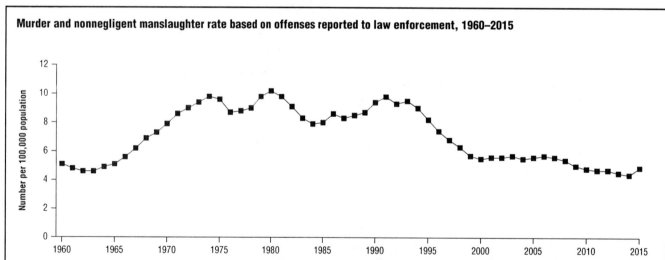

Murder and nonnegligent manslaughter rate based on offenses reported to law enforcement, 1960–2015

Notes: Offense totals are based on data from all reporting agencies and estimates for unreported areas. The 168 murder and nonnegligent homicides that occurred as a result of the bombing of the Alfred P. Murrah Federal Building in Oklahoma City in 1995 are included in the national estimate. The murder and nonnegligent homicides that occurred as a result of the events of September 11, 2001, are not included in the national estimates.

SOURCE: Adapted from "Murder Rate," in *Uniform Crime Reporting Statistics*, U.S. Department of Justice, Federal Bureau of Investigation, undated, https://www.ucrdatatool.gov/Search/Crime/State/TrendsInOneVar.cfm (accessed January 18, 2017) and "Table 1. Crime in the United States by Volume and Rate per 100,000 Inhabitants, 1996–2015," in *Crime in the United States, 2015*, U.S. Department of Justice, Federal Bureau of Investigation, September 26, 2016, https://ucr.fbi.gov/crime-in-the-u.s/2015/crime-in-the-u.s.-2015/tables/table-1 (accessed January 18, 2017)

FIGURE 2.7

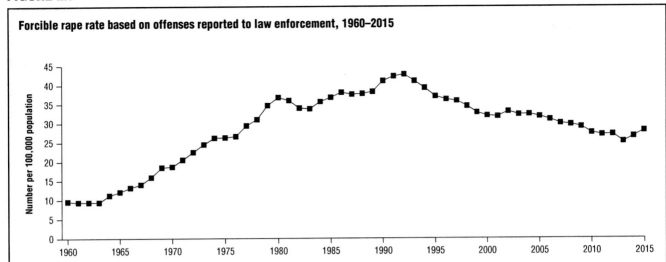

Forcible rape rate based on offenses reported to law enforcement, 1960–2015

Note: Offense totals are based on data from all reporting agencies and estimates for unreported areas. Rape data were estimated using the legacy Uniform Crime Reporting definition of rape.

SOURCE: Adapted from "Forcible Rape Rate," in *Uniform Crime Reporting Statistics*, U.S. Department of Justice, Federal Bureau of Investigation, undated, https://www.ucrdatatool.gov/Search/Crime/State/TrendsInOneVar.cfm (accessed January 18, 2017) and "Table 1. Crime in the United States by Volume and Rate per 100,000 Inhabitants, 1996–2015," in *Crime in the United States, 2015*, U.S. Department of Justice, Federal Bureau of Investigation, September 26, 2016, https://ucr.fbi.gov/crime-in-the-u.s/2015/crime-in-the-u.s.-2015/tables/table-1 (accessed January 18, 2017)

FIGURE 2.8

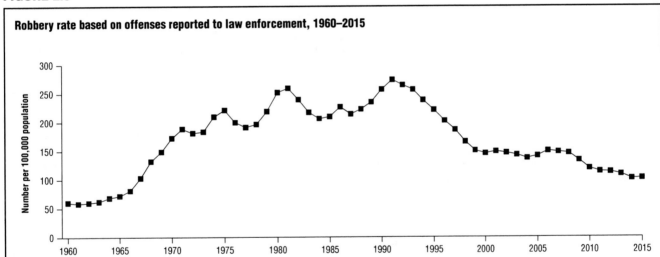

Robbery rate based on offenses reported to law enforcement, 1960–2015

Note: Offense totals are based on data from all reporting agencies and estimates for unreported areas.

SOURCE: Adapted from "Robbery Rate," in *Uniform Crime Reporting Statistics*, U.S. Department of Justice, Federal Bureau of Investigation, undated, https://www.ucrdatatool.gov/Search/Crime/State/TrendsInOneVar.cfm (accessed January 18, 2017) and "Table 1. Crime in the United States by Volume and Rate per 100,000 Inhabitants, 1996–2015," in *Crime in the United States, 2015*, U.S. Department of Justice, Federal Bureau of Investigation, September 26, 2016, https://ucr.fbi.gov/crime-in-the-u.s/2015/crime-in-the-u.s.-2015/tables/table-1 (accessed January 18, 2017)

Property Crime Trends

Figure 2.10 shows the larceny-theft rate per 100,000 population between 1960 and 2015. The rate soared from the 1960s through the early 1990s, peaking at 3,229.1 offenses in 1991. It then plunged over the following years, reaching 1,775.4 larceny-thefts per 100,000 population in 2015. The burglary rate reached its climax in 1980, at 1,684.1 offenses per 100,000 population. (See Figure 2.11.) The rate fell to 491.4 offenses per 100,000 population in 2015. As shown in Figure 2.12, the motor vehicle theft rate peaked in 1991 at 659 thefts per 100,000 population. It dropped substantially to 215.4 motor vehicle thefts per 100,000 population in 2014. The rate ticked up to 220.2 motor vehicle thefts per 100,000 population in 2015.

WHY DID CRIME RISE AND FALL?

According to Arthur J. Lurigio of Loyola University Chicago, in "Crime and Communities: Prevalence,

FIGURE 2.9

Aggravated assault rate based on offenses reported to law enforcement, 1960–2015

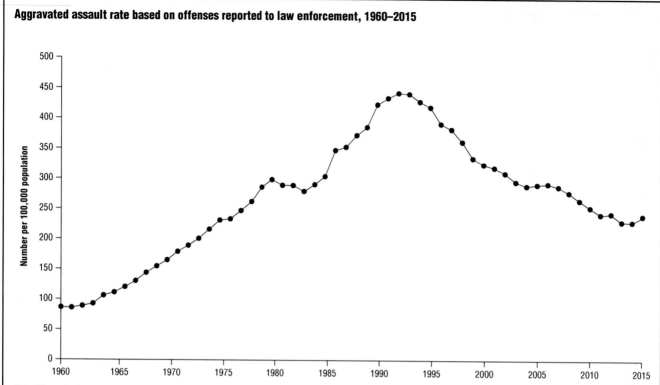

Note: Offense totals are based on data from all reporting agencies and estimates for unreported areas.

SOURCE: Adapted from "Aggravated Assault Rate," in *Uniform Crime Reporting Statistics*, U.S. Department of Justice, Federal Bureau of Investigation, undated, https://www.ucrdatatool.gov/Search/Crime/State/TrendsInOneVar.cfm (accessed January 18, 2017) and "Table 1. Crime in the United States by Volume and Rate per 100,000 Inhabitants, 1996–2015," in *Crime in the United States, 2015*, U.S. Department of Justice, Federal Bureau of Investigation, September 26, 2016, https://ucr.fbi.gov/crime-in-the-u.s/2015/crime-in-the-u.s.-2015/tables/table-1 (accessed January 18, 2017)

FIGURE 2.10

Larceny-theft rate based on offenses reported to law enforcement, 1960–2015

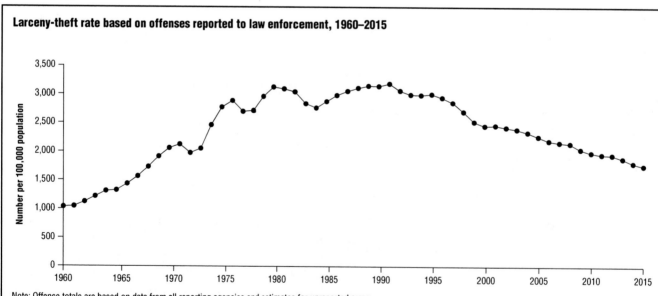

Note: Offense totals are based on data from all reporting agencies and estimates for unreported areas.

SOURCE: Adapted from "Larceny-Theft Rate," in *Uniform Crime Reporting Statistics*, U.S. Department of Justice, Federal Bureau of Investigation, undated, https://www.ucrdatatool.gov/Search/Crime/State/TrendsInOneVar.cfm (accessed January 18, 2017) and "Table 1. Crime in the United States by Volume and Rate per 100,000 Inhabitants, 1996–2015," in *Crime in the United States, 2015*, U.S. Department of Justice, Federal Bureau of Investigation, September 26, 2016, https://ucr.fbi.gov/crime-in-the-u.s/2015/crime-in-the-u.s.-2015/tables/table-1 (accessed January 18, 2017)

FIGURE 2.11

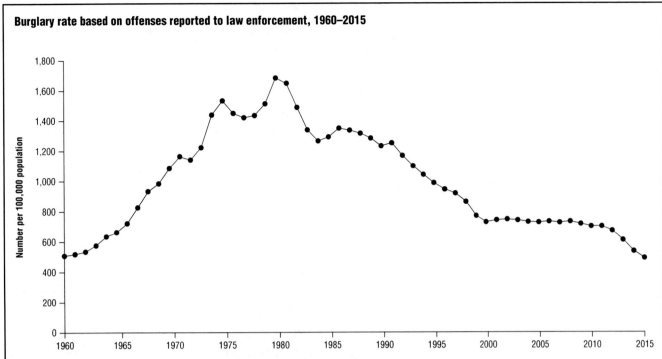

Burglary rate based on offenses reported to law enforcement, 1960–2015

Note: Offense totals are based on data from all reporting agencies and estimates for unreported areas.

SOURCE: Adapted from "Burglary Rate," in *Uniform Crime Reporting Statistics*, U.S. Department of Justice, Federal Bureau of Investigation, undated, https://www.ucrdatatool.gov/Search/Crime/State/TrendsInOneVar.cfm (accessed January 18, 2017) and "Table 1. Crime in the United States by Volume and Rate per 100,000 Inhabitants, 1996–2015," in *Crime in the United States, 2015*, U.S. Department of Justice, Federal Bureau of Investigation, September 26, 2016, https://ucr.fbi.gov/crime-in-the-u.s/2015/crime-in-the-u.s.-2015/tables/table-1 (accessed January 18, 2017)

FIGURE 2.12

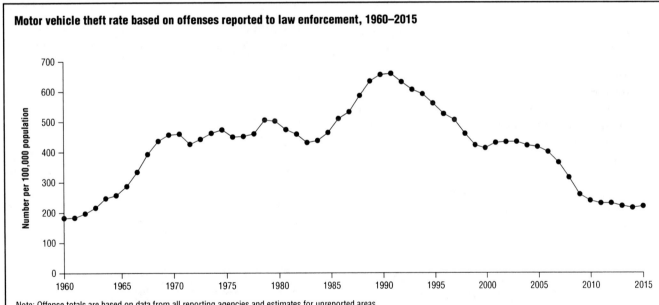

Motor vehicle theft rate based on offenses reported to law enforcement, 1960–2015

Note: Offense totals are based on data from all reporting agencies and estimates for unreported areas.

SOURCE: Adapted from "Motor Vehicle Theft Rate," in *Uniform Crime Reporting Statistics*, U.S. Department of Justice, Federal Bureau of Investigation, undated, https://www.ucrdatatool.gov/Search/Crime/State/TrendsInOneVar.cfm (accessed January 18, 2017) and "Table 1. Crime in the United States by Volume and Rate per 100,000 Inhabitants, 1996–2015," in *Crime in the United States, 2015*, U.S. Department of Justice, Federal Bureau of Investigation, September 26, 2016, https://ucr.fbi.gov/crime-in-the-u.s/2015/crime-in-the-u.s.-2015/tables/table-1 (accessed January 18, 2017)

Impact, and Programs" (Lawrence B. Joseph, ed., *Crime, Communities, and Public Policy*, 1995), the national crime rate fell from 1900 until the Prohibition era (1920–1933). Crime spiked during Prohibition and then fell and leveled off until World War II (1939–1945). Crime dropped dramatically during the war because many young men were away. Following the war, a baby boom occurred, meaning that there was a dramatic increase in births. The baby boom lasted from the late 1940s into the 1960s, resulting in a huge surge of teen-agers and young adults in the population from the 1960s through the 1980s.

Historical crime rates for violent crimes and property crimes increased dramatically from 1960 through the 1980s and 1990s. A variety of social, economic, and even environmental reasons have been proposed to explain this increase:

- Huge influx in youth due to the baby boom
- Decrease in high-paying blue-collar manufacturing jobs for low-skilled workers
- Growth of ghettos and low-income housing projects in the inner cities
- Breakdown of the traditional family structure
- New drug culture, particularly heroin and cocaine during the 1970s and crack cocaine during the 1980s
- Growth of youth gangs
- Easy availability of firearms
- Better crime-tracking methods
- Exposure of infants and children to lead in paint and gasoline before the late 1970s (lead exposure has been linked to a range of developmental and behavioral issues, including inattention, irritability, aggressive-ness, and violent behavior)

During the early 1990s the crime rate began a dra-matic decline. Many of the conditions that had been blamed for the crime surge continued into the 1990s and the first decade of the 21st century, even as the crime rate decreased. The breakdown of the traditional family, the growth of youth gangs, and the loss of high-paying blue-collar jobs continued to occur even as the crime rate plummeted. Likewise, crime-tracking methods continued to improve over time. Sociologists and criminologists have struggled to explain why the crime rate increased and then decreased. During the 1990s and early years of the first decade of the 21st century, the strong economy was credited for the crime decline. In 2007, however, the United States entered an economic downturn called the Great Recession that saw huge spikes in unemployment and financial hardships for millions of people. Although the recession officially ended in 2009, the subsequent economic recovery was weak and slow to develop. Nevertheless, crime rates did not surge during and imme-diately after the Great Recession. As a result, analysts have posited noneconomic causes as the possible reasons for the overall decrease in crime:

- Tougher sentencing rules took hard-core criminals off the streets and kept them behind bars for longer periods
- Tougher gun control laws made firearms less acces-sible to criminals
- The U.S. population aged and baby boomers became older and less prone to criminal behavior
- Some ghettos and low-income housing projects that had been hotbeds for crime in the inner cities were dismantled
- There were more police officers per capita
- Policing methods improved
- People increased their crime prevention efforts, such as the use of security systems and neighborhood watch programs
- Widespread cell phone use led to much quicker report-ing of crimes and the capture of photos and videos of perpetrators
- The proliferation of credit cards, debit cards, and online shopping reduced the carrying of cash
- The crack cocaine epidemic subsided
- The national legalization of abortion in 1973 pre-vented unwanted babies from being born and poten-tially growing up to become criminals
- Lead exposure in infants and children and fetal alco-hol syndrome (due to alcohol consumption during pregnancy) decreased dramatically after the 1970s
- New medications, such as antidepressants and antipsy-chotics, provided better treatment for mental health and behavioral disorders, such as attention deficit hyper-activity disorder

CRIME REBOUND?

Trend analysis became more complicated after there was an uptick in the violent crime rate between 2014 and 2015. (See Table 2.1.) The rates for murder and non-negligent manslaughter, rape (legacy and revised defini-tions), robbery, aggravated assault, and motor vehicle theft all increased slightly between 2014 and 2015. There was more bad news in mid-2016, when the FBI released preliminary UCR statistics for the first six months of 2016. As shown in Table 2.8, the nation's violent crime rate increased 5.3% when comparing January to June 2015 with January to June 2016. Much of the rise was due to a surge in violent crime in large cities with pop-ulations of at least 1 million—murder (up 21.6%), rape (revised definition; up 11.3%), robbery (up 6.3%), and aggravated assault (up 11.4%).

Chicago, in particular, became a focal point of media and public attention as its murder rate soared. In "762 Murders. 12 Months. 1 American City" (CNN.com, January 2, 2017),

TABLE 2.8

Percentage change in crime rates January to June 2015–16

Population group	Number of agencies	Population	Violent crime[a]	Murder	Rape (revised definition)[b]	Rape (legacy definition)[c]	Robbery	Aggravated assault	Property crime	Burglary	Larceny-theft	Motor vehicle theft	Arson
Total	13,366	272,120,479	+5.3	+5.2	+3.5	+4.4	+3.2	+6.5	−0.6	−3.4	−0.8	+6.6	−1.1
Cities:													
1,000,000 and over	10	25,844,935	+9.7	+21.6	+11.3	—	+6.3	+11.4	+2.1	−5.4	+3.3	+5.9	+5.3
500,000 to 999,999	21	15,272,484	+5.2	+2.3	−0.1	−2.4	+2.0	+7.8	+0.1	−2.7	−0.2	+7.1	+0.7
250,000 to 499,999	46	15,694,486	+4.3	+6.1	+11.0	+2.2	−0.2	+5.9	−0.6	−4.3	−0.5	+4.9	−4.8
100,000 to 249,999	208	30,929,824	+5.1	+2.6	+3.1	−4.6	+3.9	+6.1	+0.2	−3.1	*	+7.6	−0.7
50,000 to 99,999	422	29,443,924	+4.1	−3.8	+7.4	+6.4	+3.3	+4.0	+0.5	−1.8	+0.1	+8.8	−1.3
25,000 to 49,999	763	26,325,532	+4.0	−5.8	+3.7	+7.6	+1.7	+5.0	−0.5	−1.5	−0.8	+5.7	−3.0
10,000 to 24,999	1,617	25,871,294	+1.1	−6.4	−5.6	+5.7	+1.4	+2.3	−2.5	−2.0	−3.3	+7.0	−6.6
Under 10,000	6,676	20,950,502	+2.4	+16.7	+0.1	−11.5	+3.1	+2.8	−3.5	−2.8	−4.3	+8.8	−2.4
Counties:													
Metropolitan[d]	1,569	59,667,439	+6.3	+10.9	+2.9	+16.2	+1.8	+7.8	−1.5	−5.2	−1.1	+5.9	−0.3
Nonmetropolitan[e]	2,034	22,120,059	+1.6	−14.7	−4.8	+1.1	+13.5	+2.7	−3.9	−4.0	−4.7	+4.3	−3.1

[a]The violent crime figures include the offenses of murder, rape (revised definition), rape (legacy definition), robbery, and aggravated assault.
[b]The figures shown in this column for the offense of rape were reported using the revised Uniform Crime Reporting (UCR) definition of rape.
[c]The figures shown in this column for the offense of rape were reported using the legacy UCR definition of rape.
[d]Includes crimes reported to sheriffs' departments, county police departments, and state police within Metropolitan Statistical Areas.
[e]Includes crimes reported to sheriffs' departments, county police departments, and state police outside Metropolitan Statistical Areas.
*Less than one-tenth of 1 percent.
Note: No agencies over 1,000,000 in population submitted rape data using the legacy UCR definition in 2016; therefore, the UCR Program could not provide a 2–year comparison for this agency group size.

SOURCE: "Table 1. January to June 2015–2016 Percent Change by Population Group," in *Preliminary Semiannual Uniform Crime Report, January–June, 2016*, U.S. Department of Justice, Federal Bureau of Investigation, 2016, https://ucr.fbi.gov/crime-in-the-u.s/2016/preliminary-semiannual-uniform-crime-report-januaryjune-2016/tables/table-1 (accessed January 20, 2017)

Amanda Wills, Sergio Hernandez, and Marlena Baldacci provide data from the Chicago Police Department regarding the number of first- and second-degree murders and reckless homicides in the city. Chicago experienced 762 murders in 2016, a number that was up dramatically from the 2001 to 2015 average of 497 murders per year. The city's 2016 murder rate of around 28 homicides per 100,000 population approached levels last seen during the early 1990s, when the murder rate exceeded 30 homicides per 100,000 population.

Analysts are unable to explain the uptick in violent crime that emerged nationwide and in some large cities in 2015 and 2016 after decades of improvement. It remains to be seen if the surge is a temporary blip or the beginning of a sustained rebound in the nation's crime rate.

CHAPTER 3
CRIME VICTIMS

Millions of U.S. residents are victimized by crime each year. Some public and private organizations conduct surveys to estimate the national extent of victimization and the types of crimes that victims have experienced. For example, since 2000 Gallup, Inc., has surveyed Americans annually (excluding 2012) about whether or not they or someone in their household was victimized during the previous 12 months by seven specific crimes, ranging from vandalism to assault. In *Americans' Reports of Crime Victimization at High Ebb* (November 10, 2016, http://www.gallup.com/poll/197351/americans-reports-crime-victimization-high-ebb.aspx), Lydia Saad of Gallup notes that in 2016 the largest fraction (17%) said that they or someone in their household had experienced having money or property stolen from them. Property vandalism was the second-most common crime, with 14% of respondents saying they or someone in their household had experienced it. The prevalence rates for the other five crimes—home break-ins, car thefts, muggings or physical assaults, armed robberies, and sexual assaults—were all 5% or below.

According to Saad, in 2016 more than a quarter (29%) of the survey participants told Gallup that they or someone in their household had been a victim of at least one of the crimes during the previous year. A smaller percentage (16%) said they had been personally victimized. For both measures the percentages have been fairly consistent since 2000. The 29% rate for household crime victimization was the highest percentage over the period of record, but was only slightly higher than the previous high of 27% recorded in 2005, 2013, and 2015.

THE NATIONAL CRIME VICTIMIZATION SURVEY

As is described in Chapter 2, the Federal Bureau of Investigation (FBI) operates the Uniform Crime Reporting (UCR) Program, which compiles national crime data that are submitted by thousands of law enforcement agencies from throughout the country. The UCR Program provides data on the types of crimes that are reported to law enforcement agencies. It also includes some data on the victims of these crimes. Another, more detailed examination of crime victims is spearheaded by the Bureau of Justice Statistics (BJS), an agency within the U.S. Department of Justice (DOJ). This program is called the National Crime Victimization Survey (NCVS).

Every year since 1972 the BJS has overseen the annual survey conducted by the U.S. Census Bureau in which data are collected from thousands of individuals and households on the frequency, characteristics, and consequences of criminal victimizations. The data are used to calculate national crime estimates. The data are available online from the BJS's NCVS Victimization Analysis Tool (NVAT; https://www.bjs.gov/index.cfm?ty=nvat). In addition, selected data are presented and discussed in annual publications. Jennifer Truman and Rachel E. Morgan of the BJS indicate in *Criminal Victimization, 2015* (October 2016, https://www.bjs.gov/content/pub/pdf/cv15.pdf) that a nationally representative sample of 163,880 individuals aged 12 years and older from 95,760 households was interviewed in 2015.

The BJS divides criminal victimizations into three categories: violent crimes, personal larceny crimes, and property crimes. Violent crimes include rape and sexual assault, robbery, aggravated assault, and simple assault. Personal larceny crimes include pocket picking and purse snatching. Both categories are known collectively as personal crimes because the victims are individuals. Victimization rates for personal crimes are expressed as the number of victims per 1,000 U.S. residents aged 12 years and older. By contrast, the victimization rates for property crimes (household burglary, motor vehicle theft, and other thefts) are expressed as the number of incidents per 1,000 U.S. households. (Note that murder and other killing crimes are not counted in the NCVS because the data are gathered only through interviews with victims.)

According to the BJS, in *Survey Methodology for Criminal Victimization in the United States* (April 16, 2010, https://www.bjs.gov/content/pub/pdf/ncvs_methodology.pdf), neither the interviewers nor the victims classify events as specific crimes during the interviews. A computer program later performs crime classification based on victim answers to specific detailed questions about the nature of each event. The NVAT website provides the following definitions for the crimes considered in the NCVS:

- Aggravated assault—an attack or attempted attack with a weapon, regardless of whether the victim is injured, or an attack without a weapon when serious injury results.

- Burglary—unlawful or forcible entry or attempted entry into a residence (house, garage, storage shed, or any other structure on the premises) or hotel room. This crime usually, but not always, involves theft. Note that forcible entry is not required, as burglary occurs when the person entering has no legal right to be present in the structure.

- Motor vehicle theft—unlawful taking, or attempted taking, of a self-propelled road vehicle owned by another, with the intent of permanently or temporarily depriving the owner of possession. Excludes vehicle parts.

- Purse snatching or pocket picking—theft or attempted theft of property or cash directly from the victim by stealth, without force or the threat of force.

- Rape—unlawful penetration or attempted penetration of a person against the will of the victim, with use or threatened use of force, including psychological coercion and physical force. Also includes incidents where penetration is from a foreign object, such as a bottle. Attempted rape includes verbal threats of rape.

- Robbery—unlawful taking or attempted taking of property that is in the immediate possession of another, by force or threat of force, with or without a weapon, and with or without injury.

- Sexual assault—this includes a wide range of sexual victimizations (excluding rape or attempted rape) that may or may not involve force. The assaults, or attempted assaults, generally involve unwanted sexual contact between victim and offender, such as grabbing or fondling. Verbal threats are also included.

- Simple assault—an attack or attempted attack without a weapon that results in either no injury, minor injury (e.g., bruises, black eyes, cuts, scratches, or swelling), or an undetermined injury requiring less than two days of hospitalization.

- Theft—the unlawful taking or attempted unlawful taking of property or cash without personal contact with the victim, by an offender with a legal right to be in the house (e.g., a maid, delivery person, or guest).

According to the BJS (April 5, 2017, https://www.bjs.gov/index.cfm?ty=tp&tid=93), for events that include more than one crime (e.g., rape and burglary), only the most serious crime is counted for NCVS purposes using the following hierarchy: rape, sexual assault, robbery, aggravated assault, simple assault, burglary, motor vehicle theft, and theft.

It should be noted that the BJS used a different overall methodology during the 2006 NCVS data collection effort. As a result, Truman and Morgan warn that victimization estimates for 2006 may not be comparable to estimates from other years.

Comparing NCVS and UCR Data

The NCVS was created because of a concern that the FBI's UCR Program did not fully portray the true volume of crime in the United States. The UCR provides data on crimes that are reported to law enforcement authorities, but not all crimes are reported by victims.

Some observers believe the NCVS is a better indicator than the UCR of the volume of crime in the United States. Nonetheless, like all surveys, the NCVS is subject to error. The accuracy of the survey data depends on people's truthful and complete reporting of incidents and events that have happened to them. Also, the NCVS and the UCR define and track some crimes differently. For example, Truman and Morgan indicate that the NCVS covers simple assaults and sexual assaults, two crime categories that are excluded from the UCR. In addition, the UCR Program counts crimes committed against people less than 12 years old, whereas the NCVS only counts crimes against people aged 12 years and older. Thus, direct comparisons between UCR and NCVS data are difficult.

The NCVS and the UCR are generally considered the primary sources of statistical information on crime in the United States. Like all reporting systems, both have their shortcomings, but each provides valuable insights into crime in the United States.

CRIME VICTIMS AND VICTIMIZATIONS IN 2015

In *Criminal Victimization, 2015*, Truman and Morgan report the number of victims who experienced certain crimes in 2015 and the number of victimizations that occurred. Note that these are different measures. For example, a person who was robbed twice in 2015 is counted twice in the victimization count but only once in the victim count. The number of victimizations reflects the number of victims that were present during a criminal incident. Because there can be multiple victims from a single criminal incident (e.g., a home invasion robbery in which several victims are present), the number of victimizations in 2015 may be larger than the number of criminal incidents that occurred that year.

Violent Crimes

As stated earlier, the NCVS considers rape/sexual assault, robbery, and aggravated and simple assault as violent crimes. With the exception of simple assault these crimes are also considered "serious violent crimes." As shown in Table 3.1, nearly 2.7 million people aged 12 years and older experienced at least one violent victimization in 2015. Note that the victim counts provided for specific violent crime categories in Table 3.1 do not sum to the total victim count for each year. This is because victims of multiple crimes are counted each time for the crime type, but only once for the violent crime total. For example, a person who was robbed and assaulted in 2015 is counted once in the robbery total and once in the assault total, but only once in the violent crime total.

Truman and Morgan estimate that 0.98% of the population aged 12 years and older "experienced at least one violent victimization" in 2015. (See Table 3.1.) The prevalence rate was down from 1.11% in 2014.

Domestic violence is a crime in which the offender and victim have a close personal relationship; that is, they are family members or current or former spouses, boyfriends, or girlfriends. As noted in Table 3.1, in 2015 there were 493,310 victims of domestic violence aged 12 years and older. Nearly two-thirds of them (310,090, or 62.9%) were victimized by their intimate partners—current or former spouses, boyfriends, or girlfriends. By contrast, 1.1 million people were violently victimized by strangers in 2015.

Table 3.2 provides a breakdown by crime type for the 5 million violent victimizations estimated to have occurred in 2015 to U.S. residents aged 12 years and older. More than 1.8 million of the victimizations were associated with "serious violent crimes." Overall, the largest number of victimizations (4 million) were assaults, including 3.2 million simple assaults and 816,760 aggravated assaults. In addition, there were 578,580 robbery victimizations and 431,840 rapes/sexual assaults.

Table 3.3 provides information about weapon use during certain types of violent victimizations in 2015. Overall, weapons were used by offenders in 53.5% of serious violent victimizations. The percentages by crime

TABLE 3.1

Number of victims and prevalence rate, by type of crime, 2014 and 2015

Type of crime	Number of persons victimized[a]		Prevalence rate[b]	
	2014[h]	2015	2014[h]	2015
Violent crime[c]	2,948,540	2,650,670	1.11%	0.98%
Rape/sexual assault[d]	150,420	204,000	0.06	0.08
Robbery	435,830	375,280	0.16	0.14
Assault	2,449,820	2,175,520	0.92	0.81
Aggravated assault	681,280	560,720	0.26	0.21
Simple assault	1,842,100	1,690,190	0.69	0.63
Domestic violence[e]	596,270	493,310	0.22	0.18
Intimate partner violence[f]	319,950	310,090	0.12	0.12
Stranger violence	1,274,100	1,117,340	0.48	0.41
Violent crime involving injury	856,760	778,300	0.32	0.29
Serious violent crime[g]	1,235,290	1,099,400	0.46%	0.41%
Serious domestic violence[e]	239,330	212,690	0.09	0.08
Serious intimate partner violence[f]	128,090	141,530	0.05	0.05
Serious stranger violence	600,650	479,870	0.23	0.18
Serious violent crime involving weapons	815,380	644,370	0.31	0.24
Serious violent crime involving injury	440,690	399,360	0.17	0.15
Property crime	10,352,520	10,030,500	7.99%	7.60%
Burglary	2,166,890	2,175,380	1.67	1.65
Motor vehicle theft	429,840	465,650	0.33	0.35
Theft	8,297,290	7,941,030	6.41	6.02

BJS = Bureau of Justice Statistics
NCVS = National Crime Victimization Survey
[a]Number of persons age 12 or older who experienced at least one victimization during the year for violent crime, and number of households that experienced at least one victimization during the year for property crime.
[b]Percent of persons age 12 or older who experienced at least one victimization during the year for violent crime, and percent of households that experienced at least one victimization during the year for property crime.
[c]Excludes homicide because the NCVS is based on interviews with victims and therefore cannot measure murder.
[d]BJS has initiated projects examining collection methods for self-report data on rape and sexual assault.
[e]Includes victimization committed by intimate partners and family members.
[f]Includes victimization committed by current or former spouses, boyfriends, or girlfriends.
[g]In the NCVS, serious violent crime includes rape or sexual assault, robbery, and aggravated assault.
[h]Comparison year.
Note: Detail may not sum to total because a person or household may experience multiple types of crime.

SOURCE: Jennifer L. Truman and Rachel E. Morgan, "Table 9. Number of Victims and Prevalence Rate, by Type of Crime, 2014 and 2015," in *Criminal Victimization, 2015*, U.S. Department of Justice, Bureau of Justice Statistics, October 2016, https://www.bjs.gov/content/pub/pdf/cv15.pdf (accessed January 19, 2017)

TABLE 3.2

Violent victimizations, number and rate, by type of crime, 2014 and 2015

Type of violent crime	Number		Rate per 1,000 persons age 12 or older	
	2014[f]	2015	2014[f]	2015
Violent crime[a]	5,359,570	5,006,620	20.1	18.6
Rape/sexual assault[b]	284,350	431,840	1.1	1.6
Robbery	664,210	578,580	2.5	2.1
Assault	4,411,010	3,996,200	16.5	14.8
Aggravated assault	1,092,090	816,760	4.1	3.0
Simple assault	3,318,920	3,179,440	12.4	11.8
Domestic violence[c]	1,109,880	1,094,660	4.2	4.1
Intimate partner violence[d]	634,610	806,050	2.4	3.0
Stranger violence	2,166,130	1,821,310	8.1	6.8
Violent crime involving injury	1,375,950	1,303,290	5.2	4.8
Serious violent crime[e]	2,040,650	1,827,170	7.7	6.8
Serious domestic violence[c]	400,030	460,450	1.5	1.7
Serious intimate partner violence[d]	265,890	333,210	1.0	1.2
Serious stranger violence	930,690	690,550	3.5	2.6
Serious violent crime involving weapons	1,306,900	977,840	4.9	3.6
Serious violent crime involving injury	692,470	658,040	2.6	2.4

BJS = Bureau of Justice Statistics

NCVS = National Crime Victimization Survey

[a]Excludes homicide because the NCVS is based on interviews with victims and therefore cannot measure murder.

[b]BJS has initiated projects examining collection methods for self-report data on rape and sexual assault.

[c]Includes victimization committed by intimate partners and family members.

[d]Includes victimization committed by current or former spouses, boyfriends, or girlfriends.

[e]In the NCVS, serious violent crime includes rape or sexual assault, robbery, and aggravated assault.

[f]Comparison year.

Note: Detail may not sum to total due to rounding. Total population age 12 or older was 266,665,160 in 2014 and 269,526,470 in 2015.

SOURCE: Jennifer L. Truman and Rachel E. Morgan, "Table 1. Violent Victimization, by Type of Violent Crime, 2014 and 2015," in *Criminal Victimization, 2015*, U.S. Department of Justice, Bureau of Justice Statistics, October 2016, https://www.bjs.gov/content/pub/pdf/cv15.pdf (accessed January 19, 2017)

type were aggravated assaults (89%), robberies (34.7%), and rapes/sexual assaults (11.7%).

The violent crime victimization rate in 2015 was 18.6 victimizations per 1,000 population aged 12 years and older. (See Table 3.2.) Simple assault had the highest rate (11.8), followed by aggravated assault (3), robbery (2.1), and rape/sexual assault (1.6). As shown in Figure 3.1, the violent crime victimization rate has declined dramatically since 1993, when it was around 80 victimizations per 1,000 population aged 12 years and older.

Table 3.4 categorizes violent victimizations in 2015 by victim-offender relationship. Overall, strangers were the offenders in the largest share (36.4%) of the victimizations. They were followed by well-known/casual acquaintances (34.4%) and intimate partners (16.1%). As shown in Table 3.2, nearly 1.1 million of the violent victimizations in 2015 were classified as domestic violence. Nearly three-quarters (806,050, or 73.6%) of them were committed by intimate partners.

VICTIM DEMOGRAPHICS FOR VIOLENT CRIMES. Table 3.5 provides a breakdown of the number of people victimized and the prevalence rates for violent crimes in 2014 and 2015. In 2015 nearly 2.7 million people were victimized—1.2 million males and 1.4 million females. White non-Hispanic victims (1.7 million) outnumbered non-Hispanic African Americans, people of Hispanic origin, and people of other racial groups. However, non-Hispanic African Americans had the highest prevalence rate (1.19%) for violent crime. Children aged 12 to 17 years had the highest prevalence rate (1.64%) when comparing victims by age group. Likewise, separated people had the highest prevalence rate (1.65%) when comparing victims by marital status.

Table 3.6 categorizes violent crime and serious violent crime victimization rates by victim demographics in 2014 and 2015. In 2015 the highest rate (25.7 victimizations per 1,000 population) was experienced by people who were Native American, Alaskan Native, Asian, native Hawaiian, other Pacific Islander, or of two or more races but not of Hispanic or Latino origin. Children aged 12 to 17 years had a much higher rate (31.3 per 1,000 population aged 12 years and older) than other age groups. Likewise, the victimization rate for separated people (39.5 per 1,000 population aged 12 years and older) was higher than the rates for people with other marital statuses.

Table 3.6 also provides a breakdown by annual household income for people who were victimized by violent crimes in 2015. The NCVS data indicate that individuals from lower income households experienced much higher victimization rates than did individuals from higher income households. The victimization rate for people from households $9,999 or less per year was 39.2 per 1,000 people aged 12 years and older. The next-highest victimization rate

TABLE 3.3

Serious violent victimizations, by weapon use and weapon category, 2015

Crime type	Number	Percent
Serious violent victimization	**1,827,171**	**100%**
Yes, offender had weapon	977,842	53.5%
Firearm	284,910	15.6%
Knife	330,204	18.1%
Other type weapon	265,372	14.5%
Type weapon unknown	97,355	5.3%
No, offender did not have weapon	738,549	40.4%
No weapon	738,549	40.4%
Do not know if offender had weapon	110,781	6.1%
Do not know if offender had weapon	110,781	6.1%
Rape/Sexual Assault	**431,837**	**100%**
Yes, offender had weapon	50,654	11.7%
Firearm	8,298	1.9%
Knife	7,701	1.8%
Other type weapon	573	—
Type weapon unknown	34,081	7.9%
No, offender did not have weapon	313,234	72.5%
No weapon	313,234	72.5%
Do not know if offender had weapon	67,949	15.7%
Do not know if offender had weapon	67,949	15.7%
Robbery	**578,578**	**100%**
Yes, offender had weapon	200,568	34.7%
Firearm	92,305	16%
Knife	51,827	9%
Other type weapon	51,768	8.9%
Type weapon unknown	4,668	0.8%
No, offender did not have weapon	335,178	57.9%
No weapon	335,178	57.9%
Do not know if offender had weapon	42,831	7.4%
Do not know if offender had weapon	42,831	7.4%
Aggravated Assault	**816,757**	**100%**
Yes, offender had weapon	726,620	89%
Firearm	184,306	22.6%
Knife	270,676	33.1%
Other type weapon	213,031	26.1%
Type weapon unknown	58,606	7.2%
No, offender did not have weapon	90,137	11%
No weapon	90,137	11%

Notes: Special tabulations from the NCVS Victimization Analysis Tool (NVAT). Detail may not sum to total due to rounding and/or missing data.

SOURCE: Adapted from "Number of Serious Violent Victimizations, Rape/Sexual Assaults, Robberies, and Aggravated Assaults by Weapon Use and Weapon Category, 2015," in *NCVS Victimization Analysis Tool (NVAT)*, U.S. Department of Justice, Office of Justice Programs, Bureau of Justice Statistics, 2017, http://www.bjs.gov/index.cfm?ty=nvat (accessed January 19, 2017)

FIGURE 3.1

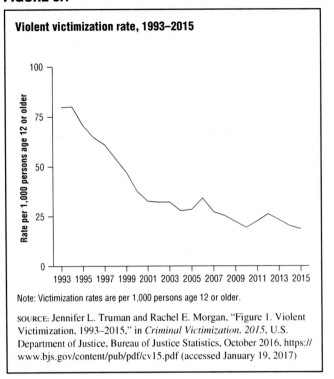

Violent victimization rate, 1993–2015

Note: Victimization rates are per 1,000 persons age 12 or older.

SOURCE: Jennifer L. Truman and Rachel E. Morgan, "Figure 1. Violent Victimization, 1993–2015," in *Criminal Victimization, 2015*, U.S. Department of Justice, Bureau of Justice Statistics, October 2016, https://www.bjs.gov/content/pub/pdf/cv15.pdf (accessed January 19, 2017)

older for suburban dwellers and 14 per 1,000 population aged 12 years and older for rural dwellers.

Property Crimes

As noted earlier, the NCVS includes household burglaries (forced and unforced), motor vehicle thefts, and other thefts (excluding purse snatching and pocket picking) in the category of property crimes. As shown in Table 3.1, 10 million households experienced at least one property victimization in 2015. Truman and Morgan calculate that 7.6% of all U.S. households suffered property crimes in 2015. Most of the victimized households (7.9 million) experienced thefts.

According to NCVS data, more than 14.6 million property victimizations occurred at households in 2015. (See Table 3.8.) Thefts made up 11.1 million of the total victimizations, followed by 2.9 million household burglaries and 564,160 motor vehicle thefts.

As shown in Table 3.8, in 2015 the victimization rate for all property crimes was 110.7 per 1,000 households. The victimization rates for individual property crimes were:

- Motor vehicle theft—4.3 per 1,000 households
- Burglary—22 per 1,000 households
- Theft—84.4 per 1,000 households

Overall, the property victimization rate has declined significantly since 1993, when it was above 350 victimizations per 1,000 households. (See Figure 3.2.)

(27.7 per 1,000 people aged 12 years and older) was for those with a household income of $10,000 to $14,999 per year. These two rates were more than twice the overall rate of 12.8 violent victimizations per 1,000 people aged 12 years and older for those with a household income of $75,000 or more.

As shown in Table 3.7, in 2015 people living in the West (21.3 per 1,000 population aged 12 years and older) and Midwest (19.6 per 1,000 population aged 12 years and older) experienced higher victimization rates for violent crimes than did people in other regions. People living in urban areas had a rate of 22.7 violent victimizations per 1,000 population aged 12 years and older. This compared with rates of 17.3 per 1,000 population aged 12 years and

NCVS data indicate that households in the West had the highest property victimization rate in 2015, at 144.7 per 1,000 households. (See Table 3.7.) People living in urban areas had a rate of 135.4 victimizations per 1,000 households, compared with rates of 98.4 for suburban households and 95.7 for rural households.

Personal Larceny Crimes

Truman and Morgan do not provide victimization estimates for personal larceny crimes, such as pocket picking and purse snatching. However, the data are available online through the NVAT (https://www.bjs.gov/index.cfm?ty=nvat). In 2015 there were an estimated 88,857 victimizations of U.S. residents aged 12 years and older. This value is far lower than the 481,384 victimizations reported for 1993. The personal larceny victimization rate in 2015 was 0.3 per 1,000 population aged 12 years and older. The rate was down from 1993, when it was 2.3 per 1,000 population aged 12 years and older.

REPORTING VICTIMIZATIONS TO THE POLICE

Almost half (46.5%) of all violent crime victimizations covered in the 2015 NCVS were reported by the victims to the police. (See Table 3.9.) The percentage has hovered between around 40% and 50% since the early 1990s. (See Figure 3.3.) The reporting rate in 2015 was highest for victims of robbery (61.9%) and aggravated assault (61.9%), followed by simple assault (41.7%) and rape/sexual assault (32.5%). A majority of domestic violence crimes (57.7%), intimate partner violence crimes

TABLE 3.4

Breakdown of violent victimizations by victim-offender relationship, 2015

Crime type	2015
Violent victimization	100%
Intimates	16.1%
Other relatives	5.8%
Well-known/casual acquaintances	34.4%
Stranger	36.4%
Do not know relationship	3.1%
Do not know number of offenders	4.3%

Notes: Special tabulations from the NCVS Victimization Analysis Tool (NVAT). Detail may not sum to total due to rounding and/or missing data.

SOURCE: "Percent of Violent Victimizations by Victim-Offender Relationship, 2015," in *NCVS Victimization Analysis Tool (NVAT)*, U.S. Department of Justice, Office of Justice Programs, Bureau of Justice Statistics, 2017, http://www.bjs.gov/index.cfm?ty=nvat (accessed January 19, 2017)

TABLE 3.5

Prevalence of violent crime, by victim demographic characteristics, 2014 and 2015

Victim demographic characteristic	Number of persons victimized[a]		Prevalence rate[b]	
	2014[e]	2015	2014[e]	2015
Total	2,948,540	2,650,670	1.11%	0.98%
Sex				
Male	1,497,430	1,227,870	1.15%	0.94%
Female	1,451,110	1,422,800	1.06	1.03
Race/Hispanic origin				
White[c]	1,848,860	1,667,090	1.06%	0.96%
Black[c]	453,650	394,770	1.38	1.19
Hispanic	457,320	400,720	1.11	0.93
Other[c, d]	188,710	188,090	1.00	0.94
Age				
12–17	422,460	407,850	1.68%	1.64%
18–24	478,740	445,760	1.58	1.46
25–34	650,560	476,630	1.51	1.09
35–49	703,980	686,380	1.16	1.13
50–64	579,770	497,800	0.93	0.79
65 or older	113,030	136,250	0.25	0.29
Marital status				
Never married	1,482,570	1,343,010	1.61%	1.44%
Married	806,200	692,470	0.63	0.54
Widowed	77,420	92,330	0.53	0.62
Divorced	410,540	428,830	1.58	1.58
Separated	151,630	84,370	2.99	1.65

[a]Number of persons age 12 or older who experienced at least one victimization during the year for violent crime.
[b]Percent of persons age 12 or older who experienced at least one victimization during the year for violent crime.
[c]Excludes persons of Hispanic or Latino origin.
[d]Includes American Indian and Alaska Natives; Asian, Native Hawaiian, and other Pacific Islanders; and persons of two or more races.
[e]Comparison year.
Note: Detail may not sum to total due to rounding.

SOURCE: Jennifer L. Truman and Rachel E. Morgan, "Table 10. Prevalence of Violent Crime, by Victim Demographic Characteristics, 2014 and 2015," in *Criminal Victimization, 2015*, U.S. Department of Justice, Bureau of Justice Statistics, October 2016, https://www.bjs.gov/content/pub/pdf/cv15.pdf (accessed January 19, 2017)

TABLE 3.6

Rate of violent victimization, by victim demographic characteristics, 2014 and 2015

Victim demographic characteristic	Violent crime[a]		Serious violent crime[b]	
	2014[f]	2015	2014[f]	2015
Total	**20.1**	**18.6**	**7.7**	6.8
Sex				
Male	21.1	15.9	8.3	5.4
Female	19.1	21.1	7.0	8.1
Race/Hispanic origin				
White[c]	20.3	17.4	7.0	6.0
Black[c]	22.5	22.6	10.1	8.4
Hispanic	16.2	16.8	8.3	7.1
Other[c, d]	23.0	25.7	7.7	10.4
Age				
12–17	30.1	31.3	8.8	7.8
18–24	26.8	25.1	13.6	10.7
25–34	28.5	21.8	8.6	9.3
35–49	21.6	22.6	8.9	7.8
50–64	17.9	14.2	7.0	5.7
65 or older	3.1	5.2	1.3	1.5
Marital status				
Never married	27.9	26.2	10.7	9.4
Married	12.4	9.9	4.0	3.5
Widowed	8.7	8.5	2.9	2.9
Divorced	30.3	35.3	14.2	13.0
Separated	52.8	39.5	27.7	20.6
Household income[e]				
$9,999 or less	39.7	39.2	18.7	17.7
$10,000–$14,999	36.0	27.7	16.8	12.0
$15,000–$24,999	25.3	25.9	8.4	8.2
$25,000–$34,999	19.7	16.3	8.3	5.5
$35,000–$49,999	19.0	20.5	8.1	7.1
$50,000–$74,999	16.4	16.3	5.4	5.9
$75,000 or more	15.1	12.8	4.7	4.5

NCVS = National Crime Victimization Survey

[a]Includes rape or sexual assault, robbery, aggravated assault, and simple assault. Excludes homicide because the NCVS is based on interviews with victims and therefore cannot measure murder.

[b]In the NCVS, serious violent crime includes rape or sexual assault, robbery, and aggravated assault.

[c]Excludes persons of Hispanic or Latino origin.

[d]Includes American Indian and Alaska Natives; Asian, Native Hawaiian, and other Pacific Islanders: and persons of two or more races.

[e]Household income was imputed for 2014 and 2015.

[f]Comparison year.

Note: Victimization rates are per 1,000 persons age 12 or older.

SOURCE: Jennifer L. Truman and Rachel E. Morgan, "Table 7. Rate of Violent Victimization, by Victim Demographic Characteristics, 2014 and 2015," in *Criminal Victimization, 2015*, U.S. Department of Justice, Bureau of Justice Statistics, October 2016, https://www.bjs.gov/content/pub/pdf/cv15.pdf (accessed January 19, 2017)

(54.1%), and violent crimes involving injury (57%) were reported by the victims to the police.

Only 34.6% of all property crime victimizations tallied in the 2015 NCVS were reported to the police. (See Table 3.9.) The percentage has hovered between around 30% and 40% since the early 1990s. (See Figure 3.3.) In 2015 victims of motor vehicle theft were, by far, the most likely to have reported the crime, with 69% of the thefts reported to the police. This compares with 50.8% of household burglaries and 28.6% of other thefts.

Table 3.10 breaks down victimizations rates for crimes that were and were not reported to the police by the type of crime. Overall, violent victimizations reported to the police in 2015 had a rate of 8.6 per 1,000 people aged 12 years and older. The rate for violent victimizations not reported to the police was 9.5 per 1,000 people aged 12 years and older. For property crimes the rate of victimizations reported to the police (38.3 per 1,000 people aged 12 years and older) was much lower than the rate of victimizations not reported to the police (71.3 per 1,000 people aged 12 years and older).

Reasons Victims Do Not Report Victimizations

In *Criminal Victimization, 2015*, Truman and Morgan do not provide the reasons given by victims for reporting or not reporting victimizations to the police. However, historical data on this subject are presented by Lynn Langton et al. in *Victimizations Not Reported to the Police, 2006–2010* (August 2012, https://www.bjs.gov/content/pub/pdf/vnrp0610.pdf), the most recent report on this topic as of April 2017.

TABLE 3.7

Rate of violent and property victimization, by household location, 2014 and 2015

Household location	Violent crime[a]		Serious violent crime[b]		Property crime[c]	
	2014[d]	2015	2014[d]	2015	2014[d]	2015
Total	**20.1**	**18.6**	**7.7**	**6.8**	**118.1**	**110.7**
Region						
Northeast	18.9	17.1	6.2	5.1	85.8	81.6
Midwest	20.6	19.6	7.5	7.5	111.8	105.0
South	20.2	16.9	7.6	5.8	116.2	107.6
West	20.3	21.3	8.9	8.8	153.0	144.7
Location of residence						
Urban	22.2	22.7	9.3	8.6	148.8	135.4
Suburban	19.3	17.3	6.9	6.3	101.7	98.4
Rural	18.3	14.0	6.5	4.2	103.2	95.7

NCVS = National Crime Victimization Survey

[a]Includes rape or sexual assault, robbery, aggravated assault, and simple assault. Excludes homicide because the NCVS is based on interviews with victims and therefore cannot measure murder.

[b]In the NCVS, serious violent crime includes rape or sexual assault, robbery, and aggravated assault.

[c]Includes household burglary, motor vehicle theft, and theft.

[d]Comparison year.

Note: Victimization rates are per 1,000 persons age 12 or older for violent crime and per 1,000 households for property crime.

SOURCE: Jennifer L. Truman and Rachel E. Morgan, "Table 8. Rate of Violent and Property Victimization, by Household Location, 2014 and 2015," in *Criminal Victimization, 2015*, U.S. Department of Justice, Bureau of Justice Statistics, October 2016, https://www.bjs.gov/content/pub/pdf/cv15.pdf (accessed January 19, 2017)

TABLE 3.8

Property victimizations, number and rate, by type of crime, 2014 and 2015

Type of property crime	Number		Rate per 1,000 households	
	2014*	2015	2014*	2015
Total	**15,288,470**	**14,611,040**	**118.1**	**110.7**
Burglary	2,993,480	2,904,570	23.1	22.0
Motor vehicle theft	534,370	564,160	4.1	4.3
Theft	11,760,620	11,142,310	90.8	84.4

*Comparison year.

Note: Detail may not sum to total due to rounding. Total number of households was 129,492,740 in 2014 and 131,962,260 in 2015.

SOURCE: Jennifer L. Truman and Rachel E. Morgan, "Table 3. Property Victimization, by Type of Property Crime, 2014 and 2015," in *Criminal Victimization, 2015*, U.S. Department of Justice, Bureau of Justice Statistics, October 2016, https://www.bjs.gov/content/pub/pdf/cv15.pdf (accessed January 19, 2017)

According to Langton et al., more than half (58%) of victimizations occurring between 2006 and 2010 were not reported by victims to the police. Interviewers asked the crime victims who had not reported their victimizations to the police why they chose not to do so. The largest single reason given for not reporting a violent crime (attempted or completed rape/sexual assault, robbery, or aggravated or simple assault) was that the victim considered the incident to be a private or personal matter. About one-third (34%) of those asked gave this reason. Other oft-cited reasons were that the victimization was "not important enough" to report to the police (18%), the police would not or could not help (16%), or the victim feared reprisal from the offender or feared getting the offender in trouble (13%).

Langton et al. indicate that 60% of property crimes between 2006 and 2010 were not reported to the police by their victims. The primary reasons cited by victims were that they believed the police would or could not help them (36%) or that the crime was "not important enough" to report (30%). Smaller percentages of property crime victims said they chose not to report because the incident was a private or personal matter (15%) or because they feared reprisal from the offender or getting the offender in trouble (3%).

VICTIMIZATIONS AT SCHOOL

The U.S. Department of Education (ED) and the DOJ collaborate to compile and publish data about crimes in school environments. In *Indicators of School Crime and Safety: 2015* (May 2016, https://www.bjs.gov/content/pub/pdf/iscs15.pdf), the agencies note that the data are collected from a variety of sources, including the NCVS, national youth and school surveys, and law enforcement agencies. In general, the statistics cover two major groups of students: those aged 12 to 18 years (who attend the upper grades at elementary schools or attend secondary schools) and those attending postsecondary schools (colleges and universities).

Schools Serving Students Aged 12 to 18 Years

According to the ED and the DOJ, in *Indicators of School Crime and Safety: 2015*, nearly two-thirds (65%) of public schools recorded one or more violent incidents during the 2013–14 school year, equating to around 757,000 crimes. Figure 3.4 provides a breakdown of the violent crimes by type. Physical attacks or fights without

FIGURE 3.2

Property victimization rate, 1993–2015

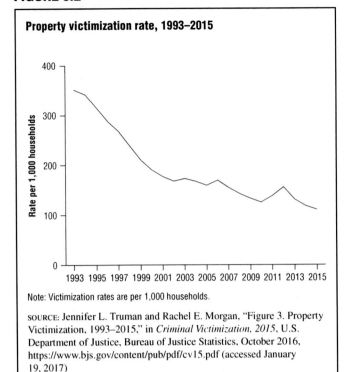

Note: Victimization rates are per 1,000 households.

SOURCE: Jennifer L. Truman and Rachel E. Morgan, "Figure 3. Property Victimization, 1993–2015," in *Criminal Victimization, 2015*, U.S. Department of Justice, Bureau of Justice Statistics, October 2016, https://www.bjs.gov/content/pub/pdf/cv15.pdf (accessed January 19, 2017)

TABLE 3.9

Percentage of victimizations reported to police, by type of crime, 2014 and 2015

Type of crime	2014[f]	2015
Violent crime[a]	46.0%	46.5%
Rape/sexual assault[b]	33.6	32.5
Robbery	60.9	61.9
Assault	44.6	45.8
Aggravated assault	58.4	61.9
Simple assault	40.0	41.7
Domestic violence[c]	56.1	57.7
Intimate partner violence[d]	57.9	54.1
Stranger violence	48.8	42.1
Violent crime involving injury	54.9	57.0
Serious violent crime[e]	55.8%	54.9%
Serious domestic violence[c]	60.0	60.8
Serious intimate partner violence[d]	56.7	49.6
Serious stranger violence	65.4	54.3
Serious violent crime involving weapons	57.6	56.3
Serious violent crime involving injury	61.0	59.0
Property crime	37.0%	34.6%
Burglary	60.0	50.8
Motor vehicle theft	83.3	69.0
Theft	29.0	28.6

BJS = Bureau of Justice Statistics
NCVS = National Crime Victimization Survey
[a]Excludes homicide because the NCVS is based on interviews with victims and therefore cannot measure murder.
[b]BJS has initiated projects examining collection methods for self-report data on rape and sexual assault.
[c]Includes victimization committed by intimate partners and family members.
[d]Includes victimization committed by current or former spouses, boyfriends, or girlfriends.
[e]In the NCVS, serious violent crime includes rape or sexual assault, robbery, and aggravated assault.
[f]Comparison year.

SOURCE: Jennifer L. Truman and Rachel E. Morgan, "Table 4. Percent of Victimizations Reported to Police by Type of Crime, 2014 and 2015," in *Criminal Victimization, 2015*, U.S. Department of Justice, Bureau of Justice Statistics, October 2016, https://www.bjs.gov/content/pub/pdf/cv15.pdf (accessed January 19, 2017)

a weapon (57.5%) were the most common crime, followed by threats of physical attack without a weapon (47.1%) and threats of physical attack with a weapon (8.7%).

In 2014 there were approximately 850,100 nonfatal victimizations at school, meaning inside school buildings, on school property, or on the way to or from school. Just over half of the victimizations (486,400, or 57%) were violent victimizations involving rape, sexual assault, robbery, aggravated assault, or simple assault. The other 363,700 victimizations, or 43% of the total, were theft victimizations (excluding motor vehicle thefts).

The ED and the DOJ indicate that the total victimization rate of students aged 12 to 18 years at school decreased from 181 victimizations per 1,000 students in 1992 to 33 victimizations per 1,000 students in 2014, a decline of 82%. (See Figure 3.5.) For the sake of comparison, the victimization rate in 2014 for this age group away from school was 24 per 1,000 students. There were stark differences in the victimization rates at school by location:

- Rural areas—52.8 victimizations per 1,000 students

- Urban areas—32.5 victimizations per 1,000 students

- Suburban areas—27.6 victimizations per 1,000 students

Figure 3.6 shows the percentage of students reporting various types of victimizations at school during the previous six months between 1995 and 2013. In 1995 nearly 10% of students reported some type of victimization. By 2013 this value had fallen to around 3%. Figure 3.7 provides demographic data about the students who

reported being criminally victimized in 1995 and 2013. In both years males were slightly more likely to be victims than females. In 2013 African American (3.2%) and Hispanic (3.2%) students had slightly higher rates than white students (3%). Likewise, students in sixth grade and ninth grade had higher victimization rates than students in other grades.

Overall, 6% of teachers at public schools and 3% of teachers at private schools reported being physically attacked by students during the 2011–12 school year. The rate was higher among elementary school teachers (8.2%) than among secondary school teachers (2.6%). (See Figure 3.8.)

Postsecondary Schools

The ED and the DOJ note in *Indicators of School Crime and Safety: 2015* that there were 27,600 criminal incidents on degree-granting postsecondary school campuses in 2013. (See Figure 3.9.) This equates to a rate of 18.4 crimes per 10,000 full-time equivalent students. The

FIGURE 3.3

Percentage of victimizations reported to police, by type of crime, 1993–2015

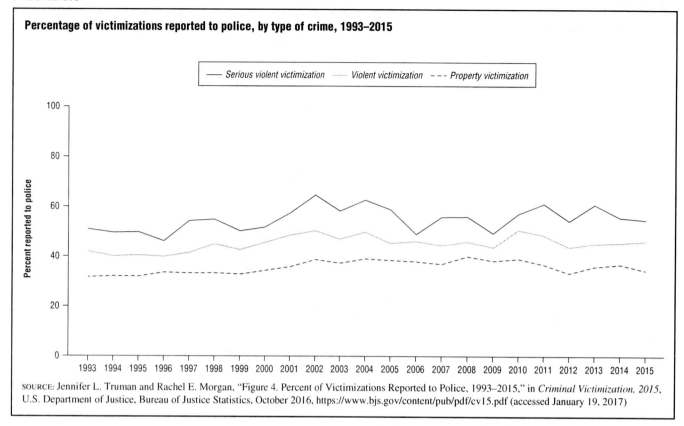

SOURCE: Jennifer L. Truman and Rachel E. Morgan, "Figure 4. Percent of Victimizations Reported to Police, 1993–2015," in *Criminal Victimization, 2015*, U.S. Department of Justice, Bureau of Justice Statistics, October 2016, https://www.bjs.gov/content/pub/pdf/cv15.pdf (accessed January 19, 2017)

number and rate of on-campus crimes were down dramatically from 2001. These declines were primarily due to a sharp drop in the number of burglaries and a slight drop in the number of motor vehicle thefts. Nevertheless, there was a steep rise in the number of forcible sex offenses, from 2,200 in 2001 to 5,000 in 2013, an increase of 126%. Although not shown in Figure 3.9, on-campus drug violations also grew dramatically, with arrests up 70% between 2001 and 2013. Drug crime is discussed in detail in Chapter 4.

SEXUAL OFFENSES. Sexual offenses committed on college campuses became the focus of intense public and political scrutiny during the early 21st century. Awareness about the problem was heightened by female students who spoke openly about being sexually assaulted by male students and criticized their universities for failing to take administrative actions against the accused perpetrators. In some cases the victims were incapacitated during the assaults. This could have been due to alcohol consumption or the effects of drugs that they may have unwittingly taken. (Chapter 4 describes so-called date rape drugs that have become infamous for their association with sexual assaults.)

The extent of sexual misconduct on college campuses is widely debated and difficult to ascertain with certainty. As of April 2017, two major surveys funded or conducted by the DOJ provide insight into the problem but also present far different estimates of its prevalence:

- In *The Campus Sexual Assault (CSA) Study* (October 2007, https://www.ncjrs.gov/pdffiles1/nij/grants/221153.pdf), Christopher P. Krebs et al. present web-based survey results from "two large, public universities." Data collected from 6,800 undergraduate students reveal that "13.7% of undergraduate women had been victims of at least one completed sexual assault since entering college."

- In *Rape and Sexual Assault Victimization among College-Age Females, 1995–2013* (December 2014, https://www.bjs.gov/content/pub/pdf/rsavcaf9513.pdf), Sofi Sinozich and Lynn Langton present findings from the NCVS regarding sexual offenses committed against women aged 18 to 24 years. Based on victim accounts, the overall rate of rape and sexual assault for female college students was calculated at 6.1 per 1,000 and for female nonstudents 7.6 per 1,000.

The Association of American Universities (AAU) is a nonprofit organization that represents the interests of dozens of public and private research universities in North America. David Cantor et al. discuss in *Report on the AAU Campus Climate Survey on Sexual Assault and Sexual Misconduct* (September 21, 2015, https://www.aau.edu/uploadedFiles/AAU_Publications/AAU_Reports/Sexual_Assault_Campus_Survey/AAU_Campus_Climate_Survey_12_14_15.pdf) the results of a 2015 web-based survey of 150,072 students at 27 participating schools. Overall, 23.1% of female undergraduate students reported

TABLE 3.10

Rate of victimizations reported and not reported to police, by type of crime, 2014 and 2015

Type of crime	Reported to police 2014[f]	Reported to police 2015	Not reported to police 2014[f]	Not reported to police 2015
Violent crime[a]	9.2	8.6	10.5	9.5
Rape/sexual assault[b]	0.4	0.5	0.7	1.1
Robbery	1.5	1.3	1.0	0.8
Assault	7.4	6.8	8.9	7.6
Aggravated assault	2.4	1.9	1.7	1.1
Simple assault	5.0	4.9	7.2	6.5
Domestic violence[c]	2.3	2.3	1.7	1.7
Intimate partner violence[d]	1.4	1.6	0.9	1.4
Stranger violence	4.0	2.8	4.1	3.6
Violent crime involving injury	2.8	2.8	2.3	2.0
Serious violent crime[e]	4.3	3.7	3.3	3.0
Serious domestic violence[c]	0.9	1.0	0.6	0.7
Serious intimate partner violence[d]	0.6	0.6	0.4	0.6
Serious stranger violence	2.3	1.4	1.2	1.1
Serious violent crime involving weapons	2.8	2.0	2.0	1.5
Serious violent crime involving injury	1.6	1.4	1.0	1.0
Property crime	43.7	38.3	72.8	71.3
Burglary	13.9	11.2	8.8	10.5
Motor vehicle theft	3.4	3.0	0.7	1.3
Theft	26.4	24.1	63.3	59.5

BJS = Bureau of Justice Statistics
NCVS = National Crime Victimization Survey
[a]Excludes homicide because the NCVS is based on interviews with victims and therefore cannot measure murder.
[b]BJS has initiated projects examining collection methods for self-report data on rape and sexual assault.
[c]Includes victimization committed by intimate partners and family members.
[d]Includes victimization committed by current or former spouses, boyfriends, or girlfriends.
[e]In the NCVS, serious violent crime includes rape or sexual assault, robbery, and aggravated assault.
[f]Comparison year.
Note: Victimization rates are per 1,000 persons age 12 or older for violent crime or per 1,000 households for property crime. Excludes victimizations in which it was unknown whether the victimization was reported to police.

SOURCE: Jennifer L. Truman and Rachel E. Morgan, "Table 5. Rate of Victimizations Reported and Not Reported to Police, by Type of Crime, 2014 and 2015," in *Criminal Victimization, 2015*, U.S. Department of Justice, Bureau of Justice Statistics, October 2016, https://www.bjs.gov/content/pub/pdf/cv15.pdf (accessed January 19, 2017)

"nonconsensual sexual contact involving physical force or incapacitation." This finding was widely reported in the media with some prominent sources suggesting that the percentage applied across the national population of female college students. For example, Richard Pérez-Peña reported on this study with the headline "1 in 4 Women Experience Sexual Assault on Campus" (NYTimes.com, September 21, 2015). However, in "AAU Climate Survey on Sexual Assault and Sexual Misconduct" (2017, https://www.aau.edu/Climate-Survey.aspx?id=16525), the AAU warns that the percentage is not nationally representative.

The far differing prevalence rates found in these studies reveal the difficulties involved in quantifying the extent of the sexual assault problem on college campuses. Sinozich and Langton note that the ways in which acts of sexual misconduct are defined by survey takers can affect the results, as can the medium that is used (e.g., web-based surveys versus in-person surveys).

CONSEQUENCES OF CRIMINAL VICTIMIZATION

Crime victims suffer a number of consequences from being victimized, including physical injuries, mental distress, and economic losses. The economic costs borne by crime victims include direct costs, such as the value of items that have been stolen, and indirect costs, such as the expenses of the criminal justice system, which must be shared by the entire society.

Physical Injuries

As shown in Table 3.2, NCVS data indicate that in 2015, 1.3 million violent victimizations (or 26% of the total of 5 million) involved injury to the victims. (Note that only people aged 12 years and older are included.) An estimated 658,040 victimizations due to serious violent crimes (rape/sexual assault, robbery, or aggravated assault) left victims physically injured. This number accounted for more than one-third (36%) of the 1.8 million serious violent victimizations that occurred that year.

Socio-emotional Impacts

Crime victims may also suffer social and emotional impacts due to victimizations. Lynn Langton and Jennifer Truman of the BJS discuss in *Socio-emotional Impact of Violent Crime* (September 2014, https://www.bjs.gov/content/pub/pdf/sivc.pdf) NCVS data collected between 2009 and 2012 regarding the socio-emotional impacts of violent criminal victimizations. Victims were quizzed about the level of distress they experienced because of the crimes. The results are shown in Figure 3.10 by crime type. Overall, the highest levels of severe or moderate distress were seen for people who had experienced rape, sexual assault, or robbery. As illustrated in Figure 3.11, distress levels reported by the victims of serious violent crimes (rape/sexual assault, robbery, and aggravated assault) varied significantly depending on the victim-offender relationship. People victimized by relatives or intimate partners had much higher levels of distress than did people victimized by close friends, other acquaintances, or strangers.

Victims who experienced moderate or severe distress were more likely to report the crime to police and/or to receive victim services than victims who experienced no distress or mild distress.

Langton and Truman present comprehensive data on violent crime victims that experienced one or more of the following socio-emotional problems:

- Moderate or severe distress

- Significant problems at work or school (e.g., trouble with bosses, coworkers, or peers)

FIGURE 3.4

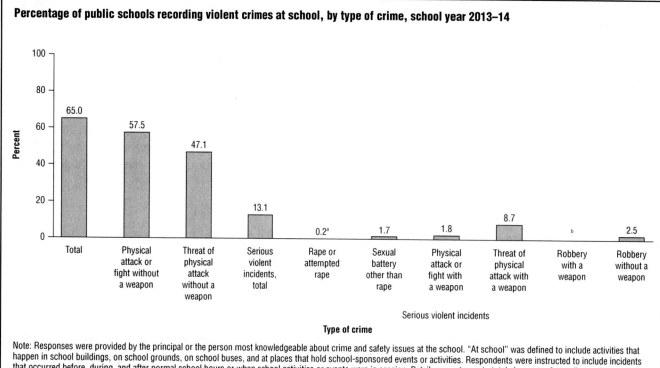

Percentage of public schools recording violent crimes at school, by type of crime, school year 2013–14

Note: Responses were provided by the principal or the person most knowledgeable about crime and safety issues at the school. "At school" was defined to include activities that happen in school buildings, on school grounds, on school buses, and at places that hold school-sponsored events or activities. Respondents were instructed to include incidents that occurred before, during, and after normal school hours or when school activities or events were in session. Detail may not sum to totals because of rounding and because schools that recorded more than one type of crime incident were counted only once in the total percentage of schools recording or reporting incidents.
[a]Interpret data with caution. The coefficient of variation (CV) for this estimate is between 30 and 50 percent.
[b]Reporting standards are not met. Either there are too few cases for a reliable estimate or the coefficient of variation (CV) is 50 percent or greater.

SOURCE: Anlan Zhang, Lauren Musu-Gillette, and Barbara A. Oudekerk, "Figure 6.1. Percentage of Public Schools Recording Incidents of Violent Crime at School, by Type of Crime: School Year 2013–14," in *Indicators of School Crime and Safety: 2015*, U.S. Department of Education, National Center for Education Statistics, and U.S. Department of Justice, Bureau of Justice Statistics, May 2016, https://www.bjs.gov/content/pub/pdf/iscs15.pdf (accessed January 19, 2017)

- Significant problems with family members or friends (e.g., more arguments, inability to trust, or feelings of emotional distance)

Overall, 57% of the violent crime victims suffered socio-emotional problems. The percentage was highest for victims of rape/sexual assault (75%) and lowest for victims of simple assault (51%). Socio-emotional problems were most prevalent in victims who had endured firearm violence (74%) and those who had to receive medical treatment because of their injuries (77%). More people who were victimized by their intimate partners (85%) experienced socio-emotional problems than did people victimized by other types of offenders.

Table 3.11 lists specific physical and emotional symptoms suffered by the violent crime victims who experienced socio-emotional problems. The highest percentages of victims reported experiencing worry or anxiety (72%), anger (70%), or feeling unsafe (65%). Trouble sleeping was the most common physical symptom reported by the victims. Nearly half (47%) said they experienced this problem. The prevalence rates of the specific symptoms were highest for victims of serious violence and for people victimized by their intimate partners.

VICTIMS' RIGHTS

For many years victims received little consideration in justice proceedings; to some it seemed that victims were victimized again by the very system to which they had turned for help. In *Final Report of the President's Task Force on Victims of Crime* (December 1982, https://ojp.gov/ovc/publications/presdntstskforcrprt/87299.pdf), Lois Haight Herrington observes that "somewhere along the way, the system began to serve lawyers and judges and defendants, treating the victim with institutionalized disinterest."

The report describes a number of problems that were commonly cited by crime victims. For example, police questioning seemed to accuse rape victims of enticing their attacker or participating willingly in the act. Assault victims found that hospitals were more concerned about whether they could pay for treatment than about helping them recover from the incident. In their efforts to make sure that each defendant received a fair trial, judges and lawyers appeared to be more concerned about the accused offenders than the victims. Crime victims were not informed of court dates, sentencing hearings, or probation or parole hearings concerning their cases. They were not informed when their attacker escaped or was

FIGURE 3.5

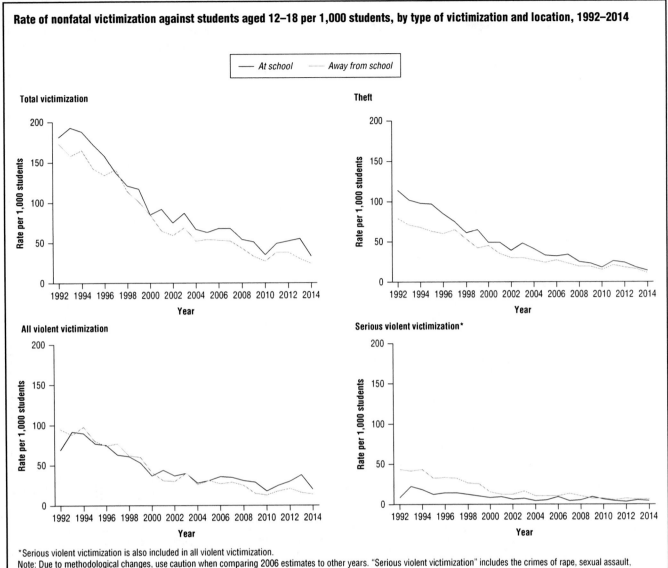

Rate of nonfatal victimization against students aged 12–18 per 1,000 students, by type of victimization and location, 1992–2014

— At school   ⋯⋯ Away from school

Total victimization

Theft

All violent victimization

Serious violent victimization*

*Serious violent victimization is also included in all violent victimization.

Note: Due to methodological changes, use caution when comparing 2006 estimates to other years. "Serious violent victimization" includes the crimes of rape, sexual assault, robbery, and aggravated assault. "All violent victimization" includes serious violent crimes as well as simple assault. "Theft" includes attempted and completed purse-snatching, completed pickpocketing, and all attempted and completed thefts, with the exception of motor vehicle thefts. Theft does not include robbery, which involves the threat or use of force and is classified as a violent crime. "Total victimization" includes thefts and violent crimes. "At school" includes inside the school building, on school property, or on the way to or from school. Although Indicators 2 and 3 present information on similar topics, Indicator 2 is based solely on data collected in National Crime Victimization Survey (NCVS), whereas Indicator 3 is based on data collected in the School Crime Supplement (SCS) to the NCVS as well as demographic data collected in the NCVS. Indicator 2 uses data from all students ages 12–18 who responded to the NCVS, while Indicator 3 uses data from all students ages 12–18 who responded to both the NCVS and the SCS. The population size for students ages 12–18 was 25,773,800 in 2014. Detail may not sum to totals due to rounding. Estimates may vary from previously published reports.

SOURCE: Anlan Zhang, Lauren Musu-Gillette, and Barbara A. Oudekerk, "Figure 2.1. Rate of Nonfatal Victimization against Students Ages 12–18 per 1,000 Students, by Type of Victimization and Location: 1992 through 2014," in *Indicators of School Crime and Safety: 2015*, U.S. Department of Education, National Center for Education Statistics, and U.S. Department of Justice, Bureau of Justice Statistics, May 2016, https://www.bjs.gov/content/pub/pdf/iscs15.pdf (accessed January 19, 2017)

released from prison. Also, victims participating in a trial were sometimes kept outside the courtroom without ever being called to the witness stand.

The Crime Victims' Rights Movement

Beginning in the 1960s a growing victims' rights movement spurred the creation of victim assistance and compensation programs throughout the country. In 1976 a California probation officer named James Rowland introduced the first victim impact statements. These written statements provided the judiciary with information about the specific and often devastating impact of crimes on victims—a viewpoint that had not previously been considered by the criminal justice system.

By the early 1980s a number of programs had been developed at the state and local levels on behalf of crime victims. In 1981 President Ronald Reagan (1911–2004) proclaimed the first National Victims' Rights Week. In 1982 he spearheaded passage of the federal Victim and Witness Protection Act, which was designed to protect

FIGURE 3.6

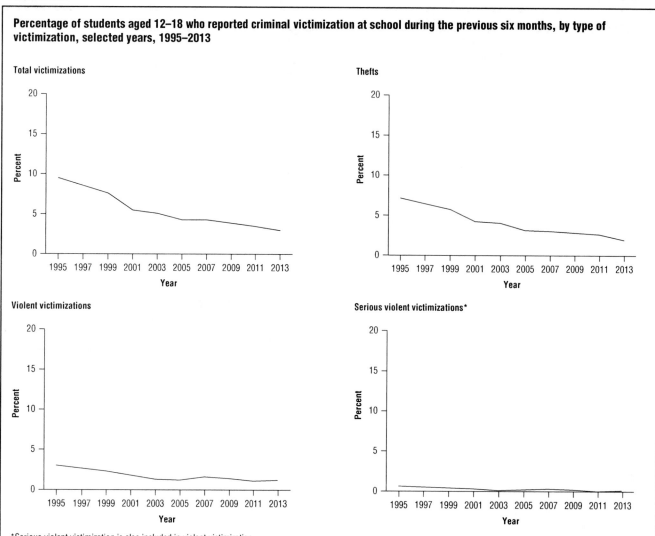

Percentage of students aged 12–18 who reported criminal victimization at school during the previous six months, by type of victimization, selected years, 1995–2013

*Serious violent victimization is also included in violent victimization.

Note: "Total victimization" includes theft and violent victimization. "Theft" includes attempted and completed purse-snatching, completed pickpocketing, and all attempted and completed thefts, with the exception of motor vehicle thefts. Theft does not include robbery, which involves the threat or use of force and is classified as a violent crime. "Serious violent victimization" includes the crimes of rape, sexual assault, robbery, and aggravated assault. "Violent victimization" includes the serious violent crimes as well as simple assault. "At school" includes the school building, on school property, on a school bus, and, from 2001 onward, going to and from school. Detail may not sum to totals because of rounding and because students who reported both theft and violent victimization are counted only once in total victimization. Although Indicators 2 and 3 present information on similar topics, Indicator 2 is based solely on data collected in the National Crime Victimization Survey (NCVS), whereas Indicator 3 is based on data collected in the School Crime Supplement (SCS) to the NCVS as well as demographic data collected in the NCVS. Indicator 2 uses data from all students ages 12–18 who responded to the NCVS, while Indicator 3 uses data from all students ages 12–18 who responded to both the NCVS and the SCS.

SOURCE: Anlan Zhang, Lauren Musu-Gillette, and Barbara A. Oudekerk, "Figure 3.1. Percentage of Students Ages 12–18 Who Reported Criminal Victimization at School during the Previous 6 Months, by Type of Victimization: Selected Years, 1995 through 2013," in *Indicators of School Crime and Safety: 2015*, U.S. Department of Education, National Center for Education Statistics, and U.S. Department of Justice, Bureau of Justice Statistics, May 2016, https://www.bjs.gov/content/pub/pdf/iscs15.pdf (accessed January 19, 2017).

and assist victims and witnesses of federal crimes. The law permits victim impact statements in sentencing hearings to provide judges with information concerning financial, psychological, and/or physical harm that is suffered by victims. It provides for restitution (monetary compensation) to victims and prevents victims and/or witnesses from being intimidated by threatening verbal harassment. The law also establishes penalties for acts of retaliation by defendants against those who testify against them.

Since the 1980s numerous crime laws passed at the federal and state levels have included provisions that

pertain specifically to victims and their rights during criminal proceedings. In 1983 the DOJ created the Office for Victims of Crime (OVC; https://ojp.gov/ovc/). The following year Congress passed the Victims of Crime Act. The act established the Crime Victims Fund, which is administered by the OVC and supports federal and state programs for victim services and compensation. Deposits to the fund come from fines, penalty assessments, and bond forfeitures that are collected from convicted federal criminal offenders and from donations from private entities. According to the OVC (2017, https://www.ovc.gov/pubs/reporttonation2015/), during fiscal years

FIGURE 3.7

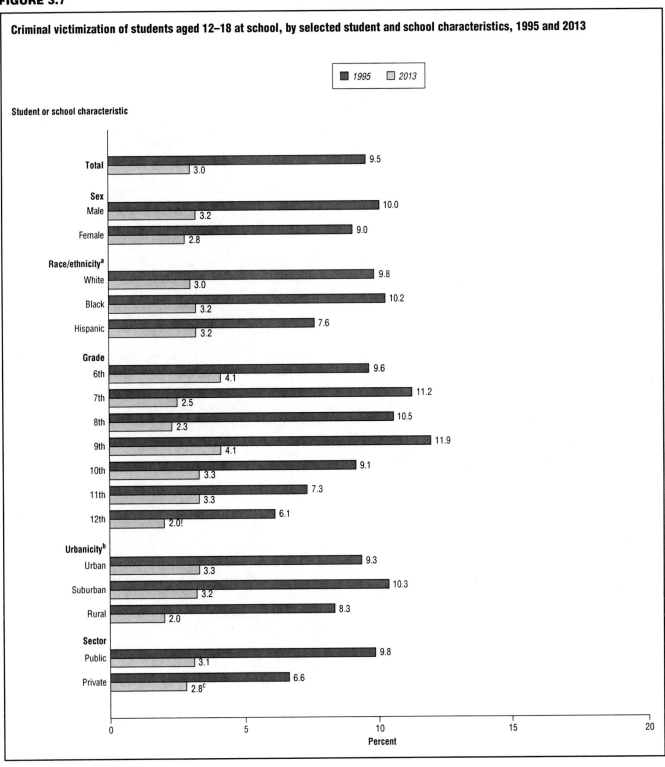

Criminal victimization of students aged 12–18 at school, by selected student and school characteristics, 1995 and 2013

2013 and 2014 the fund "provided more than $1.4 billion to support direct assistance to more than 7 million crime victims through a variety of services—from emergency food and shelter to crisis counseling and advocacy—as well as compensation for financial losses associated with the crime."

Some states have passed constitutional amendments to ensure that victims' rights are preserved and protected in their criminal justice systems. Diverse organizations have begun offering services to victims of crime. These organizations include domestic violence shelters, rape crisis centers, and child abuse programs. Law enforcement agencies, hospitals, and social services agencies also provide victims' services. The types of services provided include crisis intervention, counseling, emergency shelter and transportation, and legal services.

FIGURE 3.7

Criminal victimization of students aged 12–18 at school, by selected student and school characteristics, 1995 and 2013 [CONTINUED]

[a]Race categories exclude persons of Hispanic ethnicity. Separate date for Asians were not collected in 1995; therefore, data for this group are not shown.
[b]Refers to the Standard Metropolitan Statistical Area (MSA) status of the respondent's household as defined in 2000 by the U.S. Census Bureau. Categories include "central city of an MSA (urban)," in MSA but not in central city (suburban)," and "not MSA (rural)."
[c]Interpret data with caution. The coefficient of variation (CV) for this estimate is between 30 and 50 percent.
Note: "Total victimization" includes theft and violent victimization. "At school" includes the school building, on school property, on a school bus, and, from 2001 onward, going to and from school. Although Indicators 2 and 3 present information on similar topics, Indicator 2 is based solely on data collected in the National Crime Victimization Survey (NCVS), whereas Indicator 3 is based on data collected in the School Crime Supplement (SCS) to the NCVS as well as demographic data collected in the NCVS. Indicator 2 uses data from all students ages 12–18 who responded to the NCVS, while Indicator 3 uses data from all students ages 12–18 who responded to both the NCVS and the SCS.

SOURCE: Anlan Zhang, Lauren Musu-Gillette, and Barbara A. Oudekerk, "Figure 3.2. Percentage of Students Ages 12–18 Who Reported Criminal Victimization at School during the Previous 6 Months, by Selected Student and School Characteristics: 1995 and 2013," in *Indicators of School Crime and Safety: 2015*, U.S. Department of Education, National Center for Education Statistics, and U.S. Department of Justice, Bureau of Justice Statistics, May 2016, https://www.bjs.gov/content/pub/pdf/iscs15.pdf (accessed January 19, 2017)

FIGURE 3.8

Victimization of school teachers by students, school year 2011–12

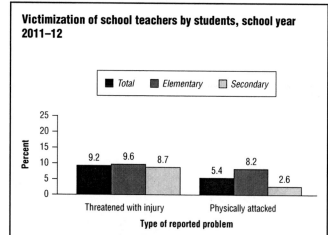

Note: Teachers who taught only prekindergarten students are excluded. Instructional level divides teachers into elementary or secondary based on a combination of the grades taught, main teaching assignment, and the structure of the teachers' class(es). Please see the glossary for a more detailed definition.

SOURCE: Anlan Zhang, Lauren Musu-Gillette, and Barbara A. Oudekerk, "Figure 5.3. Percentage of Public and Private School Teachers Who Reported That They Were Threatened with Injury or That They Were Physically Attacked by a Student from School during the Previous 12 Months, by Instructional Level: School Year 2011–12," in *Indicators of School Crime and Safety: 2015*, U.S. Department of Education, National Center for Education Statistics, and U.S. Department of Justice, Bureau of Justice Statistics, May 2016, https://www.bjs.gov/content/pub/pdf/iscs15.pdf (accessed January 19, 2017)

The OVC (https://www.ovc.gov/help/index.html) provides a list of crime victim organizations, helplines, and other resources for crime victims. The online database VictimLaw (https://www.victimlaw.org), which is funded by the OVC, serves as a clearinghouse of information regarding victims' rights at the federal, state, and tribal levels.

THE USE OF VICTIM SERVICE AGENCIES. During NCVS interviews, crime victims are quizzed about whether or not they used victim service agencies after being victimized. These agencies include public and private groups that provide victims with a variety of services and other support. As shown in Table 3.12, Truman and Morgan estimate that 9.1% of the victims of violent crimes (rape/sexual assault, robbery, aggravated assault, and simple assault) received assistance from such agencies in 2015. The highest percentage of crime victims who received assistance were those who experienced intimate partner violence (18.3%).

NATIONAL CRIME VICTIMS' RIGHTS WEEK. The OVC encourages local communities to observe a National Crime Victims' Rights Week. The event is held annually in April and includes rallies, candlelight vigils, and other activities that are designed to honor or memorialize crime victims and highlight their rights in the criminal justice system.

Victims' Participation at Sentencing

According to the National Center for Victims of Crime (2012, http://www.victimsofcrime.org/help-for-crime-victims/get-help-bulletins-for-crime-victims/victim-impact-statements), every state allows courts to consider or ask for information from victims concerning how their life has been affected by the offense. Most states permit victim input at sentencing and most allow written victim impact statements. Although impact statements are typically used at sentencing and parole hearings, they can also be used at bail hearings, pretrial release hearings, and plea-bargaining hearings.

Offender Restitution Programs

Restitution programs require those who have harmed an individual to repay the victim. In the past, the criminal justice system focused primarily on punishing the criminal and leaving the victims to rely on civil court cases for damage repayment. By the early 21st century most states permitted criminal courts to allow restitution payments as a condition of probation and/or parole. In addition, courts had the statutory authority to order restitution, and several states had passed constitutional amendments that specifically enumerated a victim's right to restitution.

Most restitution laws provide for restitution to the direct victim(s) of a crime, including the surviving family

FIGURE 3.9

Number of on-campus crimes and number of on-campus crimes per 10,000 full-time-equivalent students in degree-granting postsecondary institutions, by selected type of crime, 2001–2013

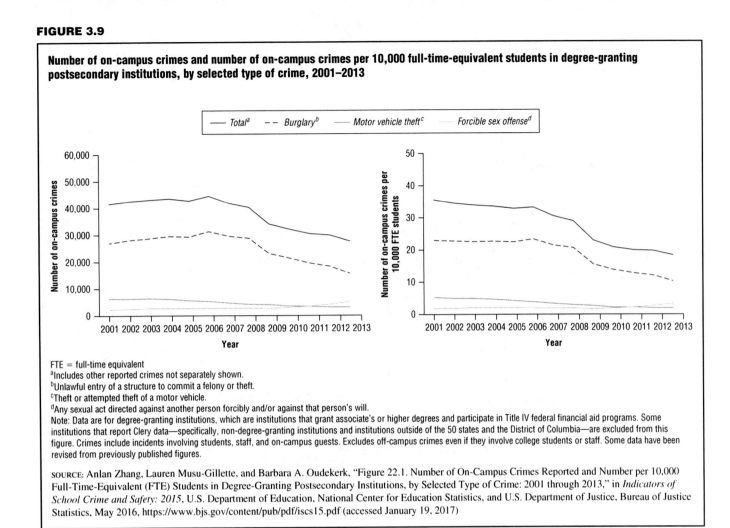

FTE = full-time equivalent
[a]Includes other reported crimes not separately shown.
[b]Unlawful entry of a structure to commit a felony or theft.
[c]Theft or attempted theft of a motor vehicle.
[d]Any sexual act directed against another person forcibly and/or against that person's will.
Note: Data are for degree-granting institutions, which are institutions that grant associate's or higher degrees and participate in Title IV federal financial aid programs. Some institutions that report Clery data—specifically, non-degree-granting institutions and institutions outside of the 50 states and the District of Columbia—are excluded from this figure. Crimes include incidents involving students, staff, and on-campus guests. Excludes off-campus crimes even if they involve college students or staff. Some data have been revised from previously published figures.

SOURCE: Anlan Zhang, Lauren Musu-Gillette, and Barbara A. Oudekerk, "Figure 22.1. Number of On-Campus Crimes Reported and Number per 10,000 Full-Time-Equivalent (FTE) Students in Degree-Granting Postsecondary Institutions, by Selected Type of Crime: 2001 through 2013," in *Indicators of School Crime and Safety: 2015*, U.S. Department of Education, National Center for Education Statistics, and U.S. Department of Justice, Bureau of Justice Statistics, May 2016, https://www.bjs.gov/content/pub/pdf/iscs15.pdf (accessed January 19, 2017)

members of homicide victims. Restitution is usually only provided to victims of crimes for which a defendant was convicted. Many states allow victims to claim medical expenses and property damage or loss, and several permit families of homicide victims to claim costs for loss of support. In assessing damages, the courts must consider the offender's ability to pay.

Civil Suits

A victim can sue in civil court for damages even if the offender has not been found guilty of a criminal offense. In addition, any restitution amounts that remain unpaid at the end of an offender's parole or probation period may be converted into civil judgments. Victims often pursue civil suits because it is easier to win civil cases than criminal

cases. In a criminal case, a jury or judge can find an alleged offender guilty only if the proof is "beyond a reasonable doubt." In a civil case, the burden of proof requires merely a "preponderance of the evidence" against the accused. Proof is still needed that a crime was committed, that there were damages, and that the accused is liable to pay for those damages. Nonetheless, even when victims secure a civil judgment, they often have trouble collecting their damage payments. Such has been the case with O. J. Simpson (1947–), a former professional football player, who was acquitted in 1995 of killing his former wife and her friend. In 1997 the victims' families won a multimillion-dollar civil judgment against Simpson. However, quirks of state laws shielded his pension and primary residence from seizure to pay the debts.

FIGURE 3.10

Level of distress experienced by violent crime victims, by type of crime, 2009–12

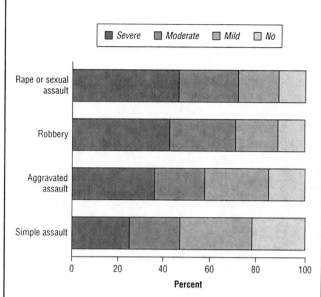

Note: Excludes victimizations in which the level of distress was unknown.

SOURCE: Lynn Langton and Jennifer Truman, "Figure 3. Level of Distress Experienced by Violent Crime Victims, by Type of Crime, 2009–2012," in *Socio-Emotional Impact of Violent Crime*, U.S. Department of Justice, Office of Justice Programs, Bureau of Justice Statistics, September 2014, http://www.bjs.gov/content/pub/pdf/sivc .pdf (accessed January 19, 2017)

FIGURE 3.11

Level of distress experienced by serious violent crime victims, by victim–offender relationship, 2009–12

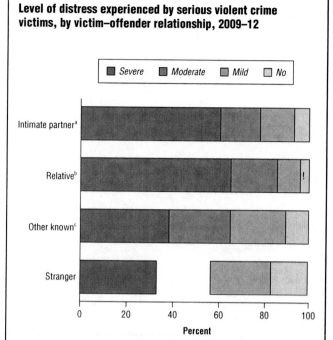

!interpret with caution. Based on 10 or fewer sample cases, or the coeffient of variation is greater than 50%.
[a]Includes victimizations committed by current or former spouses, boyfriends, and girlfriends.
[b]Includes victimizations committed by family members (excluding intimate partners).
[c]Includes victimizations committed by close friends or other acquaintances.
Note: Excludes victimizations in which the level of distress was unknown and the victim–offender relationship was unknown.

SOURCE: Lynn Langton and Jennifer Truman, "Figure 4. Level of Distress Experienced by Serious Violent Crime Victims, by Victim–Offender Relationship, 2009–2012," in *Socio-Emotional Impact of Violent Crime*, U.S. Department of Justice, Office of Justice Programs, Bureau of Justice Statistics, September 2014, http://www.bjs.gov/content/pub/pdf/sivc.pdf (accessed January 19, 2017)

TABLE 3.11

Physical and emotional symptoms suffered by violent crime victims who experienced socio-emotional problems as a result of the victimization, by type of crime and victim–offender relationship, 2009–12

Symptom	Type of crime			Victim–offender relationship		
	Total violence	Serious violence	Simple assault	Intimate partner[a]	Other known[b]	Stranger
Emotional	91%	96%	87%	92%	91%	89%
Worried or anxious	72	78	67	79	73	65
Angry	70	76	67	72	72	68
Unsafe	65	73	60	69	63	66
Violated	61	69	56	72	57	57
Vulnerable	60	64	58	69	58	57
Distrustful	56	66	50	60	57	52
Sad or depressed	53	58	50	72	54	37
Other	12	13	12	13	11	14
Physical	61%	67%	57%	74%	61%	53%
Trouble sleeping	47	51	44	61	45	38
Fatigue	34	36	33	52	33	24
Upset stomach	31	32	30	46	29	22
Muscle tension	31	34	28	39	31	25
Headaches	30	37	25	40	31	22
Problems with eating/drinking	27	33	23	43	26	16
High blood pressure	15	16	15	18	17	11
Other	9	12	7	12	8	8

[a]Includes victimizations committed by current or former spouses, boyfriends, or girlfriends.
[b]Includes victimizations committed by family members (excluding intimate partners), close friends, or other acquaintances.
Note: Includes victims who experienced symptoms for a month or more. Victims who did not report experiencing socio-emotional problems (one or more of the following: moderate to severe distress, problems with family or friend relationships, or problems at work or school) were not asked about physical and emotional symptoms and were excluded from the analysis. Excludes victimizations in which the level of distress was unknown.

SOURCE: Lynn Langton and Jennifer Truman, "Table 1. Physical and Emotional Symptoms Suffered by Violent Crime Victims Who Experienced Socio-Emotional Problems as a Result of the Victimization, by Type of Crime and Victim–Offender Relationship, 2009–2012," in *Socio-Emotional Impact of Violent Crime*, U.S. Department of Justice, Office of Justice Programs, Bureau of Justice Statistics, September 2014, http://www.bjs.gov/content/pub/pdf/sivc.pdf (accessed January 19, 2017)

TABLE 3.12

Percentage of violent victimizations in which assistance from a victim service agency was received, by type of crime, 2014 and 2015

Type of crime	2014[d]	2015
Violent crime[a]	10.5%	9.1%
Serious violent crime[b]	12.3	14.4
Simple assault	9.5	6.0
Intimate partner violence[c]	28.2%	18.3%
Violent crime involving injury	14.9%	16.9%
Violent crime involving weapon	7.2%	15.0%

NCVS = National Crime Victimization Survey
[a]Includes rape or sexual assault, robbery, aggravated assault, and simple assault. Excludes homicide because the NCVS is based on interviews with victims and therefore cannot measure murder.
[b]In the NCVS, serious violent crime includes rape or sexual assault, robbery, and aggravated assault.
[c]Includes victimization committed by current or former spouses, boyfriends, or girlfriends.
[d]Comparison year.

SOURCE: Jennifer L. Truman and Rachel E. Morgan, "Table 6. Percent of Violent Victimizations in Which Assistance from a Victim Service Agency Was Received, by Type of Crime, 2014 and 2015," in *Criminal Victimization, 2015*, U.S. Department of Justice, Bureau of Justice Statistics, October 2016, https://www.bjs.gov/content/pub/pdf/cv15.pdf (accessed January 19, 2017)

CHAPTER 4
DRUG CRIMES

Drug crimes have grown to be an enormous national problem. In *Southwest Border Violence: Issues in Identifying and Measuring Spillover Violence* (February 28, 2013, https://fas.org/sgp/crs/homesec/R41075.pdf), Kristin M. Finklea of the Congressional Research Service (CRS) states, "The United States is the largest consumer of illegal drugs and sustains a multi-billion dollar market in illegal drugs."

U.S. history regarding the criminalization of drug use has been checkered. During the 1700s a number of potions containing opium and promising cures for a variety of ailments were available as so-called patent medicines, and physicians routinely prescribed opium medications to their patients. In 1805 the discovery of morphine by the German pharmacist Friedrich Sertürner (1793–1841) introduced another powerful drug to the medicines of the day. By the end of the 19th century, cocaine, codeine, and dozens of similar drugs were in common use. However, doctors were increasingly concerned about the side effects and addictiveness of these drugs and began issuing stern warnings about them to the public.

The Progressive movement and religious revival that swept the United States during the late 1800s and early 1900s made drug abuse socially unacceptable. Legislators at the state and federal levels responded by passing laws that prohibited the use of specific drugs, including opium and marijuana. By the 1950s many Americans considered drug abuse to be a problem only among marginalized populations, such as the African American inhabitants of inner-city ghettos and beatniks (nonconformist youths who defied societal conventions).

The 1960s ushered in a completely new drug culture to the United States: recreational drug use among middle- and upper-class white youths in suburban and rural areas. Marijuana and a relatively new hallucinogenic drug called D-lysergic acid diethylamide (LSD) surged in popularity. Other drugs of choice during this era were

amphetamines (also called speed or uppers). Amphetamines stimulate the central nervous system. The drugs were widely dispensed by U.S. military authorities during World War II (1939–1945) to keep soldiers alert during battle. After the war amphetamines remained popular among students and workers who wanted to stay awake for long periods. People also used them to lose weight because amphetamines suppress the appetite. According to John M. Roll et al., in *Methamphetamine Addiction: From Basic Science to Treatment* (2009), amphetamines could be easily purchased over the counter (without a prescription) during the 1950s. By the end of the 1960s, new laws had been passed to combat the growing problems with LSD and amphetamine abuse.

In 1969 President Richard M. Nixon (1913–1994) asked Congress to pass extensive legislation giving the federal government more control over the problem of drug abuse. The result was the Comprehensive Drug Abuse Prevention and Control Act (CDAPCA) of 1970. The act gave the U.S. attorney general greater jurisdiction over drug crimes and provided for the rehabilitation of drug addicts. It placed new restrictions on the pharmaceutical industry and the medical professionals to better control and monitor the supply and dispensing of prescription drugs. The following year Nixon (http://www.presidency.ucsb.edu/ws/?pid=3047) made a statement to the public in which he called drug abuse "public enemy number one" and called for an "all-out offensive" against it. Over time, Nixon's statement became known as the declaration of the War on Drugs. In 1973 the U.S. Drug Enforcement Administration (DEA) was created to coordinate drug control efforts for the federal government.

Over the decades the War on Drugs has precipitated the arrests of millions of people. The 21st century, however, has witnessed dramatic shifts in public and political attitudes about how the war should be waged. For example, some states have decided to allow marijuana to be legally grown, sold, and used by adults. Imprisoning non-violent drug offenders for long periods has come under fire. The nature of drug abuse is also evolving. Misuse of prescription drugs and drug overdoses have become major public health problems. All these factors complicate the nation's long-lasting fight against drug crimes.

DRUG OFFENSES AND ARRESTS

Titles II and III of the CDAPCA are called the Controlled Substances Act (CSA). The CSA places illicit drugs and certain legal drugs into one of five schedules or categories based on the characteristics of the drugs and their potential for abuse. (See Table 4.1.)

Table 4.2 provides information about some common drugs or drug categories, including their CSA schedule numbers, and how they are typically administered. Cocaine, heroin, and marijuana are derived primarily from organic sources. Cocaine and heroin originate from opium poppies. Marijuana is from *Cannabis*, a genus of flowering plants. Some drugs are considered synthetic or manufactured drugs because their origins are not primarily organic. Examples include amphetamines, methamphetamines, MDMA drugs (e.g., ecstasy), and LSD.

Many drug offenses are felonies and are punishable by at least one year in prison. Some drug offenses (e.g., the possession of small amounts of marijuana in some jurisdictions) are misdemeanors. People convicted of misdemeanor drug crimes may receive a fine and/or a sentence of less than one year in a local jail. Some jurisdictions treat the possession of very small amounts of marijuana (e.g., less than 1 ounce [28 g]) as an infraction, rather than as a misdemeanor. Infractions are minor offenses, such as traffic violations, that are punishable only with fines, not with incarceration.

Drug laws are complex and can differ between jurisdictions. In general, the seriousness of an offense and the harshness of its penalty are based on the type and amount of drug involved and whether the offender possesses the drug for his or her own use or is a seller, manufacturer, or distributor. First-time offenders may receive less harsh charges and sentences than repeat offenders.

There is substantial overlap between federal law and state laws regarding drug offenses. In many cases perpetrators could be prosecuted by either federal or state authorities. People arrested for drug offenses on federal property (e.g., national parks), drug trafficking or distributing drugs across state lines, and those arrested by federal officers (e.g., DEA officers) fall under federal jurisdiction. In other cases federal and state prosecutors may negotiate which jurisdiction should have precedence. Federal authorities tend to handle cases involving the trafficking of large amounts of drugs and those in which conspiracies, organized crime groups, and/or firearms are a factor.

As is shown in Figure 2.1 in Chapter 2, more than 30,000 people had drug cases filed against them in federal court during fiscal year (FY) 2012 (October 1, 2011, to September 30, 2012). Excluding immigration cases, drug cases far outnumbered other types of federal prosecutions from the late 1990s through FY 2012. In "Statistics and Facts" (2017, https://www.dea.gov/resource-center/statistics.shtml), the DEA notes that it made roughly 30,000 to 31,000 arrests each year on drug charges in 2013, 2014, and 2015.

Many more drug cases are handled at the state and local levels. Statistics about them are collected by the Federal Bureau of Investigation (FBI) as part of its Uniform Crime Reporting (UCR) Program. The Bureau of Justice Statistics (BJS) presents in "Drugs and Crime Facts: Total Estimated Drug Law Violation Arrests in

TABLE 4.1

Schedules under the Controlled Substances Act

Schedule	Definition	Examples
I	No currently accepted medical use in the United States, a lack of accepted safety for use under medical supervision, and a high potential for abuse.	Heroin, lysergic acid diethylamide (LSD), marijuana (cannabis), peyote, methaqualone, and 3,4-methylenedioxymethamphetamine ("Ecstasy").
II	A high potential for abuse which may lead to severe psychological or physical dependence.	Narcotics: oxycodone and fentanyl. Stimulants: amphetamine, methamphetamine, and methylphenidate (Ritalin). Other: amobarbital, glutethimide, and pentobarbital.
III	A potential for abuse less than substances in Schedules I or II and abuse may lead to moderate or low physical dependence or high psychological dependence.	Narcotics: products containing not more than 90 milligrams of codeine per dosage unit (Tylenol with Codeine) and buprenorphine. Non-Narcotics: benzphetamine, phendimetrazine, ketamine, and anabolic steroids such as Depo-Testosterone.
IV	A low potential for abuse relative to substances in Schedule III.	Alprazolam (Xanax), clonazepam (Klonopin), diazepam (Valium), lorazepam (Ativan), and triazolam (Halcion).
V	A low potential for abuse relative to substances listed in Schedule IV and consist primarily of preparations containing limited quantities of certain narcotics.	Cough preparations containing not more than 200 milligrams of codeine per 100 milliliters or per 100 grams (Robitussin AC, Phenergan with Codeine), and ezogabine.

SOURCE: Adapted from "Definition of Controlled Substance Schedules," in *Controlled Substance Schedules*, U.S. Department of Justice, Drug Enforcement Administration, January 2017, https://www.deadiversion.usdoj.gov/schedules/ (accessed January 19, 2017)

TABLE 4.2

Characteristics of commonly abused drugs

Name or category	Examples of street and commercial names	Type	Common forms	Common ways taken	Controlled Substances Act schedule
Cocaine	Blow, Bump, C, Candy, Charlie, Coke, Crack, Flake, Rock, Snow, Toot	Stimulant	White powder, whitish rock crystal	Snorted, smoked, injected	Schedule II
DMT	DMT, Dimitri	Hallucinogen	White or yellow crystalline powder	Smoked, injected	Schedule I
GHB	G, Georgia Home Boy, Goop, Grievous Bodily Harm, Liquid Ecstasy, Liquid X, Soap, Scoop	Depressant	Colorless liquid, white powder	Swallowed (often combined with alcohol or other beverages)	Schedule I
Heroin	Brown sugar, China White, Dope, H, Horse, Junk, Skag, Skunk, Smack, White Horse	Opioid	White or brownish powder, or black sticky substance known as "black tar heroin"	Injected, snorted, smoked	Schedule I
Ketamine	Cat Valium, K, Special K, Vitamin K	Hallucinogen	Liquid, white powder	Injected, snorted, smoked (powder added to tobacco or marijuana cigarettes), swallowed	Schedule III
Khat (pronounced "cot")	Abyssinian Tea, African Salad, Catha, Chat, Kat, Oat	Psychoactive	Fresh or dried leaves	Chewed, brewed as tea	Cathinone is a Schedule I drug, making khat use illegal, but the khat plant is not controlled
LSD	Acid, Blotter, Blue Heaven, Cubes, Microdot, Yellow Sunshine	Hallucinogen	Tablet; capsule; clear liquid; small, decorated squares of absorbent paper that liquid has been added to	Swallowed, absorbed through mouth tissues (paper squares)	Schedule I
Marijuana (Cannabis)	Blunt, Bud, Dope, Ganja, Grass, Green, Herb, Joint, Mary Jane, Pot, Reefer, Sinsemilla, Skunk, Smoke, Trees, Weed; Hashish: Boom, Gangster, Hash, Hemp	Psychoactive	Greenish-gray mixture of dried, shredded leaves, stems, seeds, and/or flowers; resin (hashish) or sticky, black liquid (hash oil)	Smoked, eaten (mixed in food or brewed as tea)	Schedule I (Sale of marijuana is legal in some states)
MDMA (Ecstasy and Molly)	Adam, Clarity, Eve, Lover's Speed, Peace, Uppers	Psychoactive	Colorful tablets with imprinted logos, capsules, powder, liquid	Swallowed, snorted	Schedule I
Mescaline (Peyote)	Buttons, Cactus, Mesc	Hallucinogen	Fresh or dried buttons, capsule	Swallowed (chewed or soaked in water and drunk)	Schedule I
Methamphetamine	Crank, Chalk, Crystal, Fire, Glass, Go Fast, Ice, Meth, Speed	Stimulant	White powder or pill; crystal meth looks like pieces of glass or shiny blue-white "rocks" of different sizes	Swallowed, snorted, smoked, injected	Schedule II
PCP	Angel Dust, Boat, Hog, Love Boat, Peace Pill	Hallucinogen	White or colored powder, tablet, or capsule; clear liquid	Injected, snorted, swallowed, smoked (powder added to mint, parsley, oregano, or marijuana)	Schedule I, II
Codeine-based prescription Opioids	Captain Cody, Cody, Lean, Schoolboy, Sizzurp, Purple Drank; Codeine (various brand names)	Pain reliever	Tablet, capsule, liquid	Injected, swallowed (often mixed with soda and flavorings)	Schedule II, III, V
Prescription Barbiturates	Barbs, Phennies, Red Birds, Reds, Tooies, Yellow Jackets, Yellows	Sedative	Pill, capsule, liquid	Swallowed, injected	Schedule II, III, IV
Prescription Amphetamines	Bennies, Black Beauties, Crosses, Hearts, LA Turnaround, Speed, Truck Drivers, Uppers	Stimulant	Tablet, capsule	Swallowed, snorted, smoked, injected	Schedule II
Psilocybin	Little Smoke, Magic Mushrooms, Purple Passion, Shrooms	Hallucinogen	Fresh or dried mushrooms	Swallowed (eaten, brewed as tea, or added to other foods)	Schedule I
Rohypnol (Flunitrazepam)	Circles, Date Rape Drug, Forget Pill, Forget-Me Pill, La Rocha, Lunch Money, Mexican Valium, Mind Eraser, Pingus, R2, Reynolds, Rib, Roach, Roach 2, Roaches, Roachies, Roapies, Rochas Dos, Roofies, Rope, Rophies, Row-Shay, Ruffies, Trip-and-Fall, Wolfies	Sedative	Tablet	Swallowed (as a pill or as dissolved in a drink), snorted	Schedule IV; Rohypnol is not approved for medical use in the United States; it is available as a prescription sleep aid in other countries

TABLE 4.2

Characteristics of commonly abused drugs [CONTINUED]

Name or category	Examples of street and commercial names	Type	Common forms	Common ways taken	Controlled Substances Act schedule
Salvia	Magic mint, Maria Pastora, Sally-D, Shepherdess's Herb, Diviner's Sage	Hallucinogen	Fresh or dried leaves	Smoked, chewed, or brewed as tea	Not Scheduled; but labeled drug of concern by DEA and illegal in some states
Steroids (anabolic)	Juice, Gym Candy, Pumpers, Roids	Steroids (anabolic)	Tablet, capsule, liquid drops, gel, cream, patch, injectable solution	Injected, swallowed, applied to skin	Schedule III
Synthetic Cannabinoids (Synthetic Marijuana)	K2, Spice, Black Mamba, Bliss, Bombay Blue, Fake Weed, Fire, Genie, Moon Rocks, Skunk, Smacked, Yucatan, Zohai	Herbal mixtures containing man-made cannabinoid chemicals	Dried, shredded plant material that looks like potpourri and is sometimes sold as "incense"	Smoked, swallowed (brewed as tea)	Schedule I
Synthetic Cathinones (bath salts)	Bloom, Cloud Nine, Cosmic Blast, Flakka, Ivory Wave, Lunar Wave, Scarface, Vanilla Sky, White Lightning	Stimulant	White or brown crystalline powder sold in small plastic or foil packages labeled "not for human consumption" and sometimes sold as jewelry cleaner; tablet, capsule, liquid	Swallowed, snorted, injected	Schedule I (Some formulations have been banned by the DEA)

SOURCE: Adapted from "Commonly Abused Drugs Charts," in *Drugs of Abuse*, U.S. Department of Health and Human Services, National Institutes of Health, National Institute on Drug Abuse, January 2016, https://www.drugabuse.gov/drugs-abuse/commonly-abused-drugs-charts#DEA (accessed January 19, 2017)

the United States, 1980–2007" (2017, https://www.bjs.gov/content/dcf/tables/arrtot.cfm) UCR data, indicating there were 580,900 arrests for drug crimes in 1980. (See Figure 4.1.) By 1988 the number had soared to more than a million a year and continued to grow. Drug arrests peaked in 2006 at nearly 1.9 million and slowly began to decline. According to the FBI, in *Crime in the United States, 2015* (September 2016, https://ucr.fbi.gov/crime-in-the-u.s/2015/crime-in-the-u.s.-2015/), arrests for drug abuse violations in 2015 totaled nearly 1.5 million. It was the largest number of arrests for any specific crime type.

FIGURE 4.1

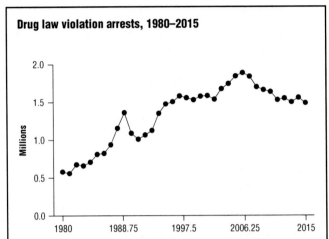

Drug law violation arrests, 1980–2015

SOURCE: Adapted from "Total Estimated Drug Law Violation Arrests in the United States," in *Drugs and Crime Facts*, U.S. Department of Justice, Bureau of Justice Statistics, August 17, 2009, https://www.bjs.gov/content/dcf/enforce.cfm (accessed January 20, 2017) and "Table 29. Estimated Number of Arrests, United States, 2015," in *Crime in the United States, 2015*, U.S. Department of Justice, Federal Bureau of Investigation, September 26, 2016, https://ucr.fbi.gov/crime-in-the-u.s/2015/crime-in-the-u.s.-2015/tables/table-29 (accessed January 20, 2017)

Table 4.3 breaks down state and local drug arrests in 2015 by drug law violation and drug type. The majority (83.9%) of the arrests were for possession, whereas only 16.1% were for sale/manufacturing. Overall, marijuana was involved in more than four out of 10 (43.2%) of all arrests—4.6% of sale/manufacturing arrests and 38.6% of possession arrests. Heroin or cocaine and their derivatives were involved in 25.4% of all arrests—5.5% of sale/manufacturing arrests and 19.9% of possession arrests. Only 6.9% of the total arrests—1.8% of sale/manufacturing arrests and 5.1% of possession arrests—were related to synthetic or manufactured drugs, such as methamphetamine. Arrests for other types of drugs accounted for 24.4% of the total arrests by making up 4.2% of sale/manufacturing arrests and 20.2% of possession arrests.

DRUG FACTORS IN OTHER CRIMINAL OFFENSES

Crimes such as assault, murder, and robbery clearly have victims. Drug abuse is different in that people other than the users are not specifically victimized by the offenses. However, drug abusers may commit other crimes, such as stealing (to support their habits), or engage in violent behavior.

Drug Trafficking and Violence

Drug trafficking is strongly associated with other criminal acts, particularly violent ones. In *U.S.-Mexican Security Cooperation: The Mérida Initiative and Beyond* (January 18, 2017, https://fas.org/sgp/crs/row/R41349.pdf), Clare Ribando Seelke and Kristin Finklea of the CRS estimate that more than 100,000 people have died in Mexico since 2006 because of drug crime–related violence. Mexico is a major source and transit country for many of the illegal drugs smuggled into the United States, including cocaine,

TABLE 4.3

Arrests for drug abuse violations, by type and region, 2015

Drug abuse violations	United States total	Northeast	Midwest	South	West
Total*	100	100	100	100	100
Sale/manufacturing:					
Total	16.1	19.9	15.9	16.6	13.4
Heroin or cocaine and their derivatives	5.5	10.9	3.7	5.1	4
Marijuana	4.6	5.2	6.3	4	3.7
Synthetic or manufactured drugs	1.8	1.5	1.1	3.4	0.5
Other dangerous nonnarcotic drugs	4.2	2.3	4.7	4.1	5.2
Possession:					
Total	83.9	80.1	84.1	83.4	86.6
Heroin or cocaine and their derivatives	19.9	18	10.9	14.7	33.5
Marijuana	38.6	46.1	50.7	46.5	16.5
Synthetic or manufactured drugs	5.1	3.5	5.2	7.6	2.8
Other dangerous nonnarcotic drugs	20.2	12.6	17.3	14.7	33.8

*Because of rounding, the percentages may not add to 100.0.

SOURCE: "Arrests Table: Arrests for Drug Abuse Violations Percent Distribution by Region, 2015," in *Crime in the United States, 2015*, U.S. Department of Justice, Federal Bureau of Investigation, September 26, 2016, https://ucr.fbi.gov/crime-in-the-u.s/2015/crime-in-the-u.s.-2015/persons-arrested/persons-arrested (accessed January 20, 2017)

marijuana, and methamphetamine. Much of this illicit business is conducted by drug cartels or drug trafficking organizations (DTOs) that engage in extremely violent behaviors. Finklea explains in *Southwest Border Violence: Issues in Identifying and Measuring Spillover Violence*, "Mexican DTOs have formed relationships with U.S. street gangs, prison gangs, and outlaw motorcycle gangs. Although these gangs have historically been involved with retail-level drug distribution, their ties to the Mexican DTOs have allowed them to become increasingly involved at the wholesale level as well. These gangs facilitate the movement of illicit drugs to urban, suburban, and rural areas of the United States."

Finklea notes that it is extremely difficult to quantify how many U.S. criminal acts are associated with drug trafficking because law enforcement authorities do not compile such data on a widespread basis. For example, the FBI's UCR Program contains very limited information about the role of drugs in other criminal offenses. As is shown in Table 2.4 in Chapter 2, the FBI indicates that 468 murders in 2015 were related to "narcotic drug laws" and 75 murders were associated with "brawl due to influence of narcotics." However, no statistics are provided about the role of drugs in other criminal offenses.

Drug Use Reported by Prison Inmates and Arrestees

Some clues about the link between drug use and criminal behavior can be gleaned from studies of prison inmates. Between 1974 and 2004 the BJS conducted the periodic "Survey of Inmates in State and Federal Correctional Facilities" that included questions about drug use. In *Drug Use and Dependence, State and Federal Prisoners, 2004* (January 2007, https://www.bjs.gov/content/pub/pdf/dudsfp04.pdf), Christopher J. Mumola and Jennifer C. Karberg of the BJS reported on drug-related findings from the 2004 survey. In 2004, 56% of all state prisoners reported using drugs in the month before committing their offense(s). This percentage had changed little from 1997, when 57% of state prisoners reported previous drug use. A slightly lower percentage of federal prison inmates, 50%, reported drug use in the month before their offense in 2004, compared with 45% in 1997. Nearly one-third (32.1%) of state prison inmates and 26.4% of federal prison inmates in 2004 said they had committed their current offense while under the influence of drugs. A follow-up survey of inmates had not been conducted as of April 2017.

Since 2007 the Office of National Drug Control Policy (ONDCP) within the Executive Office of the President has operated the Arrestee Drug Abuse Monitoring (ADAM) program. The ONDCP's ADAM II program replaces an earlier ADAM I program that was operated by the National Institute of Justice. The ONDCP notes in *ADAM II 2013 Annual Report* (January 2014, https://

obamawhitehouse.archives.gov/sites/default/files/ondcp/policy-and-research/adam_ii_2013_annual_report.pdf) that the ADAM II program monitors drug use trends among newly arrested males. From 2007 to 2011 the program included 10 jail systems throughout the country; in 2012 and 2013 only five jail systems were included. Participation by arrestees is voluntary, and they are not limited to people arrested for drug crimes. The results indicate that the majority of arrestees subjected to urine drug testing at each location in 2013 tested positive for at least one drug. The drugs tested included amphetamine, barbiturates, benzodiazepines, cocaine, marijuana, methadone, methamphetamine, opiates, oxycodone, phencyclidine, and propoxyphene.

Marijuana was the most commonly used drug in all locations, with a range of 33.5% to 59.4% of arrestees testing positive for it. It was followed by cocaine, from 6.6% to 33.3%; opiates, from 6% to 17.9%; and methamphetamine, from 0.3% to 50.6%. Usage of the latter three drugs varied substantially from one city to another. Overall, the ONDCP reports that ADAM II results consistently show that marijuana has been the most commonly used illegal substance among booked arrestees since the original program began in 2000.

Drug-Facilitated Sexual Abuse

Two commonly abused drugs called flunitrazepam and gamma-hydroxybutyrate (GHB) are associated with sexual assaults. In "Drug Facilitated Sexual Assault" (2017, https://www.rainn.org/articles/drug-facilitated-sexual-assault), the Rape, Abuse, and Incest National Network notes that alcohol and some drugs are used by perpetrators to facilitate sexual assaults. The substances lower victims' inhibitions, minimize their resistance to assault, and impair their memories. Since the 1990s there have been some well-publicized cases in which so-called date rape drugs were secretly slipped into the drinks of people who were then sexually assaulted. For example, Joe Sterling reports in "Sex Assault, Date-Rape Drug Allegations Rattle Northwestern" (CNN.com, February 7, 2017) that in February 2017 campus police at Northwestern University were investigating claims that five female students had been secretly given drugs while attending fraternity party events. Three of the women said they were sexually assaulted during the incidents.

NATIONAL SURVEY ON DRUG USE AND HEALTH

The Substance Abuse and Mental Health Services Administration (SAMHSA), which is part of the U.S. Department of Health and Human Services, conducts an annual survey on the illicit use of drugs by the U.S. population. In *Key Substance Use and Mental Health Indicators in the United States: Results from the 2015 National Survey on Drug Use and Health* (September 2016, https://www.samhsa.gov/data/sites/default/files/NSDUH-FFR1-2015/NSDUH-FFR1-2015/NSDUH-FFR1-2015.pdf),

FIGURE 4.2

Self-reported illicit use of drugs during previous month by persons aged 12 or older, by type of drug, 2015

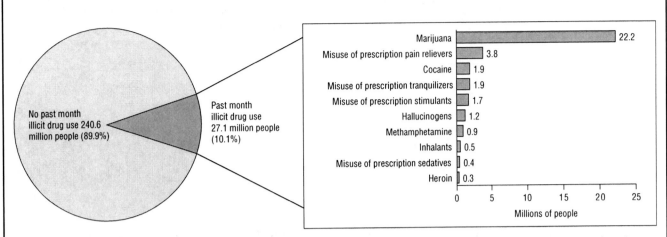

Notes: Estimated numbers of people refer to people aged 12 or older in the civilian, noninstitutionalized population in the United States. The numbers do not sum to the total population of the United States because the population for National Survey on Drug Use and Health (NSDUH) does not include people aged 11 years old or younger, people with no fixed household address (e.g. homeless or transient people not in shelters), active-duty military personnel, and residents of institutional group quarters, such as correctional facilities, nursing homes, mental institutions, and long-term care hospitals. The estimated numbers of current users of different illicit drugs are not mutually exclusive because people could have used more than one type of illicit drug in the past month.

SOURCE: "Figure 1. Numbers of Past Month Illicit Drug Users among People Aged 12 or Older: 2015," in *Key Substance Use and Mental Health Indicators in the United States: Results from the 2015 National Survey on Drug Use and Health*, U.S. Department of Health and Human Services, Substance Abuse and Mental Health Services Administration, Center for Behavioral Health Statistics and Quality, September 2016, https://www.samhsa.gov/data/sites/default/files/NSDUH-FFR1-2015/NSDUH-FFR1-2015/NSDUH-FFR1-2015.pdf (accessed January 20, 2017)

SAMHSA notes that in 2015 it surveyed 68,073 people in the civilian noninstitutionalized population (people who are not in the U.S. military, hospitals, jail, or similar facilities) of the United States.

SAMHSA finds that in 2015, 27.1 million Americans aged 12 years and older reported illicit use of drugs within the previous month. (See Figure 4.2.) The vast majority (22.2 million) had used marijuana. Much smaller numbers had misused prescription pain relievers (3.8 million) or used cocaine (1.9 million).

Figure 4.3 shows past-month illicit drug use by people aged 12 years and older in 2015 by age group. Overall, 10.1% of the U.S. population aged 12 years and older admitted illicit use of drugs during the previous month. It was most common among teens and young adults aged 18 to 25 years (22.3%), followed by younger teens aged 12 to 17 years (8.8%). Adults aged 26 years and older (8.2%) were the least likely to report illicit drug use.

Student Surveys

Monitoring the Future is an annual survey funded by the National Institute on Drug Abuse (NIDA), which is part of the National Institutes of Health. The survey assesses drug use among students in the eighth, 10th, and 12th grades. According to the NIDA, in "Monitoring the Future Study: Trends in Prevalence of Various Drugs" (2017, https://www.drugabuse.gov/trends-statistics/monitoring-future/monitoring-future-study-trends-in-pre

FIGURE 4.3

Self-reported illicit use of drugs during previous month by persons aged 12 or older, by age group, 2015

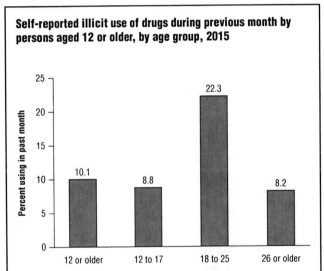

SOURCE: "Figure 2. Past Month Illicit Drug Use among People Aged 12 or Older, by Age Group: Percentages, 2015," in *Key Substance Use and Mental Health Indicators in the United States: Results from the 2015 National Survey on Drug Use and Health*, U.S. Department of Health and Human Services, Substance Abuse and Mental Health Services Administration, Center for Behavioral Health Statistics and Quality, September 2016, https://www.samhsa.gov/data/sites/default/files/NSDUH-FFR1-2015/NSDUH-FFR1-2015/NSDUH-FFR1-2015.pdf (accessed January 20, 2017)

valence-various-drugs), 17.2% of eighth graders, 33.7% of 10th graders, and 48.3% of 12th graders had used illicit drugs at some point during their lifetime. These values had

FIGURE 4.4

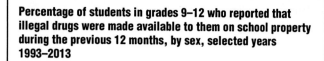

Percentage of students in grades 9–12 who reported that illegal drugs were made available to them on school property during the previous 12 months, by sex, selected years 1993–2013

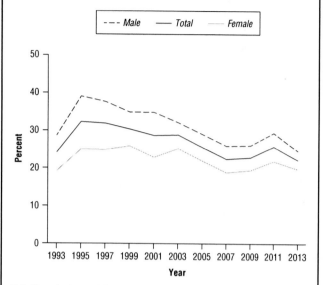

Note: "On school property" was not defined for survey respondents.

SOURCE: Anlan Zhang, Lauren Musu-Gillette, and Barbara A. Oudekerk, "Figure 9.1. Percentage of Students in Grades 9–12 Who Reported That Illegal Drugs Were Made Available to Them on School Property during the Previous 12 Months, by Sex: Selected Years, 1993 through 2013," in *Indicators of School Crime and Safety: 2015*, U.S. Department of Education, National Center for Education Statistics, and U.S. Department of Justice, Bureau of Justice Statistics, May 2016, https://www.bjs.gov/content/pub/pdf/iscs15.pdf (accessed January 19, 2017).

decreased by around two to five percentage points since 2013. In 2016 marijuana was the most commonly abused drug, followed by prescription drugs of any type, amphetamine, and inhalants.

Chapter 3 describes *Indicators of School Crime and Safety: 2015* (May 2016, https://www.bjs.gov/content/pub/pdf/iscs15.pdf), a publication by the U.S. Departments of Education and Justice about crimes in school environments. The data are compiled from a variety of sources, including youth surveys. As shown in Figure 4.4, in 2013 nearly a quarter (22%) of students in grades nine to 12 reported that illegal drugs were offered, sold, or given to them on school property. This value was down from its peak of 32% in 1995.

COCAINE AND CRACK

Nonmedical use of cocaine has been illegal since the passage of the Harrison Narcotics Act of 1914. In 1970 cocaine was classified as a CSA Schedule II drug because it is considered highly addictive. During the 1970s and 1980s cocaine use soared in the United States with the rise of large well-funded drug cartels in South America,

particularly in Colombia. The cartels used their extensive criminal networks to import the drug into the United States and sell it for premium prices. Cocaine in powdered form became the drug of choice for wealthy celebrities and professionals. It developed a reputation as a trendy, glamorous, and nonaddictive drug that was too expensive for street users.

The Crack Epidemic

During the early 1980s a cheaper form of cocaine called crack cocaine was introduced to street users. Unlike powdered cocaine, the crack version was a crystal that could be smoked. It was also more potent than the same amount of powdered cocaine and provided a much quicker high. Crack soon became the drug of choice among low-income users, particularly in inner cities with large minority populations, and the country experienced a so-called crack epidemic. Gang wars and other crack-related crimes skyrocketed. Americans were appalled by media reports about crack-induced street crime and crack-addicted babies born to mothers abusing the drug. The social effects of the crack epidemic are described by the DEA in *DEA History in Depth* (January 2009, https://www.dea.gov/about/history/1985-1990.pdf): "The crack trade had created a violent sub-world, and crack-related murders in many large cities were skyrocketing. For example, a 1988 study by the Bureau of Justice Statistics found that in New York City, crack use was tied to 32% of all homicides and 60% of drug-related homicides. On a daily basis, the evening news reported the violence of drive-by shootings and crack users trying to obtain money for their next hit."

The Crackdown on Crack

In 1986 Congress passed the Anti-drug Abuse Act, a comprehensive law that imposed mandatory minimum prison sentences for people convicted of federal drug crimes. The new law made an important distinction between crack cocaine and powdered cocaine. A person convicted of possessing only 0.2 of an ounce (5 g) of crack cocaine faced the same mandatory prison sentence as a person convicted of possessing 17.6 ounces (500 g) of powdered cocaine. In other words, there was a 100 to 1 sentencing disparity between the two forms of the drug. At the time, politicians defended the disparity as a reasonable response to the harm that crack cocaine was doing to U.S. society. However, the law soon became controversial because relatively low-level crack users and suppliers (many of whom were low-income African Americans) received harsher sentences than users and suppliers of much larger amounts of powdered cocaine. Because most of the latter offenders were white, activists decried the law as racist.

After nearly two decades of controversy, the issue was addressed by the U.S. Supreme Court in *Kimbrough v.*

United States (552 U.S. 85 [2007]). The case involved Derrick Kimbrough, an African American defendant who had pleaded guilty in federal court to offenses involving both powdered and crack cocaine. The original court sentenced Kimbrough in accordance with the federal guidelines for powdered cocaine, rather than with the harsher crack cocaine sentence structure. The Supreme Court ruled in December 2007 that federal judges can use discretion in such cases and impose shorter sentences for crack cocaine offenses than called for by federal guidelines, to reduce the powder-crack disparity. That same month the U.S. Sentencing Commission (USSC) ruled that crack cocaine sentences imposed by federal courts in the past could be shortened accordingly following petition by the convicted defendants. The USSC also recommended that Congress eliminate the 100 to 1 disparity in crack sentencing compared with sentencing for powdered cocaine offenses.

In August 2010 President Barack Obama (1961–) signed the Fair Sentencing Act. The act eliminated the five-year mandatory minimum prison sentence for first-time crack cocaine possession and increased to 1 ounce (28 g) the amount of crack cocaine that is required for the imposition of mandatory minimum prison terms for drug trafficking. In other words, the 100 to 1 sentencing disparity between crack cocaine and powdered cocaine was reduced to an 18 to 1 sentencing disparity.

The Crack Epidemic Ends

During the 1990s crack lost favor as a drug of choice as marijuana grew in popularity. The end of the crack epidemic saw a brief downturn in the total number of drug arrests by state and local authorities. According to the BJS, in "Drugs and Crime Facts: Total Estimated Drug Law Violation Arrests in the United States, 1980–2007," arrests dropped from 1.4 million in 1989 to 1 million in 1992. (See Figure 4.1.) This decline coincided with a national drop in overall crime that is described in Chapter 2. The overall crime rate continued its downward trend, but arrests for drug crimes resurged due in large part to soaring use of marijuana.

Self-Reported Cocaine Use

In *Key Substance Use and Mental Health Indicators in the United States*, SAMHSA indicates that in 2015 an estimated 1.9 million Americans aged 12 years and older were current users of cocaine (used the drug in the previous month). This number included about 394,000 current users of crack. Figure 4.5 shows the percentage of people aged 12 years and older who reported past-month use of cocaine between 2002 and 2015. In general, usage fell over this period; there was, however, a slight uptick between 2012 and 2015.

FIGURE 4.5

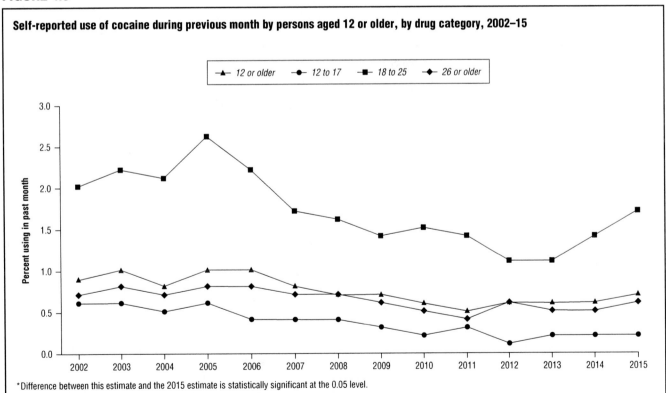

Self-reported use of cocaine during previous month by persons aged 12 or older, by drug category, 2002–15

*Difference between this estimate and the 2015 estimate is statistically significant at the 0.05 level.

SOURCE: "Figure 7. Past Month Cocaine Use among People Aged 12 or Older, by Age Group: Percentages, 2002–2015," in *Key Substance Use and Mental Health Indicators in the United States: Results from the 2015 National Survey on Drug Use and Health*, U.S. Department of Health and Human Services, Substance Abuse and Mental Health Services Administration, Center for Behavioral Health Statistics and Quality, September 2016, https://www.samhsa.gov/data/sites/default/files/NSDUH-FFR1-2015/NSDUH-FFR1-2015/NSDUH-FFR1-2015.pdf (accessed January 20, 2017)

MARIJUANA

According to the BJS, in "Drugs and Crime Facts: Number of Arrests, by Drug Type, 1982–2007" (2017, https://www.bjs.gov/content/dcf/tables/drugtype.cfm), marijuana arrests at the state and local levels fell throughout the 1980s, dropping to 287,900 arrests in 1991. Over the following decade arrests more than doubled and continued to rise through 2007, before declining. As noted earlier, there were nearly 1.5 million total arrests in 2015 for drug crimes, and 43.2% of them involved marijuana. Thus, approximately 648,000 arrests in 2015 were associated with marijuana.

Gallup, Inc., has occasionally polled American adults about their use of marijuana. Justin McCarthy of Gallup indicates in *One in Eight U.S. Adults Say They Smoke Marijuana* (August 8, 2016, http://www.gallup.com/poll/194195/adults-say-smoke-marijuana.aspx) that in 2016 more than four out of 10 (43%) respondents admitted having tried marijuana at some point during their life. This value was up dramatically from only 4% in 1969.

In *Key Substance Use and Mental Health Indicators in the United States*, SAMHSA indicates that in 2015 an estimated 22.2 million Americans aged 12 years and older were current users of marijuana. Figure 4.6 shows the percentage of people aged 12 years and older who reported past-month use of marijuana between 2002 and 2015. In general, usage grew over this period among adults aged 18 to 25 years and aged 26 years and older but fell slightly among youths aged 12 to 17 years.

Marijuana Decriminalization

Stuart Biegel of the University of California, Los Angeles, reports in *Beyond Our Control?: Confronting the Limits of Our Legal System in the Age of Cyberspace* (2003) that marijuana arrests in the United States doubled from 7,000 to 15,000 between 1964 and 1966. By 1969 the national total for marijuana arrests had increased nearly 700% to 118,903. Court systems became overrun with cases involving marijuana possession, which at that time could elicit a prison sentence as long as five years for possession of only a single marijuana cigarette (or joint). In response, many jurisdictions began lowering the penalties for possession of small amounts of marijuana, such as from a misdemeanor to an infraction payable only by a fine. This practice is called decriminalization and is not the same as legalization, which makes an action legal when it was previously illegal. In *State Marijuana Legalization Initiatives: Implications for Federal Law Enforcement* (December 4, 2014, https://fas.org/sgp/crs/misc/R43164.pdf), Lisa N. Sacco and Kristin Finklea of the CRS explain, "A state decriminalizes conduct by removing the accompanying criminal penalties; however, civil penalties remain. If, for instance, a state decriminalizes the possession of marijuana in small amounts, possession of marijuana still violates state law; however, possession of marijuana within the specified small amount is considered a civil offense and subject to a civil penalty, not criminal prosecution."

FIGURE 4.6

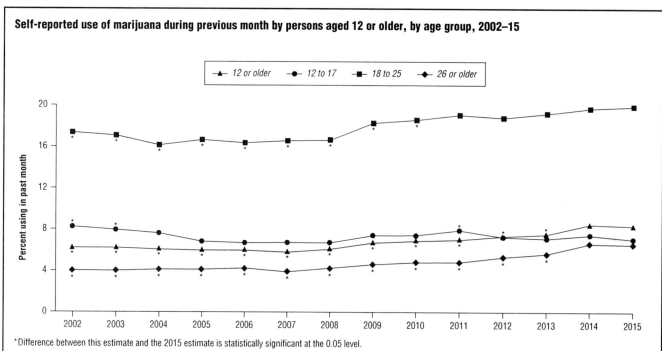

Self-reported use of marijuana during previous month by persons aged 12 or older, by age group, 2002–15

*Difference between this estimate and the 2015 estimate is statistically significant at the 0.05 level.

SOURCE: "Figure 3. Past Month Marijuana Use among People Aged 12 or Older, by Age Group: Percentages, 2002–2015," in *Key Substance Use and Mental Health Indicators in the United States: Results from the 2015 National Survey on Drug Use and Health*, U.S. Department of Health and Human Services, Substance Abuse and Mental Health Services Administration, Center for Behavioral Health Statistics and Quality, September 2016, https://www.samhsa.gov/data/sites/default/files/NSDUH-FFR1-2015/NSDUH-FFR1-2015/NSDUH-FFR1-2015.pdf (accessed January 20, 2017)

Marijuana decriminalization began in Oregon in 1973 and then spread to other states and to dozens of cities and counties. Typically, the laws specify threshold amounts of the drug and offender age limits. For example, in 2014 Maryland decriminalized the possession of less than 0.35 of an ounce (10 g) of marijuana. Jenna Johnson reports in "Having a Small Amount of Pot in Md. Is No Longer a Criminal Case" (WashingtonPost.com, October 1, 2014) that people aged 21 years and older caught with less than 0.35 of an ounce of marijuana must pay a fine; younger offenders must also "attend a drug education program." In 2016 Nashville and Memphis, Tennessee, passed local decriminalization measures that were decried by some state authorities, including the state's attorney general. As of April 2017, the measures were suspended after the Tennessee governor Bill Haslam (1958–) signed a law (http://wapp.capitol.tn.gov/apps/Bill info/default.aspx?BillNumber=HB0173&ga=110) clarifying that state law preempts any local laws regarding drug regulations and penalties.

During the late 1990s some states began decriminalizing the use of small amounts of marijuana for medical reasons, such as to relieve pain or nausea. According to the National Conference of State Legislatures, in "State Medical Marijuana Laws" (http://www.ncsl.org/research/health/state-medical-marijuana-laws.aspx), as of March 2017, 28 states, the District of Columbia, Guam, and Puerto Rico had passed laws allowing "comprehensive public medical marijuana and cannabis programs." Another 17 states allowed medical use of some low-dosage products under limited circumstances.

Despite these changes at the state level, marijuana remains illegal under federal law, and some of those who use or traffic in medical marijuana have been prosecuted by the federal government. In *Medical Marijuana: The Supremacy Clause, Federalism, and the Interplay between State and Federal Laws* (November 9, 2012, https://fas.org/sgp/crs/misc/R42398.pdf), Todd Garvey of the CRS notes that in 2009 the U.S. attorney general issued a memorandum indicating that the federal government did not intend to prioritize the enforcement of federal laws against marijuana users acting in compliance with state laws. Although the Obama administration held this viewpoint, as of April 2017 it was not clear what stance would be taken by President Donald Trump (1946–), who took office in January 2017.

Marijuana Legalization

In November 2012 voters in Colorado and Washington approved ballot initiatives that legalized the possession of small amounts of marijuana for recreational use and called on their state governments to license and regulate marijuana sales. These actions posed direct challenges to federal laws against marijuana use. The Department of

Justice responded in August 2013 with the memorandum "Guidance Regarding Marijuana Enforcement" (https://www.justice.gov/iso/opa/resources/305201382913275685 7467.pdf) by the U.S. deputy attorney general James M. Cole (1952–), who indicated the federal government would not block the state legalization movement so long as the states "implement strong and effective regulatory and enforcement systems that will address the threat those state laws could pose to public safety, public health, and other law enforcement interests." Over subsequent years, voters in Alaska (2014), California (2016), the District of Columbia (2014), Maine (2016), Massachusetts (2016), Nevada (2016), and Oregon (2014) also passed legalization initiatives.

THE COLORADO EXPERIENCE. Colorado already allowed medicinal use of marijuana when it legalized the drug for recreational use by people aged 21 years and older. The new law (https://www.colorado.gov/pacific/sites/default/files/Section%2016%20-%20%20Retail.pdf) and the associated regulations are complex. The Marijuana Enforcement Division (https://www.colorado.gov/pacific/enforcement/marijuanaenforcement) within the Colorado Department of Revenue (CDOR) is responsible for licensing and regulating the state's medical and retail marijuana industries and provides lists of licensed commercial growers, testers, product manufacturers, and stores. In "Colorado Struggles to Adjust Marijuana Supply" (DenverPost.com, September 2, 2014), Kristen Wyatt notes that previously the state "limited pot-growers to the number of medical marijuana patients they served." With recreational use allowed, the state has begun implementing new production caps designed to prevent oversupply that could make its way out of the state. According to Wyatt, "Commercial growers will need to prove they're selling 85 percent of their inventory before getting permission to add plants."

In January 2014 Colorado became the first jurisdiction in the country to allow retail stores to begin selling marijuana legally. It was joined later in the year by Washington State. According to Michael Martinez, in "10 Things to Know about Nation's First Recreational Marijuana Shops in Colorado" (CNN.com, January 1, 2014), Colorado permits state residents to buy up to an ounce (28.4 grams) at a time. People visiting from out of state are limited to a quarter of an ounce (7.1 grams) per purchase. Retail sales have a 25% excise tax added on top of a state sales tax of 2.9%. Individual communities can impose additional taxes or refuse to allow retail sales. Colorado adults are allowed to grow up to six marijuana plants in an "enclosed and locked" area for their personal use. In "Marijuana Retailers in Colo. Woo Shoppers with Holiday Deals" (BostonGlobe.com, November 24, 2014), Wyatt points out that marijuana legally grown and sold in Colorado cannot leave the state per federal laws against interstate drug trafficking.

Colorado has weathered several court challenges against its authority to legalize marijuana. The attorneys general of the bordering states Oklahoma and Nebraska have repeatedly insisted that marijuana flows into their jurisdictions from Colorado in violation of federal laws. In March 2016 the U.S. Supreme Court refused to hear their proposed lawsuit. Alicia Wallace, however, reports in "Bid to Take Down Colorado Marijuana Laws Revived in Court" (DenverPost.com, January 17, 2017) that the two states joined a separate lawsuit against Colorado that a federal appeals court began considering in January 2017. As of April 2017, no decision had been reached in the case.

According to Tom Huddleston Jr., in "Colorado Topped $1 Billion in Legal Marijuana Sales in 2016" (Fortune.com, December 13, 2016), the state's legal marijuana retailers sold more than $1 billion worth of product in 2016. The CDOR indicates in "Marijuana Tax Data" (2017, https://www.colorado.gov/pacific/revenue/colorado-marijuana-tax-data) that in February 2017, $17.7 million in taxes, licenses, and fees were remitted to the state for marijuana sales. The opportunities for the state to raise funds and to reduce spending on marijuana law enforcement were two drivers behind the legalization effort. However, critics worry that other crimes, such as driving under the influence, will rise with increasing retail marijuana sales. As of April 2017, there were insufficient data on the issue to make a determination.

PUBLIC OPINION ON LEGALIZATION. Since 1969 Gallup has conducted polls that gauge American public opinion about legalizing marijuana use. In *Support for Legal Marijuana Use up to 60% in U.S.* (October 19, 2016, http://www.gallup.com/poll/196550/support-legal-marijuana.aspx), Art Swift of Gallup notes that only 12% of respondents in 1969 thought that marijuana should be legalized. By 2016 that percentage had soared to 60%. Similar levels of support have been found by the Pew Research Center. According to Abigail Geiger of Pew, in "Support for Marijuana Legalization Continues to Rise" (October 12, 2016, http://www.pewresearch.org/fact-tank/2016/10/12/support-for-marijuana-legalization-continues-to-rise/), 57% of those polled in 2016 said they support legalization.

MISUSE OF PRESCRIPTION DRUGS

During the 1980s and 1990s pharmaceutical companies introduced many new drugs to the market. Some of these prescription-only drugs became popular targets of abuse, particularly pain relievers, sedatives, stimulants, and tranquilizers. Together, these types of drugs are known as psychotherapeutics (the word *therapeutics* refers to medications that are designed to treat medical conditions; the prefix *psycho* indicates that the medications can affect the mind, emotions, and behavior).

Examples include Adderall, amphetamines, fentanyl, hydrocodone, oxycodone, Ritalin, and Vicodin. SAMHSA provides in *Key Substance Use and Mental Health Indicators in the United States* survey results regarding misuse of prescription psychotherapeutics. The agency defines the term *misuse* as use in any way that is not directed by a doctor, including:

- Use without a prescription of one's own
- Use in greater amounts than prescribed
- Use more often than prescribed
- Use for longer periods than prescribed

SAMHSA finds that in 2015 an estimated 6.4 million Americans aged 12 years and older were current misusers of psychotherapeutic drugs. As shown in Figure 4.7, nearly six out of 10 (59.3%) of these people misused prescription pain relievers. The remaining 40.7% misused sedatives, stimulants, and/or tranquilizers. Figure 4.8 provides a breakdown of misusers by age group and prescription drug type. Young adults aged 18 to 25 years were far more likely than people of other ages to be current misusers of pain relievers, stimulants, and tranquilizers.

FIGURE 4.7

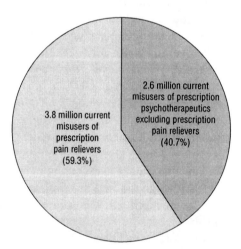

Self-reported misuse of prescription psychotherapeutics during previous month by persons aged 12 or older, by drug type, 2015

[6.4 million current misusers of prescription psychotherapeutics]

2.6 million current misusers of prescription psychotherapeutics excluding prescription pain relievers (40.7%)

3.8 million current misusers of prescription pain relievers (59.3%)

SOURCE: "Figure 5. Misuse of Prescription Pain Relievers and Other Prescription Psychotherapeutics among People Aged 12 or Older Who Were Current Misusers of Any Prescription Psychotherapeutics: 2015," in *Key Substance Use and Mental Health Indicators in the United States: Results from the 2015 National Survey on Drug Use and Health*, U.S. Department of Health and Human Services, Substance Abuse and Mental Health Services Administration, Center for Behavioral Health Statistics and Quality, September 2016, https://www.samhsa.gov/data/sites/default/files/NSDUH-FFR1-2015/NSDUH-FFR1-2015/NSDUH-FFR1-2015.pdf (accessed January 20, 2017)

FIGURE 4.8

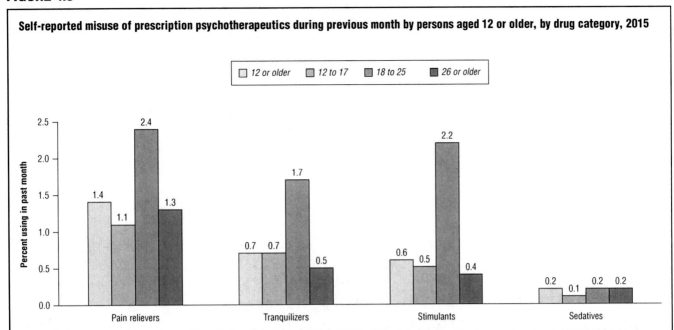

Self-reported misuse of prescription psychotherapeutics during previous month by persons aged 12 or older, by drug category, 2015

SOURCE: "Figure 6. Past Month Misuse of Prescription Pain Relievers, Tranquilizers, Stimulants, and Sedatives among People Aged 12 or Older, by Age Group: Percentages, 2015," in *Key Substance Use and Mental Health Indicators in the United States: Results from the 2015 National Survey on Drug Use and Health,* U.S. Department of Health and Human Services, Substance Abuse and Mental Health Services Administration, Center for Behavioral Health Statistics and Quality, September 2016, https://www.samhsa.gov/data/sites/default/files/NSDUH-FFR1-2015/NSDUH-FFR1-2015/NSDUH-FFR1-2015.pdf (accessed January 20, 2017)

Prescription drug misuse has grown to be a vexing public health problem in the United States. Many of these drugs are highly addictive. Misusers may begin taking them for valid medical reasons, but become addicted to them. Doctors have been accused of overprescribing the drugs. Law enforcement agency efforts are primarily directed at pain clinics, pharmacies, and doctors' offices that illegally prescribe or sell the drugs. In addition, there are numerous media reports about the illegal diversion (theft by deception) of prescription drugs from hospitals, nursing homes, and other facilities. As awareness about the problem has grown during the early 21st century, doctors have taken steps to limit prescriptions for the most addictive of the drugs. Likewise, drug manufacturers have implemented changes to their formulations to make some of the drugs less easy to crush. (Crushed pills can be inhaled or injected for a quicker and more intense physiological response.)

Opioid pain relievers, such as oxycodone and hydrocodone, are particularly popular narcotics among those who misuse prescription psychotherapeutics. As supplies of these legal drugs have tightened, some misusers have turned to illegal opioids, such as heroin, that are sold on the streets.

HEROIN

As noted earlier, heroin originates from opium poppies. As shown in Table 4.2, the drug is an opioid that may be injected, smoked, or snorted. Heroin is a Schedule I drug under the CSA because it has no accepted medical use in the United States and a very high potential for abuse.

It is difficult to quantify how many arrests made in the United States are due to heroin, because the BJS lumps arrests for heroin with those for cocaine, which is another opioid. In "Drugs and Crime Facts: Number of Arrests, by Drug Type, 1982–2007," the agency indicates that during the late 1980s and early 1990s arrests for heroin and cocaine soared to around 600,000 to 700,000 per year. Over subsequent years, however, arrests fell to less than half a million annually. As shown in Table 4.3, in 2015 heroin or cocaine and their derivatives were involved in 25.4% of all arrests. Considering that there were around 1.5 million drug arrests in 2015, heroin or cocaine and their derivatives accounted for approximately 381,000 arrests that year.

According to SAMHSA, in *Key Substance Use and Mental Health Indicators in the United States,* an estimated 329,000 Americans aged 12 years and older were current users of heroin in 2015. Figure 4.9 provides a breakdown by age group between 2002 and 2015. The overall percentage of current users remained relatively flat over this period with a slight upward trend in 2014 and 2015. In general, current usage was higher in young adults aged 18 to 25 years than in other age groups. SAMHSA estimates that in 2015 about 828,000 people aged 12 years and older were past-year users of heroin. As shown in Figure 4.10, young adults aged 18 to 25

FIGURE 4.9

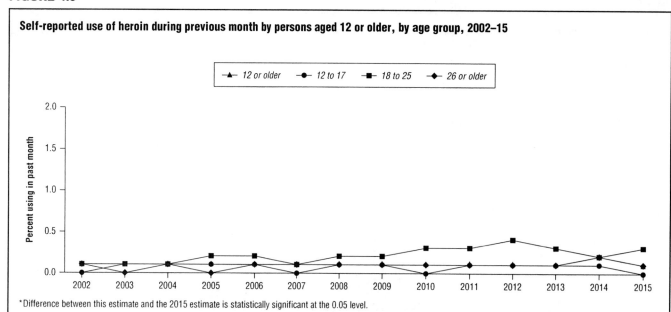

Self-reported use of heroin during previous month by persons aged 12 or older, by age group, 2002–15

[Legend: 12 or older; 12 to 17; 18 to 25; 26 or older]

*Difference between this estimate and the 2015 estimate is statistically significant at the 0.05 level.

SOURCE: "Figure 8. Past Month Heroin Use among People Aged 12 or Older, by Age Group: Percentages, 2002–2015," in *Key Substance Use and Mental Health Indicators in the United States: Results from the 2015 National Survey on Drug Use and Health*, U.S. Department of Health and Human Services, Substance Abuse and Mental Health Services Administration, Center for Behavioral Health Statistics and Quality, September 2016, https://www.samhsa .gov/data/sites/default/files/NSDUH-FFR1-2015/NSDUH-FFR1-2015/NSDUH-FFR1-2015.pdf (accessed January 20, 2017)

FIGURE 4.10

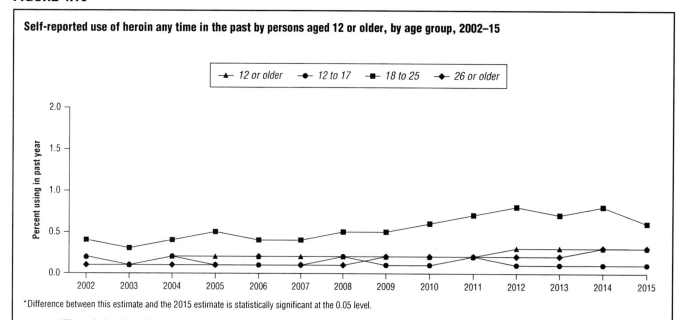

Self-reported use of heroin any time in the past by persons aged 12 or older, by age group, 2002–15

[Legend: 12 or older; 12 to 17; 18 to 25; 26 or older]

*Difference between this estimate and the 2015 estimate is statistically significant at the 0.05 level.

SOURCE: "Figure 9. Past Year Heroin Use among People Aged 12 or Older, by Age Group: Percentages, 2002–2015," in *Key Substance Use and Mental Health Indicators in the United States: Results from the 2015 National Survey on Drug Use and Health*, U.S. Department of Health and Human Services, Substance Abuse and Mental Health Services Administration, Center for Behavioral Health Statistics and Quality, September 2016, https://www.samhsa .gov/data/sites/default/files/NSDUH-FFR1-2015/NSDUH-FFR1-2015/NSDUH-FFR1-2015.pdf (accessed January 20, 2017)

were more likely than people of other age groups to be past-year users between 2002 and 2015.

OPIOID OVERDOSES

The Centers for Disease Control and Prevention (CDC) reports in "Opioid Overdose" (February 9, 2017, https:// www.cdc.gov/drugoverdose/) that "the United States is in the midst of an opioid overdose epidemic. Opioids (including prescription opioids and heroin) killed more than 33,000 people in 2015, more than any year on record." In "Increases in Drug and Opioid-Involved Overdose Deaths—United States, 2010–2015" (*Morbidity and Mortality Weekly Report*, vol. 65, nos. 50–51, December 30,

2016), Rose A. Rudd et al. of the CDC indicate that overdose rates "increased sharply" between 2010 and 2015 and are largely blamed on heroin and a synthetic opioid called fentanyl. Fentanyl is a powerful painkiller that is a legal psychotherapeutic. It is also manufactured illegally by criminals for sale on the streets either by itself or mixed with heroin. The NIDA notes in "Fentanyl" (June 2016, https://www.drugabuse.gov/publications/drugfacts/fentanyl) that authorities believe that many opioid overdoses linked to fentanyl have been caused by nonprescription versions of the drug.

METHAMPHETAMINE

Methamphetamine (or meth) is a stimulant in the amphetamine group. The drug can be synthesized from a naturally occurring chemical called ephedrine. This so-called precursor chemical is commonly synthesized, as are two other methamphetamine precursors: phenylpropanolamine and pseudoephedrine. Both of the latter are widely used in cold and sinus medications, many of which can be purchased without a prescription.

Beginning in the 1990s methamphetamine abuse became a major problem in some parts of the United States as illicit methamphetamine laboratories flourished. Many of the laboratories were operated in homes, putting the residents (particularly children) at great danger of fires and explosions because of the volatile nature of the chemicals involved.

As the methamphetamine epidemic attracted national attention, legislators rushed to pass laws making it more difficult for amateur chemists to obtain the ephedrine-type precursors that are used to synthesize methamphetamine. The Comprehensive Methamphetamine Control Act of 1996 added the precursor chemicals to Schedule II of the CSA. That act and a subsequent law, the Methamphetamine Trafficking Penalty Enhancement Act of 1998, increased the penalties for manufacturing and selling methamphetamine. After 2000, legislators tackled the easy availability of precursor chemicals in over-the-counter cold and sinus medications. In 2006 federal law was changed to set limits on how much of these precursor-containing products an individual could purchase at one time, as well as within a 30-day period. Furthermore, businesses were required to track who was purchasing these products and to keep the products in an area where customers could not access them directly, such as in a locked case.

The U.S. Government Accountability Office (GAO) analyzes in *Drug Control: State Approaches Taken to Control Access to Key Methamphetamine Ingredient Show Varied Impact on Domestic Drug Labs* (January 2013, http://www.gao.gov/assets/660/651709.pdf) DEA data regarding seizures of methamphetamine laboratories, dump sites, chemicals, and glassware around the country. The number of seizures peaked in 2004 at 24,155 and then declined sharply to 6,951 in 2007. According to the GAO, this decrease was likely the result of state and federal restrictions on the sale of cold and allergy medications. In *2016 National Drug Threat Assessment Summary* (November 2016, https://www.dea.gov/resource-center/2016%20NDTA%20Summary.pdf), the DEA indicates that less than 5,000 methamphetamine laboratories were seized in 2015. The agency believes that production of the drug has shifted largely to Mexico and that the drug is smuggled across the border into the United States. SAMHSA estimates in *Key Substance Use and Mental Health Indicators in the United States* that 897,000 people aged 12 years and older were current users of the drug in 2015.

CHAPTER 5
WHITE-COLLAR CRIME

OFFENSES AND ARRESTS

The term *white-collar crime* was first used by the American criminologist Edwin Hardin Sutherland (1883–1950) in 1939 to define a violation of the criminal law committed by "a person of respectability and high social status in the course of his occupation" (Cornell University Law School, "White Collar Crime," June 2016, https://www.law.cornell.edu/wex/White-collar_crime). Over time, the definition has become much broader. In "White-Collar Crime" (2017, https://www.fbi.gov/investigate/white-collar-crime), the Federal Bureau of Investigation (FBI) notes that white-collar crimes are "characterized by deceit, concealment, or violation of trust and are not dependent on the application or threat of physical force or violence." Examples include bribery, computer hacking, confidence games, copyright violations, counterfeiting, embezzlement, environmental crimes, fraud, identity theft, money laundering, and swindles. Table 5.1 briefly describes dozens of types of white-collar crimes based on information from the FBI.

White-collar crimes are prohibited by federal and/or state laws. Some offenses fall directly under federal authority, particularly currency counterfeiting, mail fraud, and wire fraud. Mail fraud involves offenses perpetrated by use of the U.S. Postal Service or other interstate delivery services, such as FedEx. Wire fraud covers offenses committed via telecommunication systems, such as the telephone or the Internet. Because fraudsters frequently use one of these two methods to communicate with victims, many white-collar offenses are federal crimes. Federal authorities also focus on offenses involving corporate financial misdeeds, income tax fraud, public official corruption, and frauds perpetrated against insurance companies, financial institutions, and federal government programs, such as Medicaid (a state and federal health insurance program for low-income people) and Medicare (a federal health insurance program for people aged 65 years and older and people with disabilities).

White-collar criminals who operate across state lines and/or have international connections are also subject to federal prosecution. In fact, foreign nationals are increasingly implicated in fraudulent activities that victimize Americans. Prosecuting these cases can be challenging, especially when the offenders are in countries that have relatively unfriendly relations with the United States.

The FBI's Uniform Crime Reporting (UCR) Program gathers crime data from local law enforcement agencies throughout the country and publishes selected data in an annual report. Arrest data for 2015 are provided in *Crime in the United States, 2015* (September 2016, https://ucr.fbi.gov/crime-in-the-u.s/2015/crime-in-the-u.s.-2015/). The UCR Program provides 2015 arrest data for only three crime types widely considered white-collar crimes:

- Fraud—133,138 arrests
- Forgery and counterfeiting—55,333 arrests
- Embezzlement—15,909 arrests

The FBI (https://ucr.fbi.gov/crime-in-the-u.s/2015/crime-in-the-u.s.-2015/resource-pages/offense-definitions/offense definitions_final.pdf) defines these crimes as:

- Fraud—"The intentional perversion of the truth for the purpose of inducing another person or other entity in reliance upon it to part with something of value or to surrender a legal right. Fraudulent conversion, obtaining of money or property by false pretenses, confidence games, and bad checks, except forgeries and counterfeiting, are included."

- Forgery and counterfeiting—"The altering, copying, or imitating of something, without authority or right, with the intent to deceive or defraud by passing the copy or thing altered or imitated as that which is original or genuine; or the selling, buying, or possession of an altered, copied, or imitated thing with the intent to deceive or defraud. Attempts are included."

TABLE 5.1

White-collar crimes

Fraud	Description and/or examples
Adoption scams	Women promise their unborn children to more than one couple or aren't even pregnant; phony domestic adoption agencies or facilitators; unsanctioned international adoptions.
Advance fee schemes	The victim pays money to someone in anticipation of receiving something of greater value—such as a loan, contract, investment, or gift—and then receives little or nothing in return.
Anti-aging product fraud	Con artists market and sell bogus products advertised as having anti-aging benefits.
ATM skimming	Surreptitious surveillance equipment installed on ATMs allows criminals to record customers' account information and PINs, create their own bank cards, and steal from customer accounts.
Bankruptcy fraud	Lying under oath or providing false documentation during bankruptcy proceedings or concealing or transferring financial assets. Using false identities to file for bankruptcy multiple times in multiple locations; bribing a bankruptcy trustee; intentionally running up credit card bills with no intention of paying them off (also known as "credit card bust-outs").
Corporate fraud	Accounting schemes designed to deceive investors, auditors, and analysts about the true financial condition of a corporation or business entity; insider trading; utilizing companies to perpetrate large-scale, high-yield fraud schemes, such as Ponzi schemes.
Credit card fraud	Criminals use stolen credit cards or the credit card numbers of victims to make purchases, apply for credit cards using the identities of others, or create counterfeit credit cards.
Financial institution fraud	Insider fraud (embezzlement and misapplication), check fraud, counterfeit negotiable instruments, check kiting, and fraud contributing to the failure of financial institutions.
Foreclosure fraud	Con artists take money from homeowners in danger of foreclosure by offering bogus services such as mortgage loan modifications or other means touted as a way to avoid foreclosure.
Funeral fraud (prepaid funeral scams)	Victims pay in advance for funeral services that are never provided. Typically the victims are led to believe their money will be invested in a life insurance policy that will pay off in the event of their death.
Gameover malware	Spam e-mails—purportedly from the National Automated Clearing House Association (NACHA), the Federal Reserve Bank, or the Federal Deposit Insurance Corporation (FDIC)—that can infect recipients' computers with malware and allow access to their bank accounts.
Grandparent scam	Typically involves a phone call or an e-mail from someone who identifies himself or herself as the victim's grandchild or other relative and claims to need money wired as soon as possible for an emergency.
Health care fraud	Fraudulent billings to health care programs including medically unnecessary services billed to health care insurers.
Hedge fund fraud	Hedge funds are minimally regulated private investment partnerships that historically accept only high-wealth investors. Fraud is perpetrated when investors are given false information about the fund's performance or otherwise deceived.
House stealing	Criminals assume the identities of homeowners and then fill out transfer property forms and file deeds with the authorities to transfer ownership of the homes to themselves.
Identity theft	Someone wrongfully obtains another's personal information without their knowledge in order to commit theft or fraud.
Income tax refund fraud	Schemes in which criminals file false income tax forms with stolen identities in order to obtain tax refunds.
Insider trading	The trading of securities or stocks by "insiders" with material, non-public information pertaining to significant, often market-moving developments to benefit themselves or others financially.
Insurance fraud	Fraudsters obtain insurance under false circumstances or file bogus or inflated claims.
Internet fraud	Fraud perpetrated over the internet, for example, via phishing or malware.
Internet pharmacy fraud	Online businesses that fill orders without prescriptions and sell drugs that may be expired, counterfeit, mislabeled, adulterated, or contaminated.
Investment fraud	Schemes in which investors in securities, stocks, commodities, real estate, or businesses are deceived and defrauded.
Jury duty scam	People claiming to be court officials call victims and threaten them with arrest for not reporting for jury duty. The perpetrators ask for personal information including a credit card number which they claim is for the purpose of paying a fine and avoiding arrest.
Letter of credit fraud	Legitimate letters of credit are issued by banks to ensure payment for goods shipped in international trade. Payment on a letter of credit generally requires that the paying bank receive documentation certifying that the goods ordered have been shipped and are en route to their intended destination. Con artists present fake letters of credit to banks to lure them to pay for goods that were not shipped or were inferior.
Lottery scams	Scam artists sell victims fake lottery tickets or notify victims they have won large amounts in foreign lotteries and request money to pay for taxes or fees.
Mass marketing fraud	Scams that exploit mass communication techniques like bulk mail, e-mail, or telemarketing.
Mortgage fraud	Material misstatements, misrepresentations, or omissions relating to real estate transactions; includes foreclosure rescue schemes, loan modification schemes, illegal property flipping, builder bailout/condo conversion, equity skimming, silent second, home equity conversion mortgage, bogus commercial real estate loans, and air loans (i.e., loans obtained by brokers for properties and applicants that do not actually exist).
Natural disaster fraud	Frauds perpetrated in the aftermath of natural disasters involving fake insurance claims or theft of government-provided assistance.
Nigerian letter or "419" fraud	An advance fee scheme in which a letter or e-mail from Nigeria offers the recipient the "opportunity" to share in a percentage of millions of dollars that the author—a self-proclaimed government official—is trying to transfer illegally out of Nigeria. The victim is asked to transmit bank information and pay "expenses" with fake promises of reimbursement.
Online auction fraud	Schemes designed to defraud sellers or buyers participating in online auctions.
Online auto auction fraud	Con artists offer vehicles for sale—often at below-market prices—on legitimate websites, but convince victims to conclude the transactions at other websites controlled by the criminals. The victims are often convinced to purchase buyer protection plans and instructed to wire funds to the fake sellers.
Online dating scams	Con artists establish relationships through online dating sites and then ask for money from unsuspecting victims.
Online rental housing scheme	Online scheme in which victims prepay for rental or vacation housing not actually owned by the individuals pretending to be the owners.
Phishing	Victims receive faked e-mails that appear to be from their banks or other trusted institutions and are designed to con them into providing personal information (PINs, social security numbers, credit card information, etc.).
Ponzi schemes	"Ponzi" schemes promise high financial returns or dividends not available through traditional investments. Instead of investing the funds of victims, however, the con artist pays "dividends" to initial investors using the funds of subsequent investors. The scheme generally falls apart when the operator flees with all of the proceeds or when a sufficient number of new investors cannot be found to allow the continued payment of "dividends."
Prime bank note fraud	An investment scheme that supposedly offers extremely high yields in a relatively short period of time. The con artists claim to have access to "bank guarantees" that they can buy at a discount and sell at a premium.

- Embezzlement—"The unlawful misappropriation or misapplication by an offender to his/her own use or purpose of money, property, or some other thing of value entrusted to his/her care, custody, or control."

According to the UCR Program, there were 10.8 million total arrests in 2015; thus, arrests for these three white-collar crimes made up only a very small portion (1.9%) of the total arrests.

TABLE 5.1

White-collar crimes [CONTINUED]

Fraud	Description and/or examples
Pump-and-dump stock scheme	Con artists hype a small company with little actual worth. Unsuspecting investors purchase the stock in droves, pumping up the price. But when the fraudsters behind the scheme sell their shares at the peak price and stop hyping the stock, the price plummets, and innocent investors lose their money.
Pyramid schemes	Marketing and investment frauds in which an individual is offered a distributorship or franchise to market a particular product. The real profit is earned, not by the sale of the product, but by the sale of new distributorships. Emphasis on selling franchises rather than the product eventually leads to a point where the supply of potential investors is exhausted and the pyramid collapses.
Ransomware	Malware that causes the victim's computer to lock up, and the monitor to display a message claiming to be from the FBI or other authority stating there has been a violation of federal law, for example, viewing of child pornography. To unlock their computers, users are instructed to pay a fine using a prepaid money card service.
Redemption/strawman/bond fraud	Con artists claim that the U.S. government or the Treasury Department control bank accounts—often referred to as "U.S. Treasury Direct Accounts"—for all U.S. citizens that can be accessed by submitting the appropriate paperwork to state and federal authorities. Individuals promoting this scam often charge large fees for "kits" that teach individuals how to perpetrate this scheme.
Reverse mortgage scams	Scams engineered by unscrupulous professionals in real estate, financial services, and related companies to steal the equity from the property of unsuspecting senior citizens or to use these seniors to unwittingly aid the fraudsters in stealing equity from a flipped property.
Scareware	Faked pop-up messages appear on computers telling users they have a computer virus and must buy antivirus software to solve the problem.
Securities and commodities fraud	Schemes involving the purchase and selling of securities, such as stock, and commodities.
Senior citizen fraud	Scams that target senior citizens.
Smishing	Criminals set up an automated dialing system to text or call people in a particular region or area code (or sometimes they use stolen customer phone numbers from banks or credit unions). The victims receive messages like: "There's a problem with your account," or "Your ATM card needs to be reactivated," and are directed to a phone number or website asking for personal information.
Social Security card fraud	These crimes typically involve falsified social security cards that can be used by illegal aliens or for other criminal purposes.
Spear phishing	A type of "phishing" in which con artists target a group of people with something in common, such as membership in a particular organization. The phishing e-mails appear to come from a legitimate organization with which the targeted individuals are familiar.
Sports memorabilia fraud	Fraud committed by forgers and counterfeiters who prey on sports fans and try to sell them faked memorabilia, such as baseballs with forged signatures of famous players.
Staged auto accident fraud	Frauds in which con artists purposely cause unsuspecting drivers to crash into cars driven by the con artists so they can file bogus and inflated insurance claims against the innocent drivers' insurance companies.
Stock options backdating	Company executives look back over their company's stock performance and pick a low point on the stock chart to set the options price, thereby boosting the value of the options—and the executive's portfolio. When the practice isn't documented in financial statements, it amounts to fraud.
Surrogacy scam	Con artists take advantage of couples who desperately want children by offering them seemingly legitimate surrogacy situations in exchange for money.
Telemarketing fraud	Frauds in which con artists use telecommunications systems to contact victims.
Telephone denial of service fraud	Using automated dialing programs, crooks flood victims' phone lines with multiple calls. While the lines are tied up, the criminals—masquerading as the victims themselves—raid the victims' bank accounts and online trading or other money management accounts.
Timeshare schemes	Victims—mostly owners trying to sell—are scammed by criminals posing as representatives of timeshare resale companies or by actual employees of companies that are committing fraud.
Vishing	A type of "phishing" in which con artists target victims with Voice Over Internet Protocol, or VoIP, which enables telephone calls to be made over the internet.
Work-at-home scams	Con artists recruit victims for supposed work-at-home jobs that require payment of a fee up front. In another scam "mystery shoppers" are sent a check and told to shop for certain items and send them to the con artists. The ruse continues until the check bounces.

ATM = automated teller machine.
PIN = personal identification number.

SOURCE: Adapted from "Common Fraud Schemes," in *Scams and Safety*, U.S. Department of Justice, Federal Bureau of Investigation, 2017, https://www.fbi.gov/scams-and-safety/common-fraud-schemes (accessed January 20, 2017) and "Major Threats & Programs," in *What We Investigate: White-Collar Crime*, U.S. Department of Justice, Federal Bureau of Investigation, 2017, https://www.fbi.gov/investigate/white-collar-crime (accessed January 20, 2017)

IDENTITY THEFT

One of the most pervasive white-collar crimes is identity theft, which is defined in various terms in federal and state law. In general, identity thieves steal personal information from victims, such as their Social Security, driver's license, credit card, or other identification numbers, and then set up new bank or credit card accounts or otherwise misrepresent themselves as their victims to obtain money, goods, or services fraudulently.

Identity thievery is accomplished in various ways. In some cases the thieves steal or find (e.g., in the garbage) paper records containing the information they seek. Since the late 20th century more and more financial transactions are handled remotely using cell phones, computers, and the Internet. Perpetrators may steal phones, tablets, or computers to obtain stored identity information or hack (digitally access without permission) these devices or the computer networks used to transfer or store sensitive data.

Large-scale thefts of identity information are called data breaches. These are crimes in which the computer records of businesses, government agencies, universities, or other organizations are breached to obtain the personal and/or financial data of large numbers of people. The Privacy Rights Clearinghouse (https://www.privacyrights.org) is an organization that educates consumers about personal privacy issues. It maintains an on-site listing (https://www.privacyrights.org/data-breaches) of more than 5,400 data breaches that have been reported publicly since 2005. According to Jim Finkle and Anya George Tharakan, in "Yahoo Says One Billion Accounts Exposed in Newly Discovered Security Breach" (Reuters.com, December 15, 2016), Yahoo Inc. disclosed in December

2016 that it had recently discovered that data were stolen in August 2013 from more than 1 billion of its user accounts. This would make it the largest known data breach in history.

Identity thieves may also use trickery and deception to get people to voluntarily provide identifying information to them, such as through phone calls, e-mail, or over the Internet. These methods are described in more detail later in this chapter.

Identity Theft in Tax Refund Fraud

During the 21st century the Internal Revenue Service (IRS) has seen a huge increase in income tax fraud facilitated by identity theft. In "With Personal Data in Hand, Thieves File Early and Often" (NYTimes.com, May 26, 2012), Lizette Alvarez notes that fraudsters use stolen identities to file false tax returns with the IRS showing that refunds are due to the filers. Identity thieves typically file tax returns early in the filing season and obtain refunds before returns are filed by the legitimate owners of the stolen names and Social Security numbers. (See Figure 5.1.) The legitimate returns are subsequently rejected by the IRS system as duplicate returns. This is the point at which many legitimate tax filers first learn that their identities have been stolen.

David Adams indicates in "Florida Hit by 'Tsunami' of Tax Identity Fraud" (Reuters.com, February 17, 2013) that 48,000 tax identity theft cases were identified by the U.S. Department of the Treasury in 2008, but the number soon soared to more than a million. In *Efforts Continue to Result in Improved Identification of Fraudulent Tax Returns Involving Identity Theft; However, Accuracy of Measures Needs Improvement* (February 7, 2017, https://www.treasury.gov/tigta/auditreports/2017reports/201740017 fr.pdf), the Treasury Inspector General for Tax Administration notes that in 2014 the IRS processed 4.7 million tax returns it believes were fraudulent because of identity theft. The agency discovered the fraud early in 3.5 million of the returns, thereby preventing the payout of $21.5 billion in tax refunds to identity thieves. Identity thieves, however, succeeded in obtaining $3.1 billion in refunds through the other 1.2 million fraudulent returns. The Treasury Inspector General for Tax Administration indicates that the IRS implemented several new security procedures in 2015 and 2016 to combat tax refund fraud committed by identity theft. It remains to be seen if these measures will be effective at remedying the problem.

FINANCIAL CYBERCRIME

Cybercrime is perpetrated for a variety of reasons. One motivation is financial gain, such as through identity theft or fraud. Cyber resources can also be used by criminals as a means for disrupting the computer transactions of targeted businesses, organizations, or government agencies. Three typical methods of cybercrime are described in this chapter: deception, malware, and hacking.

Deception

One common cybercrime is the deceiving of people online into voluntarily divulging their personal or financial information or turning over their money. One type of traditional white-collar crime is called a confidence game. People who engage in confidence games are known as con artists. They gain the confidence of their victims by establishing a personal and/or business relationship with them and then take their victims' money using deception and trickery. In the modern world confidence games can be easily perpetrated over the Internet thanks in large part to the popularity of online shopping and auction sites. Con artists pose as legitimate sellers, gain the trust of potential buyers, and then take payment for merchandise that is never delivered.

Another means of deception used by cybercriminals, particularly for identity theft, is called phishing. This is an activity in which Internet fraudsters impersonate legitimate businesses, government agencies, or organizations to trick victims into providing desired information. The anonymous nature of Internet-based transactions makes it particularly easy for criminals to create deceptive websites, e-mail messages, or text messages through which they can interact with potential victims and trick them into turning over information and/or money.

Criminals engaged in Internet fraud may also use spam as a means to find potential victims. Spam refers to unsolicited bulk e-mail. The e-mails are unsolicited because the recipients have not chosen to receive the messages. Generally, spam involves simultaneously sending identical e-mail messages to large numbers of e-mail accounts. For example, spam e-mails containing a phishing ploy could be sent to many thousands of individuals in the hope that at least a few of the recipients will fall for the scam.

Malware

Another tool used by cybercriminals is malware, which is short for malicious software. Malware takes many forms, and its effects can range from being mildly irritating to seriously damaging, depending on how the malware is programmed. Users may unknowingly put malware on their computers by downloading music, games, or other types of software in which the malware is hidden. Clicking on website links or e-mail attachments can also provide a way for malware to access a computer.

The computer networking company Cisco Systems notes in "What Is the Difference: Viruses, Worms, Trojans, and Bots?" (2017, http://www.cisco.com/c/en/us/about/security-center/virus-differences.html) that some of the most common types of malware are viruses, worms,

FIGURE 5.1

Methods by which the Internal Revenue Service detects identity theft refund fraud

Example: Identity theft (IDT) refund fraud IRS detects after a duplicate return is filed

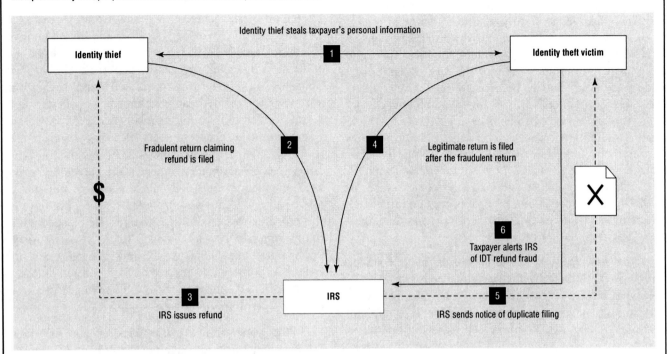

Example: IDT refund fraud IRS detects during information return matching

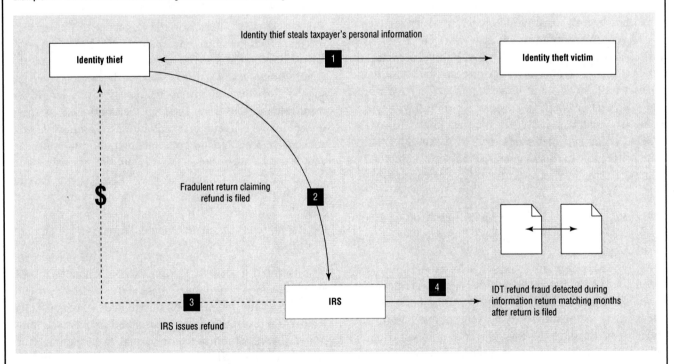

Notes: Numbers represent the order in which these actions occur in the examples.

SOURCE: "Figure 2. Examples of Identity Theft Refund Fraud That IRS Detects," in *Identity Theft: Additional Actions Could Help IRS Combat the Large, Evolving Threat of Refund Fraud*, U.S. Government Accountability Office, August 2014, http://www.gao.gov/assets/670/665368.pdf (accessed January 20, 2017)

Trojans, and bots. Viruses and worms are capable of replicating themselves and spreading to other computers. Viruses attach themselves to host programs, such as executable files, while worms operate more independently. By contrast, Trojans cannot replicate themselves. In addition, they are malware programs that appear to be legitimate. They get their name from a legendary story in which Greek soldiers constructed and then hid within a huge wooden horse. Their enemies mistook the horse for a gift and pulled it inside the walls of the city of Troy. The soldiers secretly exited the horse and opened the city gates, allowing the rest of their army to invade and conquer Troy. In a similar manner Trojan malware can open "back doors" to computers and networks that allow criminals to use them for their own purposes. Cisco Systems indicates that bots (which is short for robots) can be programmed to conduct automated processes, such as recording keystrokes, gathering passwords and financial information, or interacting with websites and other computers for criminal purposes.

Individual malware programs often have colorful names given to them by their creators or by the people who work to discover and destroy the harmful software. In addition, malware programs are often lumped into descriptive categories based on their means of operation or intended purposes. For example, the term *spyware* is broadly used to refer to malware that secretly collects information about a computer user. Likewise, *hijackers* are computer programs that allow criminals to seize control of others' computers for their own purposes. Malware classifications are not always mutually exclusive. For example, a Trojan or other piece of malware could conduct both spying and hijacking. The Daprosy worm, first reported in 2009, is an example of a keylogger. It monitors whatever is typed on the keyboard of an infected computer, and sends reports of this information to its originator. In this manner the malware's creator can gain access to Internet usernames, passwords, and other sensitive information.

In the press release "Two Major International Hackers Who Developed the 'SpyEye' Malware Get over 24 Years Combined in Federal Prison" (April 20, 2016, https://www.justice.gov/usao-ndga/pr/two-major-international-hackers-who-developed-spyeye-malware-get-over-24-years-combined), the U.S. Department of Justice (DOJ) notes that in April 2016 two foreign nationals were sentenced to a combined 24 years and six months in prison for developing and distributing the malware SpyEye. The software was sold to cybercriminals around the world who used it to infect and control more than 50 million computers and inflict nearly $1 billion in "financial harm."

Hacking

Criminals who are particularly savvy in computer programming may engage in hacking (gaining unauthorized access to computers by identifying and exploiting system vulnerabilities). Criminal hackers use their expertise to crack passwords and security codes to access stored information or hijack computers (take control of computers and instruct them to perform certain tasks).

James Verini details in "The Great Cyberheist" (NYTimes.com, November 10, 2010) the life and crimes of Albert Gonzalez (1981–), who is considered to be one of the most financially successful hackers in U.S. history. Gonzalez was first arrested in 2003 and became an informant for the federal government to help the U.S. Secret Service capture top members of the Shadowcrew, a semiorganized group of sophisticated cybercriminals. However, Gonzalez secretly continued his own hacking career. He masterminded schemes for breaching corporate computer systems and gained access to millions of credit and debit card account numbers. In 2008 the FBI arrested Gonzalez on multiple charges. He pleaded guilty and in March 2010 was sentenced to 20 years in prison. Verini notes that Gonzalez's crimes allegedly cost the victimized corporations more than $400 million in losses. As of April 2017, he was serving his sentence in a low-security federal prison in Mississippi.

Some cybercriminals use hacking not for direct financial gain but to damage or disrupt the operations of computers used by others, particularly businesses or government agencies. These attacks may be designed to impose economic losses on the targets or to punish them for perceived wrongs. For example, in 2014 Sony Pictures Entertainment suffered a large-scale hack attack in which movie scripts, films, internal documents, and personal information about celebrities and Sony employees were released publicly. In 2016 the computers of major figures in the Democratic National Committee were hacked. Internal documents and records, including private e-mails, were leaked to the public by the hackers. President Barack Obama (1961–) accused the Russian government of conducting the cyber operations to influence the November 2016 presidential election, which saw the Republican candidate Donald Trump (1946–) emerge victorious.

COMPUTER CRIME LEGISLATION. Since the 1980s numerous laws have been passed to address growing problems with crimes committed via cyberspace. In 1986 Congress passed the Computer Fraud and Abuse Act (CFAA), which makes it illegal to perpetrate fraud on a computer. The law has been amended multiple times. Robert Tappan Morris (1965–) was the first person ever to be charged under the CFAA after allegedly releasing the first-known computer worm on the Internet. He did not serve prison time but was put on probation for his crime and had to perform community service and pay a fine. As of April 2017, Morris was a computer science professor at the Massachusetts Institute of Technology.

The Controlling the Assault of Non-Solicited Pornography and Marketing (CAN-SPAM) Act of 2003 established requirements for those who send commercial e-mail. CAN-SPAM requires that all spam contain a legitimate return address as well as instructions on how to opt out of receiving additional spam from the sender. Spam must also state in the subject line if the e-mail is pornographic in nature. Violators of these rules are subject to heavy fines.

The first person convicted by a jury in a CAN-SPAM case was Jeffrey Brett Goodin (1961–). He was found guilty in January 2007 of operating an Internet-based scheme to obtain personal and credit card information. Goodin sent e-mails to AOL users that appeared to be from AOL's billing department. The messages, which instructed recipients to update their AOL billing information or lose service, referred users to web pages that were actually scam pages set up by Goodin to collect the users' personal and credit card information. Goodin was sentenced to 70 months in federal prison and released in November 2011.

In "Computer Crime Statutes" (December 5, 2016, http://www.ncsl.org/research/telecommunications-and-in formation-technology/computer-hacking-and-unauthorized-access-laws.aspx), the National Conference of State Legislatures provides a listing of state laws related to cybercrime. The organization notes that as of December 2016, all 50 states had enacted computer crime laws. Although the laws cover different types of activities, common offenses involve unauthorized access, computer trespassing, phishing, and malware. For example, California's Consumer Protection against Computer Spyware Act makes it illegal for anyone to install software on someone else's computer deceptively and use it to modify settings, including the user's home page, default search page, or bookmarks. The act also outlaws collecting, through intentionally deceptive means, personally identifiable information by logging keystrokes, tracking website visits, or extracting personal information from a user's hard drive.

INTELLECTUAL PROPERTY CRIMES

According to the World Intellectual Property Organization (2017, http://www.wipo.int/about-ip/en), intellectual property consists of "creations of the mind, such as inventions; literary and artistic works; designs; and symbols, names and images used in commerce." These include industrial property such as trademarks, chemical formulas, patents, and designs and copyrighted material such as literary works, films, musical compositions and recordings, graphic and architectural designs, works of art in any medium, and domain names.

In the United States intellectual property is protected by the joint efforts of the U.S. Patent and Trademark Office, the U.S. Copyright Office, the DOJ's Computer Crime and Intellectual Property Section (CCIPS), the U.S. Department of Commerce, and two agencies that focus on international aspects of intellectual property: the U.S. Customs and Border Protection, which monitors incoming goods arriving from other nations, and the Office of the U.S. Trade Representative, which negotiates on behalf of U.S. interests and develops and implements trade agreements and policies.

Intellectual property fraud takes many forms. A scan of 2016 CCIPS press releases (2017, https://www.justice.gov/criminal-ccips/ccips-press-releases-2016) reveals many releases concerning counterfeiting of copyright-protected merchandise. The U.S. Patent and Trademark Office warns inventors in "Scam Prevention" (July 14, 2016, https://www.uspto.gov/patents-getting-started/using-legal-services/scam-prevention) to be wary of scams perpetrated by individuals or firms pretending to be invention promoters. The fraudsters may charge inventors large up-front fees and promise to research, develop, and promote their inventions, but do not actually provide these services. The agency notes that the American Inventors Protection Act of 1999 requires invention promoters to disclose to potential customers certain information about their operations and past clients, such as the total number of customers that the promoter knows received a "net financial profit as a direct result of the invention promotion services" provided by the promoter. In "Be Aware of Trademark and Patent Scams" (NatLaw Review.com, October 15, 2011), Monica Riva Talley of the Washington, D.C., law firm Sterne, Kessler, Goldstein & Fox P.L.L.C. warns holders of patents and trademarks not to fall prey to e-mails and letters that appear to be from government agencies and illegally solicit fees for various services related to intellectual property.

COUNTERFEITING MONEY

Making counterfeit U.S. currency or altering genuine currency to increase its value is punishable by a fine, imprisonment, or both. Possession of counterfeit U.S. currency is also a crime, as is manufacturing counterfeit U.S. coins.

In response to the growing use of computer-generated counterfeit paper money, the Department of the Treasury began redesigning currency notes; for example, a watermark was added to notes of higher denominations to make them harder to copy accurately. According to the Bureau of Engraving and Printing, in "The History of American Currency" (2017, https://www.uscurrency.gov/content/history-american-currency), another change in currency design was made in 2013 to add additional security features to the $100 bill. Two of these features are a blue ribbon across the center of the bill and symbols that appear to change shape as the bill is tilted back and forth. The many security features added to the design and manufacture of U.S. currency have made it easier to detect bogus notes. Nevertheless, the counterfeiting of cash remains a vexing problem. In "They Make the Finest Counterfeit Money in the World. The U.S. Just Recovered $30 Million Worth" (WashingtonPost.com, November 22, 2016), Peter Holley describes a joint U.S.-Peruvian operation that resulted in the seizure of $30 million in fake U.S. dollars and 50,000 euros. The bills were created by Peruvian gangs that employ skilled artists and cutters to create authentic-looking money. Holley notes that these organizations are "responsible for producing and distributing an estimated 60 percent of the world's counterfeit U.S. notes."

CORPORATE FRAUD AND SECURITIES FRAUD

Corporate fraud and securities (or investment) fraud are particularly troublesome because they can involve large numbers of victims and inflict high monetary losses. Three notable cases from the early 21st century demonstrate these principles.

Enron Corporation

The collapse of the Enron Corporation is one of the most glaring examples of corporate crime and falsification of corporate data in recent history. Based in Houston, Texas, Enron was an energy broker that traded in electricity and other energy commodities. During the late 1990s Enron devised increasingly complex contracts with buyers and sellers that allowed Enron to profit from the difference in the selling price and the buying price of commodities such as electricity. Enron executives created a number of partnerships—in effect, companies that existed only on paper whose sole function was to hide debt and make Enron appear to be much more profitable than it actually was.

In December 2001 Enron filed for bankruptcy protection, listing $13.1 billion in liabilities and $24.7 billion in assets—$38 billion less than the assets it claimed only two months earlier. As a result, thousands of Enron employees lost their jobs. In addition, many Enron staff—who had been encouraged by company executives to invest monies from their 401(k) retirement plans in Enron stock—had their retirement savings reduced to almost nothing as a result of the precipitous decline in value of Enron stock. Over subsequent years many lawsuits were filed against Enron, its accounting firm Arthur Andersen, and former Enron executives. Also, several top Enron executives were convicted of fraud and conspiracy charges and sentenced to prison. Dozens of other people were also charged in the scandal. In June 2002 Arthur Andersen was convicted of destroying Enron documents during a federal investigation. In 2005 the U.S. Supreme Court overturned this conviction because of flaws in the instructions that had been given to the jury. However, the firm was effectively driven out of the accounting business.

The Enron scandal helped lead to the passage of the Sarbanes-Oxley Act (SOX), which was signed into law in July 2002. The law was designed to rebuild public trust in the U.S. corporate sector by imposing new criminal and civil penalties for security violations and establishing a new certification system for internal audits. SOX also grants independent auditors more access to company data and requires increased disclosure of compensation methods and systems, especially for upper management.

Bernard Madoff's Ponzi Scheme

One of the most famous white-collar crimes in history was the enormous Ponzi scheme managed by Bernard Madoff (1938–), an influential Wall Street executive. At the time of Madoff's arrest, the U.S. Securities and Exchange Commission (SEC) reported in the press release "SEC Charges Bernard L. Madoff for Multi-billion Dollar Ponzi Scheme" (December 12, 2008, https://www.sec.gov/news/press/2008/2008-293.htm) that Madoff estimated the fraud losses to his victims to total "at least $50 billion."

Ponzi schemes are named after Charles Ponzi (1883–1949), an Italian immigrant who defrauded investors in Boston, Massachusetts, during the early 20th century. The victims of a Ponzi scheme are lured with promises of large, quick returns on their investments. Rather than generating legitimate profits, however, the swindler makes payments to his or her clients out of the funds that they and others have invested. If the swindler can convince enough people to continue investing large enough sums in the scheme, he or she can maintain the illusion of a legitimately profitable enterprise for years, all while diverting funds from his or her clients for personal use. However, this arrangement is inherently unstable. Eventually, circumstances will develop where the swindler is unable to give his or her clients the money that they expect and the scheme will be exposed (provided the swindler does not run off with all of the money first).

When Madoff's list of clients was made public in early February 2009, it included thousands of institutions and individuals, including investment funds, pension funds, charitable organizations, financiers, Hollywood celebrities, and many private investors who expressed alarm at the sudden, unsought media exposure of their personal finances. In March 2009 Madoff pleaded guilty to 11 felony counts against him in federal court, including securities fraud, investment adviser fraud, mail fraud, wire fraud, money laundering, making false statements, filing false information with the SEC, and theft from an employee benefit plan. In June 2009 Madoff was sentenced to 150 years in prison. As of April 2017, he was serving his sentence in a medium-security federal prison in North Carolina.

Wells Fargo Fake Account Scandal

In 2016 federal regulators accused thousands of employees of the Wells Fargo banking company of creating unauthorized accounts for unsuspecting customers. Matt

Egan explains in "5,300 Wells Fargo Employees Fired over 2 Million Phony Accounts" (CNN.com, September 9, 2016) that the employees were under intense pressure to make sales (i.e., recruit new customers to open accounts and convince existing customers to open additional accounts). According to Egan, 5,300 employees were ultimately fired by the company for creating more than 2 million fake accounts. The employees benefited from the scheme by meeting their sales targets and earning bonuses. Egan notes that "employees moved funds from customers' existing accounts into newly-created ones without their knowledge or consent." As a result, some customers incurred fees because there was insufficient money in their original (authentic) accounts. In addition, employees filled out credit card applications using customers' names and personal and financial information. Again, these activities were conducted without the knowledge or consent of the customers. Some of these credit card accounts racked up fees, including interest charges, for the unwitting victims.

In September 2016 Wells Fargo was assessed federal, state, and local fines totaling $185 million. Its CEO, John Stumpf (1953–), resigned and several top executives were fired; they reportedly lost tens of millions of dollars in revoked pay and other compensation. The company promised to reimburse customers for all the fees incurred on unauthorized accounts. In "Wells Fargo Says Sales Scandal Could Hurt Growth Permanently" (Fortune.com, April 13, 2017), Lucinda Shen notes that Wells Fargo continued to suffer financially in April 2017 because of damage to the company's reputation and loss of customer confidence. Shen states, "Despite the hundreds of millions spent, Wells Fargo may never grow as fast as it did before the fake accounts problem."

PUBLIC CORRUPTION

The abuse of public trust may be found wherever the interest of individuals or businesses overlaps with government interest. It ranges from the health inspector who accepts a bribe from a restaurant owner, to the police officer who "shakes down" a drug dealer, to the council member or legislator who accepts money to vote a certain way. These crimes are often difficult to uncover because typically few willing witnesses are available.

According to the DOJ, in *Report to Congress on the Activities and Operations of the Public Integrity Section for 2015* (September 14, 2016, https://www.justice.gov/criminal/file/891961/download), the number of people convicted federally for offenses involving the abuse of public office has remained relatively stable since 2002, when it stood at 1,011. In 2015, 1,102 federal, state, and local officials and private citizens were indicted, and 904 were convicted, in public corruption cases.

Because public officials have sworn to uphold the law and to act in the interest of the communities they represent, their failure to do so is considered particularly reprehensible, and cases of public corruption often receive much media attention. Common public corruption charges include perjury (lying when one is legally required to tell the truth), obstruction of justice, and bribery. "Pay-to-play" is a form of bribery in which a public official demands benefits (often in the form of campaign contributions) in exchange for government appointments or contracts. Some notable public corruption cases in the 21st century include:

- Rod R. Blagojevich (1956–)—the Illinois governor was impeached and removed from office in January 2009 following his arrest the previous month on federal charges of solicitation of bribery, mail fraud, and abuse of power. Later that year the federal charges were expanded in a 19-count indictment that included wire fraud, attempted extortion, and racketeering conspiracy, among other charges. In August 2010 Blagojevich was convicted of only one of the charges against him: making false statements to investigators. A mistrial was declared for the other charges against him. In 2011 he was retried and convicted of multiple charges, including wire fraud, attempted extortion, and bribery. Blagojevich was sentenced to 14 years in prison and fined more than $20,000. As of April 2017, he was serving his sentence in a low-security federal prison in Colorado.

- Jesse Jackson Jr. (1965–; D-IL)—in February 2013 the former U.S. representative Jesse Jackson Jr., the son of the civil rights leader and politician Jesse Jackson (1941–), was charged with misusing hundreds of thousands of dollars in campaign funds. Later that month he pleaded guilty to the charges and was sentenced to two and a half years in prison.

- Bob McDonnell (1954–)—the former Virginia governor and his wife were indicted on multiple federal charges only weeks after he left office in January 2014. They were accused of accepting lavish gifts and financial benefits from a businessman in the state. The McDonnells were both found guilty on several charges. In June 2016, however, the U.S. Supreme Court overturned Bob McDonnell's conviction after finding that the jury had been given improper instructions. His wife's conviction was also subsequently overturned.

WHITE-COLLAR CRIME VICTIMIZATIONS

Information about the prevalence of white-collar crime can be gleaned from victim surveys and complaint centers operated by various government and private organizations. The results reflect the observations of participants about events that happened to them or their

TABLE 5.2

Victims aged 16 or older who experienced at least one identity theft incident during the previous year, by type of theft, 2012 and 2014

| | Anytime during the past 12 months[a] | | | | Most recent incident | | | | | |
| | Number of victims | | Percent of all persons | | Number of victims | | Percent of all persons | | Percent of all victims | |
Type of identity theft	2012	2014[e]	2012	2014[e]	2012	2014[e]	2012	2014[e]	2012	2014[e]
Total	16,580,500	17,576,200	6.7%	7.0%	16,580,500	17,576,200	6.7%	7.0%	100%	100%
Existing account	15,323,500	16,392,600	6.2%	6.6%	14,022,100	15,045,200	5.7%	6.0%	84.6%	85.6%
Credit card	7,698,500	8,598,600	3.1	3.4	6,676,300	7,329,100	2.7	2.9	40.3	41.7
Bank	7,470,700	8,082,600	3.0	3.2	6,191,500	6,735,800	2.5	2.7	37.3	38.3
Other	1,696,400	1,452,300	0.7	0.6	1,154,300	980,300	0.5	0.4	7.0	5.6
New account	1,125,100	1,077,100	0.5%	0.4%	683,400	683,300	0.3%	0.3%	4.1%	3.9%
Personal information	833,600	713,000	0.3%	0.3%	622,900	546,400	0.3%	0.2%	3.8%	3.1%
Multiple types	d	d	d	d	1,252,000	1,297,700	0.5%	0.6%	7.6%	7.4%
Existing account[b]	d	d	d	d	824,700	921,500	0.3	0.4	5.0	5.2
Other[c]	d	d	d	d	427,400	376,200	0.2	0.2	2.6	2.1

[a]Identify theft classified as a single type.
[b]Includes victims who experienced two or more of the following: unauthorized use of a credit card, bank account, or other existing account.
[c]Includes victims who experienced two or more of the following: unauthorized use of an existing account, misuse of personal information to open a new account, or misuse of personal information for other fraudulent purposes.
[d]Not applicable.
[e]Comparison year.
Note: Numbers and percentages will not sum to total due to victims who reported multiple incidents of identity theft.

SOURCE: Erika Harrell, "Table 1. Persons Age 16 or Older Who Experienced at Least One Identity Theft Incident in the Past 12 Months, by Type of Theft, 2012 and 2014," in *Victims of Identity Theft, 2014*, U.S. Department of Justice, Bureau of Justice Statistics, September 2015, https://www.bjs.gov/content/pub/pdf/vit14.pdf (accessed January 20, 2017)

households. It should be noted that not all of these events necessarily rise to the level of criminality. In addition, organizations use different terms to refer to events that might legally be deemed white-collar crimes; for example, they might define identity theft in different ways.

National Crime Victimization Survey

As is noted in Chapter 3, the DOJ's Bureau of Justice Statistics (BJS) performs a detailed examination of U.S. crime victims through its National Crime Victimization Survey (NCVS). This annual survey measures the levels of victimization resulting from specific criminal acts. The data collected are extrapolated to the entire U.S. population to provide estimates of criminal victimization at the national level. In "Identity Theft" (April 12, 2017, https://www.bjs.gov/index.cfm?ty=tp&tid=42), the BJS defines identity theft for NCVS purposes as including the following types of activities:

- Unauthorized use or attempted use of an existing account

- Unauthorized use or attempted use of personal information to open a new account

- Misuse of personal information for a fraudulent purpose

Lynn Langton of the BJS notes in *Identity Theft Reported by Households, 2005–2010* (November 2011, https://www.bjs.gov/content/pub/pdf/itrh0510.pdf) that the agency first added questions about identity theft to the NCVS survey in 2004. At that time the data were collected for entire households. Eventually, the BJS began surveying individuals about their experiences with identity theft. As of April 2017, the most recent BJS report on this topic was *Victims of Identity Theft, 2014* (September 2015, https://www.bjs.gov/content/pub/pdf/vit14.pdf) by Erika Harrell.

According to Harrell, in 2014 an estimated 17.6 million people aged 16 years and older were victimized by identity theft during the previous year. (See Table 5.2.) As shown in Figure 5.2, this represented 7% of the total population within that age group. Overall, 3% of the population experienced misuse of an existing credit card account and 3% experienced misuse of an existing bank account. These percentages were similar to those recorded in 2012.

The financial impact of the identity theft incidents was enormous, with the total loss estimated at $24.7 billion in 2012 and $15.4 billion in 2014. (See Table 5.3.) This includes both direct and indirect losses. Harrell defines a direct loss as "the monetary amount the offender obtained from misusing the victim's account or personal information, including the estimated value of goods, services, or cash obtained." Indirect losses include victim expenses such as fees, for example, bank fees for bounced checks. (Note that victims may have been reimbursed for some or all of the direct and indirect financial losses resulting from the identity theft incidents.)

The NCVS survey indicates that around 8% of identity theft victims in 2014 reported the incidents to police. (See Figure 5.3.) Those who suffered personal information fraud were far more likely to file a report than victims of other types of identity theft.

As shown in Figure 5.4, nearly one-third (32%) of identity theft victims in 2014 knew how their information had been fraudulently obtained. Victims who suffered multiple types of identity theft and those who had personal information stolen were the most likely to know how their information had been obtained. According to Harrell, 45% of identity theft victims discovered they had been victimized when a financial institution contacted them about suspicious activity related to their accounts. (See Table 5.4.)

During the 2014 NCVS, participants were asked if they had ever experienced identity theft "at any point in their lives." Overall, the results indicate that an estimated 36.5 million people aged 16 years and older had been victimized. (See Table 5.5.) This number represented 14.6% of the total population in that age group.

Consumer Sentinel Network

The Federal Trade Commission (FTC) operates a complaint database known as the Consumer Sentinel Network (CSN) that compiles consumer complaints about identity theft, consumer fraud, and related offenses. The data are made available to law enforcement agencies, such as the FBI, to assist in their investigations of white-collar crimes. The FTC publishes an annual report that summarizes CSN data collected within the previous year. According to the FTC, in *Consumer Sentinel Network Data Book for January–December 2015* (February 2016, https://www.ftc.gov/system/files/documents/reports/consumer-sentinel-network-data-book-january-december-2015/160229csn-2015databook.pdf), the CSN compiles complaints that are filed with the FTC and other federal and state agencies and private organizations (such as the Council of Better Business Bureaus) in North America.

Table 5.6 shows the number of complaints that were registered each year between 2001 and 2015. In 2015 the CSN received 3.1 million complaints, the highest number ever recorded. Overall, 40.4% (1.2 million) of the complaints that year involved fraud. Table 5.7 lists the top-20 complaint categories that were processed by the CSN in 2015. Debt collection (29%) was the most prevalent

FIGURE 5.2

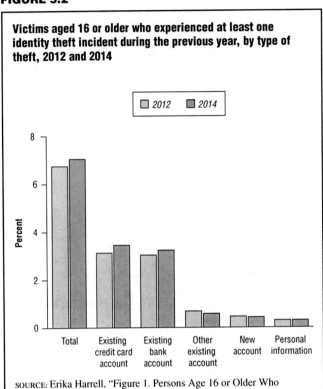

Victims aged 16 or older who experienced at least one identity theft incident during the previous year, by type of theft, 2012 and 2014

SOURCE: Erika Harrell, "Figure 1. Persons Age 16 or Older Who Experienced at Least One Identity Theft Incident in the Past 12 Months, by Type of Theft, 2012 and 2014," in *Victims of Identity Theft, 2014*, U.S. Department of Justice, Bureau of Justice Statistics, September 2015, https://www.bjs.gov/content/pub/pdf/vit14.pdf (accessed January 20, 2017)

TABLE 5.3

Total financial loss due to identity theft, 2012 and 2014

	2012				2014			
Percentile	Amount	Cumulative percent	Cumulative amount*	Amount in previous percentile groups	Amount	Cumulative percent	Cumulative amount*	Amount in previous percentile groups
10th	$20	10.3%	$11,657,500	$11,657,500	$30	12.1%	$21,186,200	$21,186,200
20th	60	22.2	72,023,900	60,366,400	70	20.6	71,964,300	50,778,100
30th	100	36.4	220,912,200	148,888,300	100	33.2	211,583,400	139,619,100
40th	200	47.2	461,721,100	240,808,900	200	45.4	490,817,200	279,233,800
50th	300	55.9	749,671,200	287,950,100	300	53.9	781,482,400	290,665,200
60th	400	61.4	993,847,100	244,175,900	500	67.2	1,485,320,500	703,838,100
70th	600	71.0	1,570,533,600	576,686,500	600	71.6	1,787,747,400	302,426,900
80th	1,000	81.6	2,596,494,100	1,025,960,500	1,000	82.5	2,875,212,900	1,087,465,500
90th	2,000	90.5	4,192,313,700	1,595,819,600	2,000	90.3	4,256,993,600	1,381,780,700
100th	703,700	100.0	24,696,323,900	20,504,010,200	105,500	100.0	15,395,709,600	11,138,716,000

*The amount of financial loss to victims, up to and including percentile.

SOURCE: Erika Harrell, "Table 7. Total Financial Loss Due to Identity Theft, 2012 and 2014," in *Victims of Identity Theft, 2014*, U.S. Department of Justice, Bureau of Justice Statistics, September 2015, https://www.bjs.gov/content/pub/pdf/vit14.pdf (accessed January 20, 2017)

FIGURE 5.3

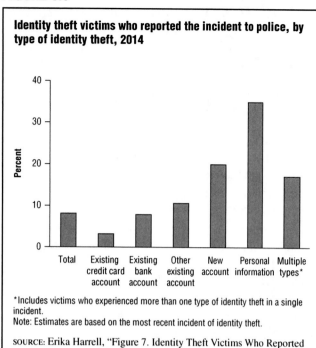

Identity theft victims who reported the incident to police, by type of identity theft, 2014

*Includes victims who experienced more than one type of identity theft in a single incident.
Note: Estimates are based on the most recent incident of identity theft.

SOURCE: Erika Harrell, "Figure 7. Identity Theft Victims Who Reported the incident to Law Enforcement, 2014," in *Victims of Identity Theft, 2014*, U.S. Department of Justice, Bureau of Justice Statistics, September 2015, https://www.bjs.gov/content/pub/pdf/vit14.pdf (accessed January 20, 2017)

FIGURE 5.4

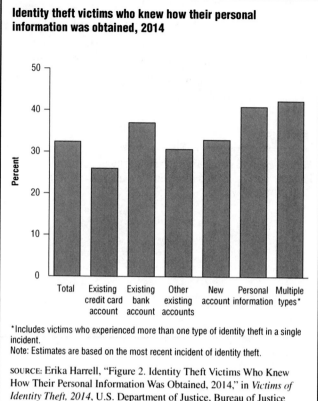

Identity theft victims who knew how their personal information was obtained, 2014

*Includes victims who experienced more than one type of identity theft in a single incident.
Note: Estimates are based on the most recent incident of identity theft.

SOURCE: Erika Harrell, "Figure 2. Identity Theft Victims Who Knew How Their Personal Information Was Obtained, 2014," in *Victims of Identity Theft, 2014*, U.S. Department of Justice, Bureau of Justice Statistics, September 2015, https://www.bjs.gov/content/pub/pdf/vit14.pdf (accessed January 20, 2017)

complaint. It was followed by complaints about identity theft (16%) and imposter scams (11%).

Internet Crime Complaint Center

The Internet Crime Complaint Center (IC3) is a joint effort of the FBI, the DOJ's Bureau of Justice Assistance, and the National White Collar Crime Center. The IC3 collects complaints about Internet (and other types of) fraud from consumers and refers them, as appropriate, to law enforcement agencies. In *2015 Internet Crime Report* (May 2016, https://pdf.ic3.gov/2015_IC3Report.pdf), the IC3 notes that it received 288,012 complaints in 2015. In total, nearly 3.5 million complaints had been received since the IC3 began in 2000. The total dollar loss to victims in 2015 was an estimated $1.1 billion.

In terms of victim counts, the three most prevalent types of crimes reported to the IC3 in 2015 were:

- Nonpayment/nondelivery (67,375 victims)—nonpayment means that victims shipped goods or provided services to customers, but never received payment for them. Nondelivery means that victims ordered goods or services and paid for them but never received what they ordered.

- 419/overpayment (30,855 victims)—the FBI explains in "Internet Crime Schemes" (2017, https://www.ic3.gov/crimeschemes.aspx) that "419" refers to Section 419 of the Nigerian Criminal Code. In this scam, a victim is contacted (often by e-mail) and asked to help facilitate the transfer of a large sum of money in exchange for a commission. The victim must first pay a sum that purportedly covers some of the costs associated with the financial transfer. Once that is done, the victim never receives the promised commission. In an overpayment scheme a victim is sent a payment (typically a check) and instructed to cash the check and keep a portion of the payment in exchange for forwarding the remainder of the payment to someone else. By the time the victim's bank finds out that the original check is fraudulent, the victim has already forwarded some of his or her own money to the fraudster.

- Identity theft (21,949 victims)—as noted earlier, this crime involves the use without permission of personally identifying information or account information to commit fraud or other illegal acts.

TABLE 5.4

Most common ways that victims discovered identity theft, by type of theft, 2014

Most common ways victim discovered identity theft	Any identity theft	Existing account misuse[a]	Other identity theft[b]
Contacted by financial institution about suspicious activity	45.0%	47.9%	15.3%
Noticed fraudulent charges on account	18.2	19.7	4.0
Noticed money missing from account	9.0	9.5	3.2
Contacted by company or agency	4.7	3.1	21.1
Contacted financial institution to report a theft	6.9	7.4	2.1[c]
Credit card declined, check bounced/account closed due to insufficient funds	4.7	4.9	2.3[c]
Received a bill or contacted about an unpaid bill	3.2	2.1	13.8
Notified by family member	0.5	0.3	1.7[c]
Discovered through credit report/credit monitoring service	1.4	1.0	5.9
Problem applying for a loan/government benefits/problem with income taxes	1.6	0.2[c]	15.7
Notified by police	0.4	[d,c]	4.6
Received merchandise/card that the victim did not receive product victim ordered	0.6	0.4	3.1
Another way[e]	3.7	3.4	7.3

[a]Comparison group.

[b]Includes identity theft incidents involving the misuse of personal information to open a new account or for other fraudulent purposes.

[c]Interpret with caution; estimate is based on 10 or fewer sample cases or coefficient of variation is greater than 50%.

[d]Less than 0.05%.

[e]Includes someone other than a family member notified victim; victim noticed suspicious computer activity, including a hacked computer; victim noticed suspicious contact, including phishing; account information missing or stolen; or victim discovered through news media.

Note: Estimates are based on the most recent incident of identity theft.

SOURCE: Erika Harrell, "Table 4. Most Common Ways Victims Discovered Identity Theft, by Type of Theft, 2014," in *Victims of Identity Theft, 2014*, U.S. Department of Justice, Bureau of Justice Statistics, September 2015, https://www.bjs.gov/content/pub/pdf/vit14.pdf (accessed January 20, 2017)

TABLE 5.5

Victims aged 16 or older who experienced identity theft at any point in their lives, type of identity theft they experienced outside of the past year, and ongoing problems resulting from identity theft, 2014

	Number of persons	Percent of all persons	Percent with unresolved problems resulting from identity theft[a]
Experienced at least one incident of identity theft during lifetime			
No	212,478,300	85.2%	[d]
Yes	36,467,000	14.6	7.1%
Experienced at least one incident of identity theft outside of past 12 months			
No	226,869,800	91.0%	[d]
Yes	21,964,800	8.8	6.6%
Type of identity theft experienced			
Existing account	16,948,300	6.8	3.5
Credit card	9,876,800	4.0	2.9
Bank account	6,405,800	2.6	4.0
Other account	665,700	0.3	8.3
New account	1,547,100	0.6	16.7
Personal information	1,860,900	0.7	14.1
Multiple types	1,590,800	0.6	20.2
Existing account[b]	780,500	0.3	12.3
Other[c]	810,200	0.3	27.8

[a]Based on number of persons who experienced the identity theft.

[b]Includes victims who experienced two or more of the following: unauthorized use of a credit card, bank account, or other existing account.

[c]Includes victims who experienced two or more of the following: unauthorized use of an existing account, misuse of personal information to open a new account, or misuse of personal information for other fraudulent purposes.

[d]Not applicable.

Note: Detail may not sum to total due to a small number of victims who did not know whether they experienced identity theft during their lifetime or outside of the past 12 months.

SOURCE: Erika Harrell, "Table 11. Persons Age 16 or Older Who Experienced Identity Theft at Any Point in Their Lives, Type of Identity Theft They Experienced Outside of the Past Year, and Ongoing Problems from Identity Theft That Occurred Outside of the Past Year, 2014," in *Victims of Identity Theft, 2014*, U.S. Department of Justice, Bureau of Justice Statistics, September 2015, https://www.bjs.gov/content/pub/pdf/vit14.pdf (accessed January 20, 2017)

TABLE 5.6

Consumer Sentinel Network complaints, by type of complaint, 2001–15

Calendar year	Consumer Sentinel Network complaint count			Total complaints
	Fraud	Identity theft	Other	
2001	137,306	86,250	101,963	325,519
2002	242,783	161,977	146,862	551,622
2003	331,366	215,240	167,051	713,657
2004	410,298	246,909	203,176	860,383
2005	437,585	255,687	216,042	909,314
2006	423,672	246,214	236,243	906,129
2007	505,563	259,314	305,570	1,070,447
2008	620,832	314,587	325,705	1,261,124
2009	708,781	278,360	441,836	1,428,977
2010	820,072	251,074	399,160	1,470,306
2011	1,041,517	279,191	577,835	1,898,543
2012	1,112,627	369,145	631,843	2,113,615
2013	1,212,719	290,102	672,534	2,175,355
2014	1,578,565	332,647	718,775	2,629,987
2015	1,246,849	490,220	1,346,310	3,083,379

Note: Complaint counts from calendar year 2001 to calendar year 2010 represent historical figures as per the Consumer Sentinel Network's five-year data retention policy. These complaint figures exclude National Do Not Call Registry complaints.

SOURCE: "Consumer Sentinel Network Complaint Type Count: Calendar Years 2001 through 2015," in *Consumer Sentinel Network Data Book for January–December 2015*, Federal Trade Commission, February 2016, https://www.ftc.gov/system/files/documents/reports/consumer-sentinel-network-data-book-january-december-2015/160229csn-2015databook.pdf (accessed January 20, 2017)

TABLE 5.7

Top-20 Consumer Sentinel Network complaint categories, 2015

Rank	Category	No. of complaints	Percentages*
1	Debt collection	897,655	29%
2	Identity theft	490,220	16%
3	Impostor scams	353,770	11%
4	Telephone and mobile services	275,754	9%
5	Prizes, sweepstakes and lotteries	140,136	5%
6	Banks and lenders	131,875	4%
7	Shop-at-home and catalog sales	96,363	3%
8	Auto-related complaints	93,917	3%
9	Television and electronic media	47,728	2%
10	Credit bureaus, information furnishers and report users	43,939	1%
11	Internet services	40,106	1%
12	Credit cards	37,750	1%
13	Health care	34,669	1%
14	Investment-related complaints	26,453	1%
15	Foreign money offers and counterfeit check scams	25,324	1%
16	Advance payments for credit services	24,433	1%
17	Travel, vacations and timeshare plans	24,171	1%
18	Business and job opportunities	17,314	1%
19	Office supplies and services	10,287	<1%
20	Mortgage foreclosure relief and debt management	10,210	<1%

CSN = Consumer Sentinel Network
FTC = Federal Trade Commission
*Percentages are based on the total number of CSN complaints (3,083,379) received by the FTC between January 1 and December 31, 2015. Four percent (126,482) of the CSN complaints received by the FTC were coded "Other (Note in Comments)."

SOURCE: Adapted from "Consumer Sentinel Network Complaint Categories: January 1–December 31, 2015," in *Consumer Sentinel Network Data Book for January–December 2015*, Federal Trade Commission, February 2016, https://www.ftc.gov/system/files/documents/reports/consumer-sentinel-network-data-book-january-december-2015/160229csn-2015databook.pdf (accessed January 20, 2017)

CHAPTER 6
CONTROLLING CRIME

Criminologists state that every criminal act involves three elements: motivation, resources, and opportunity. A person who is motivated to commit a crime and has the resources to do so (e.g., a weapon or the physical or mental prowess needed to carry out a crime) seeks criminal opportunities, such as victims or targets. Societies try to control crime by controlling these three primary elements of criminality.

Controlling crime in the United States is a multi-pronged effort that includes interrelated acts of prevention, deterrence, and punishment. Private citizens may take actions designed to prevent and deter crimes on their person and property. Examples include installing alarm systems, taking self-defense classes, and participating in neighborhood watch programs. Taxpayer funds are used by governments to establish crime-controlling entities at the local, state, and federal levels for the overall good of society. There are four major governmental components that work together to control crime:

- Law enforcement agencies
- The legal system
- The judiciary system
- The corrections system

The corrections system is described in detail in Chapters 7, 8, and 9. The remainder of this chapter addresses the three other arms of crime control.

LAW ENFORCEMENT AGENCIES

The primary role of law enforcement agencies is to investigate crimes, gather evidence, and arrest suspected perpetrators. Agencies differ by geographic jurisdictions (e.g., federal, state, or local) and by enforcement responsibilities (e.g., the types of laws they enforce or the types of crimes they investigate).

Agencies and Employees

The vast majority of law enforcement in the United States is carried out by local agencies. The Federal Bureau of Investigation (FBI) tracks local law enforcement employment as part of its Uniform Crime Reporting (UCR) Program. For 2015 the UCR Program reported that 13,160 city and county police agencies around the country had 913,161 full-time employees. (See Table 6.1.) Of these employees, 635,781 (or 70% of the total) were law enforcement officers, such as police officers or sheriff's deputies, and the remainder were civilian employees (e.g., receptionists or clerks). More than half of all local law enforcement employees worked for city governments, most for cities with populations of 250,000 or more.

In addition, all states operate some type of state police agency, state patrol, or highway patrol force. These officers patrol state highways and often provide law enforcement assistance to local agencies within their state, particularly those in rural areas or small towns.

The federal government has several law enforcement agencies with specific responsibilities. The largest agencies are:

- FBI
- U.S. Drug Enforcement Administration
- Bureau of Alcohol, Tobacco, Firearms, and Explosives
- U.S. Customs and Border Protection
- U.S. Immigration and Customs Enforcement
- U.S. Secret Service

The first three of these agencies are part of the U.S. Department of Justice (DOJ). The latter three agencies operate under the U.S. Department of Homeland Security.

OFFICERS KILLED AND ASSAULTED IN THE LINE OF DUTY. The UCR Program tracks the number of law enforcement officers that are killed and assaulted in the

TABLE 6.1

Number of full-time law enforcement employees (officers and civilians) and number of law enforcement agencies, total and by jurisdiction size, 2015

Population group	Total law enforcement employees	Percent law enforcement employees		Total officers	Percent officers		Total civilians	Percent civilians		Number of agencies	2015 estimated population
		Male	Female		Male	Female		Male	Female		
Total agencies:	**913,161**	**73.7**	**26.3**	**635,781**	**88.4**	**11.6**	**277,380**	**40.0**	**60.0**	**13,160**	**273,099,970**
Total cities	**519,134**	**75.8**	**24.2**	**402,978**	**88.3**	**11.7**	**116,156**	**32.6**	**67.4**	**10,075**	**187,551,939**
Group I (250,000 and over)	183,302	72.4	27.6	139,335	84.2	15.8	43,967	35.1	64.9	76	56,116,904
1,000,000 and over (Group I subset)	95,978	70.5	29.5	71,395	83.0	17.0	24,583	34.1	65.9	10	24,675,984
500,000 to 999,999 (Group I subset)	50,297	75.9	24.1	39,598	85.4	14.6	10,699	40.9	59.1	23	16,678,441
250,000 to 499,999 (Group I subset)	37,027	72.6	27.4	28,342	85.5	14.5	8,685	30.7	69.3	43	14,762,479
Group II (100,000 to 249,999)	63,094	73.7	26.3	48,159	88.2	11.8	14,935	26.9	73.1	195	28,956,838
Group III (50,000 to 99,999)	59,540	76.7	23.3	46,318	90.3	9.7	13,222	29.0	71.0	419	29,206,031
Group IV (25,000 to 49,999)	56,074	78.1	21.9	44,803	90.9	9.1	11,271	27.0	73.0	764	26,443,466
Group V (10,000 to 24,999)	57,693	80.1	19.9	47,085	92.1	7.9	10,608	26.7	73.3	1,612	25,662,681
Group VI (under 10,000)	99,431	79.2	20.8	77,278	90.7	9.3	22,153	39.4	60.6	7,009	21,166,019
Metropolitan counties	280,343	70.2	29.8	165,764	87.0	13.0	114,579	45.8	54.2	1,238	63,774,885
Nonmetropolitan counties	113,684	72.4	27.6	67,039	92.2	7.8	46,645	43.9	56.1	1,847	21,773,146
Suburban areas*	429,617	73.3	26.7	283,285	88.6	11.4	146,332	43.6	56.4	7,034	116,427,469

*Suburban areas include law enforcement agencies in cities with less than 50,000 inhabitants and county law enforcement agencies that are within a Metropolitan Statistical Area. Suburban areas exclude all metropolitan agencies associated with a principal city. The agencies associated with suburban areas also appear in other groups within this table.

SOURCE: "Table 74. Full-time Law Enforcement Employees by Population Group. Percent Male and Female. 2015," in *Crime in the United States 2015*, U.S. Department of Justice, Federal Bureau of Investigation, September 26, 2016, https://ucr.fbi.gov/crime-in-the-u.s/2015/crime-in-the-u.s.-2015/tables/table-74 (accessed January 21, 2017)

line of duty each year. In *Law Enforcement Officers Killed and Assaulted, 2015* (October 2016, https://ucr.fbi.gov/leoka/2015/home), the FBI indicates that between 2006 and 2015, 491 federal, state, and local law enforcement officers were feloniously killed (their deaths were caused by another person and were not accidental) in the line of duty:

- 2006—48 officers killed
- 2007—58 officers killed
- 2008—41 officers killed
- 2009—48 officers killed
- 2010—56 officers killed
- 2011—72 officers killed
- 2012—49 officers killed
- 2013—27 officers killed
- 2014—51 officers killed
- 2015—41 officers killed

Another 556,095 officers were assaulted between 2006 and 2015. Figure 6.1 provides a percentage breakdown of the circumstances under which these law enforcement officers were killed or assaulted. The largest percentage (18.7%) of felonious killings occurred during arrest situations, followed by traffic pursuits or stops (16.9%).

In "Number of Police Officers Killed by Firearms Rose in 2016, Study Finds" (NPR.org, December 30, 2016), Camila Domonoske notes that an estimated 64 officers were killed by firearms in 2016. Two events resulted in eight of the deaths. In early July five officers died after being ambushed in Dallas—Lorne Ahrens, Michael Krol, Michael Smith, Brent Thompson, and Patrick Zamarripa. Later in the same month three officers were killed during an ambush in Baton Rouge, Louisiana—Brad Garafola, Matthew Gerald, and Montrell Jackson. In both cases, the perpetrators were killed by police during the incidents.

Key Law Enforcement Agency Components

Law enforcement agencies differ in their geographic and criminal jurisdictions, but there are some components that are considered key to modern crime control, particularly at the local level. These components are

FIGURE 6.1

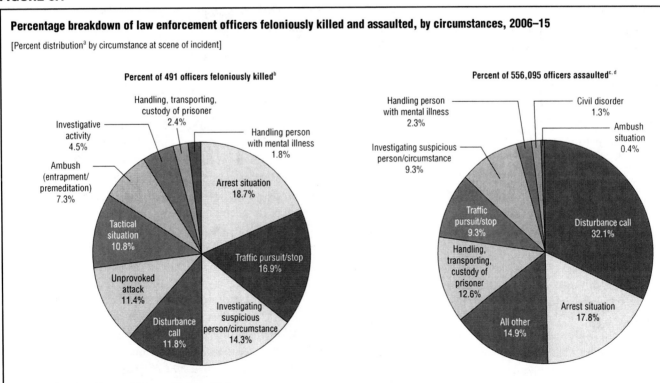

Percentage breakdown of law enforcement officers feloniously killed and assaulted, by circumstances, 2006–15

[Percent distribution[a] by circumstance at scene of incident]

Percent of 491 officers feloniously killed[b]

Handling, transporting, custody of prisoner 2.4%
Investigative activity 4.5%
Handling person with mental illness 1.8%
Ambush (entrapment/premeditation) 7.3%
Arrest situation 18.7%
Tactical situation 10.8%
Traffic pursuit/stop 16.9%
Unprovoked attack 11.4%
Disturbance call 11.8%
Investigating suspicious person/circumstance 14.3%

Percent of 556,095 officers assaulted[c, d]

Handling person with mental illness 2.3%
Civil disorder 1.3%
Investigating suspicious person/circumstance 9.3%
Ambush situation 0.4%
Traffic pursuit/stop 9.3%
Disturbance call 32.1%
Handling, transporting, custody of prisoner 12.6%
Arrest situation 17.8%
All other 14.9%

[a]Because of rounding, the percentages may not add to 100.0.
[b]The circumstance category of "All other" does not apply to the data collected for law enforcement officers feloniously killed.
[c]The circumstance categories of "Ambush (entrapment/premeditation)" and "Unprovoked attack" are included in the "Ambush situation" data collected for law enforcement officers assaulted.
[d]The circumstance categories of "Investigative activity" and "Tactical situation" are included in the "All other" data collected for law enforcement officers assaulted.

SOURCE: "Figure 4. Law Enforcement Officers Feloniously Killed and Assaulted: Percent Distribution by Circumstances at Scene of Incident, 2006–2015," in *Law Enforcement Officers Killed and Assaulted, 2015*, U.S. Department of Justice, Federal Bureau of Investigation, Fall 2016, https://ucr.fbi.gov/leoka/2015/figures/figure_4_2015.pdf (accessed January 21, 2017)

proactive policing, detectives, high-technology tools, and forensic science.

PROACTIVE POLICING. Local law enforcement agencies may assign uniformed officers to regularly patrol specific neighborhoods for the purpose of developing relationships with the residents and business owners in the area. These officers are known informally as "beat cops" because each officer patrols a particular "beat" within the community. The use of beat cops is an example of community policing, whereby law enforcement agencies seek to forge a cooperative bond with people in the community to better fight crime.

Community policing was commonly practiced in the United States in the early part of the 20th century. Beginning in the 1950s and 1960s, however, police departments shifted beat cops from their foot patrols to patrol cars so that larger areas could be covered. Eventually, law enforcement agencies became almost completely reactive; that is, they reacted after a crime was committed with officers dispatched in response to 911 calls.

Community policing is an example of proactive policing. Proactive means taking action before a situation or event becomes a problem. Proactive policing is intended to prevent crimes from occurring in the first place. Some jurisdictions install video cameras in public places, such as parks or street corners, to deter criminal activity. Local law enforcement agencies also work with private citizens and business owners to encourage the reporting of suspicious-acting people or situations that present opportunities to criminals.

DETECTIVES. Many law enforcement agencies also employ detectives. These are plainclothes officers who are specially trained to investigate particular crimes (such as homicides). Detectives interview witnesses and suspects, gather facts, examine records, and collect evidence. They may also participate in the apprehension of perpetrators.

HIGH-TECHNOLOGY TOOLS. As noted earlier, some jurisdictions deter criminal activity by employing video cameras in public areas. Video cameras are also useful for solving crimes that have already occurred, as video images can help detectives identify perpetrators and provide evidence for the prosecution. During the late 20th century law enforcement agencies began employing a variety of high-technology resources devoted to crime control. For example, agencies equipped their patrol cars with personal computers and global positioning systems to better provide officers with the data they need to perform their job. Another option that has become popular in some jurisdictions, particularly large cities, is the employment of gunfire locators. These devices recognize and record the sound of gunfire and determine the location of its source. The information can be instantly

transmitted to patrol officers so that they can quickly go to the scene. Facial recognition software is another high-tech tool used by some law enforcement agencies. The software can scan crowds of people and notify officers if any viewed faces match photos of suspects. Advanced biometric technology is also increasingly being employed for crime fighting, such as to digitally take fingerprints or scan the irises of arrestees.

FORENSIC SCIENCE. Forensic science is the application of scientific knowledge and methods to solve crime. Forensic investigators (or criminalists) are employed by some law enforcement agencies. These specialists commonly investigate crime scenes where they collect and analyze physical evidence. They may perform deoxyribonucleic acid (DNA) or firearms analyses or conduct laboratory tests on blood, semen, hair, tissue, fibers, and other evidentiary materials that are associated with criminal acts.

Police Controversies

In the 21st century some law enforcement departments have come under intense criticism for the killing of unarmed civilians during encounters with their officers. Incidents involving white officers and African American civilians have severely stoked racial tensions in the United States. There is also growing concern about the increased militarization of the nation's police departments.

RACIALLY CHARGED CASES. Several incidents in which African Americans have died during or after encounters with police officers have gained particular notoriety since 2014. In "Looking for Accountability in Police-Involved Deaths of Blacks" (NYTimes.com, November 16, 2016), Haeyoun Park and Jasmine C. Lee review 13 high-profile cases that have inflamed public anger and spurred complaints about racial bias. For example, on July 17, 2014, an African American man was subjected to a chokehold by a New York City police officer during an arrest for a minor offense. The incident was captured on video and shows the victim, Eric Garner (1970–2014), gasping, "I can't breathe." Garner died as a result of the chokehold. Despite the fact that the use of chokeholds for restraining suspects has been banned by the New York City Police Department since 1993, a grand jury declined to indict the officer who had employed this technique on Garner. This decision prompted public demonstrations and criticism. On August 9, 2014, the African American teenager Michael Brown Jr. (1996–2014) was shot and killed by a white police officer in Ferguson, Missouri, a suburb of St. Louis. The shooting sparked prolonged public protests in Ferguson and other parts of the country. After a grand jury decided not to indict the officer, the protests increased in intensity and sometimes resulted in rioting and property destruction.

According to Park and Lee, officers were indicted on state criminal charges (e.g., for murder or manslaughter) in most of the 11 other high-profile cases. As of April 2017 trials had taken place in three of the cases (the deaths of Walter L. Scott in North Charleston, South Carolina; Freddie Gray in Baltimore; and Samuel DuBose in Cincinnati). All three trials ended in mistrials or acquittals for the officers that were charged.

Police-involved shootings can trigger federal investigations of officers for violating the civil rights of the victims. Federal law (Title 18, Section 242; https://www.justice.gov/crt/deprivation-rights-under-color-law) prohibits a person acting "under color of any law" from willfully depriving another person of a right or privilege protected by the U.S. Constitution or laws of the United States. The DOJ notes, "Persons acting under color of law within the meaning of this statute include police officers, prison guards and other law enforcement officials, as well as judges, care providers in public health facilities, and others who are acting as public officials." In March 2015 federal investigators announced that Darren Wilson, the officer involved in the Brown Jr. killing, would not face criminal charges for civil rights violations. As of April 2017, federal civil rights investigations into the other police-involved deaths described by Park and Lee were still ongoing.

The racial tensions spurred by the deaths of African Americans during and after police encounters have profoundly impacted U.S. society. "Black Lives Matter" has become both a catchphrase and the name of an activist movement for people pressing for social justice, particularly respect for the human and civil rights of African Americans. The movement has also become a lightning rod for critics who claim its followers incite (or tolerate) violence against police. The two perpetrators in the 2016 ambush killings of police officers in Dallas and Baton Rouge were both allegedly motivated by anger over police killings of African Americans. (The Dallas ambush occurred around the time of the conclusion of a peaceful rally that had been held to protest such killings.)

MILITARY EQUIPMENT AND TACTICS. Some police departments around the country have acquired military-type weapons and equipment, such as armored vehicles, and deploy officers trained in military tactics. These measures have grown increasingly controversial, particularly as the nation's violent crime rate has decreased. In "The Rise of the SWAT Team in American Policing" (NYTimes.com, September 7, 2014), Clyde Haberman traces this militarization trend back to the 1960s, when the first special weapons and tactics (SWAT) units were created in Los Angeles in the wake of deadly rioting in the Watts neighborhood. As the nation's war on drugs intensified over subsequent decades, SWAT-like units became routinely used in drug raids. Haberman notes that critics decry the tactics employed by these units, claiming that the "show of force … often far exceeds the threat to them." However, others argue these tactics are necessary because drug gangs are often heavily armed with powerful weapons.

In 1990 the National Defense Authorization Act included provisions for transferring U.S. military equipment to local police departments. These transfers attracted little public attention until the summer of 2014, when rioting broke out in Ferguson over the police killing of Brown Jr. Local police responded to the rioting equipped with military-type body armor, weapons, and vehicles. Media images of this response against mostly unarmed protestors caused a public outcry. Haberman states, "What the world saw were lawmen looking more like combat troops in the Mideast than peacekeepers in the Midwest."

The furor prompted calls by community activists and some legislators to demilitarize local police departments. President Barack Obama (1961–) ordered federal agencies to reexamine their policies regarding transfers of military weapons and gear to local police departments. Evan Perez explains in "Police Militarization: The Ferguson Issue That Wasn't" (CNN.com, December 8, 2014) that the Obama administration decided to continue the transfer program, but instituted stricter tracking methods for the equipment and called for more training for officers using the equipment. During the 2016 presidential election, Donald Trump (1946–) vowed to discontinue the restrictions if he was elected. As of April 2017, the Trump administration had not taken action on the issue.

Police and Public Surveys

In "Key Findings on How Police View Their Jobs amid Protests and Calls for Reform" (January 11, 2017, http://www.pewresearch.org/fact-tank/2017/01/11/police-key-findings/), Renee Stepler summarizes the results of a Pew Research Center survey conducted during the summer of 2016. Nearly 8,000 police officers nationwide were asked to share their views on various topics related to their jobs, particularly the use of deadly force. Stepler notes that nearly three-quarters of the officers (72%) said that "outside of required training, they have never fired their service firearm while on duty." The vast majority (86%) of all respondents said that the recent spate of fatal incidents between police and African Americans had "made their jobs harder." Pew found stark differences in the perceptions of white and African American officers on the incidents. Nearly three-quarters (72%) of white officers said that the fatal encounters were "isolated incidents rather than signs of a broader problem." However, only 43% of the African American officers shared this viewpoint. A larger percentage of African American officers (57%) thought the incidents were symptomatic of a broader problem in U.S. society. This breakdown is very similar to that obtained during a separate Pew survey of the public at large. In that survey, Stepler notes, 60% of Americans said that the deaths of African Americans during encounters with police are signs of a broader problem.

Arrests

One of the most important aspects of crime control that law enforcement agencies practice is the apprehension and arrest of suspected perpetrators. According to the FBI, in 2015 law enforcement agencies made 10.8 million arrests for all criminal infractions, excluding traffic violations. (See Table 6.2.)

The FBI notes that there were 505,681 arrests for violent crimes (murder and nonnegligent manslaughter, rape, robbery, and aggravated assault) and nearly 1.5 million arrests for property crimes (burglary, larceny-theft, motor vehicle theft, and arson) in 2015. (See Table 6.2.) Of the arrests for specific offenses on which the FBI collects statistics, the five crimes with the most arrests were:

TABLE 6.2

Estimated number of arrests, by offense, 2015

Total[a]	10,797,088
Murder and nonnegligent manslaughter	11,092
Rape[b]	22,863
Robbery	95,572
Aggravated assault	376,154
Burglary	216,010
Larceny-theft	1,160,390
Motor vehicle theft	77,979
Arson	8,834
Violent crime[c]	505,681
Property crime[c]	1,463,213
Other assaults	1,081,019
Forgery and counterfeiting	55,333
Fraud	133,138
Embezzlement	15,909
Stolen property; buying, receiving, possessing	88,576
Vandalism	191,015
Weapons; carrying, possessing, etc.	145,358
Prostitution and commercialized vice	41,877
Sex offenses (except rape and prostitution)	51,388
Drug abuse violations	1,488,707
Gambling	4,825
Offenses against the family and children	94,837
Driving under the influence	1,089,171
Liquor laws	266,250
Drunkenness	405,880
Disorderly conduct	386,078
Vagrancy	25,151
All other offenses	3,218,880
Suspicion	1,389
Curfew and loitering law violations	44,802

[a]Does not include suspicion.
[b]The rape figure in this table is an aggregate total of the data submitted based on both the legacy and revised Uniform Crime Reporting definitions.
[c]Violent crimes are offenses of murder and nonnegligent manslaughter, rape, robbery, and aggravated assault. Property crimes are offenses of burglary, larceny-theft, motor vehicle theft, and arson.

SOURCE: "Table 29. Estimated Number of Arrests, United States, 2015," in *Crime in the United States, 2015*, U.S. Department of Justice, Federal Bureau of Investigation, September 26, 2016, https://ucr.fbi.gov/crime-in-the-u.s/2015/crime-in-the-u.s.-2015/tables/table-29 (accessed January 20, 2017)

- Drug abuse violations—1,488,707 arrests
- Larceny-theft—1,160,390 arrests
- Driving under the influence—1,089,171 arrests
- Assaults, other than aggravated assaults—1,081,019 arrests
- Drunkenness—405,880 arrests

Based on data from 9,581 law enforcement agencies, Table 6.3 provides the percentage changes in the number of people arrested between 2006 and 2015. Overall, arrests were down 22.3% over this period. Arrests of adults (those aged 18 years and older) were down 16.7% overall. (Overall juvenile arrests also declined during this period; for arrest data about people under the age of 18 years, see Chapter 10.) Adult arrests were down 9.4% for violent crimes and up 16.4% for property crimes between 2006 and 2015. The largest decreases for adult arrestees were reported for suspicion (down 61.7%), liquor law violations (down 53.9%), and fraud (down 52.6%). Among specific crimes, arrests increased between 2006 and 2015 only for larceny-theft (up 30.7%).

ARRESTEE DEMOGRAPHICS. Age data were reported to the FBI in 2015 for 8.3 million arrestees. (See Table 6.4.) Of this number, 709,333 were under the age of 18 years and nearly 7.6 million were aged 18 years and older. As is explained in Chapter 10, people under the age of 18 years are considered juveniles in most states and are typically handled by the juvenile court system.

In Table 6.5 the FBI provides a gender breakdown for 8.3 million arrestees in 2015. Male arrestees outnumbered female arrestees by a margin of almost three to one (73.1% male to 26.9% female).

Of the 8.2 million arrests reported to the UCR Program that included race information in 2015, 69.7% of the arrestees were white and 26.6% were African American. (See Table 6.6.) The remaining arrestees were Native American or Alaskan Native (2.1%), Asian American (1.2%), or Native Hawaiian or other Pacific Islander (0.3%).

OFFENSES CLEARED BY ARREST OR EXCEPTIONAL MEANS. Figure 6.2 shows the percentage of known offenses that were cleared by arrest or exceptional means in 2015. Offenses cleared by exceptional means are those for which there can be no arrest, such as in a murder-suicide, when the perpetrator is known to be deceased.

Because murder is considered the most serious crime, it receives the most police attention and, therefore, has the highest arrest rate of all felonies. In 2015, 61.5% of murders and nonnegligent manslaughters were cleared by arrest or exceptional means. (See Figure 6.2.) The only other offense for which more than half of the crimes were cleared in 2015 was aggravated assault (54%). Clearance

TABLE 6.3

Arrests and percentage change in arrests, by offense, 2006–15

	Number of persons arrested					
	Total all ages			18 years of age and over		
Offense charged	2006	2015	Percent change	2006	2015	Percent change
Total[a]	8,676,456	6,739,363	−22.3	7,396,261	6,160,825	−16.7
Murder and nonnegligent manslaughter	7,104	6,201	−12.7	6,462	5,780	−10.6
Rape[b]	14,120	13,945	—	12,009	11,706	—
Robbery	68,437	54,003	−21.1	50,236	44,250	−11.9
Aggravated assault	271,740	231,828	−14.7	235,756	214,111	−9.2
Burglary	188,122	136,465	−27.5	136,169	114,409	−16.0
Larceny-theft	679,290	753,665	+10.9	498,667	651,767	+30.7
Motor vehicle theft	72,650	46,463	−36.0	54,999	38,916	−29.2
Arson	10,445	5,737	−45.1	5,222	3,926	−24.8
Violent crime[c]	361,401	305,977	−15.3	304,463	275,847	−9.4
Property crime[c]	950,507	942,330	−0.9	695,057	809,018	+16.4
Other assaults	792,178	678,537	−14.3	639,782	594,848	−7.0
Forgery and counterfeiting	68,319	34,911	−48.9	66,031	34,279	−48.1
Fraud	181,863	86,484	−52.4	176,773	83,708	−52.6
Embezzlement	13,008	9,923	−23.7	12,059	9,532	−21.0
Stolen property; buying, receiving, possessing	79,077	57,918	−26.8	65,045	51,318	−21.1
Vandalism	189,867	124,058	−34.7	113,665	96,265	−15.3
Weapons; carrying, possessing, etc.	114,104	86,443	−24.2	86,397	74,829	−13.4
Prostitution and commercialized vice	33,402	17,663	−47.1	32,669	17,394	−46.8
Sex offenses (except rape and prostitution)	50,656	32,356	−36.1	40,708	26,713	−34.4
Drug abuse violations	1,078,156	928,122	−13.9	965,024	865,087	−10.4
Gambling	2,807	1,657	−41.0	2,515	1,524	−39.4
Offenses against the family and children	79,568	58,377	−26.6	76,220	56,169	−26.3
Driving under the influence	925,818	675,960	−27.0	912,871	671,666	−26.4
Liquor laws	408,511	174,230	−57.3	313,782	144,700	−53.9
Drunkenness	368,271	251,424	−31.7	357,178	247,896	−30.6
Disorderly conduct	422,187	240,723	−43.0	292,239	195,064	−33.3
Vagrancy	18,106	15,017	−17.1	14,631	14,419	−1.4
All other offenses (except traffic)	2,477,981	1,997,799	−19.4	2,229,152	1,890,549	−15.2
Suspicion	1,125	480	−57.3	922	353	−61.7
Curfew and loitering law violations	60,669	19,454	−67.9	—	—	—

[a]Does not include suspicion.

[b]The 2006 rape figures are based on the legacy definition, and the 2015 rape figures are aggregate totals based on both the legacy and revised Uniform Crime Reporting definitions. For this reason, a percent change is not provided.

[c]Violent crimes are offenses of murder and nonnegligent manslaughter, rape, robbery, and aggravated assault. Property crimes are offenses of burglary, larceny-theft, motor vehicle theft, and arson.

SOURCE: Adapted from "Table 32. Ten-Year Arrest Trends: Totals, 2006–2015," in *Crime in the United States, 2015*, U.S. Department of Justice, Federal Bureau of Investigation, September 26, 2016, https://ucr.fbi.gov/crime-in-the-u.s/2015/crime-in-the-u.s.-2015/tables/table-32 (accessed January 21, 2017)

rates were much lower for the other crimes, particularly motor vehicle theft (13.1% clearance rate) and burglary (12.9% clearance rate).

Making an arrest does not mean the alleged offender is guilty or will be convicted of the crime. Law enforcement agencies do not determine the guilt or innocence of suspected perpetrators. That task is left up to the judicial system.

THE LEGAL SYSTEM

Although *mala in se* (morally wrong or inherently wrong) behaviors are universally condemned as wrong, punishments for these crimes can vary significantly between societies. Many of the legal decisions concerning *mala in se* crimes have evolved over time through what is known as common law. Common law refers to the legal precedents that are established by court decisions over time, as opposed to laws that are passed by legislative bodies. The U.S. legal system relies heavily on common-law decisions dating back to the legal system that was used in England before the establishment of the United States.

People enter the U.S. criminal justice system through a variety of means. They may be issued a citation for a traffic violation witnessed by a law enforcement officer. They may be arrested for a more serious crime by a law enforcement officer who has probable cause to believe they committed a crime. They may be arrested because of issuance of a warrant for their arrest by a court. An arrest warrant is a legal document signed by a judge or a magistrate who believes there is compelling evidence that the person named in the warrant has committed a particular crime.

A person charged with a crime falls under the legal and judicial system of the government body with appropriate jurisdiction, such as the city, county, state, or federal government. These systems may differ in structure and mode of operation, but under U.S. law they all must provide certain legal rights to arrested people.

TABLE 6.4

Arrests, by age, 2015

Offense charged	Total all ages	Ages under 18	Ages 18 and over	18	19	20	21	22	23	24	25–29	30–34	35–39	40–44	45–49	50–54	55–59	60–64	65 and over
Total	8,305,919	709,333	7,596,586	273,160	298,988	302,084	309,730	314,334	318,362	315,966	1,379,975	1,121,695	841,019	626,209	541,069	453,198	279,782	130,856	90,159
Total percent distribution[a]	100.0	8.5	91.5	3.3	3.6	3.6	3.7	3.8	3.8	3.8	16.6	13.5	10.1	7.5	6.5	5.5	3.4	1.6	1.1
Murder and nonnegligent manslaughter	8,533	605	7,928	454	469	466	472	465	458	414	1,472	1,055	690	446	347	310	199	103	108
Rape[b]	17,504	2,745	14,759	761	724	683	641	568	497	552	2,187	2,096	1,668	1,349	1,025	890	523	283	312
Robbery	73,230	14,176	59,054	5,155	4,483	3,927	3,706	3,333	3,253	2,870	11,220	7,515	4,875	3,066	2,537	1,770	911	293	140
Aggravated assault	288,815	21,993	266,822	7,002	7,942	8,691	10,020	10,606	10,892	10,921	49,508	41,106	31,409	23,556	19,948	16,439	10,180	4,723	3,879
Burglary	166,609	27,473	139,136	8,297	7,603	6,748	6,714	6,400	6,235	5,978	26,532	21,027	14,609	9,440	8,293	6,180	3,212	1,246	622
Larceny-theft	900,077	120,967	779,110	40,062	37,084	33,313	31,704	31,411	31,506	31,116	139,353	114,463	83,749	61,570	53,989	43,630	25,744	12,046	8,370
Motor vehicle theft	59,831	11,169	48,662	2,846	2,508	2,376	2,269	2,196	2,299	2,154	9,895	7,967	5,470	3,477	2,518	1,586	732	235	134
Arson	6,802	2,083	4,719	188	174	180	162	171	181	172	733	718	492	371	352	388	231	120	86
Violent crime[c]	388,082	39,519	348,563	13,372	13,618	13,767	14,839	14,972	15,100	14,757	64,387	51,772	38,642	28,417	23,857	19,409	11,813	5,402	4,439
Violent crime percent distribution[a]	100.0	10.2	89.8	3.4	3.5	3.5	3.8	3.9	3.9	3.8	16.6	13.3	10.0	7.3	6.1	5.0	3.0	1.4	1.1
Property crime[c]	1,133,319	161,692	971,627	51,393	47,369	42,617	40,849	40,178	40,221	39,420	176,513	144,175	104,320	74,858	65,152	51,784	29,919	13,647	9,212
Property crime percent distribution[a]	100.0	14.3	85.7	4.5	4.2	3.8	3.6	3.5	3.5	3.5	15.6	12.7	9.2	6.6	5.7	4.6	2.6	1.2	0.8
Other assaults	831,684	100,980	730,704	19,677	20,837	22,966	27,180	28,584	29,585	29,717	132,963	112,028	87,498	67,150	56,395	46,272	27,292	12,582	9,978
Forgery and counterfeiting	42,681	791	41,890	1,071	1,518	1,840	1,454	1,628	1,737	1,835	8,435	7,109	5,244	3,621	2,773	1,988	1,020	392	225
Fraud	102,339	3,474	98,865	2,146	2,794	3,332	3,210	3,448	3,609	3,794	18,412	16,365	12,882	9,704	7,597	5,513	3,290	1,534	1,235
Embezzlement	12,247	450	11,797	597	727	693	613	590	592	498	2,118	1,567	1,172	894	692	520	300	152	72
Stolen property; buying, receiving, possessing	68,341	7,990	60,351	3,021	2,896	2,723	2,895	2,711	2,786	2,787	12,109	9,797	6,847	4,381	3,335	2,218	1,158	444	243
Vandalism	147,191	32,145	115,046	6,489	5,960	5,551	6,032	5,798	5,735	5,242	21,780	16,246	11,378	7,825	6,480	5,144	2,992	1,336	1,058
Weapons; carrying, possessing, etc.	111,316	14,779	96,537	4,802	4,993	4,875	5,200	5,210	5,113	4,999	19,258	13,820	9,272	6,146	4,651	3,616	2,347	1,176	1,059
Prostitution and commercialized vice	31,534	442	31,092	849	1,217	1,324	1,531	1,530	1,520	1,386	6,055	4,307	3,302	2,605	2,072	1,628	938	462	366
Sex offenses (except rape and prostitution)	39,393	6,699	32,694	1,235	1,223	1,162	1,128	1,026	1,028	923	4,356	4,090	3,573	2,946	2,771	2,643	1,894	1,180	1,516
Drug abuse violations	1,144,021	76,172	1,067,849	53,900	57,847	55,280	53,268	52,807	51,912	49,946	205,891	156,861	109,234	73,329	59,919	46,557	26,193	10,504	4,401
Gambling	3,607	357	3,250	194	168	165	134	139	133	104	504	354	281	248	251	184	185	115	91
Offenses against the family and children	72,418	2,628	69,790	897	1,014	1,193	1,517	1,863	2,105	2,363	13,044	13,546	11,591	7,955	5,594	3,886	1,951	787	484
Driving under the influence	833,833	5,064	828,769	10,593	16,240	20,362	32,328	34,643	36,388	36,175	152,191	118,442	90,822	73,910	66,488	59,941	41,420	22,020	16,806
Liquor laws	204,665	33,155	171,510	30,639	33,468	28,000	5,069	3,623	3,118	2,728	10,843	9,380	8,204	7,701	8,406	8,865	6,424	3,193	1,849
Drunkenness	314,856	4,243	310,613	5,606	7,002	7,345	11,430	10,755	10,587	10,568	45,607	40,605	33,778	29,756	31,456	31,190	20,513	9,468	4,947
Disorderly conduct	298,253	55,102	243,151	9,850	9,111	9,194	12,069	11,314	10,584	10,083	41,008	32,051	24,685	19,523	18,207	16,329	10,479	4,990	3,674
Vagrancy	19,414	825	18,589	436	427	441	447	472	518	475	2,415	2,300	2,006	1,668	2,025	2,111	1,646	813	389
All other offenses (except traffic)	2,471,772	128,770	2,343,002	56,351	70,523	79,221	88,495	93,015	95,947	98,133	441,911	366,753	276,185	203,494	172,901	143,345	87,987	40,648	28,093
Suspicion	1,045	148	897	42	36	33	42	28	44	33	175	127	103	78	47	55	21	11	22
Curfew and loitering law violations	33,908	33,908	—	—	—	—	—	—	—	—	—	—	—	—	—	—	—	—	—

[a]Because of rounding, the percentages may not add to 100.0.
[b]The rape figures in this table are aggregate totals of the data submitted based on both the legacy and revised Uniform Crime Reporting definitions.
[c]Violent crimes are offenses of murder and nonnegligent manslaughter, rape, robbery, and aggravated assault. Property crimes are offenses of burglary, larceny-theft, motor vehicle theft, and arson.

SOURCE: Adapted from "Table 38. Arrests by Age, 2015," in *Crime in the United States, 2015*, U.S. Department of Justice, Federal Bureau of Investigation. September 26, 2016, https://ucr.fbi.gov/crime-in-the-u.s/2015/crime-in-the-u.s.-2015/tables/table-38 (accessed January 21, 2017)

TABLE 6.5

Arrests, by sex, 2015

Offense charged	Number of persons arrested			Percent male	Percent female
	Total	Male	Female		
Total	**8,305,919**	**6,067,584**	**2,238,335**	**73.1**	**26.9**
Murder and nonnegligent manslaughter	8,533	7,549	984	88.5	11.5
Rape[a]	17,504	16,990	514	97.1	2.9
Robbery	73,230	62,721	10,509	85.6	14.4
Aggravated assault	288,815	221,993	66,822	76.9	23.1
Burglary	166,609	135,064	31,545	81.1	18.9
Larceny-theft	900,077	511,557	388,520	56.8	43.2
Motor vehicle theft	59,831	47,169	12,662	78.8	21.2
Arson	6,802	5,460	1,342	80.3	19.7
Violent crime[b]	388,082	309,253	78,829	79.7	20.3
Property crime[b]	1,133,319	699,250	434,069	61.7	38.3
Other assaults	831,684	598,000	233,684	71.9	28.1
Forgery and counterfeiting	42,681	27,596	15,085	64.7	35.3
Fraud	102,339	62,721	39,618	61.3	38.7
Embezzlement	12,247	6,093	6,154	49.8	50.2
Stolen property; buying, receiving, possessing	68,341	53,621	14,720	78.5	21.5
Vandalism	147,191	115,695	31,496	78.6	21.4
Weapons; carrying, possessing, etc.	111,316	101,366	9,950	91.1	8.9
Prostitution and commercialized vice	31,534	11,355	20,179	36.0	64.0
Sex offenses (except rape and prostitution)	39,393	36,361	3,032	92.3	7.7
Drug abuse violations	1,144,021	886,022	257,999	77.4	22.6
Gambling	3,607	2,883	724	79.9	20.1
Offenses against the family and children	72,418	51,598	20,820	71.3	28.7
Driving under the influence	833,833	625,927	207,906	75.1	24.9
Liquor laws	204,665	145,238	59,427	71.0	29.0
Drunkenness	314,856	253,565	61,291	80.5	19.5
Disorderly conduct	298,253	214,118	84,135	71.8	28.2
Vagrancy	19,414	15,080	4,334	77.7	22.3
All other offenses (except traffic)	2,471,772	1,826,711	645,061	73.9	26.1
Suspicion	1,045	802	243	76.7	23.3
Curfew and loitering law violations	33,908	24,329	9,579	71.8	28.2

[a]The rape figures in this table are aggregate totals of the data submitted based on both the legacy and revised Uniform Crime Reporting definitions.
[b]Violent crimes are offenses of murder and nonnegligent manslaughter, rape, robbery, and aggravated assault. Property crimes are offenses of burglary, larceny-theft, motor vehicle theft, and arson.
Note: Because of rounding, the percentages may not add to 100.0.

SOURCE: Adapted from "Table 42. Arrests by Sex, 2015," in *Crime in the United States, 2015*, U.S. Department of Justice, Federal Bureau of Investigation, September 26, 2016, https://ucr.fbi.gov/crime-in-the-u.s/2015/crime-in-the-u.s.-2015/tables/table-42 (accessed January 21, 2017)

The Rights of the Arrested

People placed under arrest (with or without a warrant) must be told their Miranda rights before being questioned about their alleged crime by law enforcement officials. Miranda rights stem from the 1966 U.S. Supreme Court decision *Miranda v. Arizona* (384 U.S. 436). The court ruled that arrested individuals must be told about their constitutional rights to an attorney and against self-incrimination before they are subjected to any questioning about their alleged crime. Although the so-called Miranda warning takes several forms, it must cover the following basic concepts:

- The arrestee has the right to remain silent during police questioning.

- Anything the arrestee says to the police can be used against him or her at trial.

- The arrestee has the right to an attorney.

- If the arrestee cannot afford an attorney, one will be appointed for him or her at the government's expense.

In addition, arrested individuals have the right to know the charges against them and to see any arrest warrants that are used to make the arrest. According to the American Bar Association, in "Steps in a Trial: Arrest Procedures" (2017, http://www.americanbar.org/groups/public_education/resources/law_related_education_network/how_courts_work/arrestprocedure.html), a person arrested without a warrant can be held by the police for only a limited period (typically 48 hours) before making his or her first court appearance, or arraignment, before a judge or magistrate.

The Role of Prosecutors

Government jurisdictions have their own unique legal systems. Each system is typically headed by a public official. At the state level this official may be called the state attorney. At the lower levels of government, such as counties or cities, officials may be called district attorneys, county or city attorneys, or simply prosecutors. A prosecutor represents the legal authority of his or her geographical area and supervises the legal

TABLE 6.6

Arrests, by race, 2015

Offense charged	Total arrests — Race						Percent distribution[a]					
	Total	White	Black or African American	American Indian or Alaska Native	Asian	Native Hawaiian or other Pacific Islander	Total	White	Black or African American	American Indian or Alaska Native	Asian	Native Hawaiian or other Pacific Islander
Total	8,248,709	5,753,212	2,197,140	174,020	101,064	23,273	100.0	69.7	26.6	2.1	1.2	0.3
Murder and nonnegligent manslaughter	8,508	3,908	4,347	102	126	25	100.0	45.9	51.1	1.2	1.5	0.3
Rape[b]	17,370	11,809	4,907	301	271	82	100.0	68.0	28.2	1.7	1.6	0.5
Robbery	73,023	32,439	39,052	562	668	302	100.0	44.4	53.5	0.8	0.9	0.4
Aggravated assault	287,566	184,024	92,237	5,836	4,631	838	100.0	64.0	32.1	2.0	1.6	0.3
Burglary	165,948	112,992	48,907	1,686	1,963	400	100.0	68.1	29.5	1.0	1.2	0.2
Larceny-theft	893,707	621,585	244,722	14,311	11,078	2,011	100.0	69.6	27.4	1.6	1.2	0.2
Motor vehicle theft	59,533	40,000	17,499	917	763	354	100.0	67.2	29.4	1.5	1.3	0.6
Arson	6,762	4,952	1,519	177	88	26	100.0	73.2	22.5	2.6	1.3	0.4
Violent crime[c]	386,467	232,180	140,543	6,801	5,696	1,247	100.0	60.1	36.4	1.8	1.5	0.3
Property crime[c]	1,125,950	779,529	312,647	17,091	13,892	2,791	100.0	69.2	27.8	1.5	1.2	0.2
Other assaults	826,920	544,870	254,600	15,039	9,910	2,501	100.0	65.9	30.8	1.8	1.2	0.3
Forgery and counterfeiting	42,436	27,419	14,001	293	644	79	100.0	64.6	33.0	0.7	1.5	0.2
Fraud	101,556	67,594	31,495	1,157	1,171	139	100.0	66.6	31.0	1.1	1.2	0.1
Embezzlement	12,169	7,378	4,482	83	203	23	100.0	60.6	36.8	0.7	1.7	0.2
Stolen property; buying, receiving, possessing	68,057	44,561	21,783	751	832	130	100.0	65.5	32.0	1.1	1.2	0.2
Vandalism	146,090	101,481	39,778	2,816	1,667	348	100.0	69.5	27.2	1.9	1.1	0.2
Weapons; carrying, possessing, etc.	110,822	63,967	44,284	1,099	1,244	228	100.0	57.7	40.0	1.0	1.1	0.2
Prostitution and commercialized vice	31,362	17,084	12,513	111	1,599	55	100.0	54.5	39.9	0.4	5.1	0.2
Sex offenses (except rape and prostitution)	39,184	28,650	9,058	614	729	133	100.0	73.1	23.1	1.6	1.9	0.3
Drug abuse violations	1,136,950	803,809	307,140	11,717	12,436	1,848	100.0	70.7	27.0	1.0	1.1	0.2
Gambling	3,597	1,296	2,028	23	230	20	100.0	36.0	56.4	0.6	6.4	0.6
Offenses against the family and children	71,865	47,312	21,425	2,552	538	38	100.0	65.8	29.8	3.6	0.7	0.1
Driving under the influence	825,218	681,628	108,590	16,042	16,421	2,537	100.0	82.6	13.2	1.9	2.0	0.3
Liquor laws	201,550	160,772	27,742	9,788	2,749	499	100.0	79.8	13.8	4.9	1.4	0.2
Drunkenness	313,390	239,556	44,676	25,660	3,037	461	100.0	76.4	14.3	8.2	1.0	0.1
Disorderly conduct	295,835	189,321	91,716	11,912	2,311	575	100.0	64.0	31.0	4.0	0.8	0.2
Vagrancy	19,268	13,247	5,143	668	195	15	100.0	68.8	26.7	3.5	1.0	0.1
All other offenses (except traffic)	2,455,238	1,683,297	688,146	49,114	25,197	9,484	100.0	68.6	28.0	2.0	1.0	0.4
Suspicion	1,085	479	297	293	11	5	100.0	44.1	27.4	27.0	1.0	0.5
Curfew and loitering law violations	33,700	17,782	15,053	396	352	117	100.0	52.8	44.7	1.2	1.0	0.3

[a]Because of rounding, the percentages may not add to 100.0.

[b]The rape figures in this table are aggregate totals of the data submitted based on both the legacy and revised Uniform Crime Reporting definitions.

[c]Violent crimes are offenses of murder and nonnegligent manslaughter, rape, robbery, and aggravated assault. Property crimes are offenses of burglary, larceny-theft, motor vehicle theft, and arson.

SOURCE: Adapted from "Table 43.A. Arrests by Race and Ethnicity, 2015," in *Crime in the United States, 2015*, U.S. Department of Justice, Federal Bureau of Investigation, September 26, 2016, https://ucr.fbi.gov/crime-in-the-u.s/2015/crime-in-the-u.s.-2015/tables/table-43 (accessed January 21, 2017)

FIGURE 6.2

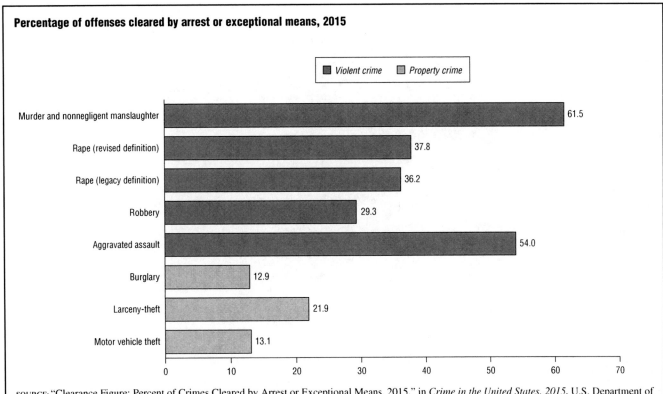

Percentage of offenses cleared by arrest or exceptional means, 2015

▨ Violent crime   ▨ Property crime

Offense	Value
Murder and nonnegligent manslaughter	61.5
Rape (revised definition)	37.8
Rape (legacy definition)	36.2
Robbery	29.3
Aggravated assault	54.0
Burglary	12.9
Larceny-theft	21.9
Motor vehicle theft	13.1

SOURCE: "Clearance Figure: Percent of Crimes Cleared by Arrest or Exceptional Means, 2015," in *Crime in the United States, 2015*, U.S. Department of Justice, Federal Bureau of Investigation, September 26, 2016, https://ucr.fbi.gov/crime-in-the-u.s/2015/crime-in-the-u.s.-2015/offenses-known-to-law-enforcement/clearances/clearances (accessed January 21, 2017)

prosecution of suspected criminals. These cases are often referred to prosecutors' offices by law enforcement agencies. Some states also use grand juries to file criminal charges against suspected criminals. Grand juries consist of local citizens who are summoned by a court to serve for a specified period. They do not determine the guilt or innocence of the accused, but they do determine if there is enough evidence to bind over the accused to stand trial. If so, the grand jury issues a formal charge called an indictment.

Some district attorneys are elected into office, whereas others are appointed by higher public officials. A prosecutor acts on behalf of the people within a jurisdiction to ensure that its criminal laws are enforced and that criminals are prosecuted. If a case goes to trial, the prosecutor is responsible for presenting the evidence against the defendant. Not all criminal cases proceed to trial. In fact, many are settled through alternative means, such as plea bargains.

PLEA BARGAINS. In a plea bargain the prosecutor and the defendant's attorney reach an agreement about how a case should be settled before it goes to trial. A typical example involves an offer from the prosecutor for the defendant to plead guilty to a lesser charge than the one originally filed against him or her. Another common plea bargain occurs when the defendant agrees to plead guilty

to a charge in exchange for a recommendation by the prosecutor for a lighter sentence than would be expected to result from a guilty verdict if the case went to trial. Prosecutors are motivated to negotiate plea bargains because criminal trials can be long and costly, and their outcomes are not certain. Defendants may choose to plea bargain to avoid the publicity and legal expense of a trial and the likely harsher sentence that will result from a guilty verdict. The American Bar Association indicates in "Steps in a Trial: Plea Bargaining" (2017, http://www.americanbar.org/groups/public_education/resources/law_related_education_network/how_courts_work/pleabargaining.html) that plea bargains resolve most of the criminal cases in most jurisdictions in the United States.

THE JUDICIARY SYSTEM

The judiciary system tries perpetrators in a court of law and, if they are found guilty, sentences them to a period of incarceration or some other form of punishment, restitution (an amount of money that is set by a court to be paid to the victim of a crime for property losses or injuries caused by the crime), and/or mental health treatment such as drug rehabilitation.

The judiciary system includes all criminal courts and the judges and juries that operate within them. There are two main levels of the judiciary system in the United States: federal courts and state/local courts.

TABLE 6.7

Federal courts

U.S. Supreme Court

U.S. Courts of Appeals

First Circuit
Second Circuit
Third Circuit
Fourth Circuit
Fifth Circuit
Sixth Circuit
Seventh Circuit
Eighth Circuit
Ninth Circuit
Tenth Circuit
Eleventh Circuit
District of Columbia Circuit
Federal Circuit

U.S. District Courts

Alabama Middle
Alabama Northern
Alabama Southern
Alaska
Arizona
Arkansas Eastern
Arkansas Western
California Central
California Eastern
California Northern
California Southern
Colorado
Connecticut
Delaware
District of Columbia
Florida Middle
Florida Northern
Florida Southern
Georgia Middle
Georgia Northern
Georgia Southern
Guam
Hawaii
Idaho
Illinois Central
Illinois Northern
Illinois Southern
Indiana Northern
Indiana Southern
Iowa Northern
Iowa Southern
Kansas
Kentucky Eastern
Kentucky Western
Louisiana Eastern
Louisiana Middle
Louisiana Western
Maine
Maryland
Massachusetts
Michigan Eastern
Michigan Western
Minnesota
Mississippi Northern
Mississippi Southern
Missouri Eastern
Missouri Western
Montana
Nebraska
Nevada
New Hampshire
New Jersey
New Mexico
New York Eastern

TABLE 6.7

Federal courts [CONTINUED]

New York Northern
New York Southern
New York Western
North Carolina Eastern
North Carolina Middle
North Carolina Western
North Dakota
Northern Mariana Islands
Ohio Northern
Ohio Southern
Oklahoma Eastern
Oklahoma Northern
Oklahoma Western
Oregon
Pennsylvania Eastern
Pennsylvania Middle
Pennsylvania Western
Puerto Rico
Rhode Island
South Carolina
South Dakota
Tennessee Eastern
Tennessee Middle
Tennessee Western
Texas Eastern
Texas Northern
Texas Southern
Texas Western
Utah
Vermont
Virgin Islands
Virginia Eastern
Virginia Western
Washington Eastern
Washington Western
West Virginia Northern
West Virginia Southern
Wisconsin Eastern
Wisconsin Western
Wyoming

SOURCE: "Court Website Links," in *About Federal Courts*, U.S. Courts, undated, http://www.uscourts.gov/about-federal-courts/federal-courts-public/court-website-links (accessed January 21, 2017)

The federal court system includes three arms—U.S. District Courts, U.S. Courts of Appeals, and the U.S. Supreme Court. (See Table 6.7.) The district courts are divided into 12 regional circuits. (See Figure 6.3; note that the 12th circuit is the District of Columbia.) The district courts serve as trial courts in the federal system. Decisions issued by these courts can be appealed under certain circumstances by lawyers representing the defendant (the charged person) or by federal prosecutors. Each federal circuit has a U.S. court of appeals. The U.S. Supreme Court is the highest court in the United States. It hears a limited number of cases each year that primarily address issues related to federal law or the U.S. Constitution.

Every state has its own court system. These systems differ by state, but in general they include local or municipal courts, county-level courts, district courts, state appeals courts, and state supreme courts. Typically, local, municipal, and county courts have jurisdiction over misdemeanors, whereas district courts have jurisdiction over felony criminal cases.

FIGURE 6.3

Map of the geographical boundaries of the U.S. Courts of Appeal and U.S. District Courts

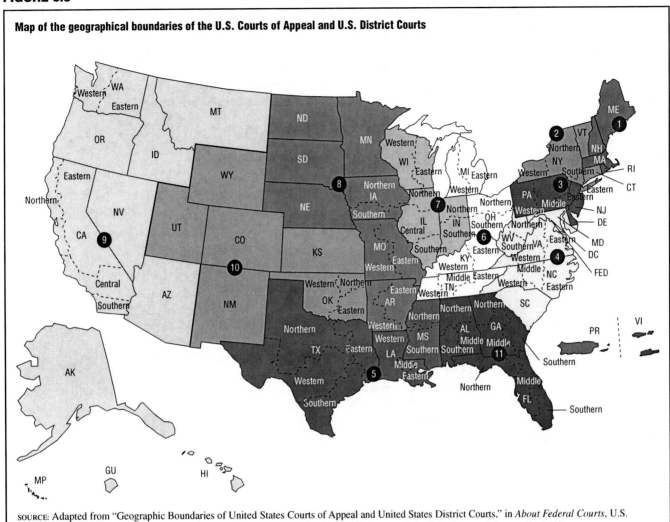

SOURCE: Adapted from "Geographic Boundaries of United States Courts of Appeal and United States District Courts," in *About Federal Courts*, U.S. Courts, undated, http://www.uscourts.gov/about-federal-courts/federal-courts-public/court-website-links (accessed January 21, 2017)

Pretrial Procedures

Arrested individuals typically appear before a judge or magistrate within 24 to 72 hours of being arrested. This first court appearance may be called an arraignment. In some large cities, arrestees do not travel to a courtroom, but are arraigned from jail via two-way video proceedings. An arraignment is not a trial, but a formal presentation of the charges against the defendant. Generally the defendant is asked for a plea, such as guilty, not guilty, or "Nolo contendere" (which is Latin for "I will not contest it"). A defendant who pleads "no contest" does not admit guilt but agrees to accept the punishment meted out for a guilty plea. Many defendants plead not guilty during their arraignment hearings, which means their cases are then scheduled for trial. Some defendants, especially those charged with minor offenses, may plead guilty or no contest. Depending on the circumstances the judge may then pass sentence or schedule a later sentencing hearing.

In many cases, arraignment hearings also include the consideration of bail, which is in effect a security deposit

intended to ensure that the defendant shows up for the trial. Bail is often in cash form, but property and other assets of value may also be posted. Defendants who post bail are allowed to remain free until their trials. Some defendants may be "released on their own recognizance," meaning that they sign a written statement promising that they will show up for trial. They are not required to provide a security deposit.

During a bail hearing the prosecutor and defense attorney provide input to the judge who decides whether or not bail should be granted and, if so, the monetary amount. These decisions are based on various factors including the seriousness of the alleged crime, the defendant's ties to the community (e.g., home ownership, employment, and family ties), and the defendant's flight risk. Defendants charged with serious violent crimes, such as murder, may not be granted bail or may be assessed a bail amount that is relatively high. The U.S. Constitution prohibits excessive bail; however, there is no universally accepted definition of what constitutes "excessive bail." In "Nevada Supreme Court Rebukes

Judge for Too-Harsh Treatment of Defendant" (Review-Journal.com, April 12, 2013), Francis McCabe notes that in 2013 the Nevada Supreme Court overruled a state judge who had set the bail amount for a defendant at $1 million "to punish him for having an attitude during a court hearing." The bail amount for the defendant, who had been arrested on drug charges, was lowered to $3,000.

Depending on the jurisdiction, there are various ways in which defendants can meet their bail obligations and avoid pretrial detention. One choice is to pay the court the entire bail amount in cash. If the defendant shows up for the trial the money (perhaps minus some administrative fees) is refunded to the defendant. If the defendant does not show up for trial, the money is forfeited (kept by the court). Alternatively, defendants, or someone close to them, may pledge property or other valuable assets they own as a security deposit. If the defendant fails to appear for trial, then the assets can be seized by the court.

Another option in many states is a bail bond company. In general, the defendant pays the company a cash fee that is usually a percentage of the entire bail amount (typically around 10%). The company takes the responsibility for the rest of the bail amount. The fee is nonrefundable; it is retained by the bail bond company. Some bail bond companies also require that property or other assets be pledged as guarantees. Then, if the defendant fails to appear for the trial, the company can take possession of the assets. Note that some states (e.g., Illinois and Kentucky) do not allow private bail bond companies to operate. In these jurisdictions bail and bond arrangements are made directly with the courts or through law enforcement agencies.

Trial and Sentencing

The U.S. Constitution guarantees defendants the right to a "speedy" trial and prohibits the imposition of "cruel and unusual punishment." Claims alleging violations of the speedy trial provision are rather common, and several have reached the U.S. Supreme Court. For example, in 2016 the U.S. Supreme Court ruled in *Betterman v. Montana* (No. 14-1457) that the right to a speedy trial applies only to the conviction phase of a trial, not the sentencing phase. The prohibition against cruel and unusual punishment is mainly a factor in capital punishment (death penalty) cases.

Some defendants have their cases dismissed or are acquitted (found not guilty) at trial. Defendants who plead guilty or are found guilty face measures including incarceration, fines, payment of restitution, and/or probation. According to Danielle Kaeble and Thomas P. Bonczar of the DOJ's Bureau of Justice Statistics (BJS), in *Probation and Parole in the United States, 2015* (December 2016, https://www.bjs.gov/content/pub/pdf/ppus15.pdf), probation is defined as "a court-ordered period of correctional supervision in the community." Convicted defendants can be sentenced to prison or probation or receive split sentences including a period of incarceration followed by a period of probation. Another alternative is a suspended sentence. In an unconditional suspended sentence the convicted defendant faces no penalty, but the conviction stays on his or her record. In a conditional suspended sentence the convicted defendant is given an amount of time in which he or she must meet certain conditions (e.g., pay restitution and/or commit no further crimes). If the conditions are met, the person avoids any prison time included in the sentence. If the conditions are not met, however, the person faces incarceration.

Alternative Sentencing

Forms of sentencing other than incarceration, probation, or a combination of the two (split sentences) are widely used in the United States. These programs can vary, but options include work-release and weekender programs, community service programs, day fines, day reporting centers, intensive probation supervision, house arrest and electronic monitoring, residential community corrections, and diversionary treatment programs. Other types of alternative sentencing options, such as mediation and restitution, are sometimes available.

WORK RELEASE AND WEEKENDER PROGRAMS. Work-release programs permit selected prisoners nearing the end of their sentence to work in the community and return to prison facilities or community residential facilities during nonworking hours. Such programs are designed to prepare inmates to return to the community in a relatively controlled environment while they are learning how to work productively. Work release also allows inmates to earn an income, reimburse the state for part of their confinement costs, build up savings for their eventual full release, and acquire more positive living habits. Those on weekender programs spend certain days in prison, usually weekends, but are free the remainder of the time. Both of these types of sentences are known as intermittent incarceration. Violent offenders and those convicted of drug offenses are usually excluded from these programs by the courts.

COMMUNITY SERVICE PROGRAMS. Community service is most often a supplement to other penalties and mainly given to white-collar criminals, juvenile delinquents, and those who commit nonserious crimes. Offenders are usually required to work for government or private nonprofit agencies cleaning parks, collecting roadside trash, setting up chairs for community events, painting community projects, and helping out at nursing homes.

DAY FINES. Under the day-fines type of alternative sentence, the offender pays a monetary sum rather than spending time in jail or prison. Day fines are fines that are assessed for a specific number of days in which the fine amount is based on the seriousness of the crime, the criminal record of the offender, and the offender's income. The fines are paid into the jurisdiction's treasury.

DAY REPORTING CENTERS. Day reporting centers (DRCs) allow offenders to reside in the community. DRCs are often populated by people with drug and alcohol problems and require offenders to appear on a frequent and regular basis to participate in services or activities that are provided by the center or other community agencies. Random drug screening and breathalyzer tests may be administered. The centers may provide employment and educational training and conduct classes on topics such as anger management, substance abuse, life skills, and cognitive skills. Failure to adhere to program requirements or to report at stated intervals can lead to commitment to prison or jail. DRC participation can also be terminated if the offender is charged with a new crime.

INTENSIVE PROBATION SUPERVISION. Intensive probation supervision (IPS) is another method of closely supervising offenders while they reside in the community. Routine probation is not designed or structured to handle high-risk probationers. Therefore, IPS was developed as an alternative that is stricter than routine probation.

The caseloads of officers assigned to IPS offenders are kept low. In most IPS programs the offender must contact a supervising officer frequently, pay restitution to victims, participate in community service, have and keep a job, and, if appropriate, undergo random and unannounced drug testing. Offenders are often required to pay a probation fee.

HOUSE ARREST AND ELECTRONIC MONITORING. Some offenders are sentenced to house arrest (or home confinement), which means that they are legally required to remain confined in their own home. They are allowed to leave only for medical purposes or to go to work, although some curfew programs permit offenders to work during the day and have a specified number of hours of free time before returning home. The idea began as a way to keep drunk drivers off the street, but it quickly expanded to include other nonviolent offenders.

The most severe type of house arrest is home incarceration, where the offender's home actually becomes a prison that he or she cannot leave except for very special reasons, such as medical emergencies. Home-detention programs require the offender to be at home when he or she is not working. Some offenders are required to perform a certain number of hours of community service and, if they are employed, to repay the cost of probation and/or restitution.

An electronic monitoring program (EMP) that is used in tandem with house arrest involves attaching a small radio transmitter to the offender in a nonremovable bracelet or anklet. Some systems send a signal to a small monitoring box, which is programmed to call a department of corrections computer if the signal is broken; other systems randomly call probationers and the computer verifies each prisoner's identity through voice recognition software. In some cases a special device in the electronic monitor sends a confirmation to the computer. Some systems have global positioning system technologies to help corrections officers ensure that offenders are not violating any territorial restrictions.

EMPs are often used to monitor the whereabouts of those who are under house arrest and permitted to work. Electronic monitoring is sometimes used to ensure that child molesters stay a specified distance from schools. EMPs cost much less than building new prison cells or housing more inmates. However, close supervision by officers is crucial to the success of EMPs. Officers must ensure that the participants are indeed working when they leave the house and that they are not using illegal drugs. Electronic monitoring equipment must also be checked periodically to make certain that the offenders have not attempted to disable the equipment.

RESIDENTIAL COMMUNITY CORRECTIONS. Residential community corrections facilities are known informally as halfway houses because they are designed as a halfway step from prison to help prisoners reintegrate into community life. Some offenders are sentenced to halfway houses directly in lieu of incarceration if their offenses and general profile indicate they will benefit from the structure and counseling available in such facilities. Many states frequently use halfway houses to relieve prison overcrowding.

Residential centers house offenders in a structured environment. Offenders work full time, maintain the residence center, perform community service, and sometimes attend educational or counseling programs. They may leave the centers only for work or approved programs such as substance-abuse treatment. One type of residential program, called a restitution center, allows offenders to work to pay restitution and child support. The centers regularly test the residents for drugs.

DIVERSIONARY TREATMENT PROGRAMS. Probation combined with mandatory treatment programs is used as an alternative sentence for nonviolent offenders convicted of drug offenses, alcohol abuse, or nonviolent sex offenses. Sentenced individuals are free on probation but typically are required to attend group therapy and supervised professional treatment sessions.

MEDIATION AND RESTITUTION. In mediation victims and offenders meet under the auspices of a community representative and work out a "reconciliation," usually involving some type of restitution and requiring the offenders to take responsibility for their actions. This technique is used mainly for minor crimes and often involves private organizations; therefore, the judiciary does not always accept its resolution. Most often, restitution is not considered the complete punishment but part of a broader punishment, such as probation or working off the restitution dollar amount while in prison.

Adjudication and Sentencing Outcomes

The U.S. Sentencing Commission (USSC) is an independent federal agency that oversees federal sentencing practices. In *Overview of Federal Criminal Cases Fiscal Year 2015* (June 2016, http://www.ussc.gov/sites/default/files/pdf/research-and-publications/research-publications/2016/FY15_Overview_Federal_Criminal_Cases.pdf), the USSC provides data about 71,184 federal criminal cases in which the offender was sentenced during fiscal year 2015 (October 2014 to September 2015). The two largest caseload categories were drug cases (31.8%) and immigration cases (29.3%). Overall, 97.1% of the defendants pleaded guilty. Nearly nine out of 10 offenders (87.3%) were sentenced to prison. Other sentences included probation with no confinement (7.2%), a combination of imprisonment and community confinement, such as a halfway house or home confinement (2.9%), and a combination of confinement and probation (2.6%).

The BJS compiles national conviction and sentencing data for the state courts. As of April 2017, the most recent data available from a nationally representative survey were for 2006. In *Felony Sentences in State Courts, 2006—Statistical Tables* (November 22, 2010, https://www.bjs.gov/content/pub/pdf/fssc06st.pdf), Sean Rosenmerkel, Matthew Durose, and Donald Farole of the BJS report that 1.1 million defendants were convicted of felonies in state courts in 2006. Nearly all of the felons (94%) pleaded guilty, many presumably as a result of plea bargains. Only 6% were convicted through a trial— 4% by juries and 2% by the bench (i.e., by a judge). In 2006 more than two-thirds (69%) of the convicted felons were sentenced to prison or jail time. Another 27% were given probation with no prison or jail time. The remaining 4% faced no prison or jail time or probation, but received other sentences including payment of fines or restitution; court-ordered testing (e.g., for drug use), treatment, or community service; or some other penalty.

CRIMINAL JUSTICE SYSTEM REFORMS

As is shown in Figure 2.4 in Chapter 2, the violent crime rate in the United States soared upwards through the early 1990s. Politicians responded to public concern with "get tough on crime" policies including mandatory minimum sentences and stiffer penalties for many offenses. Mandatory minimum sentences were driven in large part by public frustration with judges who meted out sentences that were considered too lenient. In addition, many states passed "truth-in-sentencing" laws to limit the authority of prison officials to release prisoners early, such as for good behavior. Parole policies also came under fire. (Parole is a period of supervision for inmates who are released from prison, particularly those released before completing their entire sentence.) The federal system abolished parole through the Sentencing Reform Act of 1984. Over the following decade, the public was outraged by horrific crimes committed by state parolees, including the 1993 abduction and murder in California of 12-year-old Polly Klaas. Many states greatly restricted their parole programs and some states (such as Virginia) abolished them.

As the prison population boomed, social justice advocates decried mass incarceration as a knee-jerk reaction to crime. They instead focused attention on issues related to social inequality and high incarceration rates for people of color. Critics also note that incarcerating more people for longer periods requires more prisons and increases corrections costs for maintaining prisoners. Reducing or eliminating the possibility of parole results in an increasing number of elderly prisoners, who are statistically much less likely to commit crimes than younger prisoners and who have increasing health care needs. Public concern about perceived unfairness in the criminal justice system did motivate some reforms; for example, Chapter 4 describes the relaxed sentencing guidelines that were implemented for crack cocaine possession.

The nation's "get tough on crime" policies put a tremendous strain on the prison and jail systems, which are described in detail in Chapter 7. Overcrowding became a lingering problem. The huge cost of building, operating, and maintaining prisons began to consume ever-larger portions of state budgets. This stress became especially acute during the later years of the first decade of the 21st century when the country entered a sharp economic downturn known as the Great Recession. By this time the crime rate was down dramatically from its previous heights. Advocates for reform found the public much more open to reducing the incarcerated population. The old mantra of "get tough on crime" slowly lost luster in favor of a more nuanced approach to "get smart on crime."

"Three Strikes and You're Out"

Nine years after passing the first truth-in-sentencing law, the state of Washington passed the first of the so-called three-strikes laws in December 1993. Three-strikes laws mandate a fixed sentence length for repeat offenders for specified crimes or a mix of crimes. The laws are intended to ensure that an offender receives a mandatory long sentence upon conviction for the third offense, such as life imprisonment without parole (as in the state of Washington) or 25 years without parole (as in California). These sentences guaranteed that a repeat criminal would be removed from society for a long time or, in some instances, for life. Although three-strikes laws are best known for their imposition of long sentences on a third offense, they also feature longer-than-average sentences for second offenses.

OPPOSITION AND CHALLENGES TO THREE-STRIKES LAWS. Opponents of three-strikes laws charge that the laws unfairly target African Americans, who are disproportionately represented among felony convicts. They argue that three-strikes laws remove proportion and reasonableness from sentencing when they make all third strikes punishable by the same prison sentence, whether it is for stealing a small item or killing someone. Critics also suggest that the finality of three-strikes laws may make active criminals more desperate and, thus, more violent. According to this view, if criminals know they will be sentenced to life in prison, then they have nothing to lose and might be more likely to kill witnesses or to resist arrest through violent means. The constitutionality of California's three-strikes law was considered twice by the U.S. Supreme Court. Both cases involved defendants with two strikes who triggered the third strike penalty by committing relatively minor third offenses. In *Lockyer v. Andrade* (538 U.S. 63 [2003]) and *Ewing v. California* (538 U.S. 11 [2003]) the Supreme Court upheld the California law.

AMENDING THREE-STRIKES LAWS. By the end of the first decade of the 21st century, protests about the laws, decreasing crime rates, and increasing budget pressures led many states to water down their three-strikes laws. In "Three Strikes and You're Out: Changes in California's Law" (February 2013, http://www.ncsl.org/Documents/CJ/BulletinFeb-2013.pdf), the National Conference of State Legislators indicates that at least 16 of the 24 states that enacted three-strikes laws during the early 1990s subsequently softened their laws. The most common change was the elimination of mandatory sentences in favor of allowing judges to use some discretion in setting sentences (within the range of any applicable sentencing guidelines).

In November 2012 California voters approved Proposition 36, which amended the state's three-strikes law. Aaron Sankin reports in "California Prop 36, Measure Reforming State's Three Strikes Law, Approved by Wide Majority of Voters" (HuffingtonPost.com, November 7, 2012) that the proposition revised the law so that only a serious or violent crime counts as a third strike. In addition, it gave judges the discretion to resentence offenders serving life sentences for third-strike convictions if their third crime was not serious or violent.

Other Penalty Reforms

The U.S. attorney general Eric Holder Jr. (1951–) made headlines in August 2013 when he presented new federal penalty reforms during a speech before the American Bar Association. Holder (August 12, 2013, https://www.justice.gov/opa/speech/attorney-general-eric-holder-delivers-remarks-annual-meeting-american-bar-associations) explained that "too many Americans go to too many prisons for far too long, and for no truly good law enforcement reason." He indicated that the DOJ's policies would be changed "so that certain low-level, nonviolent drug offenders who have no ties to large-scale organizations, gangs, or cartels will no longer be charged with offenses that impose draconian mandatory minimum sentences. They now will be charged with offenses for which the accompanying sentences are better suited to their individual conduct, rather than excessive prison terms more appropriate for violent criminals or drug kingpins." In addition, he urged Congress to support legislation "giving federal judges more discretion in applying mandatory minimums to certain drug offenders." Holder noted that such changes could "save our country billions of dollars while keeping us safe."

In July 2014 the USSC (http://www.ussc.gov/sites/default/files/pdf/news/press-releases-and-news-advisories/press-releases/20140718_press_release.pdf) voted to reduce sentences for most federal offenders charged with drug trafficking. The change is retroactive, meaning that existing inmates who were convicted of the covered offenses can apply to have their sentence reduced. The USSC notes, "Under the guidelines, no offender would be released unless a judge reviews the case to determine whether a reduced sentence poses a risk to public safety and is otherwise appropriate." The change went into effect in November 2015.

In November 2014 California voters approved Proposition 47 to downgrade the classification of some nonviolent felonies to misdemeanors and hence reduce the penalties for them. In "Prop. 47 Floods Courts with Pleas for Resentencing and Records Purges" (LATimes.com, November 26, 2014), Maura Dolan reports that the retroactive measure prompted hundreds of inmates to apply immediately to have their convictions reduced. Tens of thousands more are eligible for the reduction. In addition, former inmates who have been released from prison can have their records amended to reflect the change. Dolan explains that "the incentive to take advantage of the new law is strong: a felony conviction can make it impossible to get a job, obtain government student loans, receive public housing or get a license for a wide range of positions, from hairstyling to nursing."

Kristina Davis notes in "Calif Cuts Penalties for Small Drug Crimes" (UTSanDiego.com, November 4, 2014) that when it was passed the ballot measure was projected to save the state an estimated $200 million annually in prison spending. The actual savings have become a subject of controversy. In "Where Did California's Savings from Reducing Drug Penalties Go?" (SacBee.com, July 26, 2016), Rachel Cohrs indicates that the Department of Finance estimates the total saved in

2015 was $29.3 million. However, the state's Legislative Analyst's Office believes the figure should be much higher, closer to $130 million. The discrepancy stems from different formulas used to calculate how much the state would have spent on incarceration costs during 2015.

In *The 2016–17 Budget: Fiscal Impacts of Proposition 47* (February 2016, http://www.lao.ca.gov/Reports/2016/3352/fiscal-impacts-prop47-021216.pdf), Mac Taylor of the Legislative Analyst's Office indicates that funds saved due to Proposition 47 are slated for "mental health and substance use services, truancy and dropout prevention, and victim services."

The Justice Reinvestment Initiative

The DOJ's Bureau of Justice Assistance (BJA) provides federal grants at the national, state, local, and trial level to help fund criminal justice programs. In 2006 the BJA launched the Justice Reinvestment Initiative (JRI). In "FAQ" (2017, https://www.bja.gov/programs/justicereinvestment/faqs.html), the BJA notes, "The goal of the Justice Reinvestment Initiative is to manage and allocate criminal justice populations and spending more cost-effectively, thereby generating cost-savings that can be reinvested in evidence-based strategies that increase public safety." The JRI process includes these major steps:

- Garner participation commitments from multiple stakeholders, both public and private. This could include the governor's office, legislators, criminal justice authorities, correctional officials, law enforcement agencies, prosecutors, and victims and victim advocacy groups.

- Develop or improve information sharing capabilities between stakeholders.

- Collect and analyze criminal justice data.

- Develop policy options and strategies based on the data that are collected.

- Put into place evidence-based policies that increase public safety.

In "FAQ" the BJA indicates that participating entities (such as states) can receive technical assistance for each of these steps and qualify for federal grants. As of April 2017, technical and financial assistance was also available from private organizations, including the Pew Charitable Trusts.

Although the JRI was launched in 2006, it did not receive funding from Congress until 2010. The Urban Institute, an organization that researches and makes public policy recommendations, publishes progress reports for the JRI. In "The Justice Reinvestment Initiative: Experiences from the States" (July 2013, http://www.urban.org/sites/default/files/publication/22211/412994-Justice-Reinvestment-Initiative-State-Assessment-Report.PDF), the Urban Institute notes that between 2010 and 2013 JRI

participants included 17 states—Arkansas, Delaware, Georgia, Hawaii, Kansas, Kentucky, Louisiana, Missouri, New Hampshire, North Carolina, Ohio, Oklahoma, Oregon, Pennsylvania, South Carolina, South Dakota, and West Virginia. Early JRI reforms included penalty changes (e.g., reduced mandatory minimum sentences for nonviolent crimes), streamlined parole processes, expanded probation eligibility, increased community-based treatment programs, and the formation of specialty courts. The latter are also called accountability courts. They divert qualified nonviolent offenders away from prison terms and into intensive supervised treatment programs that target specific behaviors or issues. Specialty courts have been established for offenders with drug or alcohol addictions, mental health problems, or involvement in prostitution. Some accountability courts manage cases only for military veterans who have run afoul of the law.

In *Reforming Sentencing and Corrections Policy: The Experience of Justice Reinvestment Initiative States* (December 2016, http://www.urban.org/sites/default/files/publication/86691/reforming_sentencing_and_corrections_policy_final_0.pdf), the Urban Institute indicates that 28 states had participated in the JRI as of December 2016. Besides the 17 states listed earlier, more recent participants included Alabama, Alaska, Idaho, Indiana, Maryland, Michigan, Mississippi, Nebraska, Rhode Island, Utah, and Washington. The Urban Institute notes, "JRI strategies helped 15 states either decrease their prison populations or keep them below levels they were predicted to reach without reform." In addition, together, the participating states reported that criminal justice system reforms helped them achieve $1.1 billion in savings or averted costs.

Death Penalty

The ultimate penalty that can be imposed by the U.S. judiciary system is the death penalty, also known as capital punishment. The Eighth Amendment of the U.S. Constitution guarantees that "cruel and unusual punishments [not be] inflicted." In recent decades debates have raged about the morality and deterrent effect of the death penalty and whether capital punishment is cruel and unusual punishment under the Constitution. According to Tracy L. Snell of the BJS, in *Capital Punishment, 2013—Statistical Tables* (December 2014, https://www.bjs.gov/content/pub/pdf/cp13st.pdf), between 1977 and 2013 there were 1,359 executions. The Death Penalty Information Center, which opposes capital punishment, maintains a database listing the names of all those who have been executed. According to the center (2017, https://deathpenaltyinfo.org/executions-year), as of April 2017 there were 35 executions in 2014, 28 executions in 2015, 20 executions in 2016, and 6 in 2017, bringing the total since 1977 to 1,448.

KEY U.S. SUPREME COURT CASES. Three Supreme Court cases, all decided during the 1970s, have produced the current interpretation of the Eighth Amendment relative to the death penalty. In *Furman v. Georgia* (408 U.S. 238 [1972]), the court held that the death penalty in three cases under review was cruel and unusual because under the then-prevailing statutes juries had "untrammeled discretion ... to pronounce life or death in capital cases." Due process required procedural fairness, including consideration of the severity and circumstances of the crime. In the three cases decided in *Furman*, three individuals were condemned to die, two for rape and one for murder.

In response to *Furman*, states modified their statutes. North Carolina imposed a mandatory death sentence for first-degree murder. This law was tested by the Supreme Court in *Woodson v. North Carolina* (428 U.S. 280 [1976]). The court held that although the death penalty was not a cruel and unusual punishment in every circumstance, a mandatory death sentence did not satisfy the requirements laid down in *Furman*. The court stated, "North Carolina's mandatory death penalty statute for first-degree murder departs markedly from contemporary standards respecting the imposition of the punishment of death and thus cannot be applied consistently with the Eighth and Fourteenth Amendments' requirement that the State's power to punish 'be exercised within the limits of civilized standards.'" The court overturned the North Carolina law.

Woodson was decided on July 2, 1976. On that same day the court rendered its judgment in *Gregg v. Georgia* (428 U.S. 153), the case of a man who was sentenced to death for murder and robbery under new legislation that passed in Georgia following *Furman*. In this case the court upheld the death penalty, saying, in part:

> The Georgia statutory system under which petitioner was sentenced to death is constitutional. The new procedures on their face satisfy the concerns of *Furman*, since before the death penalty can be imposed there must be specific jury findings as to the circumstances of the crime or the character of the defendant, and the State Supreme Court thereafter reviews the comparability of each death sentence with the sentences imposed on similarly situated defendants to ensure that the sentence of death in a particular case is not disproportionate. Petitioner's contentions that the changes in Georgia's sentencing procedures have not removed the elements of arbitrariness and capriciousness condemned by *Furman* are without merit.

As is explained in Chapter 10, the death penalty for juveniles was deemed unconstitutional by the U.S. Supreme Court in 2005 in *Roper v. Simmons* (543 U.S. 551).

CHAPTER 7
CORRECTIONAL FACILITIES: PRISONS AND JAILS

Public views of crime and punishment have changed over the centuries. In general, most societies have moved away from the extraction of personal or family justice (vengeful acts such as blood feuds or the practice of taking "an eye for an eye") toward formal systems that are based on written codes and orderly processes. Prisons and jails have changed from being holding places where prisoners awaited deportation, maiming, whipping, or execution to places of extended—even lifelong—incarceration. Confinement itself has become the punishment.

The number of people incarcerated in the United States is substantial. As shown in Table 7.1, nearly 2.2 million people were in prisons or local jails in 2015. The incarceration rates in 2015 were 870 per 100,000 U.S. adult residents and 670 per 100,000 U.S. residents of all ages. (See Table 7.2.) Table 7.3 provides a breakdown of incarceration rates by jurisdiction at yearend 2015. At that time the rate per 100,000 U.S. adult residents was slightly lower at 860. The state with the highest rate at yearend 2015 was Louisiana with 1,370 people incarcerated per 100,000 U.S. adult residents within its jurisdiction. Other states with high rates included Oklahoma (1,340), Mississippi (1,230), Alabama (1,140), and Georgia (1,140).

THE HISTORY OF CORRECTIONS IN THE UNITED STATES

During the colonial period in U.S. history physical punishment was more common than incarceration. Stocks, pillories, branding, flogging, and maiming (such as cutting off an ear or slitting the nostrils) were typical punishments meted out to offenders. The death penalty was also used frequently. The Puritans of Massachusetts believed that humans were naturally depraved, which made it easier for some of the colonies and the first states to enforce harsh punishments. In addition, because Puritans maintained the view that individuals had no control over their fate (predestination), few early Americans supported the idea that criminals could be rehabilitated.

The Quakers, led by William Penn (1644–1718), made colonial Pennsylvania an exception to the harsh practices that were often found in the other colonies. The early criminal code of colonial Pennsylvania abolished executions for all crimes except homicide, replaced physical punishments with imprisonment and hard labor, and did not charge the prisoners for their food and housing.

The Reform Movement

The idea of individual freedom and the concept that people could change society for the better by using reason permeated American society during the 1800s. Reformers worked to abolish slavery, secure women's rights, and prohibit liquor, as well as to change the corrections system. Rehabilitation of prisoners became the goal of criminal justice, and inmates were given work to keep them busy and to defray the cost of their confinement. Prison administrators began constructing factories within prison walls or hiring inmates out as laborers in chain gangs. In rural areas inmates worked on prison-owned farms. In the South prisoners were often leased out to local farmers. Prison superintendents justified the hard labor by arguing that it taught the offenders the value of work and self-discipline. With the rise of labor unions in the North, the 1930s saw an end to the large-scale prison industry. Unions complained about competing with the inmates' free labor, especially amid the rising unemployment of the Great Depression (1929–1939). As a result, states began limiting what inmates could produce.

As crime increased from the 1970s through the early 1990s, criminal justice practices such as probation, parole, and treatment programs came under attack. Support decreased for rehabilitative programs and increased for keeping offenders incarcerated; many people subscribed

TABLE 7.1

Number of incarcerated persons in the U.S. adult correctional system, 2000 and 2005–15

Year	Total*	Local jail	Prison
2000	1,945,400	621,100	1,394,200
2005	2,200,400	747,500	1,525,900
2006	2,256,600	765,800	1,568,700
2007	2,296,400	780,200	1,596,800
2008	2,310,300	785,500	1,608,300
2009	2,297,700	767,400	1,615,500
2010	2,279,100	748,700	1,613,800
2011	2,252,500	735,600	1,599,000
2012	2,231,300	744,500	1,570,400
2013	2,222,500	731,200	1,577,000
2014	2,225,100	744,600	1,562,300
2015	2,173,800	728,200	1,526,800
Average annual percent change, 2007–2015	−0.7%	−0.9%	−0.6%
Percent change, 2014–2015	−2.3%	−2.2%	−2.3%

BJS = Bureau of Justice Statistics
*Total was adjusted to account for offenders with multiple correctional statuses.
Note: Estimates were rounded to the nearest 100 and may not be comparable to previously published BJS reports due to updated information or rounding. Counts include estimates for nonresponding jurisdictions. All probation, parole, and prison counts are for December 31; jail counts are for the last weekday in June. Detail may not sum to total due ot rounding and adjustments made to account for offenders with multiple correctional statuses. Includes offenders held in local jails or under the jurisdiction of state or federal perisons.

SOURCE: Adapted from Danielle Kaeble and Lauren E. Glaze, "Table 1. Number of Persons Supervised by U.S. Adult Correctional Systems, by Correctional Status, 2000 and 2005–2015," in *Correctional Populations in the United States, 2015*, U.S. Department of Justice, Bureau of Justice Statistics, December 2016, https://www.bjs.gov/index.cfm?ty=pbdetail&iid=5870 (accessed January 21, 2017)

TABLE 7.2

Rate of persons incarcerated in the U.S. adult correctional system, 2000 and 2005–15

Year	Number in prison or local jail per 100,000 U.S. adult residents[a]	Number in prison or local jail per 100,000 U.S. residents of all ages[b]
2000	920	690
2005	990	740
2006	1,000	750
2007	1,000	760
2008	1,000	760
2009	980	750
2010	960	730
2011	940	720
2012	920	710
2013	910	700
2014	900	690
2015	870	670

[a]Rates were computed using the estimates of the U.S. resident population of persons age 18 or older from the U.S. Census Bureau for January 1 of the following year.
[b]Rates were computed using the estimates of the U.S. resident population of persons of all ages from the U.S. Census Bureau for January 1 of the following year.
Notes: Rates were estimated to the nearest 10. Estimates may not be comparable to previously published BJS reports due to updated information or rounding. Includes offenders in the community under the authority of probation or parole agencies, under the jurisdiction of state or federal prisons, or held in local jails. Includes offenders under the jurisdiction of state or federal prisons or held in local jails.

SOURCE: Adapted from Danielle Kaeble and Lauren Glaze, "Table 4. Rate of Persons Supervised by U.S. Adult Correctional Systems, by Correctional Status, 2000 and 2005–2015," in *Correctional Populations in the United States, 2015*, U.S. Department of Justice, Bureau of Justice Statistics, December 2016, https://www.bjs.gov/index.cfm?ty=pbdetail&iid=5870 (accessed January 21, 2017)

to the idea that keeping criminals off the streets was the surest way to keep them from committing more crimes. In response, the federal government and a growing number of states introduced mandatory sentencing and life terms for habitual criminals. They also limited the use of probation, parole, and time off for good behavior. As a result, the incarceration rate skyrocketed through the early 1990s. Crime rates began falling during the late 1990s, and this trend generally continued into the 2010s. The decrease in crime rates led to a much slower growth in the incarcerated population.

TYPES OF PRISONER COUNTS

The Bureau of Justice Statistics (BJS) within the U.S. Department of Justice (DOJ) compiles detailed data on federal, state, and local correctional facilities and inmates. It is important to note that some BJS reports distinguish between two different types of prisoner counts: a custody count and a count of the number of inmates under jurisdiction. A custody count is the number of inmates physically located within a particular facility, correctional system, or state. The number of inmates under jurisdiction is the number of inmates under the legal authority of a particular jurisdiction, such as the state of California. These inmates may or may not be physically located in facilities in the same jurisdiction. Inmates under the legal authority of one type of jurisdiction, such as a state, may be physically located in a facility of another jurisdiction, such as a county jail.

CORRECTIONAL SYSTEMS

Corrections institutions are organized into tiers by level of government, and at each level (federal, state, and local) specific types of institutions provide corrections functions based on the relative severity of the offenses committed. The most restrictive form of corrections is incarceration in a prison. Both the federal and state governments operate their own prison systems; within the federal government, the military maintains its own prisons. Prison inmates serve time for serious offenses that carry a sentence of at least one year of incarceration.

State correctional facilities, including prisons, are commonly overseen by state corrections or public safety agencies. Table 7.4 lists the responsible agency for each state and the District of Columbia. Each system is administered, controlled, and funded separately. The DOJ's National Institute of Corrections provides technical

TABLE 7.3

Estimated number and rate of persons incarcerated in the U.S. adult correctional system, by jurisdiction, 2015

Jurisdiction	Number in prison or local jail, 12/31/2015ᵃ	Incarceration rate per 100,000 U.S. residents ages 18 or olderᵇ	Incarceration rate per 100,000 U.S. residents of all ages
U.S. totalᶜ	2,145,100	860	660
Federalᵈ	195,700	80	60
State	1,949,400	780	600
Alabama	42,900	1,140	880
Alaska	5,400	970	730
Arizona	54,900	1,050	800
Arkansas	24,000	1,050	800
California	201,000	670	510
Colorado	31,800	750	580
Connecticut	15,800	560	440
Delaware	6,700	890	700
District of Columbia	1,800	320	270
Florida	153,000	940	750
Georgiaᵉ	88,500	1,140	860
Hawaii	5,900	520	410
Idaho	10,900	890	660
Illinois	63,900	640	500
Indiana	43,500	860	650
Iowa	12,900	540	410
Kansas	16,600	760	570
Kentucky	33,800	990	760
Louisiana	49,000	1,370	1,050
Maine	4,000	370	300
Maryland	29,700	640	490
Massachusetts	20,100	370	300
Michigan	57,700	750	580
Minnesota	16,500	390	300
Mississippi	28,000	1,230	940
Missouri	43,400	920	710
Montana	5,600	690	540
Nebraska	8,600	600	450
Nevada	19,100	850	650
New Hampshire	4,600	430	340
New Jersey	33,900	490	380
New Mexico	15,100	950	720
New York	75,900	490	380
North Carolina	53,800	690	530
North Dakota	3,200	540	410
Ohio	70,700	790	610
Oklahomaᵉ	39,700	1,340	1,010
Oregon	21,000	660	520
Pennsylvania	83,900	830	650
Rhode Island	3,200	380	310
South Carolina	31,600	820	640
South Dakota	5,300	820	620
Tennessee	48,000	940	720
Texas	214,800	1,050	780
Utah	11,700	560	390
Vermont	1,800	350	280
Virginia	57,300	880	680
Washington	29,700	530	410
West Virginia	10,100	690	550
Wisconsin	35,000	780	610
Wyoming	3,900	880	670

TABLE 7.3

Estimated number and rate of persons incarcerated in the U.S. adult correctional system, by jurisdiction, 2015 [CONTINUED]

ᵃExcludes, by jurisdiction, an estimated 81,200 prisoners held in jail.
ᵇRates were computed using estimates of the U.S adult resident population of persons age 18 or older and persons of all ages on January 1, 2016, within jurisdiction.
ᶜTotal correctional population and total number in prison and jail include local jail counts that are based on December 31, 2015 in order to produce jurisdiction-level estimates. For this reason, excluding appendix tables 2, 3, and 4, the estimates in this table differ from the national estimates presented in other tables and figures in this report.
ᵈExcludes about 11,000 inmates that were not held in locally operated jails but rather facilities that were operated by the Federal Bureau of Prisons and functioned as jails.
ᵉTotal correctional population and community supervision population estimates include misdemeanant probation cases, not individuals, supervised by private companies and may overstate the number of offenders under supervision.
Note: Counts were rounded to the nearst 100, and rates were rounded to the nearest 10. Detail may not sum to total due to rounding and because offenders with multiple correctional statuses were excluded from totals. Counts Include estimates for nonresponding jurisdictions.

SOURCE: Adapted from Danielle Kaeble and Lauren E. Glaze, "Appendix Table 1. Estimated Number and Rate of Persons Supervised by U.S. Adult Correctional Systems, by Jurisdiction and Correctional Status, 2015," in *Correctional Populations in the United States, 2015*, U.S. Department of Justice, Bureau of Justice Statistics, December 2016, https://www.bjs.gov/index.cfm?ty=pbdetail&iid=5870 (accessed January 21, 2017)

operations, employee training, facility maintenance, inmate education, use of force, and workplace safety.

Most people sentenced to jail serve less than a year for misdemeanors and offenses against the public order. The vast majority of jails are operated at the local level by cities and counties. The federal government operates some jails as well, and within the federal government the U.S. Immigration and Customs Enforcement agency has its own detention facilities. Prisons and jails are operated under a single state authority in Alaska, Connecticut, Delaware, Hawaii, Rhode Island, and Vermont.

Prisons and jails are subject to the facility and operational standards of their specific jurisdictions. In addition, there are voluntary standards set by private organizations, such as the American Correctional Association (http://www.aca.org/ACA_Prod_IMIS/ACA_Member/Standards___Accreditation/Standards/ACA_Member/Standards_and_Accreditation/StandardsInfo_Home.aspx?hkey=7c1b31e5-95cf-4bde-b400-8b5bb32a2bad) and the National Commission on Correctional Health Care (http://www.ncchc.org/accreditation-programs). Both of these organizations offer accreditation programs for correctional systems that wish to become accredited to nationally consistent standards.

Correctional Officers and Jailers

Prisons and jails around the country employ hundreds of thousands of people. The Bureau of Labor Statistics (BLS) within the U.S. Department of Labor operates the Occupational Employment Statistics program, which annually publishes employment and wage estimates for various occupations. In "Occupational Employment and

assistance and training to corrections agencies at all levels of government. The institute (http://nicic.gov/topics/5276-state-departments-of-corrections-web-based-policy-and-procedure-manuals) maintains a listing of links to the individual policies and procedures of nearly all state correctional agencies. For example, the Ohio Department of Rehabilitation and Correction (http://www.drc.ohio.gov/policies-procedures) provides copies of dozens of its policies related to topics such as budget, business

TABLE 7.4

State correctional departments, 2017

Alabama	Alabama Department of Corrections	http://www.doc.state.al.us/
Alaska	Alaska Department of Corrections	http://www.correct.state.ak.us/corrections/index.jsf
Arizona	Arizona Department of Corrections	https://corrections.az.gov/
Arkansas	Arkansas Department of Correction	http://www.adc.arkansas.gov/
California	California Department of Corrections and Rehabilitation	http://www.cdcr.ca.gov/
Colorado	Colorado Department of Corrections	https://www.colorado.gov/cdoc/
Connecticut	Connecticut Department of Correction	http://www.ct.gov/doc/site/default.asp
Delaware	Delaware Department of Correction	http://www.doc.delaware.gov/
District of Columbia	District of Columbia Department of Corrections	http://doc.dc.gov/
Florida	Florida Department of Corrections	http://www.dc.state.fl.us/
Georgia	Georgia Department of Corrections	http://www.dcor.state.ga.us/
Hawaii	Hawaii Department of Public Safety, Corrections Division	http://hawaii.gov/psd/corrections
Idaho	Idaho Department of Correction	https://www.idoc.idaho.gov/
Illinois	Illinois Department of Corrections	https://www.illinois.gov/idoc/pages/default.aspx
Indiana	Indiana Department of Correction	http://www.in.gov/idoc/
Iowa	Iowa Department of Corrections	http://www.doc.state.ia.us/
Kansas	Kansas Department of Corrections	http://www.dc.state.ks.us/
Kentucky	Kentucky Department of Corrections	http://www.corrections.ky.gov/
Louisiana	Louisiana Department of Public Safety and Corrections	http://www.corrections.state.la.us/
Maine	Maine Department of Corrections	http://www.maine.gov/corrections/
Maryland	Maryland Department of Public Safety and Correctional Services	http://www.dpscs.state.md.us/
Massachusetts	Massachusetts Department of Correction	http://www.mass.gov/eopss/agencies/doc/
Michigan	Michigan Department of Corrections	http://www.michigan.gov/corrections
Minnesota	Minnesota Department of Corrections	http://www.doc.state.mn.us/
Mississippi	Mississippi Department of Corrections	http://www.mdoc.state.ms.us/
Missouri	Missouri Department of Corrections	http://doc.mo.gov/
Montana	Montana Department of Corrections	http://www.cor.mt.gov/default.mcpx
Nebraska	Nebraska Department of Correctional Services	http://www.corrections.nebraska.gov/
Nevada	Nevada Department of Corrections	http://doc.nv.gov/
New Hampshire	New Hampshire Department of Corrections	http://www.nh.gov/nhdoc/
New Jersey	New Jersey Department of Corrections	http://www.state.nj.us/corrections/
New Mexico	New Mexico Corrections Department	http://www.corrections.state.nm.us/
New York	New York State Department of Corrections and Community Supervision	http://www.doccs.ny.gov/
North Carolina	North Carolina Department of Public Safety	https://www.ncdps.gov/
North Dakota	North Dakota Department of Corrections and Rehabilitation	http://www.nd.gov/docr/
Ohio	Ohio Department of Rehabilitation and Correction	http://www.drc.ohio.gov/
Oklahoma	Oklahoma Department of Corrections	http://www.ok.gov/doc/
Oregon	Oregon Department of Correction	http://www.oregon.gov/DOC/index.shtml
Pennsylvania	Pennsylvania Department of Corrections	http://www.cor.pa.gov/Pages/default.aspx
Rhode Island	Rhode Island Department of Corrections	http://www.doc.ri.gov/index.php
South Carolina	South Carolina Department of Corrections	http://www.doc.sc.gov/
South Dakota	South Dakota Department of Corrections	http://doc.sd.gov/
Tennessee	Tennessee Department of Correction	http://www.tn.gov/correction/
Texas	Texas Department of Criminal Justice	http://tdcj.state.tx.us/
Utah	Utah Department of Corrections	http://corrections.utah.gov/
Vermont	Vermont Department of Corrections	http://www.doc.state.vt.us/
Virginia	Virginia Department of Corrections	http://www.vadoc.state.va.us/
Washington	Washington State Department of Corrections	http://www.doc.wa.gov/
West Virginia	West Virginia Division of Corrections	http://www.wvdoc.com/wvdoc/
Wisconsin	Wisconsin Department of Corrections	http://doc.wi.gov/Home
Wyoming	Wyoming Department of Corrections	http://doc.state.wy.us/

SOURCE: Created by Kim Masters Evans for Gale, © 2017

Wages, May 2015" (https://www.bls.gov/oes/current/oes333012.htm), the BLS indicates that as of May 2015, 427,790 people were employed nationwide as correctional officers or jailers. Of this total, 228,260 were employed by state governments, and 160,890 were employed by local governments. The remainder worked for the federal government or other entities. States with the highest number of correctional officers in 2016 included Texas (49,720 jobs), California (37,050), New York (34,460), Florida (32,930), and Pennsylvania (17,020).

PUBLIC VERSUS PRIVATE CORRECTIONAL FACILITIES

During the 1980s the rapidly rising prison and jail populations led a few jurisdictions to privatize some of their correctional facilities. The basic assumption behind this idea is that the private sector is inherently more efficient, flexible, and cost effective than the government sector because it is less constrained by bureaucracy. It is also argued that private facilities save the public the initial costs of prison construction because those costs are assumed by private contractors. This saves the government from taking on long-term debt to build housing for more prisoners. In this view, a privatized or even a partially privatized corrections system would cost taxpayers less money. Corrections functions, however, are ultimately vested in governmental hands, and private prisons must operate in accordance with the rules and regulations of their jurisdictions.

The use of private prisons has become a highly controversial issue. In "Justice Department Seeks to End Use of Private Prisons" (USNews.com, August 18, 2016), Alan Neuhauser states, "Civil liberties groups and left-leaning lawmakers long have criticized the privatization of America's prison system, declaring it impedes transparency, hinders oversight, allows for greater abuse and distorts the criminal justice system by turning prisoners into for-profit commodities for corporations."

In August 2016 the DOJ's deputy attorney general, Sally Yates, sent a memorandum (https://www.justice.gov/opa/file/886311/download) to the Federal Bureau of Prisons (BOP) advising the agency to decline to renew expiring contracts with private companies or to "substantially" reduce the scope of any renewed contracts for private prisons for federal inmates. The move was driven by declining overall inmate numbers and concerns about performance. At the time, Yates said of private prisons, "They simply do not provide the same level of correctional services, programs, and resources; they do not save substantially on costs; and as noted in a recent report by the Department's Office of Inspector General, they do not maintain the same level of safety and security." In February 2017, however, Attorney General Jeff Sessions (1946–) reversed the DOJ's earlier directive, stating (https://www.bop.gov/resources/news/20170224_doj_memo.jsp) that the Yates memorandum "changed long-standing policy and practice, and impaired the Bureau's ability to meet the future needs of the federal correctional system." Laura Jarrett reports in "DOJ Walks Back Guidance Discouraging Use of Private Prisons" (CNN.com, February 23, 2017), that the DOJ indicated the return to the previous policy would "restore (the Bureau of Prison's) flexibility to manage the federal prison inmate population based on capacity needs."

FEDERAL CORRECTIONS

The BOP was established in 1930 as an agency of the DOJ to oversee the corrections system for federal inmates and to administer federal prisons. The BOP notes in "Statistics" (https://www.bop.gov/about/statistics/population_statistics.jsp) that as of April 6, 2017, it oversaw 188,800 federal inmates. Most of the inmates (153,763, or 81% of the total) were in BOP facilities. An additional 21,408 inmates (11% of the total) were in privately managed facilities, and 13,629 inmates (8% of the total) were held in other contract facilities, such as jails or community corrections centers, or were under home confinement.

The BOP directly operated 194 facilities around the country at that time. In addition, federal inmates were incarcerated at 13 privately operated facilities. Overall, as reported in "Statistics," the 10 facilities housing the largest number of federal inmates as of April 6, 2017, were:

- Fort Dix Federal Correctional Institution (FCI), New Jersey—4,019 inmates

- Big Spring Correctional Institution (private), Texas—3,445 inmates

- Reeves Correctional Institution (private), Texas—2,332 inmates

- Adams County Correctional Institution (private), Mississippi—2,097 inmates

- Coleman Low FCI, Florida—1,921 inmates

- Dalby Correctional Institution (private), Texas—1,907 inmates

- Elkton FCI, Ohio—1,863 inmates

- Seagoville FCI, Texas—1,841 inmates

- D. Ray James Correctional Institution (private), Georgia—1,840 inmates

- Brooklyn Metropolitan Detention Center, New York—1,837 inmates

Security Levels of Federal Prisons

The BOP maintains institutions at four different security levels, and each prisoner is assigned to a particular level based on that individual's offenses and behavioral history:

- Minimum security—at the lowest security level are federal prison camps. These facilities have dormitory housing, a relatively low staff-to-inmate ratio, and limited or no perimeter fencing. They are located on or near larger institutions or military bases, where the inmates participate in work programs.

- Low-security FCIs—these FCIs have fenced perimeters and a dormitory that consists of cubicle housing. Inmates are typically involved in work programs.

- Medium-security FCIs—these facilities feature reinforced perimeter fencing, usually a double fence with an electronic detection system. In addition, inmates are housed in cells and have access to work and treatment programs.

- High-security U.S. penitentiaries—the most secure environment in the federal prison system includes highly secured perimeters with walls and reinforced fences. Inmates are held in multiple- or single-occupant cells, are closely watched, and do not have freedom to move around within the facility without supervision.

In addition, the BOP operates a number of administrative facilities. Many of them hold prisoners of several different security categories. Some are for offenders awaiting trial. Others treat inmates with serious medical needs. Special facilities may also be used to house the most dangerous, violent, or escape-prone inmates. Among the administrative facilities are metropolitan correctional centers; metropolitan detention centers; federal detention centers; federal medical centers; the Federal

Transfer Center in Oklahoma City, Oklahoma; and the Administrative-Maximum U.S. Penitentiary in Florence, Colorado.

PRISON INMATES AT YEAREND 2015

Every year the DOJ collects data on the nation's state and federal inmate population. Survey results from yearend 2015 are reported by E. Ann Carson and Elizabeth Anderson in *Prisoners in 2015* (December 2016, https://www.bjs.gov/content/pub/pdf/p15.pdf). The report provides two different types of prisoner counts: sentenced inmates and inmates under the jurisdiction of correctional authorities. The latter group includes inmates that had been convicted but not sentenced at yearend 2015, as well as those awaiting trial.

According to Carson and Anderson, 1.5 million inmates were under state or federal jurisdiction at yearend 2015. The vast majority (1.3 million, or 87%) of the inmates were under state jurisdiction and 13% (196,455) were under federal jurisdiction. Nearly 50,000 of the prisoners had not yet been sentenced, meaning that sentenced prisoners made up 97% of all inmates under the jurisdiction of state and federal prison authorities.

As shown in Figure 7.1, the total prison population grew dramatically from 1978 through the first decade of the 21st century. The population peaked in 2009 at 1.6 million before beginning to decline. Table 7.5 shows the number of prisoners under the jurisdiction of state or federal correctional authorities at yearend 2015 by jurisdiction. Texas (163,909), California (129,593), and Florida (101,424) had, by far, the largest inmate populations.

Table 7.6 shows the imprisonment rates for sentenced prisoners under the jurisdiction of federal or state authorities at yearend 2015. The overall rate was 458 sentenced prisoners per 100,000 U.S. residents aged 18 years and older. The federal rate was 55 sentenced prisoners per 100,000 U.S. residents aged 18 years and older, whereas the state rate was 402 sentenced prisoners per 100,000 U.S. adult residents. Louisiana had the highest rate (776) of any of the states, followed by Oklahoma (715), Alabama (611), Mississippi (609), and Arizona (596).

In 2015 more than 126,000 prisoners (8.3% of the total) under state jurisdiction or federal jurisdiction were incarcerated in private correctional facilities. (See Table 7.7.) The percentage was higher for state prisoners (17.8%) than for federal prisoners (6.9%). The jurisdiction with the most inmates in private prisons in 2015 was the federal system with 34,934. It was followed by Texas (14,293), Florida (12,487), and Georgia (7,953).

As shown in Table 7.8, there were 81,195 prisoners under state or federal jurisdiction held in local jails in 2015. Nearly all (80,426, or 99%) of these inmates were

under state jurisdiction. The states with the largest populations of inmates held in local jails at yearend 2015 were Louisiana (17,930), Texas (11,093), and Kentucky (9,738).

Admissions and Releases: 2014 and 2015

According to Carson and Anderson, in 2015, 608,318 people sentenced to more than one year of incarceration were admitted by state or federal correctional authorities. The vast majority of the admissions (561,406, or 92%) were to state jurisdiction; only 8% (46,912) of them were to federal jurisdiction. Overall, admissions were down by 2.8% from 2014.

Carson and Anderson report in *Prisoners in 2015* that the majority of the inmates (429,074, or 71%) admitted in 2015 were incarcerated because of new court commitments. Around a quarter (164,626, or 27%) were admitted to prison because of parole violations. As is explained in Chapter 9, parolees face incarceration for violating certain terms and conditions of their parole agreements. These include technical infractions, such as failing to follow instructions, and committing crimes while on parole.

Overall, 641,027 inmates were released from prison in 2015. This value was down by 0.7% from 2014. Nearly two-thirds (405,603, or 63%) of the inmates released in 2015 were given conditional releases, meaning that they were subject to some type of continuing supervision or conditions. Another 181,868 (or 28%) of the inmates received unconditional releases.

Prison Capacities and Overcrowding

As is shown in Figure 7.1, approximately 330,000 prisoners were under state and federal correctional jurisdiction in 1978. The incarcerated population has skyrocketed since that time, and federal and state governments have responded by building new prisons and expanding older prisons. Nevertheless, at yearend 2015 prison capacities in some jurisdictions were far less than the numbers of inmates being housed in them. This overcrowding is a cause for serious concern. When overcrowding occurs, two inmates are often assigned to a cell that is designed for one person, or temporary housing units are set up to take prison overflow. Overcrowding makes it more likely that disagreements will arise between inmates, leading to violence and injuries. In addition, diseases are more likely to spread among the inmate population.

Table 7.9 shows three types of capacity measures (as available) for state and federal prisons. The measures are defined as follows:

- Design capacity—the number of inmates that planners or architects intended for a facility

FIGURE 7.1

Prisoners under the jurisdiction of state or federal correctional authorities at yearend, 1978–2015

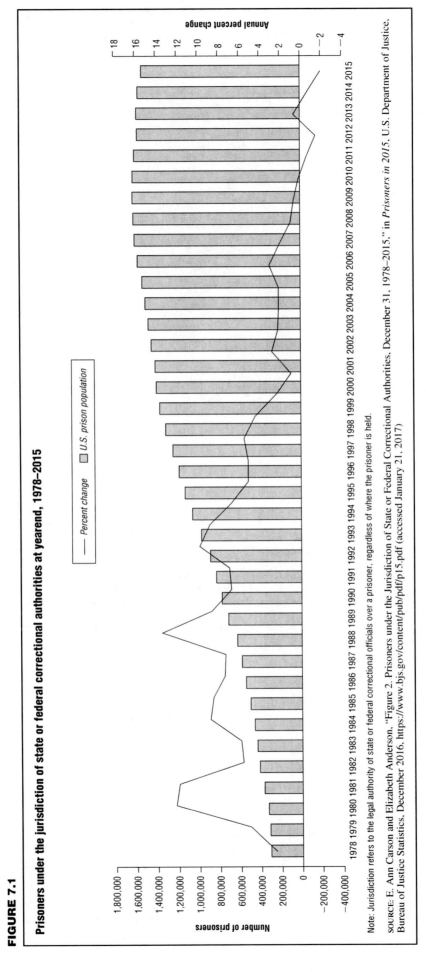

Note: Jurisdiction refers to the legal authority of state or federal correctional officials over a prisoner, regardless of where the prisoner is held.

SOURCE: E. Ann Carson and Elizabeth Anderson, "Figure 2. Prisoners under the Jurisdiction of State or Federal Correctional Authorities, December 31, 1978–2015," in *Prisoners in 2015*, U.S. Department of Justice, Bureau of Justice Statistics, December 2016, https://www.bjs.gov/content/pub/pdf/p15.pdf (accessed January 21, 2017)

TABLE 7.5

Prisoners under jurisdiction of state or federal correctional authorities, by jurisdiction, yearend 2015

Jurisdiction	Total	Jurisdiction	Total
U.S. total[a]	1,526,792	Mississippi	18,911
Federal[b]	196,455	Missouri	32,330
		Montana	3,685
State[a]	1,330,337	Nebraska	5,372
Alabama	30,810	Nevada[e]	13,071
Alaska[c]	5,338	New Hampshire	2,897
Arizona	42,719	New Jersey	20,489
Arkansas	17,707	New Mexico	7,169
California	129,593	New York	51,727
Colorado	20,168	North Carolina	36,617
Connecticut[c]	15,816	North Dakota	1,795
Delaware[c]	6,654	Ohio	52,233
Florida	101,424	Oklahoma	28,547
Georgia	52,193	Oregon[e]	15,245
Hawaii[c]	5,879	Pennsylvania	49,858
Idaho[d]	8,052	Rhode Island[c]	3,248
Illinois[d]	46,240	South Carolina	20,929
Indiana	27,355	South Dakota	3,564
Iowa	8,849	Tennessee	28,172
Kansas	9,857	Texas	163,909
Kentucky[d]	21,701	Utah	6,492
Louisiana	36,377	Vermont[c]	1,750
Maine	2,279	Virginia	38,403
Maryland	20,764	Washington	18,284
Massachusetts	9,922	West Virginia	7,118
Michigan	42,628	Wisconsin	22,975
Minnesota	10,798	Wyoming	2,424

[a]Total and state estimates include imputed counts for Nevada and Oregon, which did not submit 2015 data to National Prisoner Statistics (NPS).
[b]Includes prisoners held in nonsecure, privately operated community corrections facilities and juveniles held in contract facilities.
[c]Prisons and jails form one integrated system. Data include total jail and prison populations.
[d]State has changed reporting methodology, so 2015 counts are not comparable to those published for earlier years.
[e]State did not submit 2015 NPS data. Counts were imputed.
Note: Jurisdiction refers to the legal authority of sate or federal correctional officials over a prisoner, regardless of where the prisoner is held.

SOURCE: Adapted from E. Ann Carson and Elizabeth Anderson, "Table 2. Prisoners under Jurisdiction of State or Federal Correctional Authorities, by Jurisdiction and Sex, December 31, 2014 and 2015," in *Prisoners in 2015*, U.S. Department of Justice, Bureau of Justice Statistics, December 2016, https://www.bjs.gov/content/pub/pdf/p15.pdf (accessed January 21, 2017).

TABLE 7.6

Imprisonment rate of sentenced prisoners under the jurisdiction of state or federal correctional authorities, yearend 2015

Jurisdiction	Total[a]	Jurisdiction	Total[a]
U.S. total[a]	458	Mississippi	609
Federal[b]	55	Missouri	530
		Montana	355
State[a]	402	Nebraska	279
Alabama	611	Nevada[e]	444
Alaska[c]	306	New Hampshire	217
Arizona	596	New Jersey	228
Arkansas	591	New Mexico	335
California	329	New York	260
Colorado	364	North Carolina	352
Connecticut[c]	312	North Dakota	233
Delaware[c]	441	Ohio	449
Florida	496	Oklahoma	715
Georgia	503	Oregon[e]	376
Hawaii[c]	262	Pennsylvania	387
Idaho[d]	436	Rhode Island[c]	204
Illinois[d]	360	South Carolina	414
Indiana	412	South Dakota	413
Iowa	281	Tennessee	425
Kansas	328	Texas	568
Kentucky[d]	489	Utah	215
Louisiana	776	Vermont[c]	206
Maine	132	Virginia	457
Maryland	339	Washington	252
Massachusetts	179	West Virginia	386
Michigan	429	Wisconsin	377
Minnesota	196	Wyoming	413

[a]Total and state estimates include imputed counts for Nevada and Oregon, which did not submit 2015 data to National Prisoner Statistics (NPS).
[b]Includes prisoners held in nonsecure, privately operated community corrections facilities and juveniles held in contract facilities.
[c]Prisons and jails form one integrated system. Data include total jail and prison populations.
[d]Counts from 2015 are not comparable to counts from prior years due to a change in reporting methodology.
[e]State did not submit 2015 data to NPS. Counts were imputed.
Note: Jurisdiction refers to the legal authority of sate or federal correctional officials over a prisoner, regardless of where the prisoner is held. Counts are based on prisoners with sentences of more than 1 year.

SOURCE: Adapted from E. Ann Carson and Elizabeth Anderson, "Table 6. Imprisonment Rate of Sentenced Prisoners under the Jurisdiction of State or Federal Correctional Authorities, by Sex, December 31, 2014 and 2015," in *Prisoners in 2015*, U.S. Department of Justice, Bureau of Justice Statistics, December 2016, https://www.bjs.gov/content/pub/pdf/p15.pdf (accessed January 21, 2017)

- Operational capacity—the number of inmates that can be accommodated based on a facility's staff, existing programs, and services

- Rated capacity—the number of beds or inmates assigned by a rating official to institutions within a jurisdiction

Table 7.9 lists custody populations by jurisdiction at yearend 2015 and the custody populations as percentages of the lowest and highest capacity measures. About half of the state prison systems had custody populations that exceeded 100% of their lowest capacity rating. Put another way, when judged by the least favorable of the available ratings of their capacities (i.e., lowest capacity), the prison systems of about half the states were overcrowded at yearend 2015. Alabama (186.3%), Illinois (165.3%), and Hawaii (163.5%) had the most severe overcrowding by this measurement. Even when using the most favorable ratings of prison capacities (highest capacity), 18 states

had prisons at more than 100% capacity at yearend 2015. In addition, the federal prison system's population was at 119.7% of its rated capacity measure.

In September 2012 the U.S. Government Accountability Office (GAO) issued a report on the consequences of overcrowding in federal prisons. In *Bureau of Prisons: Growing Inmate Crowding Negatively Affects Inmates, Staff, and Infrastructure* (http://www.gao.gov/assets/650/648123.pdf), the GAO cites the following negative impacts:

- "More inmates are sharing cells and other living units, which brings together for longer periods of time inmates with a higher risk of violence and more potential victims."

- "Inmates may experience crowded bathroom facilities, reductions in shower times, shortened meal times coupled with longer waits for food service, and more limited recreational activities."

TABLE 7.7

Prisoners under the jurisdiction of state or federal correctional authorities held in the custody of private prisons, yearend 2014 and 2015

Jurisdiction	Prisoners held in private prisons[a]			
	2014	2015	Percent change 2014–2015	Percentage of total jurisdiction, 2015
U.S. total	131,723	126,272	−4.1%	8.3%
Federal[b]	40,017	34,934	−12.7%	17.8%
State	91,706	91,338	−0.4%	6.9%
Alabama	481	398	−17.3	1.3
Alaska[c]	595	593	−0.3	11.1
Arizona	6,955	6,471	−7.0	15.1
Arkansas	0	0	NA	NA
California	2,376	2,195	−7.6	1.7
Colorado	3,782	3,987	5.4	19.8
Connecticut[c]	647	524	−19.0	3.3
Delaware[c]	0	0	NA	NA
Florida	12,395	12,487	0.7	12.3
Georgia	7,901	7,953	0.7	15.2
Hawaii[b]	1,425	1,340	−6.0	22.8
Idaho	639	545	−14.7	6.8
Illinois	0	0	NA	NA
Indiana	4,420	4,204	−4.9	15.4
Iowa	0	0	NA	NA
Kansas	0	0	NA	NA
Kentucky	0	0	NA	NA
Louisiana	3,142	3,152	0.3	8.7
Maine	0	0	NA	NA
Maryland	30	30	0.0	0.1
Massachusetts	0	0	NA	NA
Michigan	0	0	NA	NA
Minnesota	0	0	NA	NA
Mississippi	4,114	3,946	−4.1	20.9
Missouri	0	0	NA	NA
Montana	1,432	1,490	4.1	40.4
Nebraska	0	0	NA	NA
Nevada	NR	NR	NA	NA
New Hampshire	0	0	NA	NA
New Jersey	2,761	2,863	3.7	14.0
New Mexico	3,072	3,026	−1.5	42.2
New York	0	0	NA	NA
North Carolina	30	29	−3.3	0.1
North Dakota	371	427	15.1	23.8
Ohio	5,370	6,050	12.7	11.6
Oklahoma	7,367	7,446	1.1	26.1
Oregon	NR	NR	NA	NA
Pennsylvania	636	605	−4.9	1.2
Rhode Island[c]	0	0	NA	NA
South Carolina	15	14	−6.7	0.1
South Dakota	10	22	120.0	0.6
Tennessee	5,116	5,172	1.1	18.4
Texas	14,368	14,293	−0.5	8.7
Utah	0	0	NA	NA
Vermont[c]	NR	NR	NA	NA
Virginia	1,570	1,568	−0.1	4.1
Washington	0	0	NA	NA
West Virginia	0	0	NA	NA
Wisconsin	0	0	NA	NA
Wyoming	255	267	4.7	11.0

NR = not reported

NA = not applicable

[a]Includes prisoners held in the jurisdiction's own private facilities and private facilities in another state.

[b]Includes federal prisoners held in nonsecure, privately operated facilities (9,153) and prisoners on home confinement (3,122). Excludes persons held in immigration detention facilities pending adjudication.

[c]Prisons and jails form one integrated system. Data include total jail and prison populations.

Note: Jurisdiction refers to the legal authority of state or federal correctional officials over a prisoner, regardless of where the prisoner is held. Totals include imputed counts for Nevada, Oregon, and Vermont, which did not submit these data to the 2015 National Prisoner Statistics.

SOURCE: Adapted from E. Ann Carson and Elizabeth Anderson, "Appendix Table 2. Prisoners under the Jurisdiction of State or Federal Correctional Authorities Held in the Custody of Private Prisons and Local Jails, December 31, 2014 and 2015," in *Prisoners in 2015*, U.S. Department of Justice, Bureau of Justice Statistics, December 2016, https://www.bjs.gov/content/pub/pdf/p15.pdf (accessed January 21, 2017)

- "The growth in the inmate population affects the availability of program opportunities, resulting in waiting lists and inmate idleness. BOP provides programs including education, vocational training, drug

TABLE 7.8

Prisoners under the jurisdiction of state or federal correctional authorities held in local jails, yearend 2014 and 2015

Jurisdiction	2014	2015	Percent change 2014–2015	Percentage of total jurisdiction, 2015
U.S. total	81,779	81,195	−0.7%	5.3%
Federal[a]	939	769	−18.1%	0.4%
State	80,840	80,426	−0.5%	6.0%
Alabama	1,702	1,788	5.1	5.8
Alaska[b]	41	46	12.2	0.9
Arizona	0	439	NC	1.0
Arkansas	2,600	1,923	−26.0	10.9
California	0	0	NA	NA
Colorado	176	82	−53.4	0.4
Connecticut[b]	0	0	NA	NA
Delaware[b]	0	0	NA	NA
Florida	1,104	1,073	−2.8	1.1
Georgia	4,946	4,902	−0.9	9.4
Hawaii[b]	0	0	NA	NA
Idaho	620	814	31.3	10.1
Illinois	0	0	NA	NA
Indiana	1,198	596	−50.3	2.2
Iowa	0	0	NA	NA
Kansas	90	78	−13.3	0.8
Kentucky	8,966	9,738	8.6	44.9
Louisiana	19,320	17,930	−7.2	49.3
Maine	26	20	−23.1	0.9
Maryland	95	163	71.6	0.8
Massachusetts	279	431	54.5	4.3
Michigan	31	295	851.6	0.7
Minnesota	997	1,211	21.5	11.2
Mississippi	5,568	4,933	−11.4	26.1
Missouri	0	0	NA	NA
Montana	515	491	−4.7	13.3
Nebraska	212	218	2.8	4.1
Nevada	NR	NR	NA	NA
New Hampshire	69	46	−33.3	1.6
New Jersey	110	101	−8.2	0.5
New Mexico	0	0	NA	NA
New York	NR	6	NA	0.0
North Carolina	0	0	NA	NA
North Dakota	12	37	208.3	2.1
Ohio	0	0	NA	NA
Oklahoma	1,079	1,173	8.7	4.1
Oregon	NR	NR	NA	NA
Pennsylvania	894	984	10.1	2.0
Rhode Island[b]	0	0	NA	NA
South Carolina	298	332	11.4	1.6
South Dakota	76	1	−98.7	0.0
Tennessee	7,987	8,416	5.4	29.9
Texas	11,395	11,093	−2.7	6.8
Utah	1,668	1,600	−4.1	24.6
Vermont[b]	NR	NR	NA	NA
Virginia	7,449	7,973	7.0	20.8
Washington	167	158	−5.4	0.9
West Virginia	1,029	1,193	15.9	16.8
Wisconsin	7	27	285.7	0.1
Wyoming	9	NR	44.4	0.5

NR = not reported

NC = not calculated

NA = not applicable

[a]Includes federal prisoners held in nonsecure, privately operated facilities (9,153) and prisoners on home confinement (3,122). Excludes persons held in immigration detention facilities pending adjudication.

[b]Prisons and jails form one integrated system. Data include total jail and prison populations.

Note: Jurisdiction refers to the legal authority of state or federal correctional officials over a prisoner, regardless of where the prisoner is held. Totals include imputed counts for Nevada, Oregon, and Vermont, which did not submit these data to the 2015 National Prisoner Statistics.

SOURCE: Adapted from E. Ann Carson and Elizabeth Anderson, "Appendix Table 2. Prisoners under the Jurisdiction of State or Federal Correctional Authorities Held in the Custody of Private Prisons and Local Jails, December 31, 2014 and 2015," in *Prisoners in 2015*, U.S. Department of Justice, Bureau of Justice Statistics, December 2016, https://www.bjs.gov/content/pub/pdf/p15.pdf (accessed January 21, 2017).

treatment, and faith-based reentry programs that help to rehabilitate inmates and support correctional management."

• "It is difficult to find meaningful work for all inmates, even though generally all inmates are required to have a job."

TABLE 7.9

Prison facility capacity, custody population, and percentage capacity, yearend 2015

Jurisdiction	Type of capacity measure			Custody population	Custody population as a percent of—	
	Rated	Operational	Design		Lowest capacity[a]	Highest capacity[a]
Federal[b]	134,461	—	—	160,946	119.7%	119.7%
Alabama[c]	—	25,763	13,318	24,814	186.3	96.3
Alaska[d]	—	5,352	—	5,247	98.0	98.0
Arizona	37,238	43,747	37,238	35,733	96.0	81.7
Arkansas	16,194	16,233	15,382	15,784	102.6	97.2
California[c]	—	127,482	87,287	116,569	133.5	91.4
Colorado	—	14,584	14,584	15,972	109.5	109.5
Connecticut	/	/	/	15,500	/	/
Delaware[c]	5,500	5,210	4,161	6,437	154.7	117.0
Florida[e]	—	105,351	—	99,485	94.4	94.4
Georgia[e]	59,332	53,961	—	52,002	96.4	87.6
Hawaii	—	3,527	2,491	4,073	163.5	115.5
Idaho[e,f]	6,903	—	—	7,238	104.9	104.9
Illinois[f]	31,864	31,864	27,981	46,240	165.3	145.1
Indiana	—	30,020	—	26,586	88.6	88.6
Iowa[g]	7,322	7,322	7,322	8,230	112.4	112.4
Kansas	9,180	9,514	9,164	9,533	104.0	100.2
Kentucky[f]	14,349	14,349	14,349	11,959	83.3	83.3
Louisiana[e]	18,121	15,524	16,764	18,447	118.8	101.8
Maine	2,256	2,478	2,478	2,190	97.1	88.4
Maryland[h]	—	23,025	—	20,921	90.9	90.9
Massachusetts	—	—	7,728	9,493	122.8	122.8
Michigan[c]	44,734	43,996	—	42,628	96.9	95.3
Minnesota	—	9,454	—	9,578	101.3	101.3
Mississippi[e]	—	23,516	—	13,967	59.4	59.4
Missouri[c]	—	32,241	—	32,295	100.2	100.2
Montana	1,692	—	—	1,686	99.6	99.6
Nebraska[c]	—	4,094	3,275	5,133	156.7	125.4
Nevada[i]	/	/	/	13,235	/	/
New Hampshire	2,583	2,700	1,966	2,661	135.4	98.6
New Jersey	17,427	18,605	23,152	17,431	100.0	75.3
New Mexico	7,093	7,882	7,882	4,078	57.5	51.7
New York	51,480	51,676	50,957	51,485	101.0	99.6
North Carolina	—	43,815	37,503	36,888	98.4	84.2
North Dakota	—	1,353	1,353	1,345	99.4	99.4
Ohio[i]	34,986	—	—	46,190	132.0	132.0
Oklahoma	16,529	19,497	16,529	19,875	120.2	101.9
Oregon[i]	—	—	14,997	14,655	97.7	97.7
Pennsylvania	48,025	48,025	48,025	48,241	100.4	100.4
Rhode Island	3,989	3,774	3,973	2,982	79.0	74.8
South Carolina	—	23,156	—	20,457	88.3	88.3
South Dakota[c]	—	3,594	—	3,514	97.8	97.8
Tennessee	15,836	15,416	—	14,628	94.9	92.4
Texas[c]	160,017	153,789	160,017	138,199	89.9	86.4
Utah	—	7,191	7,431	4,831	67.2	65.0
Vermont[i]	1,681	1,681	1,322	1,509	114.1	89.8
Virginia	—	29,633	—	30,430	102.7	102.7
Washington	—	16,828	—	17,222	102.3	102.3
West Virginia	5,159	5,987	5,159	5,925	114.8	99.0
Wisconsin	—	22,896	17,181	22,914	133.4	100.1
Wyoming	2,288	2,288	2,407	2,133	93.2	88.6

—Not available. Specific type of capacity is not measured by state.

/Not reported.

[a]Counts are based on prisoners with sentences of more than 1 year. Excludes prisoners held in local jails, other states, or private facilities unless otherwise stated. Lowest capacity represents the minimum capacity estimate submitted by the jurisdiction, while highest capacity represents the maximum capacity estimate. When a jurisdiction could only provide a single capacity estimate, it was used as both lowest and highest capacities.

[b]Due to differences in the dates when data were extracted, the federal custody count reported for the calculation of capacity includes 258 prisoners, compared to the yearend custody reported in National Prisoner Statistics (NPS) data.

[c]State defines capacity differently than BJS.

[d]State did not submit 2015 capacity data to NPS. Counts were imputed.

[e]Private facilities included in capacity and custody counts.

[f]Counts for 2015 are not comparable to prior years due to a change in reporting methodology.

[g]Both capacity and custody counts exclude prisoners in community-based work release facilities.

[h]Capacity estimate includes some beds used for pretrial prisoners not reflected in custody count.

[i]State did not submit 2015 NPS custody or capacity data. Custody count was imputed.

[j]State did not submit 2015 NPS capacity data. Data are from 2014 or state sources.

Note: Jurisdiction refers to the legal authority of state or federal correctional officials over a prisoner, regardless of where the prisoner is held.

SOURCE: E. Ann Carson and Elizabeth Anderson, "Appendix Table 1. Prison Facility Capacity, Custody Population, and Percent Capacity, December 31, 2015," in *Prisoners in 2015*, U.S. Department of Justice, Bureau of Justice Statistics, December 2016, https://www.bjs.gov/content/pub/pdf/p15.pdf (accessed January 21, 2017)

- "Crowded visiting rooms make it more difficult for inmates to visit with their families."

- "The number of staff positions generally has not increased as BOP's population has grown, affecting staff stress and overtime hours worked."

- "The increased population taxes the infrastructure that was designed for a smaller inmate population, affecting use of toilets, showers, water, and electricity, and wear and tear on food service equipment (e.g., freezer units)."

- "Increasing inmate population and staffing ratios negatively affect inmate conduct and the imposition of discipline, thereby affecting security and safety."

The negative consequences of overcrowding identified by the GAO are likely also found in state prisons that are populated over their design capacities.

As is discussed in Chapter 6, there is a growing movement in the 21st century to reform the criminal justice system by reducing penalties for certain nonviolent crimes. These measures are designed to lower incarceration spending and to ease pressure on overcrowded prisons. Similar initiatives for the nation's probation and parole systems are described in Chapter 9. In most cases, overcrowded state prisons are a state problem. Nevertheless, the federal government can become involved if the problem becomes so acute that it violates the U.S. Constitution. The Eighth Amendment forbids "cruel and unusual punishment." This prohibition has served as the basis for numerous lawsuits filed by inmates against the government regarding overcrowding.

CALIFORNIA'S LEGAL WOES. California's long-standing legal troubles in regard to prison overcrowding are described by the U.S. Supreme Court in *Brown v. Plata* (563 U.S. 493), which was decided in May 2011. Justice Anthony M. Kennedy (1936–) notes that in 1990 a suit (*Coleman v. Brown*) was brought against the state of California regarding lack of proper mental health care for prison inmates. A federal district court appointed a special master (overseer) to supervise the state's efforts to remedy the problem. According to Kennedy, in 2002 the special master reported that mental health care in California's prisons was "deteriorating due to increased overcrowding." Meanwhile, a separate lawsuit (*Plata v. Brown*) filed in 2001 resulted in the state conceding that its prison medical care violated the Eighth Amendment rights of the state's inmates. The state agreed to make improvements laid out in a remedial injunction (a court order specifying that certain actions be taken or not taken). The state's progress, however, was stymied because of continuing problems with overcrowding in the prisons.

In 2008 the original plaintiffs in both cases succeeded in having a special three-judge panel convened to assess prison overcrowding in California. The panel was allowed under the Prison Litigation Reform Act of 1995, a federal law that lays out certain legal procedures for inmate lawsuits. The panel heard testimony on the issues involved and ordered California to decrease its prison population to 137.5% of design capacity within two years. (That deadline was later extended.) The state appealed the decision, but lost in the district courts and before the U.S. Supreme Court.

In "Public Safety Realignment" (2017, http://www.cdcr.ca.gov/realignment/), the California Department of Corrections and Rehabilitation notes that the threshold determined by the three-judge panel applies only to 34 adult facilities within the state. Thus, prisoners held in other in-state facilities (e.g., private prisons) or outside the state are not counted even though the inmates are under California jurisdiction. The department reports (http://www.cdcr.ca.gov/News/docs/3JP-Mar-2017.pdf) that as of March 15, 2017, the design capacity of the covered facilities was 85,083, and the inmate population numbered 114,275, or 134.3% of design capacity. The rates at individual institutions varied from a low of 82.8% of design capacity at the California Health Care Facility in Stockton to a high of 173.8% at North Kern State Prison in Delano.

ALABAMA FEARS FEDERAL INTERVENTION. As noted earlier and shown in Table 7.9, Alabama's prisons were the most overcrowded at yearend 2015 as measured using the lowest capacity. According to Challen Stephens in "Alabama Prisons: Why We Cannot Look Away from Alabama's Shame" (AL.com, October 2, 2014), in January 2014 the DOJ notified Alabama that it had found numerous problems involving inmate sexual abuse at the state's Julia Tutwiler Prison for women. Stephens notes, "The Justice Department, citing 'catastrophically low staffing and supervision levels,' threatened a lawsuit that could lead to the courts giving the federal government control over Tutwiler." In "Time, Money, Cooperation Crucial for Lasting Criminal Justice Reform in Alabama, State Leaders Say" (AL.com, June 10, 2014), Kelsey Stein indicates that in June 2014 Alabama joined the Justice Reinvestment Initiative, a program that is described in Chapter 6. Justice Reinvestment Initiative reforms are intended to lower incarceration costs and use the money saved to fund public safety programs. The changes, such as reduced sentences, also help relieve prison overcrowding over time.

JAILS

Besides confining offenders for short terms (usually a sentence of less than one year), jails administer community justice programs that offer alternatives to incarceration. Jails also hold suspects awaiting arraignment, trial, or sentencing, and detainees such as juveniles and mental patients who are being transferred to other facilities.

Jail Inmates in 2015

Data from the DOJ survey of the nation's jail population are reported by Todd D. Minton and Zhen Zeng of the BJS in *Jail Inmates in 2015* (December 2016, https://www.bjs.gov/content/pub/pdf/ji15.pdf). During 2015 the average daily population of jail inmates was 721,300. (See Figure 7.2.) The population peaked in 2008 at 776,600 inmates and then began a general decline. As shown in Table 7.10, the average daily population fell by 2.4% from 2014 to 2015. According to Minton and Zeng, the majority (68%) of jail

FIGURE 7.2

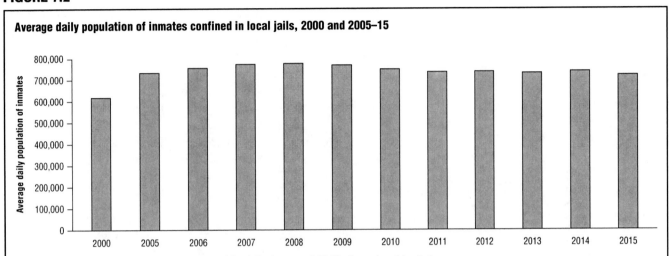

Average daily population of inmates confined in local jails, 2000 and 2005–15

Note: Average daily population is the sum of all inmates in jail each day for a year, divided by the number of days in the year.

SOURCE: Todd D. Minton and Zhen Zeng, "Figure 1. Average Daily Population of Inmates Confined in Local Jails, 2000 and 2005–2015," in *Jail Inmates in 2015*, U.S. Department of Justice, Bureau of Justice Statistics, December 2016, https://www.bjs.gov/content/pub/pdf/ji15.pdf (accessed January 21, 2017)

TABLE 7.10

Inmates confined in local jails, average daily population, and incarceration rates, midyear 2000 and 2005–2015; yearend 2015

Year	Confined inmates[a]		Average daily population[b]		Jail incarceration rate[c]	
	Total	Year-to-year percent change	Total	Year-to-year percent change	Adults and juveniles	Adults only
2000	621,100	2.5%	618,300	1.7%	220	290
2005	747,500	4.7	733,400	3.9	250	330
2006	765,800	2.4	755,300	3.0	260	340
2007	780,200	1.9	773,100	2.4	260	340
2008	785,500	0.7	776,600	0.4	260	340
2009	767,400	−2.3	768,100	−1.1	250	330
2010	748,700	−2.4	748,600	−2.5	240	320
2011	735,600	−1.8	735,600	−1.7	240	310
2012	744,500	1.2	737,400	0.2	240	310
2013	731,200	−1.8	731,400	−0.8	230	300
2014	744,600	1.8	739,000	1.0	230	300
2015[d]	728,200	−2.2	[g]	[g]	230	[f]
2015[e]	693,300[h]	[h]	721,300[d]	−2.4	[h]	[h]

[a]Unless noted for a specific year, data are based on the number of inmates confined on the last weekday in June.
[b]Sum of all inmates in jail each day for a year, divided by the number of days in the year.
[c]Number of confined inmates per 100,000 U.S. residents. Adults are defined as persons age 18 or loder, and juveniles are defined as persons age 17 or younger.
[d]Data are based on the number of inmates confined on December 31, 2015.
[d]Comparison year on confined inmates and average daily population.
[e]Data are based on the number of inmates confined on December 31, 2015.
[f]Data not collected.
[g]Data not calculated.
[h]Data not compared because the jail population goes through seasonal variation, typically with fewer inmates at yearend than at midyear.
Note: Data are adjusted for nonresponse and rounded to the nearest 100 for confined inmates and average daily population. Starting in 2015, the Annual Survey Jails collects data on the number of inmates confined on the last weekday in June (midyear) and on December 31 (yearend).

SOURCE: Todd D. Minton and Zhen Zeng, "Table 1. Inmates Confined in Local Jails, Average Daily Population, and Incarceration Rates, Midyear 2000 and 2005–2015; Yearend 2015," in *Jail Inmates in 2015*, U.S. Department of Justice, Bureau of Justice Statistics, December 2016, https://www.bjs.gov/content/pub/pdf/ji15.pdf (accessed January 21, 2017)

inmates were being held for a felony offenses. The other 32% were being held either for misdemeanors or other offenses.

TABLE 7.11

Number of annual admissions to local jails, 1999 and 2007–15

Year	Estimated total number of annual admissions[a]	Year–to–year percent change
1999	11,400,000	[c]
2007	13,100,000	[c]
2008	13,600,000	3.8%
2009	12,800,000	−5.9
2010	12,900,000	0.8
2011	11,800,000	−8.5
2012	11,600,000	−1.7
2013	11,700,000	0.9
2014	11,400,000	−2.6
2015[b]	10,900,000	−4.4
Average annual change		
1999–2014	0.0%	
2014–2015	−4.4	

[a]In 2015, the ASJ collected annual admissions. The 1999 Census of Jails and the 2007–2014 ASJ collected data on weekly admissions during the last week in June. The number of annual admissions was calculated by multiplying the weekly admissions by 365 days and dividing by 7 days.
[b]Comparison year on annual admissions.
[c]Not calculated.
Note: Data are adjusted for nonresponse and rounded to the nearest 100,000.

SOURCE: Todd D. Minton and Zhen Zeng, "Table 2. Number of Annual Admissions to Local Jails, 1999 and 2007–2015," in *Jail Inmates in 2015*, U.S. Department of Justice, Bureau of Justice Statistics, December 2016, https://www.bjs.gov/content/pub/pdf/ji15.pdf (accessed January 21, 2017)

Table 7.11 shows the number of annual admissions for 1999 and for 2007 through 2015. Overall, jail admissions climbed between 1999 and 2007 and then began to decline. There were 10.9 million admissions to local jails in 2015, down 4.4% compared with 2014.

Local Jail Sizes and Capacities

In *Jail Inmates in 2015*, Minton and Zeng note that in 2015 only 3.4% of jailed inmates were in facilities that held fewer than 50 inmates each. The largest percentage (20.8%) of inmates were in facilities that held 2,500 or more inmates each.

Overall, the nation's jails do not suffer as much overcrowding as the state and federal prisons. Figure 7.3 shows the average daily population compared to the rated capacity of local jails between 2000 and 2015. (Note that data were compiled based on midyear surveys.) Local jails had a rated capacity of 904,900 inmates at midyear 2015. The facilities were at 79.7% of rated capacity.

The percentages of capacity occupied at local jails differ greatly by jurisdiction size. Jails with fewer than 50 inmates were at 55.3% of capacity at midyear 2015, whereas those holding 2,500 or more inmates were at 79.5% of capacity, and those holding 1,000 to 2,499 inmates were at 85.8% capacity.

FIGURE 7.3

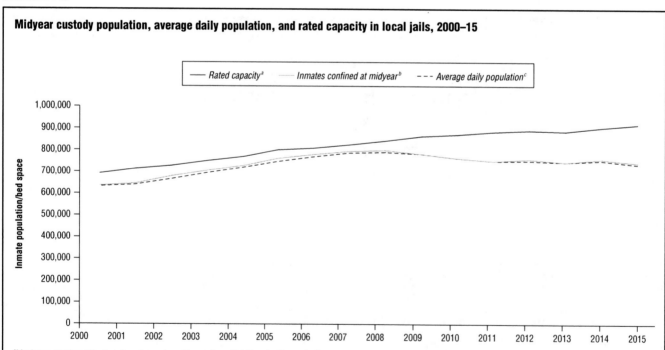

Midyear custody population, average daily population, and rated capacity in local jails, 2000–15

[a]Maximum number of beds or inmates assigned by a rating official to a facility, excluding separate temporary holding areas.
[b]Number of inmates held on the last weekday in June.
[c]Sum of all inmates in jail each day for a year, divided by the number of days in the year.

SOURCE: Todd D. Minton and Zhen Zeng, "Figure 2. Midyear Custody Population, Average Daily Population, and Rated Capacity in Local Jails, 2000–2015," in *Jail Inmates in 2015*, U.S. Department of Justice, Bureau of Justice Statistics, December 2016, https://www.bjs.gov/content/pub/pdf/ji15.pdf (accessed January 21, 2017)

Jail-Supervised People in 2015

As noted earlier, local jails perform services other than full-time confinement of inmates. Minton and Zeng indicate in *Jail Inmates in 2015* that overall, jails supervised 750,500 people at yearend 2015—693,300 inmates held in jail facilities full time and 57,100 people being supervised in other ways. Examples include community service programs, day reporting, electronic monitoring programs, home detention, treatment programs, and work programs.

COSTS OF INCARCERATION

It is important to note that the correctional system includes both incarceration and community supervision (i.e., parole and probation programs). Determining the amount that the nation spends solely on incarceration each year is difficult because of the many jurisdictions involved. Each state and local government has its own budgeting system. In addition, there are significant funds transferred between different government levels. For example, the federal government spends money directly on the federal prison system and also provides grants and other funding to state and local governments to help with their incarceration costs. Likewise, state governments provide intergovernmental funds to local jurisdictions.

As is shown in Table 1.2 in Chapter 1, the total amount spent on corrections at the federal, state, and local levels in fiscal year (FY) 2012 was $80.8 billion. Federal direct expenditures on corrections were $8.3 billion, state direct expenditures were $46.3 billion, and local direct expenditures were $26.2 billion.

Table 7.12 provides an historical perspective on state and local corrections expenditures by comparing spending for 1979–80 with that in 2012–13. The amounts are given in constant 2013 dollars, meaning that for both sets of data the dollar was assumed to have the value it had in 2013. Nationwide the expenditures increased by 324% from $16.6 billion in 1979–80 to $70.5 billion in 2012–13.

In *State Corrections Expenditures, FY 1982–2010* (April 30, 2014, https://www.bjs.gov/content/pub/pdf/scefy8210.pdf), Tracey Kyckelhahn of the BJS notes that correctional institutional costs skyrocketed from 1982 through the end of the 20th century before leveling off. Near the end of the first decade of the 21st century the United States underwent a severe economic downturn dubbed the Great Recession. As a result, many states suffered significant budget shortfalls and looked for ways to cut expenses. Some states began closing prisons to reduce their corrections expenditures. This was particularly true for states with declining inmate populations. The Sentencing Project notes in *Repurposing: New Beginnings for Closed Prisons* (December 15, 2016, http://www.sentencingproject.org/publications/repurposing-new-beginnings-closed-prisons/) that between 2011 and 2016, at least 22 states closed or announced their intentions to close 94 state prisons and juvenile facilities.

Incarceration costs are most easily ascertained for the federal government. The federal FY runs from October 1 through September 30. Thus, FY 2017 covers October 1, 2016, through September 30, 2017. In *Federal Prison System Federal Bureau of Prisons* (February 2016, https://www.justice.gov/jmd/file/822106/download), the DOJ indicates that the BOP's requested budget for FY 2017 was $7.3 billion, down slightly from the $7.5 billion in funding that was enacted for FY 2016.

WORK, EDUCATIONAL, AND COUNSELING PROGRAMS FOR INMATES

Many state and federal prisons offer inmate work, educational, and counseling programs. For example, the New York State Department of Corrections and Community Supervision (2017, http://www.doccs.ny.gov/ProgramServices/program_list_alpha.html) lists dozens of programs and services that are available to inmates in certain state prisons.

Prisoner Work Programs

State and local governments prevent prisoners from working at some jobs because they would be in competition with private enterprise or workers. In 1936 Congress barred convicts from working on federal contracts worth more than $10,000. In 1940 Congress made it illegal to transport convict-made goods through interstate commerce. These rules were changed in 1979, when Congress established the Prison Industry Enhancement Certification Program. The program allows state correctional industries that meet certain requirements to sell inmate-produced goods to the federal government and in interstate commerce. The National Correctional Industries Association, the professional organization for prison industry employees, provides training and technical assistance to the program.

Many prison administrators generally favor work programs. Some believe work keeps prisoners productive and occupied, thus leading to a safer prison environment. Another benefit is that work programs prepare prisoners for reentry into the noninstitutionalized world by helping them develop job skills and solid work habits that will be needed for post-incarceration employment. Some prisons report that inmates who work in industry are less likely to cause problems in prison or be rearrested after release than convicts who do not participate in work programs.

In addition, many inmates report they like the opportunity to work. They assert that it provides relief from boredom and gives them some extra money. Inmates find that the money they earn helps them to meet financial obligations for their families even while they are in prison.

Work Programs for Federal Inmates

The BOP explains in "Work Programs" (2017, https://www.bop.gov/inmates/custody_and_care/work_programs.jsp?) that federal prison inmates are required to work if they are medically able to do so. Their work assignments

TABLE 7.12

State and local corrections expenditures, 1979–80 and 2012–13

	State and local corrections expenditures (in constant 2013 dollars)		
	1979–80	**2012–13**	**Change**
Total (50 states)	**$16,619,181,455**	**$70,547,349,000**	**324%**
Alabama	188,039,084	680,275,000	262
Alaska	74,883,058	324,452,000	333
Arizona	234,030,418	1,383,473,000	491
Arkansas	87,151,984	539,075,000	519
California	2,722,506,379	12,763,436,000	369
Colorado	191,066,829	1,171,292,000	513
Connecticut	185,017,299	643,930,000	248
Delaware	61,049,599	280,152,000	359
Florida	677,189,835	3,886,503,000	474
Georgia	371,628,932	2,109,958,000	468
Hawaii	42,945,708	200,482,000	367
Idaho	38,928,581	311,749,000	701
Illinois	681,817,875	1,995,482,000	193
Indiana	273,632,494	982,587,000	259
Iowa	154,474,619	406,800,000	163
Kansas	113,987,464	507,132,000	345
Kentucky	207,016,134	744,106,000	259
Louisiana	327,938,207	1,279,578,000	290
Maine	55,321,916	187,730,000	239
Maryland	457,880,936	1,732,240,000	278
Massachusetts	426,307,153	1,061,575,000	149
Michigan	761,117,389	2,430,553,000	219
Minnesota	267,177,674	866,329,000	224
Mississippi	93,001,850	495,541,000	433
Missouri	227,343,153	868,674,000	282
Montana	58,275,159	231,032,000	296
Nebraska	80,694,184	361,331,000	348
Nevada	117,879,428	676,355,000	474
New Hampshire	42,266,253	181,784,000	330
New Jersey	538,870,146	2,059,640,000	282
New Mexico	75,723,437	608,867,000	704
New York	2,049,718,099	5,970,104,000	191
North Carolina	472,831,919	1,648,330,000	249
North Dakota	22,028,636	112,391,000	410
Ohio	522,315,888	1,759,207,000	237
Oklahoma	158,512,606	699,701,000	341
Oregon	246,519,868	1,041,559,000	323
Pennsylvania	757,296,947	3,182,655,000	320
Rhode Island	56,263,616	199,476,000	255
South Carolina	205,463,520	709,439,000	245
South Dakota	23,864,356	158,903,000	566
Tennessee	273,811,298	1,061,028,000	288
Texas	603,832,570	5,736,222,000	850
Utah	79,293,554	505,949,000	538
Vermont	31,335,377	134,803,000	330
Virginia	487,526,616	2,174,796,000	346
Washington	392,405,941	1,500,971,000	283
West Virginia	57,136,775	333,203,000	483
Wisconsin	317,570,563	1,433,083,000	351
Wyoming	26,290,128	213,416,000	712

SOURCE: Adapted from "Exhibit A-1. Change in PK-12 Current Expenditures and State and Local Corrections Current Expenditures from 1979–80 to 2012–13, by State," in *State and Local Expenditures on Corrections and Education: A Brief from the U.S. Department of Education, Policy and Program Studies Service*, U.S. Department of Education, Policy and Program Studies Service, July 2016, https://www2.ed.gov/rschstat/eval/other/expenditures-corrections-education/brief.pdf (accessed January 21, 2017)

typically contribute to the facility operations and maintenance in areas such as food service, plumbing, painting, or landscaping. Inmates earn $0.12 to $0.40 per hour for these in-house work assignments. In "UNICOR Socioeconomic Impact: The Straight Facts" (2017, https://www.bop.gov/inmates/custody_and_care/docs/unicorStraightFacts.pdf), the BOP also reports that more than 20,000 federal

prison inmates work annually in Federal Prison Industries factories. This program (https://www.bop.gov/inmates/custody_and_care/unicor_about.jsp) provides slightly higher wages to inmates, from $0.23 to $1.15 per hour. Work includes manufacturing jobs in areas such as furniture, electronics, textiles, and graphic arts. A high school diploma or its equivalent is required for all but entry-level positions.

CHAPTER 8
CHARACTERISTICS AND RIGHTS OF INMATES

CHARACTERISTICS OF INMATES

As of April 2017, recent national information about inmate characteristics was available from two primary sources: the Federal Bureau of Prisons (BOP) and the Bureau of Justice Statistics (BJS). Both are agencies of the U.S. Department of Justice (DOJ). Because these sources compile inmate data at different times for different inmate population subsets, they provide somewhat differing datasets of inmate counts and characteristics. In addition, some inmate counts include only adults, whereas others also include juveniles. (Detailed information about the juvenile justice system is provided in Chapter 10.) Lastly, it is important to distinguish between the different ways in which inmates are officially counted:

- Inmates under jurisdiction—the number of inmates under the jurisdiction of a governmental entity regardless of where the inmates are held and their incarceration status

- Inmates in custody—the number of inmates in the physical custody of a particular jurisdiction (i.e., the number of inmates held within the facilities of that jurisdiction)

- Sentenced inmates—the number of inmates that have been sentenced by the justice system and are serving sentences in prison or jail

Federal and State Inmates

As shown in Table 8.1, about 1.5 million adults were under the jurisdiction of federal or state prisons at yearend 2015. The inmate population was predominantly male (1.4 million or 93%) with only 111,495 female prisoners (7% of the total).

Table 8.2 provides a breakdown for the sentenced federal and state inmates at yearend 2015 by age, sex, race, and Hispanic origin. (Note that individual percentages may not sum to 100% because of rounding and other data adjustments.) The largest single age category was 30 to 34 years; 16.5% of the inmates fell into this age group. More than four out of 10 inmates (43.4%) were under the age of 35 years. The racial and ethnic breakdown for all of the prisoners was:

- Non-Hispanic African American—501,300 males and 21,700 females (523,000 inmates or 35% of the total)

- Non-Hispanic white—466,700 males and 52,700 females (519,400 inmates or 35% of the total)

- Hispanic—301,500 males and 17,900 females (319,400 inmates or 22% of the total)

- Other—122,400 males and 12,700 females (135,100 inmates or 9% of the total)

The overall adult incarceration rate at yearend 2015 was 458 prisoners per 100,000 U.S. residents of all ages. (See Table 8.3.) In *Prisoners in 2015* (December 2016, https://www.bjs.gov/content/pub/pdf/p15.pdf), E. Ann Carson and Elizabeth Anderson of the BJS note that the 2015 incarceration rate was the lowest since 1997 when the rate was 444 inmates per 100,000 U.S. residents of all ages. In 2015 the incarceration rate for males (863) was much higher than that for females (64). Table 8.3 also lists incarceration rates just for the adult population; that is, people aged 18 years and older. In 2015 the overall incarceration rate for adults was 593 per 100,000 U.S. residents aged 18 years and older. As shown in Table 8.3 and Figure 8.1, the adult incarceration rate for non-Hispanic whites was relatively flat between 2005 and 2015, whereas the adult incarceration rates for non-Hispanic African Americans and for Hispanics fell over this period.

OFFENSES OF FEDERAL INMATES. Table 8.4 provides a breakdown by most serious offense for 185,917 sentenced federal prisoners as of September 30, 2015. (Note that the individual percentages may not sum to the total because of rounding.) Nearly half (49.5%) of the inmates

TABLE 8.1

Prisoners under jurisdiction of state or federal correctional authorities, by jurisdiction and sex, yearend 2015

Jurisdiction	Total	Male	Female
U.S. total[a]	1,526,792	1,415,297	111,495
Federal[b]	196,455	183,502	12,953
State[a]	1,330,337	1,231,795	98,542
Alabama	30,810	28,220	2,590
Alaska[c]	5,338	4,761	577
Arizona	42,719	38,738	3,981
Arkansas	17,707	16,305	1,402
California	129,593	123,808	5,785
Colorado	20,168	18,322	1,846
Connecticut[c]	15,816	14,695	1,121
Delaware[c]	6,654	6,117	537
Florida	101,424	94,481	6,943
Georgia	52,193	48,578	3,615
Hawaii[c]	5,879	5,177	702
Idaho[d]	8,052	7,068	984
Illinois[d]	46,240	43,565	2,675
Indiana	27,355	24,815	2,540
Iowa	8,849	8,041	808
Kansas	9,857	9,018	839
Kentucky[d]	21,701	19,114	2,587
Louisiana	36,377	34,331	2,046
Maine	2,279	2,072	207
Maryland	20,764	19,849	915
Massachusetts	9,922	9,268	654
Michigan	42,628	40,355	2,273
Minnesota	10,798	10,027	771
Mississippi	18,911	17,595	1,316
Missouri	32,330	29,063	3,267
Montana	3,685	3,295	390
Nebraska	5,372	4,943	429
Nevada[e]	13,071	11,905	1,166
New Hampshire	2,897	2,661	236
New Jersey	20,489	19,581	908
New Mexico	7,169	6,463	706
New York	51,727	49,373	2,354
North Carolina	36,617	33,928	2,689
North Dakota	1,795	1,587	208
Ohio	52,233	47,803	4,430
Oklahoma	28,547	25,489	3,058
Oregon[e]	15,245	13,938	1,307
Pennsylvania	49,858	47,039	2,819
Rhode Island[c]	3,248	3,102	146
South Carolina	20,929	19,574	1,355
South Dakota	3,564	3,148	416
Tennessee	28,172	25,532	2,640
Texas	163,909	149,501	14,408
Utah	6,492	5,977	515
Vermont[c]	1,750	1,600	150
Virginia	38,403	35,167	3,236
Washington	18,284	16,829	1,455
West Virginia	7,118	6,253	865
Wisconsin	22,975	21,567	1,408
Wyoming	2,424	2,157	267

TABLE 8.1

Prisoners under jurisdiction of state or federal correctional authorities, by jurisdiction and sex, yearend 2015 [CONTINUED]

[a]Total and state estimates include imputed counts for Nevada and Oregon, which did not submit 2015 data to National Prisoner Statistics (NPS).
[b]Includes prisoners held in nonsecure, privately operated community corrections facilities and juveniles held in contract facilities.
[c]Prisons and jails form one integrated system. Data include total jail and prison populations.
[d]State has changed reporting methodology, so 2015 counts are not comparable to those published for earlier years.
[e]State did not submit 2015 NPS data. Counts were imputed.
Note: Jurisdiction refers to the legal authority state or federal correctional officials over a prisoner, regardless of where the prisoner is held.

SOURCE: Adapted from E. Ann Carson and Elizabeth Anderson, "Table 2. Prisoners under Jurisdiction of State or Federal Correctional Authorities, by Jurisdiction and Sex, December 31, 2014 and 2015," in *Prisoners in 2015*, U.S. Department of Justice, Bureau of Justice Statistics, December 2016, https://www.bjs.gov/content/pub/pdf/p15.pdf (accessed January 21, 2017)

prisoners as of yearend 2014. More than half (52.9%) had committed a violent offense as their most serious offense. Overall, the largest fractions of inmates had been incarcerated for murder (13%), robbery (12.8%), or rape/ sexual assault (12.4%). A violent offense was the most serious offense listed for 58.7% of Hispanic inmates, 57.8% of non-Hispanic African American inmates, and 46.6% of non-Hispanic white inmates under the jurisdiction of state correctional authorities.

Local Jail Inmates

Table 8.6 provides demographic and conviction status data for jail inmates at midyear for selected years between 2000 and 2014 and at yearend 2015. (Note that both adults and juveniles are included.) At yearend 2015 nearly all (99.5%) of the inmates were adults and most (85.7%) of them were male. Regarding racial and ethnic origin, the largest contingent of the jail inmates was non-Hispanic white (48.3%), followed by non-Hispanic African American (35.1%) and Hispanic (14.3%). The remaining inmates were non-Hispanic and were of other races. At yearend 2015, more than a third (37.3%) of the inmates in the nation's jails had been convicted of crimes, whereas 62.7% had not been convicted.

INMATE HEALTH

In "National Survey of Prison Health Care: Selected Findings" (*National Health Statistics Reports*, no. 96, July 28, 2016), Karishma A. Chari et al. note, "Prison inmates have higher rates of mental illness, chronic medical conditions, and infectious diseases compared with the general population." These conclusions are borne out by major BJS surveys of prisoners in federal, state, and local correctional facilities (see https://www.bjs.gov/index.cfm?ty=pbtp&tid=1 for a list of relevant publications and products).

Mental Health Problems

A movement began during the 1970s to deinstitutionalize the mentally ill and reintegrate them into society.

had been incarcerated for violating federal drug laws. Weapons offenses were listed for 16.3% of the inmates, and other public order offenses were listed for 12% of the inmates. Overall, 7.4% of all sentenced federal prisoners had been incarcerated for violent offenses including robbery (3.7%), homicide (1.5%), or other violent crimes (2.1%). A violent offense was the most serious offense listed for 10% of non-Hispanic African American inmates, 7% of non-Hispanic white inmates, and 2.1% of Hispanic inmates.

OFFENSES OF STATE INMATES. Table 8.5 provides a breakdown by offense for 1.3 million sentenced state

TABLE 8.2

Percentage of sentenced prisoners under the jurisdiction of state or federal correctional authorities, by age, sex, race, and Hispanic origin, yearend 2015

Age group	Male						Female				
	Total[a]	All males[a]	White[b]	Black[b]	Hispanic	Other[b]	All females[a]	White[b]	Black[b]	Hispanic	Other[b]
Total[c]	100%	100%	100%	100%	100%	100%	100%	100%	100%	100%	100%
18–19	0.8	0.8	0.5	1.2	1.0	1.1	0.5	0.4	0.9	0.6	0.8
20–24	10.5	10.6	7.7	12.5	11.9	12.7	9.2	8.0	11.5	11.2	10.2
25–29	15.6	15.4	13.3	16.3	17.3	16.2	17.8	17.5	17.5	20.1	18.1
30–34	16.5	16.3	15.4	15.9	18.3	17.3	19.0	19.0	17.1	20.7	19.7
35–39	14.6	14.6	13.7	14.5	16.1	15.0	15.2	15.6	13.8	16.2	15.7
40–44	12.1	12.1	12.2	11.8	12.4	12.6	12.5	13.1	12.4	11.7	12.6
45–49	10.3	10.3	11.6	9.9	9.0	9.5	10.5	10.6	11.5	8.9	10.2
50–54	8.6	8.7	10.6	8.4	6.5	7.1	7.9	8.3	8.3	5.6	7.1
55–59	5.4	5.5	7.0	5.2	3.7	4.3	4.1	4.4	4.6	2.8	3.1
60–64	2.8	2.9	3.9	2.5	2.0	2.2	1.8	2.1	1.8	1.1	1.6
65 or older	2.4	2.5	4.1	1.5	1.6	2.0	1.2	1.5	0.9	0.6	0.8
Number of sentenced prisoners[d]	1,476,847	1,371,879	446,700	501,300	301,500	122,400	104,968	52,700	21,700	17,900	12,700

[a]Includes American Indians and Alaska Natives; Asians, Native Hawaiians, and other Pacific Islanders; and persons of two or more races.
[b]Excludes persons of Hispanic or Latino orgin.
[c]Includes persons age 17 or younger.
[d]Race and Hispanic origin totals are rounded to the nearest 100 to accommodate differences in data collection techniques between jurisdictions.
Note: Jurisdiction refers to the legal authority of state or federal correctional officials over a prisoner, regardless of where the prisoner is held. Counts are based on prisoners with sentences of more than 1 year. Federal data include prisoners held in nonsecure, privately operated community corrections facilities and juveniles held in contract facilities. Includes imputed counts for Nevada and Oregon, which did not submit 2015 data to National Prisoner Statistics.

SOURCE: E. Ann Carson and Elizabeth Anderson, "Table 8. Percent of Sentenced Prisoners under the Jurisdiction of State or Federal Correctional Authorities, by Age, Sex, Race, and Hispanic Origin, December 31, 2015," in *Prisoners in 2015*, U.S. Department of Justice, Bureau of Justice Statistics, December 2016, https://www.bjs.gov/content/pub/pdf/p15.pdf (accessed January 21, 2017)

TABLE 8.3

Imprisonment rate of sentenced prisoners under the jurisdiction of state or federal correctional authorities, by jurisdiction and demographic characteristics, yearend 2005–15

Year	Per 100,000 U.S. residents of all ages					Per 100,000 U.S. residents age 18 or older					
	Total	Federal[a]	State	Male	Female	Total	Male	Female	White[b]	Black[b]	Hispanic
2005	492	56	436	932	65	655	1,257	86	319	2,228	1,084
2006	501	58	443	948	68	666	1,275	89	325	2,227	1,107
2007	506	59	447	955	69	670	1,282	90	324	2,232	1,123
2008	506	60	447	956	69	669	1,279	90	327	2,216	1,085
2009	504	61	443	952	67	665	1,271	88	325	2,183	1,078
2010	500	61	439	948	66	656	1,260	86	329	2,128	1,025
2011	492	63	429	932	65	644	1,236	84	326	2,058	996
2012	480	62	417	909	63	626	1,201	82	315	1,920	926
2013	478	61	417	905	65	623	1,192	83	317	1,882	898
2014	471	60	411	889	65	611	1,168	84	317	1,824	860
2015[c]	458	55	402	863	64	593	1,131	82	312	1,745	820
Percent change											
Average annual,											
2004–2014	−0.4	0.7	−0.6	−0.5	0.0	−0.7	−0.7	−0.3	−0.1%	−2.0%	−2.3%
2014–2015	−2.8%	−7.3%	−2.1%	−2.9%	−1.8%	−3.0%	−3.1%	−2.0%	−1.6%	−4.3%	−4.7%

[a]Includes prisoners held in nonsecure, privately operated community corrections facilities and juveniles held in contract facilities.
[b]Excludes persons of Hispanic or Latino origin and persons of two or more races.
[c]Total and state estimates include imputed counts for Nevada and Oregon, which did not submit 2015 data to National Prisoner Statistics.
Note: Jurisdiction refers to the legal authority of state or federal correctional officials over a prisoner, regardless of where the prisoner is held. Counts are based on prisoners with sentences of more than 1 year.

SOURCE: E. Ann Carson and Elizabeth Anderson, "Table 5. Imprisonment Rate of Sentenced Prisoners under the Jurisdiction of State or Federal Correctional Authorities, by Jurisdiction and Demographic Characteristics, December 31, 2005–2015," in *Prisoners in 2015*, U.S. Department of Justice, Bureau of Justice Statistics, December 2016, https://www.bjs.gov/content/pub/pdf/p15.pdf (accessed January 21, 2017)

This widespread trend resulted in the closing of many large mental hospitals and treatment centers. With fewer options open to them, the mentally ill came into contact with law enforcement authorities much more often.

FIGURE 8.1

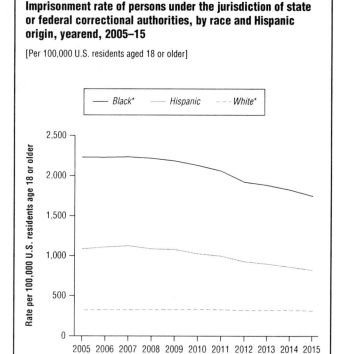

Imprisonment rate of persons under the jurisdiction of state or federal correctional authorities, by race and Hispanic origin, yearend, 2005–15

[Per 100,000 U.S. residents aged 18 or older]

*Excludes persons of Hispanic or Latino origin and persons of two or more races.
Note: Jurisdiction refers to the legal authority of state or federal correctional officials over a prisoner, regardless of where the prisoner is held. Counts are based on prisoners with sentences of more than 1 year. Federal data include prisoners held in nonsecure, privately operated community corrections facilities and juveniles held in contract facilities. Rates are per 100,000 U.S. residents age 18 or older of corresponding race or Hispanic origin.

SOURCE: E. Ann Carson and Elizabeth Anderson, "Figure 4. Imprisonment Rate of Persons under the Jurisdiction of State or Federal Correctional Authorities per 100,000 U.S. Residents Age 18 or Older, by Race and Hispanic Origin, December 31, 2005–2015," in *Prisoners in 2015*, U.S. Department of Justice, Bureau of Justice Statistics, December 2016, https://www.bjs.gov/content/pub/pdf/p15.pdf (accessed January 21, 2017).

As of April 2017, the most recent comprehensive estimates of mental illness among prisoners were published in 2006. In *Mental Health Problems of Prison and Jail Inmates* (December 2006, https://www.bjs.gov/content/pub/pdf/mhppji.pdf), Doris J. James and Lauren E. Glaze of the BJS estimate that more than half of all prison and jail inmates had a mental health problem at midyear 2005.

The Treatment Advocacy Center is a nonprofit organization devoted to issues related to the treatment of mental illness. In *The Treatment of Persons with Mental Illness in Prisons and Jails: A State Survey* (April 8, 2014, http://www.treatmentadvocacycenter.org/storage/documents/treatment-behind-bars/treatment-behind-bars.pdf), E. Fuller Torrey et al. use percentages gleaned from James and Glaze's 2006 report to estimate that in 2012 people with "severe mental illness" in the nation's state prisons and jails (356,268) far outnumbered similarly afflicted patients in state psychiatric hospitals (35,000). The researchers

note that "prisons and jails have become America's 'new asylums.'" The incarceration of so many mentally ill inmates has had negative consequences, including high inmate suicide rates and "behavioral issues disturbing to other prisoners and correctional staff." According to Torrey et al., mentally ill prisoners tend to be incarcerated for longer periods than other prisoners. This contributes to overcrowding and increases taxpayer costs for the correctional system. Also, mentally ill prisoners are more likely than other prisoners to engage in physical attacks, be victimized while they are incarcerated, be put into solitary confinement (which typically worsens their symptoms), and be rearrested after being released.

The Treatment Advocacy Center, in collaboration with the National Sheriffs' Association, surveyed correctional officials around the country to obtain information about treatment policies for mentally ill inmates. Torrey et al. note that all states except Arkansas participated in the survey. One factor that greatly complicates treatment is that some mentally ill inmates "are unaware of their own illness" and refuse to take prescribed medications. The states have varying legal procedures for correctional officials to follow when they seek to provide treatment against inmate wishes. Torrey et al. complain that these procedures are "often grossly underutilized" or fail to provide desired outcomes. For example, they explain that "many jails require the inmate to be transferred to a state psychiatric hospital for treatment; since such hospitals are almost always full, such treatment does not take place in most cases." The researchers recommend reform measures for the nation's public mental health system to help prevent mentally ill people from being incarcerated in the first place. In addition, they advocate for changes to laws and policies to ensure that mentally ill inmates receive appropriate medical treatment while they are incarcerated.

Medical Problems

In *Medical Problems of State and Federal Prisoners and Jail Inmates, 2011–12* (February 2015, https://www.bjs.gov/content/pub/pdf/mpsfpji1112.pdf), Laura M. Maruschak, Marcus Berzofsky, and Jennifer Unangst indicate that in 2011–12, nearly half of state and federal prisoners (43.9%) and jail inmates (44.7%) reported ever having a chronic health condition (i.e., cancer, high blood pressure or hypertension, stroke-related problems, diabetes or high blood sugar, heart-related problems kidney-related problems, arthritis or rheumatism, asthma, and cirrhosis of the liver). By comparison, the prevalence of these conditions was only 26.9% to 31% among general populations standardized to match the facility populations by sex, age, race, and Hispanic origin. In addition, 21% of the state and federal prisoners and 14.3% of the jail inmates reported ever having tuberculosis, hepatitis B or C, or other sexually transmitted diseases (excluding HIV or AIDS). The prevalence rates for

TABLE 8.4

Percentage of sentenced prisoners under the jurisdiction of federal correctional authority, by most serious offense, sex, race, and Hispanic origin, September 30, 2015

Most serious offense	All prisoners[a]	Male	Female	White[b]	Black[b]	Hispanic
Total	**100%**	**100%**	**100%**	**100%**	**100%**	**100%**
Violent	7.4%	7.6%	4.1%	7.0%	10.0%	2.1%
Homicide[c]	1.5	1.5	1.3	0.7	2.4	0.3
Robbery	3.7	3.9	1.6	4.7	5.6	0.9
Other	2.1	2.2	1.2	1.6	2.0	0.9
Property	6.0%	5.2%	18.2%	9.6%	6.1%	2.8%
Burglary	0.2	0.2	0.1	0.1	0.4	0.0
Fraud	4.7	4.0	15.4	7.6	4.6	2.3
Other	1.1	1.0	2.7	1.9	1.1	0.4
Drug[d]	49.5%	48.9%	58.6%	39.6%	51.0%	57.7%
Public order	36.3%	37.6%	18.3%	42.4%	32.4%	37.0%
Immigration	8.0	8.4	3.3	0.9	0.3	23.4
Weapons	16.3	17.1	4.3	14.8	25.2	7.7
Other	12.0	12.1	10.7	26.7	6.9	5.9
Other/unspecified[e]	0.8%	0.8%	0.7%	1.5%	0.5%	0.4%
Total number of sentenced prisoners	185,917	173,857	12,060	50,300	69,000	60,800

[a]Includes American Indians and Alaska Natives; Asians, Native Hawaiians, and other Pacific Islanders; and persons of two or more races.
[b]Excludes persons of Hispanic or Latino origin and persons of two or more races.
[c]Includes murder, negligent manslaughter, and nonnegligent manslaughter.
[d]Includes trafficking, possession, and other drug offenses.
[e]Includes offenses not classified.
Note: Jurisdiction refers to the legal authority of federal correctional officials over a prisoner, regardless of where the prisoner is held. Counts based on sentenced prisoners of all sentence lengths under federal jurisdiction on September 30, 2015. Detail may not sum to total due to rounding and missing offence data.

SOURCE: E. Ann Carson and Elizabeth Anderson, "Table 10. Percent of Sentenced Prisoners under the Jurisdiction of Federal Correctional Authority, by Most Serious Offense, Sex, Race, and Hispanic Origin, September 30, 2015," in *Prisoners in 2015*, U.S. Department of Justice, Bureau of Justice Statistics, December 2016, https://www.bjs.gov/content/pub/pdf/p15.pdf (accessed January 21, 2017)

the standardized generation populations were much lower at 4.6% to 4.8%. Although the prevalence of HIV/AIDS was very low among state and federal prisoners (1.3%) and among jail inmates (1.3%), it was still higher than the 0.3% to 0.4% for the standardized general populations.

Maruschak, Berzofsky, and Unangst also note that in 2011–12 large majorities of state and federal prisoners (74%) and jail inmates (62%) were overweight, obese, or morbidly obese. These designations are based on body mass index (BMI) scores calculated from height and weight measurements. Higher BMI scores indicate excessive body fat and are considered a risk factor for a variety of health problems including diabetes and high blood pressure.

Disabilities

In *Disabilities among Prison and Jail Inmates, 2011–12* (December 2015, https://www.bjs.gov/content/pub/pdf/dpji1112.pdf), Jennifer Bronson, Laura M. Maruschak, and Marcus Berzofsky note that in 2011–12 state and federal prisoners and jail inmates were three to four times more likely than standardized general populations to have a disability. The disabilities included serious difficulties with hearing, vision, or cognition. Cognitive disabilities affect brain-related tasks such as attention, memory, problem solving, and reading comprehension. Examples include attention deficit disorder, autism, and learning disorders. The prisoners and inmates were also

surveyed to determine the prevalence of ambulatory disabilities (e.g., serious difficulties with walking or climbing stairs), self-care disabilities (e.g., problems with dressing or bathing), and independent living disabilities (e.g., difficulties with activities such as going to classes, meal times, or programs). Overall, 32% of state and federal prisoners and 40% of jail inmates self-reported having at least one disability. This compares with a prevalence rate of only 9.3% to 10.9% for the standardized general populations.

SEXUAL VIOLENCE IN PRISONS AND JAILS

In response to concerns about sexual misconduct in prisons, President George W. Bush (1946–) signed into law the Prison Rape Elimination Act in September 2003. As part of this legislation, the BJS was charged with collection data on the incidence and prevalence of sexual assault within correctional facilities. As of April 2017, the most recent report on sexual violence at adult prisons and jails was by Allen J. Beck et al. in *Sexual Victimization in Prisons and Jails Reported by Inmates, 2011–12* (May 2013, https://www.bjs.gov/content/pub/pdf/svpjri1112.pdf). (Chapter 10 discusses sexual victimization in juvenile detention facilities.)

The data are based on the third National Inmate Survey, which was conducted between February 2011 and May 2012 in 233 state and federal prisons, 358 jails,

TABLE 8.5

Percentage of sentenced prisoners under the jurisdiction of state correctional authority, by most serious offense, sex, race, and Hispanic origin, yearend 2014

Most serious offense	All prisoners[a]	Male	Female	White[b]	Black[b]	Hispanic
Total	100%	100%	100%	100%	100%	100%
Violent	52.9%	54.3%	35.8%	46.6%	57.8%	58.7%
Murder[c]	13.0	13.2	11.0	10.2	14.9	14.7
Manslaughter	1.3	1.2	2.3	1.4	0.8	1.0
Rape/sexual assault	12.4	13.2	2.2	15.9	8.0	13.1
Robbery	12.8	13.2	8.0	7.4	19.4	12.9
Aggravated/simple assault	10.2	10.4	8.3	8.6	11.2	13.2
Other	3.2	3.1	4.0	3.1	3.4	3.9
Property	19.0%	18.3%	27.8%	24.8%	16.0%	13.6%
Burglary	10.1	10.3	7.2	11.9	9.7	8.0
Larceny-theft	3.6	3.2	8.0	5.2	2.8	2.4
Motor vehicle theft	0.8	0.8	0.9	1.0	0.5	0.9
Fraud	2.3	1.8	8.6	3.4	1.6	1.1
Other	2.2	2.2	3.2	3.3	1.3	1.3
Drug	15.7%	14.9%	25.1%	15.0%	14.9%	14.6%
Drug possession	3.5	3.3	6.5	3.9	3.5	3.5
Other[d]	12.2	11.7	18.5	11.2	11.3	11.1
Public order	11.6%	11.7%	10.2%	12.8%	11.0%	12.6%
Weapons	3.9	4.0	1.8	2.5	5.2	5.1
Driving under the influence	2.1	2.1	2.9	3.0	0.7	2.7
Other[e]	5.6	5.6	5.5	7.2	5.1	4.8
Other/unspecified[f]	0.8%	0.8%	1.1%	0.8%	0.4%	0.4%
Total number of sentenced prisoners[g]	1,316,409	1,222,873	93,536	451,100	456,600	261,000

[a]Includes American Indians and Alaska Natives; Asians, Native Hawaiians, and other Pacific Islanders; and persons of two or more races.
[b]Excludes persons of Hispanic or Latino origin and persons of two or more races.
[c]Includes nonnegligent manslaughter.
[d]Includes trafficking and other drug offenses.
[e]Includes court offenses; commercialized vice, morals, and decency offenses; and liquor law violations and other public order offenses.
[f]Includes juvenile offenses and other unspecified offense categories.
[g]Race and Hispanic origin totals are rounded to the nearest 100 to accommodate differences in data collection techniques between jurisdictions.
Note: Jurisdiction refers to the legal authority of state correctional officials over a prisoner, regardless of where the prisoner is held. Counts are based on prisoners with a sentence of more than 1 year. Detail may not sum to total due to rounding and missing offense data.

SOURCE: E. Ann Carson and Elizabeth Anderson, "Table 9. Percent of Sentenced Prisoners under the Jurisdiction of State Correctional Authority, by Most Serious Offense, Sex, Race, and Hispanic Origin, December 31, 2014," in *Prisoners in 2015*, U.S. Department of Justice, Bureau of Justice Statistics, December 2016, https://www.bjs.gov/content/pub/pdf/p15.pdf (accessed January 21, 2017)

and 15 special confinement facilities that were operated by U.S. Immigration and Customs Enforcement, the U.S. military, and correctional authorities on Native American tribal lands. More than 92,000 inmates participated in the survey. This number included some juveniles aged 16 or 17 years that were incarcerated in adult prisons and jails. During the survey the inmates were questioned about acts of nonconsensual sex between inmates and between inmates and facility staff. The results were extrapolated to provide estimates of sexual misconduct in the nation's entire inmate population.

According to Beck et al., the results indicate that an estimated 4% of state and federal inmates and 3.2% of jail inmates were sexually victimized in 2011–12. These rates were virtually unchanged from rates calculated in 2007. The data for 2011–12 for sexually victimized state and federal inmates indicate the following:

- 2.4% said they were sexually victimized by facility staff
- 2% said they were sexually victimized by another inmate
- 0.4% said they were sexually victimized by both facility staff and another inmate

Beck et al. note that for sexually victimized jail inmates the breakdown was as follows:

- 1.8% said they were sexually victimized by facility staff
- 1.6% said they were sexually victimized by another inmate
- 0.2% said they were sexually victimized by both facility staff and another inmate

INMATE DEATHS

The BJS initiated the Deaths in Custody Reporting Program in response to the Deaths in Custody Reporting Act of 2000. The program requires state prisons and local jails to report annually the cause of death and certain demographic data for all inmates who die in their custody.

According to Margaret E. Noonan of the BJS, in *Mortality in State Prisons, 2001–2014—Statistical Tables* (December 2016, https://www.bjs.gov/content/pub/pdf/msp0114st.pdf), the death totals for state and federal prisons in 2014 were 3,483 state prisoners and 444 federal prisoners. Data for 2001 through 2014 are summarized in

TABLE 8.6

Percentage of confined inmates in local jails, by characteristics, midyear 2000, 2005, and 2010–14; yearend 2015

Characteristic	2000	2005	Midyear 2010	2011	2012	2013	2014[f]	Yearend 2015
Sex								
Male	88.6	87.3	87.7	87.3	86.8	86.0	85.3%	85.7%[g]
Female	11.4	12.7	12.3	12.7	13.2	14.0	14.7	14.3[g]
Adult	98.8	99.1	99.0	99.2	99.3	99.4%	99.4%	99.5%[g]
Male	87.4	86.5	86.7	86.6	86.1	85.4	84.8	85.2[g]
Female	11.3	12.6	12.3	12.6	13.2	13.9	14.6	14.3[g]
Juvenile[a]	1.2	0.9	1.0	0.8	0.7	0.6%	0.6%	0.5%[g]
Held as adult[b]	1.0	0.8	0.8	0.6	0.6	0.5	0.5	0.5[g]
Held as juvenile	0.2	0.1	0.3	0.2	0.1	0.1	0.1	[h]
Race/Hispanic origin[c]								
White	41.9	44.3	44.3	44.8	45.8	47.2%	47.4%	48.3%[g]
Black/African American	41.3	38.9	37.8	37.6	36.9	35.8	35.4	35.1[g]
Hispanic/Latino	15.2	15.0	15.8	15.5	15.1	14.8	14.9	14.3[g]
American Indian/ Alaska Native[d]	0.9	1.0	1.3	1.3	1.2	1.4	1.4	1.2[g]
Asian/Native Hawaiian/ other Pacific Islander[d]	0.8	0.7	0.7	0.7	0.7	0.7	0.8	0.8[g]
Two or more races	[i]	0.1	0.1	0.2	0.2	0.2	0.1	0.2[g]
Conviction status[e]								
Convicted	44.0	38.0%	38.9	39.4	39.4	38.0%	37.2%	37.3%[g]
Unconvicted	56.0	62.0	61.1	60.6	60.6	62.0	62.8	62.7[g]

[a]Persons age 17 or younger.
[b]Includes juveniles who were tried or awaiting trial as adults.
[c]Excludes persons of Hispanic or Latino origin, unless specified.
[d]Reports prior to 2014 combined American Indians and Alaska Natives and Asians, Native Hawaiians, and other Pacific Islanders into an other race category.
[e]Includes juveniles who were tried or awaiting trial as adults.
[f]Comparison year for each characteristic.
[g]Not compared because the jail population goes through seasonal change, typically with fewer inmates at yearend than at midyear.
[h]Less than 0.05%.
[i]Not collected.
Note: Percentages are based on the total number of confined inmates. Detail may not sum to total due to rounding. Midyear estimates are based on the number of inmates confined on the last weekday in June, and yearend estimates are based on the number of inmates confined on December 31. In 2015, the Annual Survey of Jails (ASJ) collected characteristic data at yearend.

SOURCE: Todd D. Minton and Zhen Zeng, "Table 4. Percent of Confined Inmates in Local Jails, by Characteristics, Midyear 2000, 2005, and 2010–2014; Yearend 2015," in *Jail Inmates in 2015*, U.S. Department of Justice, Bureau of Justice Statistics, December 2016, https://www.bjs.gov/content/pub/pdf/ji15.pdf (accessed January 21, 2017)

Table 8.7. Overall, 45,640 state prisoners and 5,145 federal prisoners died while incarcerated over this period. The vast majority (89% of state prisoners and 88% of federal prisoners) died of illness. The next largest cause of death was suicide. It accounted for 6% of the state prisoner deaths and 4% of the federal prisoner deaths.

In *Mortality in Local Jails, 2000–2014—Statistical Tables* (December 2016, https://www.bjs.gov/content/pub/pdf/mlj0014st.pdf), Noonan indicates that 1,053 jail inmates died while incarcerated in local jails in 2014. Data for 2000 through 2014 are summarized in Table 8.8. Overall, 14,786 jail inmates died over this period. Just over half (51%) died of illness, and nearly a third (31%) died of suicide.

PRISONERS' RIGHTS

In 1871 a Virginia court, in *Ruffin v. Commonwealth* (62 Va. 790), commented that a prisoner "has, as a consequence of his crime, not only forfeited his liberty, but all his personal rights except those which the law in its humanity accords to him. He is for the time being the slave of the state." Eight decades later, in *Stroud v. Swope* (187 F. 2d. 850 [1951]), the U.S. Court of Appeals for the Ninth Circuit asserted that "it is well settled that it is not the function of the courts to superintend the treatment and discipline of prisoners in penitentiaries, but only to deliver from imprisonment those who are illegally confined." The American Correctional Association explains in *Legal Responsibility and Authority of Correctional Officers: A Handbook on Courts, Judicial Decisions, and Constitutional Requirements* (1987) that correctional administrators believed that prisoners lost all their constitutional rights after conviction. Prisoners had privileges, not rights, and privileges could be taken away arbitrarily.

A significant change in this legal view came during the 1960s. In *Cooper v. Pate* (378 U.S. 546 [1964]), the U.S. Supreme Court held that the Civil Rights Act of 1871 granted protection to prisoners. The U.S. Code states in Title 42, Chapter 21, Subchapter I, Section 1983 (which is part of the Civil Rights Act), that "every

TABLE 8.7

Number of state and federal prison inmate deaths, by cause of death, 2001–14

Cause of death	State prisoners			Federal prisoners[a]		
	Number	Percent	Mortality rate per 100,000	Number	Percent	Mortality rate per 100,000
All causes	45,640	100%	256	5,145	100%	225
Illness	40,407	89%	227	4,543	88%	199
Cancer	12,269	27	69	NA	NA	NA
Heart disease	11,685	26	66	NA	NA	NA
Liver disease	4,378	10	25	NA	NA	NA
AIDS-related	1,797	4	10	159	3	7
Respiratory disease	2,853	6	16	NA	NA	NA
All other illnesses[b]	7,425	16	42	NA	NA	NA
Suicide	2,826	6%	16	222	4%	10
Drug/alcohol intoxication	595	1%	3	NA	NA	NA
Accident[c]	450	1%	3	51	1%	2
Homicide[d]	845	2%	5	130	3%	6
Other/unknown	303	1%	2	0	0%	0
Missing	214	0.5%	1	37	1%	2

NA = not available

[a]Cause of death data for federal prisoners were not available for all causes. Excludes deaths in private facilities.

[b]Includes other specified illnesses, such as cerebrovascular disease, influenza, and other nonleading natural causes of death, as well as unspecified illnesses.

[c]Intoxication deaths of federal prisoners is included in the accidental death count.

[d]Includes homicides committed by other inmates, incidental to the staff use of force, and resulting from assaults sustained prior to incarceration.

Note: Data may have been revised from previously published statistics. Mortality rates are based on a 1-day inmate custody count.

SOURCE: Margaret E. Noonan, "Table 1. Number of State and Federal Prison Inmate Deaths, by Cause of Death, 2001–2014," in *Mortality in State Prisons, 2001–2014—Statistical Tables*, U.S. Department of Justice, Bureau of Justice Statistics, December 2016, https://www.bjs.gov/content/pub/pdf/msp0114st.pdf (accessed January 22, 2017)

TABLE 8.8

Number of local jail inmate deaths, by cause of death, 2000–14

Cause of death	Number	Percent	Mortality rate per 100,000 local jail inmates
All causes	14,786	100%	137
Illness	7,609	51%	70
Heart disease	3,415	23	32
AIDS-related	569	4	5
Cancer	536	4	5
Respiratory disease	425	3	4
Liver disease	394	3	4
All other illnesses[a]	2,270	15	21
Suicide	4,508	31%	42
Drug/alcohol intoxication	1,017	7%	9
Accident	395	3%	4
Homicide[b]	327	2%	3
Other/unknown	548	4%	5
Missing	382	3%	4

[a]Includes other specified illnesses, such as cerebrovascular disease, influenza, and other nonleading natural causes of death, as well as unspecified illnesses.

[b]Includes homicides committed by other inmates, incidental to the staff use of force, and resulting from assaults sustained prior to incarceration.

Note: Local jail mortality rates are per 100,000 inmates held in custody. Mortality rates are based on the average daily population (ADP). In 2000, ADP was estimated by taking the average of January 1 and December 31 one-day inmate population counts. Data may have been revised from previously published statistics.

SOURCE: Margaret E. Noonan, "Table 1. Number of Local Jail Inmate Deaths, by Cause of Death, 2000–2014," in *Mortality in Local Jails, 2000–2014—Statistical Tables*, U.S. Department of Justice, Bureau of Justice Statistics, December 2016, https://www.bjs.gov/content/pub/pdf/mlj0014st.pdf (accessed January 22, 2017)

person who, under color of any statute, ordinance, regulation, custom, or usage, of any State or Territory or the District of Columbia, subjects, or causes to be subjected,

any citizen of the United States or other person within the jurisdiction thereof to the deprivation of any rights, privileges, or immunities secured by the Constitution and laws, shall be liable to the party injured in an action at law, suit in equity, or other proper proceeding for redress."

With the *Cooper* decision, the court announced that prisoners had rights that were guaranteed by the U.S. Constitution and could ask the judicial system for help in challenging the conditions of their imprisonment.

The Civil Rights of Institutionalized Persons Act

Another safeguard for prisoners' rights came in 1980 with passage of the Civil Rights of Institutionalized Persons Act (CRIPA). CRIPA covers people in certain kinds of institutions that are owned, operated, or managed by or on the behalf of state or local governments. Examples include prisons, jails, juvenile correctional facilities, mental health facilities, and nursing homes. In "Rights of Persons Confined to Jails and Prisons" (2017, https://www.justice.gov/crt/rights-persons-confined-jails-and-prisons), the DOJ's Special Litigation Section explains that CRIPA gives the U.S. attorney general the authority "to review conditions and practices" within the covered facilities. (Note that this authority does not apply to federal facilities, such as federal prisons.) The DOJ does not act on behalf of individuals regarding CRIPA, but rather on cases that indicate an institution has a systematic pattern or practice that causes harm. When it finds a problem, the agency works with the state or local governments that are involved to reach a solution. If an agreement cannot be reached, then the attorney general can file a lawsuit in federal court over the matter.

The Special Litigation Section maintains a database (https://www.justice.gov/crt/special-litigation-section-cases-and-matters0#corrections) of cases that it has investigated and the legal documents associated with them. In addition, the DOJ is required by CRIPA to provide to Congress an annual report describing its enforcement efforts. In *Department of Justice Activities under the Civil Rights of Institutionalized Persons Act, Fiscal Year 2015* (May 2016, https://www.justice.gov/crt/page/file/933876/download), the most recent report available as of April 2017, the DOJ describes its activities for fiscal year 2015 (October 1, 2014, through September 30, 2015). The agency dealt with issues involving dozens of jails, prisons, and other types of correctional facilities in more than 27 states and U.S. territories.

HABEAS CORPUS REVIEW

In *Cooper v. Pate*, the Supreme Court relied on civil rights. Another source of prisoners' rights arose from the court's reliance on habeas corpus. This Latin phrase means "have the body" with the rest of the phrase "brought before me" implied. A writ of habeas corpus is therefore the command issued by one court to another court (or to a lesser authority) to produce a person and to explain why that person is being detained. Habeas corpus dates to an act of the British Parliament passed in 1679. Congress enacted the Judiciary Act of 1789 and gave federal prisoners the right to habeas corpus review. The Habeas Corpus Act of 1867 later protected the rights of newly freed slaves and extended habeas corpus protection to state prisoners. The effective meaning of habeas corpus for prisoners is that it enables them to petition federal courts to review any aspect of their case.

FIRST AMENDMENT CASES

The First Amendment of the U.S. Constitution guarantees that "Congress shall make no law respecting an establishment of religion, or prohibiting the free exercise thereof; or abridging the freedom of speech, or of the press; or the right of the people peaceably to assemble, and to petition the government for a redress of grievances."

Censorship

In *Procunier v. Martinez* (416 U.S. 396 [1974]), the Supreme Court ruled that prison officials cannot censor inmate correspondence unless they "show that a regulation authorizing mail censorship furthers one or more of the substantial governmental interests of security, order, and rehabilitation. Second, the limitation of First Amendment freedoms must be no greater than is necessary or essential to the protection of the particular governmental interest involved."

Prison officials may refuse to send letters that detail escape plans or have encoded messages but may not censor inmate correspondence simply to "eliminate unflattering or unwelcome opinions or factually inaccurate statements." Because prisoners retain rights, "when a prison regulation or practice offends a fundamental constitutional guarantee, federal courts will discharge their duty to protect constitutional rights."

However, the court recognized that it was "ill equipped to deal with the increasingly urgent problems of prison administration and reform." Running a prison takes expertise and planning, all of which, the court explained, is part of the responsibility of the legislative and executive branches. According to the court, the task of the judiciary branch is to establish a standard of review for prisoners' constitutional claims that is responsive to both the need to protect inmates' rights and the policy of judicial restraint.

In *Pell v. Procunier* (417 U.S. 817 [1974]), the court ruled that federal prison officials could prohibit inmates from having face-to-face media interviews. The court reasoned that judgments regarding prison security "are peculiarly within the province and professional expertise of corrections officials, and, in the absence of substantial evidence in the record to indicate that the officials have exaggerated their response to these considerations, courts should ordinarily defer to their expert judgment in such matters."

The U.S. Court of Appeals for the First Circuit ruled in *Nolan v. Fitzpatrick* (451 F. 2d 545 [1985]) that inmates had the right to correspond with newspapers. The prisoners were limited only in that they could not write about escape plans or include contraband material in their letters.

The Missouri Division of Corrections permitted correspondence between immediate family members who were inmates at different institutions, but it restricted other inmate correspondence from discussing legal matters and made nonfamily correspondence subject to the discretion of each prisoner's "classification/treatment team." Another Missouri regulation permitted an inmate to marry only with the superintendent's permission, which could be given only when there were "compelling reasons" to do so, such as a pregnancy. In *Turner v. Safley* (482 U.S. 78 [1987]), the Supreme Court found the first regulation constitutional and the second one unconstitutional.

The court held that the "constitutional right of prisoners to marry is impermissibly burdened by the Missouri marriage regulation." The court had ruled earlier in *Zablocki v. Redhail* (434 U.S. 374 [1978]) that prisoners had a constitutionally protected right to marry, subject to restrictions because of incarceration such as time and place and prior approval of a warden. However, the Missouri regulation practically banned all marriages.

The findings in *Turner v. Safley* have become a guide for prison regulations in the United States. In its decision, the court observed that:

> When a prison regulation impinges on inmates' constitutional rights, the regulation is valid if it is reasonably related to legitimate penological interests. ... First, there must be a "valid, rational connection" between the prison regulation and the legitimate governmental interest put forward to justify it. ... Moreover, the governmental objective must be a legitimate and neutral one. ... A second factor relevant in determining the reasonableness of a prison restriction ... is whether there are alternative means of exercising the right that remain open to prison inmates. ... A third consideration is the impact accommodation of the asserted constitutional right will have on guards and other inmates, and on the allocation of prison resources generally.

Religious Beliefs

Although inmates retain their First Amendment right to practice their religion, the courts have upheld restrictions on religious freedom when corrections departments need to maintain security, when economic considerations are involved, and when the regulation is reasonable.

The Religious Land Use and Institutionalized Persons Act was signed into law in September 2000 by President Bill Clinton (1946–). Section 3 of the law indicates that prison officials are required to accommodate inmates' religious needs in certain cases, even if this means exempting the inmates from general prison rules. The state of Ohio challenged the act's constitutionality by arguing that it violates the First Amendment's prohibition on the establishment of religion. Because the law does not require prison officials to accommodate inmates' secular needs or desires in similar ways, Ohio claimed the statute impermissibly advances religion. The state also argued that the law creates incentives for prisoners to feign religious belief to gain privileges. The Supreme Court upheld the constitutionality of the act in *Cutter v. Wilkinson* (544 U.S. 709 [2005]), reversing a ruling by the U.S. Court of Appeals for the Sixth Circuit, which had agreed with Ohio's argument.

FOURTH AMENDMENT CASES

The Fourth Amendment guarantees the "right of the people to be secure ... against unreasonable searches and seizures ... and no warrants shall issue, but upon probable cause." The courts have not been as active in protecting prisoners under the Fourth Amendment as under the First and Eighth Amendments. In *Bell v. Wolfish* (441 U.S. 520 [1979]), the Supreme Court asserted that:

> simply because prison inmates retain certain constitutional rights does not mean that these rights are not subject to restrictions and limitations.....Maintaining institutional security and preserving internal order and discipline are essential goals that may require limitation or retraction of the retained constitutional rights of both convicted prisoners and pretrial detainees. Since problems that arise in the day-to-day operation of a corrections facility are not susceptible of easy solutions, prison administrators should be accorded wide-ranging deference in the adoption and execution of policies and practices that in their judgment are needed to preserve internal order and discipline and to maintain institutional security.

Based on this reasoning, the court ruled that body searches did not violate the Fourth Amendment: "Balancing the significant and legitimate security interests of the institution against the inmates' privacy interests, such searches can be conducted on less than probable cause and are not unreasonable."

In another Fourth Amendment case, *Hudson v. Palmer* (468 U.S. 517 [1984]), the court upheld the right of prison officials to search a prisoner's cell and seize property. The court explained that "the recognition of privacy rights for prisoners in their individual cells simply cannot be reconciled with the concept of incarceration and the needs and objectives of penal institutions." However, the fact that a prisoner does not have a reasonable expectation of privacy "does not mean that he is without a remedy for calculated harassment unrelated to prison needs. Nor does it mean that prison attendants can ride roughshod over inmates' property rights with impunity. The Eighth Amendment always stands as a protection against 'cruel and unusual punishments.'"

EIGHTH AMENDMENT CASES

The Eighth Amendment states that "excessive bail shall not be required, nor excessive fines imposed, nor cruel and unusual punishments inflicted." The prohibition against "cruel and unusual punishments" has been used to challenge numerous aspects of the criminal justice system, including the death penalty, three-strikes laws, crowded prisons, lack of health or safety in prisons, and excessive violence by the guards.

Prison Conditions and Medical Care

In *Rhodes v. Chapman* (452 U.S. 337 [1981]), the Supreme Court ruled that housing prisoners in double cells was not cruel and unusual punishment. The justices maintained that "conditions of confinement, as constituting the punishment at issue, must not involve the wanton and unnecessary infliction of pain, nor may they be grossly disproportionate to the severity of the crime warranting imprisonment. But conditions that cannot be said to be cruel and unusual under contemporary standards are not unconstitutional. To the extent such conditions are restrictive and even harsh, they are part of the penalty that criminals pay for their offenses against society."

The court concluded that the Constitution "does not mandate comfortable prisons" and that only those deprivations denying the "minimal civilized measure of life's necessities" violate the Eighth Amendment.

However, Judge Richard A. Enslen (1931–2015) of the U.S. District Court ruled in *Hadix v. Caruso* (461 F.Supp.2d 574 [2006]) that officials at the Southern Michigan Correctional Facility had to stop using nonmedical restraints on prisoners because the "practice constitutes torture and violates the Eighth Amendment." In November 2006 Judge Enslen issued the opinion in the case of Timothy Souders, a mentally ill detainee who died after spending four days nude and shackled in an isolated cell. Judge Enslen ordered the prison to "immediately cease and desist from the practice of using any form of punitive mechanical restraints [and] shall timely develop practices, protocols and policies to enforce this limitation."

Chapter 7 details how a series of court decisions found that severe overcrowding and poor medical care in California's prison system constituted a violation of the Eighth Amendment.

Guards Using Force

The Supreme Court ruled in *Whitley v. Albers* (475 U.S. 312 [1986]) that guards, during prison disturbances or riots, must balance the need "to maintain or restore discipline" through force against the risk of injury to inmates. These situations require prison officials to act quickly and decisively and allow guards and administrators leeway in their actions. In *Whitley*, a prisoner was shot in the knee during an attempt to rescue a hostage. The court found that the injury suffered by the prisoner was not cruel and unusual punishment under the circumstances.

In 1983 Keith Hudson, an inmate at the state penitentiary in Angola, Louisiana, argued with Jack McMillian, a guard. McMillian placed the inmate in handcuffs and shackles to take him to the administrative lockdown area. On the way, according to Hudson, McMillian punched him in the mouth, eyes, chest, and stomach; another guard held him while the supervisor on duty watched. Hudson sued, accusing the guards of cruel and unusual punishment.

A magistrate found that the guards used "force when there was no need to do so" and that the supervisor allowed their conduct, thus violating the Eighth Amendment. However, the U.S. Court of Appeals for the Fifth Circuit reversed the decision, ruling in *Hudson v. McMillian* (929 F. 2d 1014 [1990]) that "inmates alleging use of excessive force in violation of the Eighth Amendment must prove: (1) significant injury; (2) resulting 'directly and only from the use of force that was clearly excessive to the need'; (3) the excessiveness of which was objectively unreasonable; and (4) that the action constituted an unnecessary and wanton infliction of pain."

The court agreed that the use of force was unreasonable and was a clearly excessive and unnecessary infliction of pain. Nevertheless, the court found against Hudson because his injuries were "minor" and "required no medical attention."

PREGNANT PRISONERS

Female prisoners make up a small part of the overall prison population, but their treatment is an issue for many human rights groups. One particular focus is the practice of shackling female inmates while they are pregnant, giving birth, or recovering following giving birth. Shackling can consist of handcuffs and/or chains around the ankles or midsection. It is a common practice at many prisons for inmates to be shackled under certain circumstances, such as during transport to and from court or other locations and while being treated in hospitals. Critics suggest that shackled pregnant women are in danger of seriously harming their unborn babies if they should fall. Human rights advocates also abhor the practice of shackling women inmates to their hospital beds while the women are in labor.

In "Shackling of Pregnant Women" (January 11, 2016, https://www.cga.ct.gov/med/committees/med5/2016/0111/20160111ATTACH_Restraint%20Use%20in%20Incarcerated%20Women%20Presentation.pdf), Cristian Saavedra notes that in 2008 the federal government implemented a no-shackling policy for pregnant federal inmates. In addition, as of January 2016, dozens of states had outlawed the practice or established antishackling policies. According to Saavedra, 37 states and the District of Columbia "prohibit or strictly limit the use of restraints during pregnancy, labor, birthing, and recovery, or a subset of these stages." Nevertheless, there have been complaints that the laws or policies are not being followed. In the op-ed "In Labor, in Chains: The Outrageous Shackling of Pregnant Inmates" (NYTimes.com, July 26, 2014), Audrey Quinn notes, "In many correctional systems, doctors, guards and prison officials simply are not told about anti-shackling laws, or are not trained to comply." In 2012 a group of inmates who had been shackled while pregnant at the Cook County jail in Illinois won a $4.1 million settlement against the state, which had outlawed such shackling practices in 1999. The Prison Birth Project and Prisoners' Legal Services of Massachusetts claim in "Breaking Promises: Violations of the Massachusetts Pregnancy Standards & Anti-Shackling Law" (May 2016, http://theprisonbirthproject.org/wp-content/uploads/2016/05/Breaking-Promises_May2016.pdf) that pregnant inmates in Massachusetts prisons and jails continued to be shackled during 2016 despite a state law passed in 2014 banning the practice.

DUE PROCESS COMPLAINTS

The Fifth Amendment provides that no person should "be deprived of life, liberty, or property" by the federal government "without due process of law." The 14th Amendment reaffirms this right and explicitly applies it to the states. Due process complaints brought by prisoners under the Fifth and 14th Amendments are generally centered on questions of procedural fairness. Most of the time disciplinary action in prison is taken on the word of the guard or the administrator, and the inmate has little opportunity to challenge the charges.

The Supreme Court, however, has affirmed that procedural fairness should be used in some institutional decisions. In *Wolff v. McDonnell* (418 U.S. 539 [1974]), the court declared that a Nebraska law providing for sentences to be shortened for good behavior created a "liberty interest." Thus, if an inmate met the requirements, prison officials could not deprive him of the shortened sentence without due process, according to the 14th Amendment.

At the Metropolitan Correctional Center, a federally operated short-term custodial facility in New York City that was designed mainly for pretrial detainees, inmates challenged the constitutionality of the facility's conditions. Because this was a pretrial detention center, the challenge was brought under the due process clause of the Fifth Amendment. The district court and the court of appeals found for the inmates, but the Supreme Court disagreed in *Bell v. Wolfish*.

EARLY RELEASE

Beginning in 1983 the Florida legislature enacted a series of laws authorizing the awarding of early release credits to prison inmates when the state prison population exceeded predetermined levels. In 1986 Kenneth Lynce received a 22-year prison sentence on a charge of attempted murder. He was released in 1992, based on the determination that he had accumulated five different types of early release credits totaling 5,668 days, including 1,860 days of provisional credits awarded as a result of prison overcrowding.

Shortly thereafter, the state attorney general issued an opinion interpreting a 1992 statute as having retroactively canceled all provisional credits awarded to inmates convicted of murder and attempted murder. Lynce was rearrested and returned to custody. He filed a habeas corpus petition alleging that the retroactive cancellation of provisional credits violated the ex post facto (from a thing done afterward) clause of the Constitution.

The Supreme Court agreed with Lynce. In *Lynce v. Mathis* (519 U.S. 443 [1997]), the court ruled that "to fall within the ex post facto prohibition, a law must be retrospective and 'disadvantage the offender affected by it.'"

The 1992 statute was clearly retrospective and disadvantaged Lynce by increasing his punishment.

LIMITING FRIVOLOUS PRISONER LAWSUITS

In 1995 the Supreme Court made it harder for prisoners to bring constitutional suits that challenge due process rights. In *Sandin v. Conner* (515 U.S. 472), the majority asserted that it was frustrated with the number of due process cases, some of which, it believed, clogged the judiciary with unwarranted complaints, such as claiming a "liberty interest" in not being transferred to a cell without an electrical outlet for a television set.

Sandin concerned an inmate in Hawaii who was not allowed to call witnesses at a disciplinary hearing for misconduct that had placed him in solitary confinement for 30 days. The Court of Appeals for the Ninth Circuit had held in 1993 that the inmate, Demont Conner, had a liberty interest that allowed him a range of procedural protections in remaining free from solitary confinement. The Supreme Court overruled the court of appeals, stating that the inmate had no liberty interest. Due process protections play a role only if the state's action has infringed on some separate, substantive right that the inmate possesses. For example, in *Wolff v. McDonnell* the petitioner's loss of good-time credit was a substantive right that he possessed. The punishment Conner had received "was within the range of confinement to be normally expected for one serving an indeterminate term of 30 years to life" for a number of crimes, including murder.

The court noted that "states may under certain circumstances create liberty interests which are protected by the Due Process Clause," but these should be limited to actions that impose "atypical and significant hardship on the inmate in relation to the ordinary incidents of prison life." According to the court, being put in solitary confinement in a prison where most inmates are limited to their cells most of the day anyway is not a liberty-interest issue. Because there was no liberty interest involved, how the hearing was handled was irrelevant.

Based on this ruling, the court held that a federal court should consider a complaint to be a potential violation of a prisoner's due process rights only when prison staff impose "atypical and significant hardship on the inmate." Mismanaged disciplinary hearings or temporary placement in solitary confinement are just "ordinary incidents of prison life" and should not be considered violations of the Constitution.

Chief Justice William H. Rehnquist (1924–2005) asserted that past Supreme Court decisions have "led to the involvement ... of federal courts in the day-to-day management of prisons, often squandering judicial resources with little offsetting benefit to anyone." Judges should allow prison administrators the flexibility to fine-tune the ordinary incidents of prison life.

In 1996 Congress passed the Prison Litigation Reform Act (PLRA) in an effort to limit so-called frivolous lawsuits by prisoners. The PLRA requires inmates to exhaust all possible internal prison grievance processes before filing civil rights lawsuits in federal courts. The law states that "no action shall be brought with respect to prison conditions under section 1983 of this title, or any other Federal law, by a prisoner confined in any jail, prison, or other correctional facility until such administrative remedies as are available are exhausted." After a few lower courts handed down controversial rulings on specific procedures that inmates must follow to exhaust administrative grievances, a case was brought before the U.S. Supreme Court. In the consolidated case of *Jones v. Bock* (549 U.S. 199 [2007]) and *Williams v. Overton* (No. 05-7142 [2007]), the court overturned strict legal requirements that had been imposed by the Court of Appeals for the Sixth Circuit on Michigan inmates with grievances against their prison. Lorenzo Jones claimed that prison officials forced him to do "arduous" work even though he had been seriously injured in a car accident. Timothy Williams suffered a debilitating medical condition and claimed that his medical needs were not being properly met in prison. Instead of examining the merits of these claims, the Supreme Court chose to focus on specific legal issues associated with lawsuits that the prisoners had filed under the PLRA.

The court clarified that prisoners alleging federal civil rights violations under the PLRA do not have to prove they have exhausted all administrative remedies before filing lawsuits. The burden is on the defense to prove that administrative remedies were not exhausted. In addition, lower courts cannot dismiss lawsuits including multiple claims, even if some of the claims have not been exhausted. Finally, prisoners filing such lawsuits need not have named specific defendants in the administrative grievances to retain their rights to sue those defendants in court.

Complaints about the PLRA

The PLRA is roundly criticized by human rights groups, such as the ACLU and the Southern Center for Human Rights. These groups complain that prisons have implemented complicated grievance systems with strict deadline requirements in order to thwart inmate efforts to file suits under the law. The organizations are also critical of the provision of the PLRA that specifies that inmates cannot bring federal civil action unless physical injury has occurred. Human rights advocates note that prisoners who have been raped or suffered degrading treatment at the hands of prison staff are barred from filing suits because of this provision.

INNOCENCE PROTECTION ACT

Deoxyribonucleic acid (DNA) testing has emerged as a powerful tool that can establish the innocence of a person in cases where organic matter from the perpetrator of a crime (e.g., blood, skin, or semen) has been obtained by law enforcement officials. This organic matter can be tested against DNA samples that have been taken from an accused or convicted person. If the two samples do not match, then they came from different people and the person being tested is innocent.

The Innocence Protection Act became law in 2004 as part of the Justice for All Act. The act enables people who are "convicted and imprisoned for federal offenses" and who claim to be innocent to have DNA testing on the biological evidence that was originally collected during the investigations of the crimes for which they were convicted. It mandates that the government must preserve collected biological evidence so that it can be tested after the defendant is convicted. Finally, it provides funds to allow certain agencies to test evidence to identify perpetrators of unsolved crimes.

The Innocence Project is a private organization affiliated with the Benjamin N. Cardozo School of Law at Yeshiva University. The Innocence Project (2017, https://www.innocenceproject.org/) says it "exonerates the wrongfully convicted through DNA testing and reforms the criminal justice system to prevent future injustice." In "Cases" (https://www.innocenceproject.org/all-cases/#exonerated-by-dna), the organization claims that as of April 2017, 349 people in the United States had been exonerated by postconviction DNA testing, including dozens who had served time on death row.

CHAPTER 9
PROBATION AND PAROLE

Most of the correctional population of the United States (those under the supervision of correctional authorities) are walking about freely. They are people on probation or parole. A probationer is someone who has been convicted of a crime and sentenced, but the person's sentence has been suspended on the condition that he or she behaves in a manner ordered by the court. Probation sometimes follows a brief period of incarceration; more often, it is granted by the court immediately. A parolee is an individual who has served a part of his or her sentence in jail or prison but, because of good behavior or legislative mandate, has been granted freedom before the sentence is fully served. The sentence remains in effect, however, and the parolee continues to be under the jurisdiction of a parole board. If the parolee fails to live up to the conditions of the release, he or she may be confined again. Probationers and parolees are still under official supervision and have to satisfy requirements placed on them as a condition of freedom or of early release from correctional facilities. They are sometimes referred to as being "under community supervision."

According to Danielle Kaeble and Thomas P. Bonczar of the Bureau of Justice Statistics (BJS) in *Probation and Parole in the United States, 2015* (December 2016, https://www.bjs.gov/content/pub/pdf/ppus15.pdf), an estimated 4,650,900 adults (3.8 million on probation and 870,500 on parole) were under community supervision at yearend 2015. (See Figure 9.1 and Table 9.1.) The community supervision population grew from 2005 through 2007 when it peaked at 5.1 million and then began declining. It fell, on average, by 6% annually between 2005 and 2015.

As shown in Table 9.2, at yearend 2015 the community supervision rate for adults was 1,868 per 100,000 adult U.S. residents. Approximately one out of every 53 adults in the United States was under community supervision (i.e., on probation or parole) at that time.

Table 9.3 provides a breakdown by jurisdiction for the community supervision population at yearend 2015.

(Note that data were not available for Alaska or Oregon.) In addition, Kaeble and Bonczar include the District of Columbia when referring to *states* and *state jurisdiction*; thus, this chapter does likewise. As shown in Table 9.3, the vast majority (4.5 million or 97%) of people under community supervision were under state jurisdiction, and 132,800 (3%) were under federal jurisdiction.

The 10 states with the largest numbers of adults under community supervision at yearend 2015 were:

- Texas—488,800
- Georgia—451,800
- California—349,600
- Pennsylvania—296,200
- Ohio—262,000
- Florida—225,400
- Michigan—193,900
- Illinois—151,300
- New Jersey—151,300
- New York—145,600

According to Kaeble and Bonczar in *Probation and Parole in the United States, 2015*, the number of adult probationers and parolees under state jurisdiction declined by 72,200 people, or 1.5%, between 2014 and 2015. The District of Columbia (down 10.3%), Georgia (down 10%), and California (down 6.2%) had the largest percentage declines. The states with the largest increases were North Dakota (up 11.8%), Oklahoma (up 7.3%), and Nevada (up 7.1%). Overall, there were 1,814 adults under state community supervision at yearend 2015 for every 100,000 adult residents of the United States. (See Table 9.3.)

Kaeble and Bonczar indicate that the adult community supervision population under federal jurisdiction

FIGURE 9.1

Adults under community supervision, yearend 2005–15

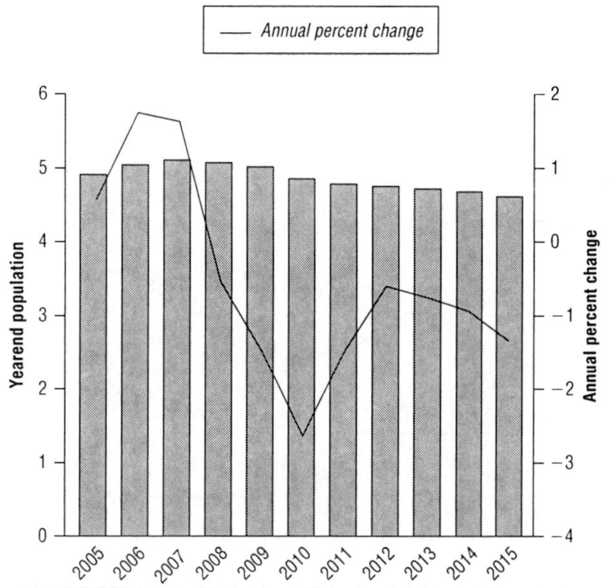

Note: Estimates are based on most recent data and may differ from previously published statistics.

SOURCE: Danielle Kaeble and Thomas P. Bonczar, "Figure 1. Adults under Community Supervision on December 31 and Annual Percent Change, 2005–2015," in *Probation and Parole in the United States, 2015*, U.S. Department of Justice, Bureau of Justice Statistics, December 2016, https://www.bjs.gov/content/pub/pdf/ppus15.pdf (accessed January 22, 2017)

TABLE 9.1

Adults under community supervision, probation, and parole, 2005–15

Year	Total	Probation	Parole
2005	4,946,600	4,162,300	784,400
2006	5,035,000	4,236,800	798,200
2007	5,119,000	4,293,000	826,100
2008	5,093,400	4,271,200	826,100
2009	5,019,900	4,199,800	824,600
2010	4,888,500	4,055,900	840,800
2011	4,818,300	3,973,800	855,500
2012	4,790,700	3,944,900	858,400
2013	4,749,800	3,912,900	849,500
2014	4,713,200	3,868,400	857,700
2015	4,650,900	3,789,800	870,500
Percent change, 2005–2015	−6.0%	−8.9%	11.0%
Percent change, 2014–2015	−1.3%	−2.0%	1.5%

Note: Counts are rounded to the nearest 100. Detail may not sum to total due to rounding. Estimates are based on most recent data and may differ from previously published statistics. Reporting methods for some probation agencies changed over time.

SOURCE: Danielle Kaeble and Thomas P. Bonczar, "Table 1. Adults under Community Supervision on Probation or Parole, Yearend 2005–2015," in *Probation and Parole in the United States, 2015*, U.S. Department of Justice, Bureau of Justice Statistics, December 2016, https://www.bjs.gov/content/pub/pdf/ppus15.pdf (accessed January 22, 2017)

increased by 3.4% between 2014 and 2015. Overall, there were 53 adults under federal community supervision at

TABLE 9.2

Rates of adults under community supervision, on probation, or on parole, 2005–15

Year	Number per 100,000 U.S. adult residents			U.S. adult residents on—		
	Community supervision[a]	Probation	Parole	Community supervision[b]	Probation	Parole
2005	2,215	1,864	351	1 in 45	1 in 54	1 in 285
2006	2,228	1,875	353	1 in 45	1 in 53	1 in 283
2007	2,239	1,878	361	1 in 45	1 in 53	1 in 277
2008	2,202	1,847	357	1 in 45	1 in 54	1 in 280
2009	2,148	1,797	353	1 in 47	1 in 56	1 in 283
2010	2,067	1,715	356	1 in 48	1 in 58	1 in 281
2011	2,017	1,663	358	1 in 50	1 in 60	1 in 279
2012	1,984	1,634	356	1 in 50	1 in 61	1 in 281
2013	1,946	1,603	348	1 in 51	1 in 62	1 in 287
2014	1,911	1,568	348	1 in 52	1 in 64	1 in 288
2015	1,868	1,522	350	1 in 53	1 in 66	1 in 286

[a]Includes adults on probation and adults on parole. For 2008 to 2015, detail does not sum to total because the community supervision rate was adjusted to exclude parolees who were also on probation.
[b]Includes adults on probation and adults on parole.
Note: Detail may not sum to total due to rounding. Rates are based on most recent data available and may differ from previously published statistics. Rates are based on the total community supervision, probation, and parole population counts as of December 31 of the reporting year and the estimated U.S. adult resident population on January 1 of each subsequent year.

SOURCE: Danielle Kaeble and Thomas P. Bonczar, "Table 2. Rates of U.S. Adult Residents on Community Supervision, Probation, and Parole, 2005–2015," in *Probation and Parole in the United States, 2015*, U.S. Department of Justice, Bureau of Justice Statistics, December 2016, https://www.bjs.gov/content/pub/pdf/ppus15.pdf (accessed January 22, 2017)

yearend 2015 for every 100,000 adult residents of the United States. (See Table 9.3.)

PROBATION

Probation Population

In 2005 there were 4.1 million probationers. (See Table 9.1 and Figure 9.2.) The number increased over subsequent years and peaked at nearly 4.3 million in 2007 before declining. There were almost 3.8 million probationers at yearend 2015.

Jurisdiction and Geographical Distribution of Probationers

As of yearend 2015, the 3.8 million people on probation represented a rate of 1,522 people on probation per 100,000 adult U.S. residents. (See Table 9.2.) In other words, one out of 66 adult U.S. residents were on probation. Table 9.4 provides a jurisdictional breakdown for the probationers. Nearly all of them (99.5%) were under state jurisdiction. Only 18,368 (0.5%) were under federal jurisdiction.

The 10 states with the highest probation populations at yearend 2015 were:

• Georgia—432,235

• Texas—378,937

TABLE 9.3

Adults under community supervision, by jurisdiction, yearend 2015

Jurisdiction	Community supervision population, December 31, 2015[a]	Number under community supervision per 100,000 adult residents, December 31, 2015[b]
U.S. total	4,650,900	1,868
Federal	132,800	53
State	4,518,100	1,814
Alabama	64,600	1,714
Alaska	—	—
Arizona	83,300	1,589
Arkansas	51,500	2,256
California	349,600	1,158
Colorado	89,200	2,102
Connecticut	45,300	1,598
Delaware	16,100	2,155
District of Columbia	9,900	1,776
Florida	225,400	1,381
Georgia	451,800	5,823
Hawaii	22,500	1,996
Idaho	37,800	3,071
Illinois	151,300	1,526
Indiana	122,500	2,423
Iowa	35,600	1,481
Kansas	20,900	951
Kentucky	70,600	2,063
Louisiana	71,900	2,014
Maine	6,700	626
Maryland	87,400	1,870
Massachusetts	66,900	1,232
Michigan	193,900	2,507
Minnesota	105,100	2,489
Mississippi	44,800	1,972
Missouri	62,600	1,329
Montana	9,700	1,198
Nebraska	13,700	955
Nevada	19,200	858
New Hampshire	6,300	590
New Jersey	151,300	2,167
New Mexico	16,800	1,054
New York	145,600	931
North Carolina	97,400	1,249
North Dakota	6,900	1,179
Ohio	262,000	2,908
Oklahoma	33,400	1,126
Oregon	—	—
Pennsylvania	296,200	2,923
Rhode Island	24,400	2,873
South Carolina	38,500	1,006
South Dakota	9,800	1,505
Tennessee	75,400	1,470
Texas	488,800	2,390
Utah	15,700	746
Vermont	6,300	1,236
Virginia	57,000	873
Washington	104,700	1,870
West Virginia	10,100	692
Wisconsin	65,600	1,462
Wyoming	5,900	1,323

- California—263,531
- Ohio—243,710
- Florida—220,769
- Pennsylvania—183,868
- Michigan—175,965
- New Jersey—136,137

—Not known.
[a]The January 1 population excludes 12,919 offenders and the December 31 population excludes 9,375 offenders under community supervision who were on both probation and parole.
[b]Rates were computed using the estimated number of U.S. residents age 15 or older in each jurisdiction on January 1, 2016.
Note: Counts are rounded to the nearest hundred. Detail may not sum to total due to rounding. Due to nonresponse or incomplete data, the community supervision population for some jurisdictions on December 31, 2015, does not equal the population on January 1, 2015, plus entries, minus exits.

SOURCE: Adapted from Danielle Kaeble and Thomas P. Bonczar, "Appendix Table 1. Adults under Community Supervision, 2015," in *Probation and Parole in the United States, 2015*, U.S. Department of Justice, Bureau of Justice Statistics, December 2016, https://www.bjs.gov/content/pub/pdf/ppus15.pdf (accessed January 22, 2017)

FIGURE 9.2

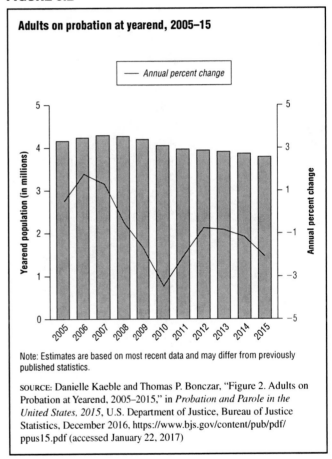

Adults on probation at yearend, 2005–15

— Annual percent change

Note: Estimates are based on most recent data and may differ from previously published statistics.

SOURCE: Danielle Kaeble and Thomas P. Bonczar, "Figure 2. Adults on Probation at Yearend, 2005–2015," in *Probation and Parole in the United States, 2015*, U.S. Department of Justice, Bureau of Justice Statistics, December 2016, https://www.bjs.gov/content/pub/pdf/ppus15.pdf (accessed January 22, 2017)

- Illinois—122,125
- Indiana—113,076

According to Kaeble and Bonczar in *Probation and Parole in the United States, 2015*, the number of adult probationers under state jurisdiction declined by 87,718 people, or 2.3%, between 2014 and 2015. The District of Columbia (down 12.9%), Georgia (down 10.2%), and California (down 7.8%) had the largest percentage

TABLE 9.4

Adults on probation, by jurisdiction, yearend 2015

Jurisdiction	Probation population, December 31, 2015	Number on probation per 100,000 U.S. adult residents, December 31, 2015[a]
U.S. total	3,789,785	1,522
Federal	18,368	7
State	3,771,417	1,514
Alabama	56,700	1,505
Alaska	NK	NK
Arizona	76,005	1,449
Arkansas	28,900	1,267
California	263,531	873
Colorado	78,883	1,860
Connecticut	42,346	1,494
Delaware	15,646	2,098
District of Columbia	5,536	990
Florida	220,769	1,353
Georgia	432,235	5,570
Hawaii	20,912	1,859
Idaho	32,898	2,675
Illinois	122,125	1,232
Indiana	113,076	2,236
Iowa	29,875	1,243
Kansas	16,588	754
Kentucky	54,049	1,579
Louisiana	40,764	1,143
Maine	6,708	624
Maryland	76,505	1,637
Massachusetts	64,934	1,195
Michigan	175,965	2,276
Minnesota	98,258	2,328
Mississippi	36,333	1,601
Missouri	44,876	953
Montana	8,610	1,063
Nebraska	12,626	882
Nevada	13,724	612
New Hampshire	3,861	361
New Jersey	136,137	1,949
New Mexico	15,048	946
New York	100,996	646
North Carolina	85,634	1,098
North Dakota	6,303	1,069
Ohio	243,710	2,706
Oklahoma	31,281	1,055
Oregon	NK	NK
Pennsylvania	183,868	1,814
Rhode Island	23,920	2,822
South Carolina	33,843	883
South Dakota	7,118	1,096
Tennessee	62,325	1,215
Texas	378,937	1,853
Utah	12,181	579
Vermont	5,170	1,021
Virginia	55,472	849
Washington	93,535	1,670
West Virginia	7,008	478
Wisconsin[b]	46,144	1,028
Wyoming	5,113	1,142

declines. The states with the largest percentage increases were Nevada (up 14.1%), North Dakota (up 11.6%), and Oklahoma (up 9.5%). Overall, there were 1,514 adults on state probation at yearend 2015 for every 100,000 U.S. adult residents. (See Table 9.4.)

Kaeble and Bonczar indicate that the adult probationer population under federal jurisdiction decreased by 3.6% between 2014 and 2015. Overall, there were seven adults on federal probation at yearend 2015 for every 100,000 adult residents of the United States. (See Table 9.4.)

TABLE 9.4

Adults on probation, by jurisdiction, yearend 2015 [CONTINUED]

NK = not known
[a]Rates were computed using the estimated U.S. adult resident population in each jurisdiction on January 1, 2016.
[b]The only exits reported were deaths.
Note: Due to nonresponse or incomplete data, the probation population for some jurisdictions on December 31, 2015, does not equal the population on January 1, 2015, plus entries, minus exits. Counts may not be actual as reporting agencies may provide estimates on some or all detailed data.

SOURCE: Adapted from Danielle Kaeble and Thomas P. Bonczar, "Appendix Table 2. Adults on Probation, 2015," in *Probation and Parole in the United States, 2015*, U.S. Department of Justice, Bureau of Justice Statistics, December 2016, https://www.bjs.gov/content/pub/pdf/ppus15.pdf (accessed January 22, 2017)

Probation Exits

Table 9.5 provides a breakdown of the nearly 1.9 million probationers who exited supervision by type of exit in 2015. Of those who left the system, 1 million (53%) did so because they had completed their probation terms successfully; that is, they either completed their full-term sentence or received an early discharge. The next largest group (233,325 or 12%) left probation because they were incarcerated. This includes probationers who were incarcerated because they violated the terms of their probation (95,541 probationers), as well as those who were incarcerated for another offense (65,209), were incarcerated for treatment (3,302), or for other or unknown circumstances (69,273). Another 40,585 or 2% absconded (escaped from supervision and had not yet been captured). The remaining probationers who left the system did so for a variety of reasons, including what are called "unsatisfactory" reasons. Unsatisfactory conclusions include those who did not successfully complete all the terms of their supervision, such as those whose sentences expired before completion and those who failed to fulfill a financial requirement such as restitution.

Demographics of Probationers

Table 9.6 provides a breakdown of the adult probation population in 2005, 2014, and 2015 for which gender, race, ethnicity, type of probation and supervision, and type and seriousness of offense were identified. (Note that these statistics do not include probationers whose status for a given characteristic was not known.) The following conclusions are drawn from the data:

- Overall, 75% of the probationers in 2015 were male, and 25% were female. This breakdown was very similar to that in 2005.

- At yearend 2015 more than half (55%) of adult probationers were non-Hispanic white, 30% were non-Hispanic African American, and 13% were Hispanic. Other races made up 2% of the total. This racial and ethnic breakdown was virtually unchanged from 2005.

TABLE 9.5

Probationers who exited supervision, by type of exit, 2015

			Incarcerated										
Jurisdiction	Total reported	Completion	With new sentence	Under current sentence	To receive treatment	Other/ unknown	Absconder	Discharged to warrant or detainer	Other unsatisfactory[a]	Death	Other[b]	Unknown or not reported
U.S. total	1,887,556	1,004,174	65,209	95,541	3,302	69,273	40,586	14,454	213,338	11,267	87,590	282,822
Federal	9,253	7,816	0	720	0	0	126	0	96	117	0	378
State	1,878,303	996,358	65,209	94,821	3,302	69,273	40,460	14,454	213,242	11,150	87,590	282,444

[a]Includes probationers discharged from supervision who failed to meet all conditions of supervision, including some with only financial conditions remaining. Also includes individuals who received jail sentence after a presentence investigation referral, had their probation sentence revoked but were not incarcerated, or who were discharged due to judicial or administrative release, new charges, diversion, mental health court, absconding, warrants, expirations of sentence, or transfer of supervision back from an interstate compact.
[b]Includes 16,025 probationers who transferred to another jurisdiction and 71,565 probationers who exited supervision for other reasons. Other reasons include probationers who had died or were deported or transferred to the jurisdiction of Immigration and Customs Enforcement or to another jurisdiction or state. Some probationers included in this count had their sentence dismissed, vacated, quashed, overturned, sealed/expunged, or were pardoned. Others were discharged through court order; deferrals; closed interest; administrative release; transfer to another program or to parole; revocation; early termination; expiration of sentence; violation of probation/new charges; incarceration; warrant; or sentencing to other sanctions.
Note: Based on reported data only.

SOURCE: Adapted from Danielle Kaeble and Thomas P. Bonczar, "Appendix Table 3. Adults Exiting Probation, by Type of Exit, 2015," in *Probation and Parole in the United States, 2015*, U.S. Department of Justice, Bureau of Justice Statistics, December 2016, https://www.bjs.gov/content/pub/pdf/ppus15.pdf (accessed January 22, 2017)

- Nearly eight out of 10 (76%) probationers were under active supervision at yearend 2015. Much smaller percentages were classified as absconders (7%), under warrant status (5%), or inactive (4%). Overall, the percentage of probationers with active status increased by four percentage points between 2005 and 2015.

- More than half (57%) of the probationers at yearend 2015 had been convicted of a felony, and 41% had been convicted of a misdemeanor. Another 2% had been convicted of other infractions, such as traffic offenses or tax crimes. The ratio of felony offenses to misdemeanor offenses in 2015 had changed since 2005, when 50% of probationers had been convicted of a felony and 49% had been convicted of a misdemeanor.

- As of yearend 2015, the two largest contingents of probationers had been convicted of property offenses (28%) or drug law violations (25%) as their most serious crime. Another 20% were on probation for a violent crime, and 13% were on probation for driving while intoxicated or driving under the influence.

PAROLE

Trends in Parole

There are two main types of parole. Discretionary parole is typically administered by parole boards. Their members examine prisoners' criminal histories and prison records and decide whether to release prisoners from incarceration. Since the mid-1990s several states have abolished discretionary parole in favor of mandatory parole. Mandatory parole is legislatively imposed at the state level and, with some exceptions, takes away parole boards' discretion. Mandatory parole provisions ensure that sentences for the same crime require incarceration for the same length of time. The prisoner can shorten his or her sentence only by good behavior—but time off for good behavior is also prohibited in some states. In some jurisdictions parole can only begin after prisoners have served 100% of their minimum incarceration time. Jeremy Travis and Sarah Lawrence of the Urban Institute report in *Beyond the Prison Gates: The State of Parole in America* (November 2002, http://www.urban.org/research/publication/beyond-prison-gates) that the share of discretionary prison releases decreased from 65% in 1976 to 24% in 1999.

The states have different prison release methods. Some states have cut back on parole supervision by releasing more prisoners directly to the community. Other states have aggressively enforced the conditions of parole, leading to the identification of more parole violations. States handle different types of offenses differently. Some allow victims or prosecutors to participate in release decisions, whereas others do not. Some states still rely heavily on parole boards to make release decisions, whereas others no longer use parole boards and have mandatory release policies for all their prisoners. Furthermore, parolees in some jurisdictions are required to wear electronic bracelets so that officials can monitor their movement.

For example, in 1983 Florida enacted sentencing guidelines that effectively eliminated the option of parole for most crimes that were committed on or after October 1, 1983. According to the Florida Parole Commission (2017, https://www.fcor.state.fl.us/release-types.shtml), the only exceptions to the parole ban are inmates who committed a capital felony murder between October 1, 1983, and May 25, 1994, and all inmates convicted of other capital felonies between October 1, 1983, and October 1, 1995.

TABLE 9.6

Characteristics of adults on probation, 2005, 2014, and 2015

Characteristic	2005	2014	2015
Sex	100%	100%	100%
Male	73	75	75
Female	23	25	25
Race/Hispanic origin[a]	100%	100%	100%
White	55	54	55
Black/African American	30	30	30
Hispanic/Latino	13	13	13
American Indian/Alaska Native	1	1	1
Asian/Native Hawaiian/other Pacific Islander	1	1	1
Two or more races	b	b	b
Status of supervision	100%	100%	100%
Active	72	73	76
Residential/other treatment program	1	1	1
Financial conditions remaining	c	1	2
Inactive	9	5	4
Absconder	10	8	7
Supervised out of jurisdiction	2	6	2
Warrant status	6	2	5
Other	b	4	4
Tyep of offense	100%	100%	100%
Felony	50	56	57
Misdemeanor	49	42	41
Other infractions	1	2	2
Most serious offense	100%	100%	100%
Violent	18%	19%	20%
Domestic violence	6	4	4
Sex offense	3	3	4
Other violent offense	10	12	13
Property	23%	28%	28%
Drug	25%	25%	25%
Public order	19%	16%	15%
DWI/DUI	14	14	13
Other traffic offense	5	2	2
Other	14%	11%	12%

[a]Excludes persons of Hispanic or Latino origin, unless specified.
[b]Less than 0.05%.
[c]Not available.
Note: Detail may not sum to total due to rounding. Estimates are based on most recent data and may differ from previously published statistics. Characteristics are based on probationers with a known type of status.

SOURCE: Danielle Kaeble and Thomas P. Bonczar, "Table 4. Characteristics of Adults on Probation, 2005, 2014, and 2015," in *Probation and Parole in the United States, 2015*, U.S. Department of Justice, Bureau of Justice Statistics, December 2016, https://www.bjs.gov/content/pub/pdf/ppus15.pdf (accessed January 22, 2017)

Parole Population

In 2005 there were 784,400 parolees. (See Table 9.1 and Figure 9.3.) The number fluctuated over subsequent years but has generally grown. There were 870,500 parolees at yearend 2015.

Geographical Distribution of Parolees

As of yearend 2015, the parole rate was 350 people on parole per 100,000 adult U.S. residents. (See Table 9.2.) In other words, one out of 286 adult U.S. residents was on parole. Table 9.7 provides a jurisdictional breakdown for the parolees. The vast majority (756,055 or 87%) of them were under state jurisdiction. The other 114,471 parolees (13%) were under federal jurisdiction.

FIGURE 9.3

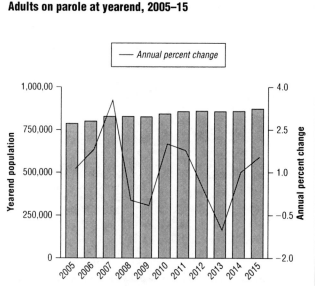

Adults on parole at yearend, 2005–15

Note: Estimates are based on most recent data and may differ from previously published statistics.

SOURCE: Danielle Kaeble and Thomas P. Bonczar, "Figure 3. Adults on Parole at Yearend, 2005–2015," in *Probation and Parole in the United States, 2015*, U.S. Department of Justice, Bureau of Justice Statistics, December 2016, https://www.bjs.gov/content/pub/pdf/ppus15.pdf (accessed January 22, 2017)

The 10 states with the highest parolee populations at yearend 2015 were:

- Pennsylvania—112,351
- Texas—111,892
- California—86,053
- New York—44,562
- Louisiana—31,187
- Illinois—29,146
- Georgia—24,130
- Arkansas—23,093
- Wisconsin—19,453
- Ohio—18,284

According to Kaeble and Bonczar in *Probation and Parole in the United States, 2015*, the number of adult parolees under state jurisdiction increased by 12,668 people, or 1.5%, between 2014 and 2015. The states with the largest increases were New Mexico (up 28.1%), North Carolina (up 17.1%), and Wyoming (up 15.7%). Delaware (down 37.1%), Oklahoma (down 17.3%), and Mississippi (down 14.8%) had the largest percentage declines. Overall, there were 350 adults on state parole at yearend 2015 for every 100,000 adult residents of the United States. (See Table 9.7.)

Kaeble and Bonczar indicate that the adult parolee population under federal jurisdiction increased by 4.7%

TABLE 9.7

Adults on parole by jurisdiction, yearend 2015

Jurisdiction	Parole population, December 31, 2015	Number on parole per 100,000 U.S. adult residents, December 31, 2015[a]
U.S. total	**870,526**	**350**
Federal	114,471	46
State	756,055	304
Alabama	8,138	216
Alaska	NK	NK
Arizona	7,379	141
Arkansas	23,093	1,012
California[b]	86,053	285
Colorado	10,269	242
Connecticut	2,939	104
Delaware	425	57
District of Columbia	4,594	822
Florida	4,611	28
Georgia	24,130	311
Hawaii	1,540	137
Idaho	4,875	396
Illinois	29,146	294
Indiana	9,434	187
Iowa	5,918	246
Kansas	4,331	197
Kentucky	16,563	484
Louisiana	31,187	874
Maine	21	2
Maryland	10,887	233
Massachusetts	1,978	36
Michigan	17,909	232
Minnesota	6,808	161
Mississippi	8,424	371
Missouri	17,694	376
Montana	1,092	135
Nebraska	1,043	73
Nevada	5,507	246
New Hampshire	2,451	229
New Jersey	15,180	217
New Mexico	2,888	182
New York	44,562	285
North Carolina	11,744	151
North Dakota	644	109
Ohio	18,284	203
Oklahoma	2,116	71
Oregon	NK	NK
Pennsylvania	112,351	1,109
Rhode Island	433	51
South Carolina	5,021	131
South Dakota	2,652	408
Tennessee	13,093	255
Texas	111,892	547
Utah	3,506	167
Vermont	1,090	215
Virginia	1,576	24
Washington	11,198	200
West Virginia	3,123	213
Wisconsin[c]	19,453	434
Wyoming	812	181

between 2014 and 2015. Overall, there were 46 adults on federal parole at yearend 2015 for every 100,000 adult U.S. residents. (See Table 9.7.)

Parole Entries and Exits

Kaeble and Bonczar estimate that federal and state governments had 475,200 entries to their parole systems in 2015. The type of entry was identified for 402,081 of these new parolees. They included 194,791 entries (48%) under discretionary parole and 97,589 entries (24%)

TABLE 9.7

Adults on parole by jurisdiction, yearend 2015 [CONTINUED]

NK = not known
[a]Rates were computed using the estimated U.S. adult resident population in each jurisdiction on January 1, 2016.
[b]Includes Post-Release Community Supervision and Mandatory Supervision parolees: 46,575 on January 1, 2015; and 29,614 entries, 31,502 exits, and 44,687 on December 31, 2015.
[c]The only exits reported were deaths.
Note: Due to nonresponse or incomplete data, the parole population for some jurisdictions on December 31, 2015, does not equal the population on January 1, 2015, plus entries, minus exits. Counts may not be actual as reporting agencies may provide estimates on some or all detailed data.

SOURCE: Adapted from Danielle Kaeble and Thomas P. Bonczar, "Appendix Table 4. Adults on Parole, 2015," in *Probation and Parole in the United States, 2015*, U.S. Department of Justice, Bureau of Justice Statistics, December 2016, https://www.bjs.gov/content/pub/pdf/ppus15.pdf (accessed January 22, 2017)

under mandatory parole. In addition, 90,151 (22%) of the new parolees went into a term of supervised release in the community, including people who received a parole term as part of their original sentence. Another 12,876 (3%) of the new parolees in 2015 were reinstatement entries, meaning that they reentered parole after being incarcerated for a parole violation. The remaining new parolees were added to parole rolls for other reasons, for example, as part of release to a drug treatment program, or for reasons that were not reported.

In 2015 Kaeble and Bonczar estimate that 463,700 parolees exited their parole systems. The type of exit was identified for 388,789 of the exiters. As shown in Table 9.8, 239,440 of them (62% of those for whom the type of exit was known) completed their obligation, meaning that they completed their full-term sentence or received an early discharge. Another 105,493 parolees (27%) were returned to incarceration—65,649 (17%) whose parole was revoked, 29,003 (7%) who committed a new offense and received a new sentence, and 10,841 (3%) who were incarcerated for other or unknown reasons. An estimated 2% of parolees (9,351) in 2015 absconded. Another 5,574 (1%) of parolees officially left the parole system, but under "unsatisfactory" conditions. For example, some still had financial obligations that they had not met. The remaining parolees who exited the system in 2015 included those who transferred to another state, died, or left for other or unknown reasons.

Characteristics of Parolees

A breakdown of adult parolees by gender, race, ethnicity, type of supervision, sentence length, and type of offense is provided in Table 9.9 for 2005, 2014, and 2015. (Note that these statistics do not include parolees whose status for a given characteristic was not known.)

The vast majority of the parolees in 2015 were men (87%), and 13% were women. As shown in Table 9.9, the ratio of males to females was nearly unchanged from 2005.

TABLE 9.8

Parolees who exited supervision, by type of exit, 2015

Jurisdiction	Total reported	Completion	Returned to incarceration				Absconder	Other unsatisfactory[a]	Death	Other[b]	Unknown or not reported
			With new sentence	With revocation	To receive treatment	Other/ unknown					
U.S. total	**388,789**	**239,440**	**29,003**	**65,649**	**2,594**	**10,841**	**9,351**	**5,574**	**5,876**	**13,894**	**6,567**
Federal	46,315	28,387	1	9,605	0	0	1,946	264	702	0	5,410
State	342,474	211,053	29,002	56,044	2,594	10,841	7,405	5,310	5,174	13,894	1,157

[a]Includes individuals who were discharged because of release to special sentence, violations, deportations, incarceration, and revocations. Includes some early terminations and expirations of sentence.

[b]Includes 1,909 parolees who were transferred to another state and 11,985 parolees who exited for other reasons. Other reasons include parolees who were deported, had their sentence overturned by the court through an appeal, were transferred to another state or jurisdiction, were discharged to probation supervision or federal custody, or received a pardon. Also includes individuals with an administrative discharge or who became inactive, or were discharged due to a pending waiver, reversal, detainer, or warrant.

SOURCE: Danielle Kaeble and Thomas P. Bonczar, "Appendix Table 6. Adults Exiting Parole, by Type of Exit, 2015," in *Probation and Parole in the United States, 2015*, U.S. Department of Justice, Bureau of Justice Statistics, December 2016, https://www.bjs.gov/content/pub/pdf/ppus15.pdf (accessed January 22, 2017)

TABLE 9.9

Characteristics of adults on parole, 2005, 2014, and 2015

Characteristic	2005	2014	2015
Sex	**100%**	**100%**	**100%**
Male	88	88	87
Female	12	12	13
Race/Hispanic origin[a]	**100%**	**100%**	**100%**
White	41	43	44
Black/African American	40	39	38
Hispanic/Latino	18	16	16
American Indian/Alaska Native	1	1	1
Asian/Native Hawaiian/other Pacific Islander	1	1	1
Two or more races	0	c	c
Status of supervision	**100%**	**100%**	**100%**
Active	83	84	83
Inactive	4	5	5
Absconder	7	6	6
Supervised out of state	4	4	4
Financial conditions remaining	e	0	0
Other	2	2	3
Maximum sentence to incarceration	**100%**	**100%**	**100%**
Less than 1 year	3	6	6
1 year or more	97	94	94
Most serious offense	**100%**	**100%**	**100%**
Violent	26%	31%	32%
Sex offense	e	7	8
Other violent	e	24	24
Property	24%	22%	21%
Drug	37%	31%	31%
Weapon	e	4%	4%
Other[b]	13%	12%	13%

[a]Excludes persons of Hispanic or Latino origin, unless specified.
[b]Includes public order offenses.
[c]Less than 0.05%.
[d]Not available.
Note: Detail may not sum to total due to rounding. Estimates are based on most recent data and may differ from previously published statistics. Characteristics based on paroless with known type of status.

SOURCE: Danielle Kaeble and Thomas P. Bonczar, "Table 6. Characteristics of Adults on Parole, 2005, 2014, and 2015," in *Probation and Parole in the United States, 2015*, U.S. Department of Justice, Bureau of Justice Statistics, December 2016, https://www.bjs.gov/content/pub/pdf/ppus15.pdf (accessed January 22, 2017)

At yearend 2015 the parolee population included 44% non-Hispanic whites and 38% non-Hispanic African Americans. (See Table 9.9.) Sixteen percent of the parolees were Hispanic. These values had changed slightly from 2005 when 41% of parolees were non-Hispanic white, 40% were non-Hispanic African American, and 18% were Hispanic.

A large percentage (83%) of adult parolees were under active supervision in 2015. (See Table 9.9.) In 2015, 6% of the parole population had absconded, which was similar to 7% in 2005.

Sentence data shown in Table 9.9 indicate that 94% of the parolees in 2015 had served a sentence of at least one year, and 6% had served less than a year.

As of yearend 2015, slightly less than one-third (31%) of parolees had been convicted of drug offenses as their most serious crime. (See Table 9.9.) Drug offenses were the largest single crime category. Nearly a third (32%) had served time for violent offenses, whereas 21% had served time for property offenses. Much smaller percentages had been convicted of other crimes (13%) and weapon offenses (4%).

IMPROVING PAROLE AND PROBATION OUTCOMES

One of the chief concerns associated with the community supervision population is recidivism. The U.S. Department of Justice's National Institute of Justice (June 17, 2014, https://www.nij.gov/topics/corrections/recidivism/Pages/welcome.aspx) defines recidivism as "a person's relapse into criminal behavior, often after the person receives sanctions or undergoes intervention for a previous crime." Recidivism is a serious problem. For example, the National Institute of Justice notes that a study begun in 2005 tracked 404,638 inmates after they were released from state prisons. More than half (56.7%) of the former inmates were rearrested within a year of their release; more than three-quarters (76.6%) were rearrested within five years of their release.

Various government and private programs are devoted to reducing the nation's recidivism rates. Many of these programs focus on enhancing the process of reentry into society when inmates are released from prison. The Department of Justice, in collaboration with the Council of State Governments, operates the National Reentry Resource Center (https://csgjusticecenter.org/jc/category/reentry/nrrc), which is a clearinghouse for education, training, and technical assistance for government agencies and private organizations working on reentry projects. The federal government annually provides millions of dollars in grant money to state, tribal, and local government and nonprofit organizations to reduce recidivism. The Council of State Governments' Justice Center (https://csgjusticecenter.org/reentry/national-criminal-justice-initiatives-map/) maintains a map that identifies nearly 1,900 grant recipients between 2006 and 2016. For example, in 2016 the Southwest Washington Workforce Development Council received a $500,000 grant through the U.S. Department of Labor's Linking to Employment Activities Pre-release initiative "to prepare inmates for jobs before release and to continue to assist them as they return home."

REFORMING THE PROBATION AND PAROLE SYSTEMS

Chapter 6 discusses penalty reforms that have been implemented during the 21st century to reduce taxpayer spending on incarceration and relieve overcrowding in prisons. The federal government has encouraged the reform movement through programs such as the Justice Reinvestment Initiative (JRI), which helps state criminal justice systems generate cost savings that can be invested in public safety programs.

Many JRI reforms involve the probation and parole systems. In *Reforming Sentencing and Corrections Policy: The Experience of Justice Reinvestment Initiative States* (December 2016, http://www.urban.org/sites/default/files/publication/86691/reforming_sentencing_and_corrections_policy_final_0.pdf), the Urban Institute indicates that as of 2016, two dozen states had enacted community supervision reforms through the JRI—Alabama, Alaska, Arkansas, Delaware, Georgia, Hawaii, Idaho, Kansas, Kentucky, Louisiana, Maryland, Mississippi, Missouri, Nebraska, New Hampshire, North Carolina, Ohio, Oklahoma, Oregon, Pennsylvania, South Carolina, South Dakota, Utah, and West Virginia.

Some jurisdictions have chosen to revise their punishments for violations of certain technical requirements of probation and parole. Example technical requirements include mandatory interviews, appointments, or drug tests. Historically, the penalty for failing to meet such technical requirements has been incarceration, typically for many months. Reform-minded jurisdictions are taking new approaches designed to reduce their incarcerated populations and corrections expenses, and also help parolees and probationers. For example, Erik Eckholm indicates in "North Carolina Cuts Prison Time for Probation Violators, and Costs" (NYTimes.com, September 11, 2014) that North Carolina implemented a "quick dip" penalty that sends some of the violators to jail for only a few days. This reduces incarceration costs and can prevent the violators from losing their job. Quick dips are an example of so-called intermediate, graduated, or proportional sanctions for parole and probation violations. In *Reforming Sentencing and Corrections Policy: The Experience of Justice Reinvestment Initiative States*, the Urban Institute indicates that Alaska implemented a graduated sanction system in which the first technical violation triggers a three-day prison stay, a second violation carries a five-day prison stay, and a third violation incurs a 10-day prison stay.

CHAPTER 10
JUVENILE CRIME

WHO IS A JUVENILE?

Juvenile courts date to the late 19th century, when Cook County, Illinois, established the first juvenile court under the Juvenile Court Act of 1899. The underlying concept was that if parents failed to provide children with proper care and supervision, then the state had the right to intervene benevolently. Other states followed Illinois, and by 1925 juvenile courts were in operation in most states. Juvenile courts favored a rehabilitative philosophy rather than a punitive philosophy and evolved less formal approaches than those in place in adult courts.

In modern law, juvenile offenses fall into two main categories: delinquency offenses and status offenses. Delinquency offenses are acts that are illegal regardless of the age of the perpetrator. Status offenses are acts that are illegal only for minors, such as truancy (failure to attend school), running away, or curfew violations. Each state defines by legislation the oldest age at which a youth falls under jurisdiction of its juvenile court. As of April 2017, that age was 17 in 43 states and the District of Columbia. The upper age was set at 16 in five states (Georgia, Michigan, Missouri, Texas, and Wisconsin) and at 15 in two states (New York and North Carolina).

New York and North Carolina use an upper age of 15. This means that youths aged 16 and 17 years fall under the jurisdiction of adult courts in these two states. However, New York provides for a "youthful offender" sentence that can be given to certain youths who are tried in adult courts. A "youthful offender" finding results in a shorter sentence than would have been imposed otherwise and no criminal record for the offender.

Many states place certain young offenders in the jurisdiction of the criminal (adult) court rather than the juvenile court based on the youth's age, offense, or previous court history.

JUVENILE ARREST STATISTICS

The report *Crime in the United States, 2015* (September 2016, https://ucr.fbi.gov/crime-in-the-u.s/2015/crime-in-the-u.s.-2015) includes Uniform Crime Reporting (UCR) statistics on crimes reported to law enforcement, arrests, and crimes cleared by arrest or exceptional means through 2015. Crimes cleared by exceptional means are those for which there can be no arrest, such as a murder-suicide, when the perpetrator is known to be deceased. In this report the Federal Bureau of Investigation (FBI) provides a partial breakdown of arrest statistics by age (i.e., the age of the arrested offender). Because the upper age classification for juveniles differs between states, the FBI does not categorize arrested individuals as adults or juveniles. For ease of terminology, however, offenders under the age of 18 years will be referred to as juveniles in this chapter.

Juvenile Arrests in 2015

As shown in Table 10.1, 709,333 people under the age of 18 years were arrested in 2015 based on UCR data from 12,706 law enforcement agencies around the country. The 10 most common offenses for arrestees in this age group were:

- Larceny-theft—120,967 arrests
- Assaults other than aggravated assaults—100,980 arrests
- Drug abuse violations—76,172 arrests
- Disorderly conduct—55,102 arrests
- Curfew and loitering law violations—33,908 arrests
- Liquor laws—33,155 arrests
- Vandalism—32,145 arrests
- Burglary—27,473 arrests
- Aggravated assault—21,993 arrests
- Weapons offenses—14,779

TABLE 10.1

Arrests of persons under 18 years of age, by age and offense, 2015

Offense charged	Ages under 18	Under 10	10–12	13–14	15	16	17
Total	709,333	5,144	42,858	149,121	134,078	171,964	206,168
Total percent distribution[a]	8.5	0.1	0.5	1.8	1.6	2.1	2.5
Murder and nonnegligent manslaughter	605	0	5	47	90	175	288
Rape[b]	2,745	24	306	768	511	529	607
Robbery	14,176	15	328	2,409	3,035	3,873	4,516
Aggravated assault	21,993	211	1,826	5,097	4,154	4,995	5,710
Burglary	27,473	225	1,656	6,291	5,730	6,617	6,954
Larceny-theft	120,967	537	6,989	25,484	22,932	30,178	34,847
Motor vehicle theft	11,169	23	265	2,129	2,633	3,089	3,030
Arson	2,083	109	484	652	360	275	203
Violent crime[c]	39,519	250	2,465	8,321	7,790	9,572	11,121
Violent crime percent distribution[a]	10.2	0.1	0.6	2.1	2.0	2.5	2.9
Property crime[c]	161,692	894	9,394	34,556	31,655	40,159	45,034
Property crime percent distribution[a]	14.3	0.1	0.8	3.0	2.8	3.5	4.0
Other assaults	100,980	1,162	10,204	27,036	19,507	21,747	21,324
Forgery and counterfeiting	791	7	16	75	82	181	430
Fraud	3,474	9	101	560	606	867	1,331
Embezzlement	450	0	5	22	18	131	274
Stolen property; buying, receiving, possessing	7,990	22	255	1,485	1,672	2,137	2,419
Vandalism	32,145	556	3,212	8,672	5,972	6,765	6,968
Weapons; carrying, possessing, etc.	14,779	163	1,182	3,265	2,553	3,428	4,188
Prostitution and commercialized vice	442	0	10	41	71	116	204
Sex offenses (except rape and prostitution)	6,699	110	822	2,248	1,200	1,174	1,145
Drug abuse violations	76,172	79	1,596	10,428	11,997	19,935	32,137
Gambling	357	1	10	34	66	114	132
Offenses against the family and children	2,628	134	186	670	500	517	621
Driving under the influence	5,064	20	4	96	223	1,150	3,571
Liquor laws	33,155	15	274	3,200	5,033	9,220	15,413
Drunkenness	4,243	20	42	476	650	996	2,059
Disorderly conduct	55,102	518	5,211	15,461	11,511	11,541	10,860
Vagrancy	825	5	40	167	194	209	210
All other offenses (except traffic)	128,770	918	5,600	24,880	25,156	32,840	39,376
Suspicion	148	5	12	34	29	37	31
Curfew and loitering law violations	33,908	256	2,217	7,394	7,593	9,128	7,320

[a]Because of rounding, the percentages may not add to 100.0.

[b]The rape figures in this table are aggregate totals of the data submitted based on both the legacy and revised Uniform Crime Reporting definitions.

[c]Violent crimes are offenses of murder and nonnegligent manslaughter, rape, robbery, and aggravated assault. Property crimes are offenses of burglary, larceny-theft, motor vehicle theft, and arson.

SOURCE: Adapted from "Table 38. Arrests by Age, 2015," in *Crime in the United States, 2015*, U.S. Department of Justice, Federal Bureau of Investigation, September 26, 2016, https://ucr.fbi.gov/crime-in-the-u.s/2015/crime-in-the-u.s.-2015/tables/table-38 (accessed January 21, 2017)

Overall, the arrests of people under the age of 18 years in 2015 totaled 39,519 for violent crimes and 161,692 for property crimes. (See Table 10.1.) The FBI includes four offenses in its definition of violent crimes: murder and nonnegligent manslaughter, rape, robbery, and aggravated assault. All these offenses involve the use or threat of violence by the perpetrator. Property crimes include burglary, larceny-theft, motor vehicle theft, and arson. The FBI counts only the most serious charge for which a single offender is arrested. Violent crimes are considered more serious than property crimes. Thus, a person arrested for rape and burglary would be counted only once in Table 10.1 (for the rape offense).

In 2015 people under the age of 18 years accounted for 10.2% of total arrests for violent crimes and 14.3% of total arrests for property crimes. (See Table 10.1.)

JUVENILE ARRESTS BY AGE AND SEX. According to the FBI, in *Crime in the United States, 2015*, 501,480 (71%) of total juvenile arrestees (709,333) in 2015 were male. More than half (54%) of the male arrests were of youths aged 17 years (149,673) or 16 years (121,649). Youths aged 15 years accounted for 92,982 of the male total, and those aged 13 to 14 years made up 101,928 of the male total. Younger male juveniles had much smaller numbers of arrests.

Female juvenile arrestees numbered 207,853 in 2015. Females accounted for 29% of the 709,333 total juvenile arrests that year. Just over half (51%) of the female arrests were of youths aged 17 years (56,495) or 16 years (50,315). Youths aged 15 years accounted for 41,096 of the female total, and those aged 13 to 14 years made up 47,193 of the female total. Younger female juveniles had much smaller numbers of arrests.

JUVENILE ARRESTS BY RACE. Table 10.2 provides a racial breakdown of 702,957 juvenile arrestees in 2015. Whites accounted for 442,364 (62.9%) of the total. There

TABLE 10.2

Arrests of persons under 18 years of age, by race and offense, 2015

Offense charged	Arrests under 18 — Race						Percent distribution[a]					
	Total	White	Black or African American	American Indian or Alaska Native	Asian	Native Hawaiian or other Pacific Islander	Total	White	Black or African American	American Indian or Alaska Native	Asian	Native Hawaiian or other Pacific Islander
Total	702,957	442,364	238,542	11,999	7,392	2,660	100.0	62.9	33.9	1.7	1.1	0.4
Murder and nonnegligent manslaughter	601	234	361	5	1	0	100.0	38.9	60.1	0.8	0.2	0.0
Rape[b]	2,715	1,802	835	42	26	10	100.0	66.4	30.8	1.5	1.0	0.4
Robbery	14,142	4,190	9,702	60	100	90	100.0	29.6	68.6	0.4	0.7	0.6
Aggravated assault	21,865	12,180	9,061	333	222	69	100.0	55.7	41.4	1.5	1.0	0.3
Burglary	27,344	15,287	11,373	344	262	78	100.0	55.9	41.6	1.3	1.0	0.3
Larceny-theft	119,712	72,434	43,232	1,751	1,815	480	100.0	60.5	36.1	1.5	1.5	0.4
Motor vehicle theft	11,111	5,535	5,296	176	71	33	100.0	49.8	47.7	1.6	0.6	0.3
Arson	2,067	1,517	469	58	17	6	100.0	73.4	22.7	2.8	0.8	0.3
Violent crime[c]	39,323	18,406	19,959	440	349	169	100.0	46.8	50.8	1.1	0.9	0.4
Property crime[c]	160,234	94,773	60,370	2,329	2,165	597	100.0	59.1	37.7	1.5	1.4	0.4
Other assaults	100,264	58,646	39,133	1,332	772	381	100.0	58.5	39.0	1.3	0.8	0.4
Forgery and counterfeiting	786	481	291	6	6	2	100.0	61.2	37.0	0.8	0.8	0.3
Fraud	3,425	1,730	1,583	60	47	5	100.0	50.5	46.2	1.8	1.4	0.1
Embezzlement	443	256	175	5	6	1	100.0	57.8	39.5	1.1	1.4	0.2
Stolen property; buying, receiving, possessing	7,941	3,442	4,322	72	88	17	100.0	43.3	54.4	0.9	1.1	0.2
Vandalism	31,840	22,359	8,562	508	308	103	100.0	70.2	26.9	1.6	1.0	0.3
Weapons; carrying, possessing, etc.	14,687	8,308	5,994	135	215	35	100.0	56.6	40.8	0.9	1.5	0.2
Prostitution and commercialized vice	442	162	267	2	6	5	100.0	36.7	60.4	0.5	1.4	1.1
Sex offenses (except rape and prostitution)	6,632	4,739	1,697	73	83	40	100.0	71.5	25.6	1.1	1.3	0.6
Drug abuse violations	75,461	56,617	16,419	1,347	836	242	100.0	75.0	21.8	1.8	1.1	0.3
Gambling	355	77	267	6	5	0	100.0	21.7	75.2	1.7	1.4	0.0
Offenses against the family and children	2,597	1,656	784	135	22	0	100.0	63.8	30.2	5.2	0.8	0.0
Driving under the influence	4,993	4,430	295	177	73	18	100.0	88.7	5.9	3.5	1.5	0.4
Liquor laws	32,663	28,684	2,184	1,326	386	83	100.0	87.8	6.7	4.1	1.2	0.3
Drunkenness	4,209	3,495	386	271	47	10	100.0	83.0	9.2	6.4	1.1	0.2
Disorderly conduct	54,686	30,061	23,100	1,058	367	100	100.0	55.0	42.2	1.9	0.7	0.2
Vagrancy	820	472	313	26	9	0	100.0	57.6	38.2	3.2	1.1	0.0
All other offenses (except traffic)	127,312	85,689	37,354	2,284	1,250	735	100.0	67.3	29.3	1.8	1.0	0.6
Suspicion	144	99	34	11	0	0	100.0	68.8	23.6	7.6	0.0	0.0
Curfew and loitering law violations	33,700	17,782	15,053	396	352	117	100.0	52.8	44.7	1.2	1.0	0.3

[a]Because of rounding, the percentages may not add to 100.0.

[b]The rape figures in this table are aggregate totals of the data submitted based on both the legacy and revised Uniform Crime Reporting definitions.

[c]Violent crimes are offenses of murder and nonnegligent manslaughter, rape, robbery, and aggravated assault. Property crimes are offenses of burglary, larceny-theft, motor vehicle theft, and arson.

SOURCE: Adapted from "Table 43B. Arrests by Race and Ethnicity, 2015," in *Crime in the United States, 2015,* U.S. Department of Justice, Federal Bureau of Investigation, September 26, 2016, https://ucr.fbi.gov/crime-in-the-u.s/2015/crime-in-the-u.s.-2015/tables/table-43 (accessed January 23, 2017)

were 238,542 African American youths arrested, making up 33.9% of the total. The number of arrests for Native Americans or Alaskan Natives (11,999, or 1.7%), Asian Americans (7,392, or 1.1%), and Hawaiians or other Pacific Islanders (2,660, or 0.4%) were much lower. Whites made up the majority of juvenile arrestees for most offenses, particularly driving under the influence (88.7%), liquor laws (87.8%), drunkenness (83%), drug offenses (75%), and arson (73.4%). African Americans accounted for the majority of juvenile arrests for five offenses, particularly gambling (75.2%), robbery (68.6%), prostitution and commercialized vice (60.4%), and murder (60.1%).

In 2015, 50.8% of juveniles arrested for violent crimes were African American and 46.8% were white. (See Table 10.2.) By contrast, the breakdown of arrests for property crimes was 59.1% white and 37.7% African American.

Juvenile Arrest Trends between 2006 and 2015

In *Crime in the United States, 2015*, the FBI uses age data from 9,581 law enforcement agencies to compile 10-year trends in arrests of people under the age of 18 years. As shown in Table 10.3, overall juvenile arrests declined by 54.8%, from nearly 1.3 million in 2006 to 578,538 in 2015. Juvenile arrests decreased for all offenses, particularly vagrancy (down 82.8%), forgery and counterfeiting (down 72.4%), and liquor laws (down 68.8%). The number of juvenile arrests for all violent crimes decreased by 47.1% between 2006 and 2015. Juvenile arrests for property crimes declined by 47.8% over the same period.

Murder: Juvenile Offenders and Victims

Table 2.2 in Chapter 2 provides demographic information about the 15,326 people arrested for murder in

TABLE 10.3

Ten-year arrest trends for persons under 18 years of age, by offense, 2006–15

[9,581 agencies; 2015 estimated population 199,921,204; 2006 estimated population 186,371,331]

Offense charged	Number of persons arrested Under 18 years of age		
	2006	2015	Percent change
Total[a]	1,280,195	578,538	−54.8
Murder and nonnegligent manslaughter	642	421	−34.4
Rape[b]	2,111	2,239	—
Robbery	18,201	9,753	−46.4
Aggravated assault	35,984	17,717	−50.8
Burglary	51,953	22,056	−57.5
Larceny-theft	180,623	101,898	−43.6
Motor vehicle theft	17,651	7,547	−57.2
Arson	5,223	1,811	−65.3
Violent crime[c]	56,938	30,130	−47.1
Property crime[c]	255,450	133,312	−47.8
Other assaults	152,396	83,689	−45.1
Forgery and counterfeiting	2,288	632	−72.4
Fraud	5,090	2,776	−45.5
Embezzlement	949	391	−58.8
Stolen property; buying, receiving, possessing	14,032	6,600	−53.0
Vandalism	76,202	27,793	−63.5
Weapons; carrying, possessing, etc.	27,707	11,614	−58.1
Prostitution and commercialized vice	733	269	−63.3
Sex offenses (except rape and prostitution)	9,948	5,643	−43.3
Drug abuse violations	113,132	63,035	−44.3
Gambling	292	133	−54.5
Offenses against the family and children	3,348	2,208	−34.1
Driving under the influence	12,947	4,294	−66.8
Liquor laws	94,729	29,530	−68.8
Drunkenness	11,093	3,528	−68.2
Disorderly conduct	129,948	45,659	−64.9
Vagrancy	3,475	598	−82.8
All other offenses (except traffic)	248,829	107,250	−56.9
Suspicion	203	127	−37.4
Curfew and loitering law violations	60,669	19,454	−67.9

[a]Does not include suspicion.
[b]The 2006 rape figures are based on the legacy definition, and the 2015 rape figures are aggregate totals based on both the legacy and revised Uniform Crime Reporting definitions. For this reason, a percent change is not provided.
[c]Violent crimes are offenses of murder and nonnegligent manslaughter, rape, robbery, and aggravated assault. Property crimes are offenses of burglary, larceny-theft, motor vehicle theft, and arson.

SOURCE: Adapted from "Table 32. Ten-Year Arrest Trends: Totals, 2006–2015," in *Crime in the United States, 2015*, U.S. Department of Justice, Federal Bureau of Investigation, September 26, 2016, https://ucr.fbi.gov/crime-in-the-u.s/2015/crime-in-the-u.s.-2015/tables/table-32 (accessed January 21, 2017)

2015. There were 667 people under 18 years of age arrested for murder that year, accounting for 4.4% of arrests for murder. The vast majority of these juvenile arrestees (616, or 92.4%) were male. Concerning the racial breakdown, 412 (61.8%) were African American and 236 (35.4%) were white.

The FBI also provides demographic data about murder victims in *Crime in the United States, 2015*. (See Table 2.3 in Chapter 2.) Of the 13,455 total victims in 2015, 1,093 (8.1%) were under the age of 18 years. More than two-thirds (761, or 69.6%) of the juvenile victims were male. The racial makeup of the juvenile victims was 49.8% (544) African American and 46.1% (504) white.

Howard N. Snyder and Melissa Sickmund of the National Center for Juvenile Justice report in *Juvenile Offenders and Victims: 2006 National Report* (March 2006, https://www.ojjdp.gov/ojstatbb/nr2006/downloads/NR2006.pdf) that murders involving a juvenile offender increased dramatically from the early 1980s to the early 1990s. In 1984 just over 1,000 murders involved a juvenile offender. By 1994 that number had climbed to more than 3,500. Then, murders by juveniles underwent a steep decline.

SCHOOL CRIME

As is noted in Chapter 3, the U.S. Department of Education and the U.S. Department of Justice (DOJ) collaborate to compile and publish data about crimes in school environments. In *Indicators of School Crime and Safety: 2015* (May 2016, https://www.bjs.gov/content/pub/pdf/iscs15.pdf), the agencies note that nearly two-thirds (65%) of public schools recorded one or more violent incidents during the 2013–14 school year, equating to about 757,000 crimes.

School Shootings

Despite the relative safety of schools, several school shootings by juveniles have received national media attention:

- April 20, 1999: 12 students and a teacher were fatally shot at Columbine High School in Littleton, Colorado, by students Eric Harris (1981–1999) and Dylan Klebold (1982–1999), who eventually killed themselves after an hour-long rampage.

- February 29, 2000: a six-year-old student was killed at Theo J. Buell Elementary School near Flint, Michigan, by Dedrick Owens (1993–), a fellow six-year-old student who brought a handgun to school.

- March 5, 2001: two students were killed and 13 wounded at Santee High School in Santana, California, when Charles A. Williams (1986–), a 15-year-old student at the school, opened fire from a school bathroom.

- April 14, 2003: one 15-year-old student was killed and three were wounded at John McDonogh High School in New Orleans, Louisiana, by gunfire from four teenagers who attended a different school.

- March 21, 2005: 16-year-old Jeff Weise (1988–2005) killed his grandfather and a companion. He then went to Red Lake High School in Red Lake, Minnesota, and killed five students, a security guard, a teacher, and finally himself.

- February 27, 2012: 17-year-old Thomas "T. J." Lane (1994–) used a firearm to kill three students in the cafeteria at Chardon High School in Chardon, Ohio. Lane attended another school and gave no reason for the killings after his capture.

- October 24, 2014: 15-year-old Jaylen Fryberg used a firearm to kill four students and wound another one in the cafeteria at Marysville High School near Seattle, Washington. He then committed suicide.

- September 28, 2016: 14-year-old Jesse Osborne allegedly opened fire at Townville Elementary School in Townville, South Carolina, wounding three students and a teacher. One of the students, a six-year old, later died from his injuries. Osborne is also accused of killing his own father prior to the school shooting.

YOUTH GANGS

Although gangs have been a part of American life since the early 18th century, modern street gangs pose a greater threat to public safety and order than ever before. Many gangs originated as social clubs. In the early 20th century most were small groups who engaged in delinquent acts or minor crimes, such as fighting with other gangs. By the late 20th century, however, they were frequently involved in violence, intimidation, and the illegal trafficking of drugs and weapons. An increasing number supported themselves by the sale of crack cocaine, heroin, and other illegal drugs, and had easy access to high-powered guns and rifles.

The National Gang Center is a DOJ-funded project that compiles information about gang activities. It also occasionally surveys law enforcement agencies about the prevalence of gangs in the United States. As of April 2017, the most recent survey results were published in 2014. In the fact sheet "Highlights of the 2012 National Youth Gang Survey" (December 2014, https://www.ojjdp.gov/pubs/248025.pdf), Arlen Egley Jr., James C. Howell, and Meena Harr summarize results from a 2012 survey of nearly 2,200 police and sheriff's departments around the country. At that time there were approximately 850,000 gang members and 30,700 gangs in the United States. It should be noted that exact statistics on national gang activity are difficult to compile because local law enforcement agencies may not be aware of gang connections in some cases or may not regularly record offenses as gang related. Egley, Howell, and Harr indicate that approximately 2,363 gang-related homicides occurred in 2012. As is shown in Table 2.4 in Chapter 2, the DOJ's Bureau of Justice Statistics (BJS) estimates that 604 murder victims died as a result of juvenile gang killings during 2015.

JUVENILE COURT CASES

Each state and the District of Columbia has its own juvenile justice system. Although no nationwide uniform procedure exists for processing juvenile cases, the cases do follow similar paths. An intake department first screens cases. The intake department can be the court itself, a state department of social services, or a prosecutor's office. The intake officer may decide that the case will be dismissed for lack of evidence, handled formally (petitioned), or resolved informally (non-petitioned). Formal processing can include placement outside the home, probation, a trial in juvenile court, or transfer to an adult court. Informal processing may consist of referral to a social services agency, a fine, some form of restitution, or informal probation. Both formal and informal processing can result in dismissal of the charges and release of the juvenile.

There are two broad types of cases within juvenile court: petitioned and non-petitioned. Petitioned cases are those in which a petition is filed requesting a hearing. Non-petitioned cases do not include such a petition and are handled more informally by the courts.

Juvenile courts may place youths in a detention facility during court processing. Detention may be needed to protect the community from the juvenile, to protect the juvenile, or both. In addition, detention is sometimes necessary to ensure a youth's appearance at scheduled hearings or evaluations.

All states allow certain juveniles to be tried in adult criminal court under some circumstances. These circumstances include the use of firearms or other weapons and a history of criminality. In some states juvenile court judges are allowed to determine whether individual suspects will be prosecuted in juvenile or adult criminal court; some states allow prosecutors to determine whether to file cases in juvenile or adult criminal court; and some states have laws that determine which court holds jurisdiction over cases, depending on the age of the suspect and the crime committed.

Although juvenile justice is governed by state laws, the federal government plays a role by setting standards for juvenile courts and providing funding to state agencies that deal with juvenile crime.

CHANGING APPROACHES TO JUVENILE DELINQUENCY

Before the 1950s the U.S. juvenile justice system was heavily focused on rehabilitation. This approach began to change as the public judged rehabilitation techniques to be ineffective. A growing number of juveniles were being institutionalized until they reached adulthood because the medical treatment they received did not seem to modify their behavior. Under the impetus of a number of U.S. Supreme Court decisions, juvenile courts became more formal to protect juveniles' rights when they were transferred to adult courts or if they were to be confined. During the 1970s the national policy became community-based management of juvenile delinquents.

Public perception changed again during the 1980s. Juvenile crime was growing, and the systems in place were perceived as being too lenient in dealing with delinquents.

This spurred a nationwide movement toward tougher treatment of juveniles. In *Juvenile Offenders and Victims: 1999 National Report* (September 1999, https://www.ncjrs.gov/html/ojjdp/nationalreport99/toc.html), Howard N. Snyder and Melissa Sickmund note that between 1992 and 1997 nearly all the states passed laws making their juvenile justice system more punitive (punishment oriented).

Laurence Steinberg argues in "Introducing the Issue" (*Future of Children*, vol. 18, no. 2, Fall 2008) that during the 1990s Americans experienced a "moral panic" about juvenile crime that fueled "get tough" on crime policies that treated many juvenile offenders as adults. However, Steinberg suggests that by the end of the first decade of the 21st century get-tough policies were softening "as politicians and the public come to regret the high economic costs and ineffectiveness of the punitive reforms and the harshness of the sanctions."

JUVENILE CRIMES: COURT STATISTICS

As noted earlier, juvenile offenses are either status offenses or delinquency offenses. Status offenses apply only to minors, not to adults. They include acts such as running away from home, truancy (failure to attend school), or violating curfew. Delinquency offenses include murder, rape and other sexual offenses, robbery, burglary, larceny-theft, and other criminal acts for which adults can also be charged.

The Office of Juvenile Justice and Delinquency Prevention (OJJDP) is a DOJ agency that compiles statistics on the nation's juvenile courts. As shown in Figure 10.1, the number of delinquency cases handled in U.S. juvenile courts increased from about 400,000 cases in 1960 to more than 1.8 million cases per year during the late 1990s. By 2013 the number had declined to nearly 1.1 million cases.

Table 10.4 provides detailed data about the nearly 1.1 million delinquency cases that were handled by juvenile courts in 2013. The number of person offense cases decreased by 34% between 2004 and 2013, property offenses declined by 42%, drug law violations decreased by 23%, and public order offenses fell by 38%.

Julie Furdella and Charles Puzzanchera of the OJJDP indicate in "Delinquency Cases in Juvenile Court, 2013" (October 2015, https://www.ojjdp.gov/pubs/248899.pdf) that male juveniles accounted for 764,800 cases, or 72% of the total delinquency caseload, in 2013, and female

FIGURE 10.1

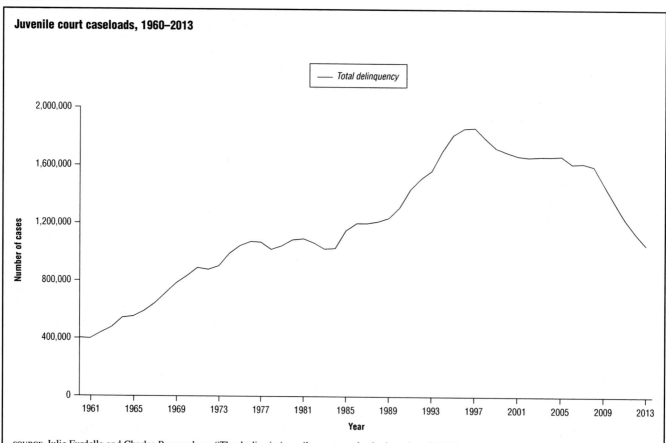

Juvenile court caseloads, 1960–2013

SOURCE: Julie Furdella and Charles Puzzanchera, "The decline in juvenile court caseloads since the mid-1990s is the most substantial decline since 1960," in *Delinquency Cases in Juvenile Court, 2013*, U.S. Department of Justice, Office of Justice Programs, Office of Juvenile Justice and Delinquency Prevention, October 2015, https://www.ojjdp.gov/pubs/248899.pdf (accessed January 23, 2017)

TABLE 10.4

Juvenile delinquency cases disposed, by most serious offense, 2013

Most serious offense	Number of cases	Percent change		
		10 year 2004–2013	5 year 2009–2013	1 year 2012–2013
Total delinquency	**1,058,500**	**−37%**	**−29%**	**−7%**
Person offenses	**278,300**	**−34**	**−24**	**−6**
Criminal homicide	900	−30	−33	−1
Forcible rape	7,500	−16	−5	−1
Robbery	22,000	2	−25	4
Aggravated assault	26,900	−42	−32	−7
Simple assault	186,400	−37	−25	−6
Other violent sex offenses	9,700	−18	−6	−3
Other person offenses	25,000	−28	−12	−11
Property offenses	**366,600**	**−42**	**−35**	**−10**
Burglary	65,300	−38	−32	−11
Larceny-theft	183,400	−38	−34	−10
Motor vehicle theft	11,600	−65	−38	0
Arson	5,000	−42	−29	−10
Vandalism	54,200	−46	−40	−13
Trespassing	29,900	−44	−38	−11
Stolen property offenses	10,200	−48	−34	−7
Other property offenses	7,100	−59	−38	−6
Drug law violations	**141,700**	**−23**	**−14**	**−4**
Public order offenses	**271,800**	**−38**	**−30**	**−7**
Obstruction of justice	132,000	−33	−28	−5
Disorderly conduct	74,500	−43	−32	−9
Weapons offenses	21,700	−44	−33	−7
Liquor law violations	9,000	−47	−47	−23
Nonviolent sex offenses	10,600	−25	−8	−2
Other public order offenses	24,000	−38	−28	−3

Notes: Data may not add to totals because of rounding. Percent change calculations are based on unrounded numbers.

SOURCE: Julie Furdella and Charles Puzzanchera, "Delinquency Cases Disposed by Most Serous Offense, 2013," in *Delinquency Cases in Juvenile Court, 2013*, U.S. Department of Justice, Office of Justice Programs, Office of Juvenile Justice and Delinquency Prevention, October 2015, https://www.ojjdp.gov/pubs/248899.pdf (accessed January 23, 2017).

TABLE 10.5

Breakdown of juvenile delinquency cases, by most serious offense and race, 2013

Most serious offense	Race profile of cases, 2013				
	Total	White	Black	American Indian	Asian
Total delinquency	**100%**	**62%**	**35%**	**2%**	**1%**
Person	100	55	42	1	1
Property	100	61	36	2	2
Drugs	100	76	21	2	1
Public order	100	62	36	1	1

Note: Detail may not add to totals because of rounding.

SOURCE: Julie Furdella and Charles Puzzanchera, "Race Profile of Cases, 2013," in *Delinquency Cases in Juvenile Court, 2013*, U.S. Department of Justice, Office of Justice Programs, Office of Juvenile Justice and Delinquency Prevention, October 2015, https://www.ojjdp.gov/pubs/248899.pdf (accessed January 23, 2017)

juveniles were involved in 293,700 (28%) of the cases. This breakdown was relatively unchanged from 2004. The racial and ethnic breakdown of juvenile delinquency cases in 2013 is shown in Table 10.5. Overall, whites (62%) accounted for the largest share of juvenile delinquents, followed by African Americans (35%), Native Americans (2%), and Asian Americans (1%). At that time whites accounted for 76% of the overall U.S juvenile population, and African Americans accounted for 16%. Thus, African American youths were highly overrepresented within the juvenile delinquent population. Table 10.5 also provides a racial breakdown of juvenile delinquents by offense type. In all offense categories, white offenders outnumbered African American offenders, but African American youth were overrepresented compared with their share of the overall population.

Figure 10.2 shows the outcome of the nearly 1.1 million delinquency cases in 2013. Just over half (55%) were petitioned, and 45% were not petitioned. In more than half (55%) of the petitioned cases the juvenile was adjudicated delinquent (found responsible by a judge for the alleged act). This is procedurally similar to a conviction in criminal court. In another 44% of the petitioned cases the juvenile was not adjudicated delinquent. Approximately 1% of the petitioned cases were waived to adult criminal court.

A majority (59%) of the juveniles whose cases were petitioned but were not adjudicated delinquent had their cases dismissed. (See Figure 10.2.) In the remainder the

FIGURE 10.2

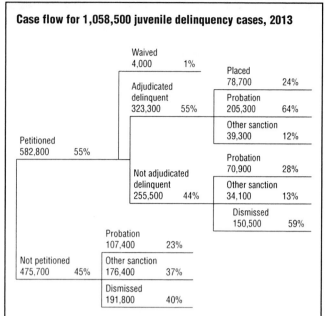

Case flow for 1,058,500 juvenile delinquency cases, 2013

Notes: Cases are categorized by their most severe or restrictive sanction. Detail may not add to totals because of rounding.

SOURCE: Julie Furdella and Charles Puzzanchera, "Case Flow for 1,058,500 Delinquency Cases in 2013," in *Delinquency Cases in Juvenile Court, 2013*, U.S. Department of Justice, Office of Justice Programs, Office of Juvenile Justice and Delinquency Prevention, October 2015, https://www.ojjdp.gov/pubs/248899.pdf (accessed January 23, 2017)

juveniles either received probation (28%) or some other sanction (13%). Probation was given in 64% of the petitioned cases where juveniles were adjudicated delinquent. Nearly one-fourth (24%) of the juveniles who were adjudicated delinquent went into residential placement, and 12% received some other sanction.

For 2013 there were 475,700 juvenile delinquency cases that were not petitioned. (See Figure 10.2.) Among these juveniles, 191,800 (40%) had their cases dismissed, 107,400 (23%) were put in probation, and 176,400 (37%) received other sanctions.

STATUS OFFENSE CASES

Status offenses are acts that are against the law only because the people who commit them are juveniles. In many communities social service agencies rather than juvenile courts are responsible for accused status offenders. Because of the differences in screening procedures, national estimates of informally handled status offense cases are not calculated. Therefore, the statistics presented in this chapter report only on status offense cases that are formally handled (petitioned) through the juvenile justice system.

According to Sarah Hockenberry and Charles Puzzanchera of the National Center for Juvenile Justice, in *Juvenile Court Statistics 2013* (July 2015, http://www.ncjj.org/pdf/jcsreports/jcs2013.pdf), the OJJDP

uses five major status offense categories: running away, truancy, liquor law violations, curfew violations, and ungovernability (also known as incorrigibility or being beyond parental control). The researchers report that 109,000 status offense cases were petitioned to juvenile courts in 2013. This number was down 13% from 1995. The following is a breakdown by offenses for 2013:

- Truancy—51% of cases

- Liquor law violations—15% of cases

- Ungovernability—9% of cases

- Curfew violations—9% of cases

- Running away—8% of cases

- Miscellaneous—8% of cases

Detention and Case Processing

The handling of status crimes has changed considerably since the mid-1980s. The Juvenile Justice and Delinquency Prevention Act of 1974 offered substantial federal funds to states that tried to reduce the detention of status offenders. The primary responsibility for status offenders was often transferred from the juvenile courts to child welfare agencies. As a result, the character of the juvenile courts' activities changed.

Before this change many juvenile detention centers held a substantial number of young people whose only offense was that their parents could no longer control them. By not routinely institutionalizing these adolescents, the courts demonstrated that children deserved the same rights as adults. A logical extension of this has been that juveniles accused of violent crimes are also now being treated legally as if they are adults.

Those involved in petitioned status offense cases are rarely held in confinement. Hockenberry and Puzzanchera indicate that only 8% of status offenders received out-of-home placement in 2013. This percentage is down from about 14% in 1995.

JUVENILES IN RESIDENTIAL PLACEMENT

Accused juveniles, delinquency offenders, and status offenders may be housed in residential placement facilities. These institutions may be under the administration of the state or be operated by private nonprofit or for-profit corporations or organizations and staffed by employees of the corporation or organization.

In *Juveniles in Residential Placement, 1997–2008* (February 2010, https://www.ncjrs.gov/pdffiles1/ojjdp/229379.pdf), Sickmund notes that juvenile residential placement facilities are also known as "detention centers, juvenile halls, shelters, reception and diagnostic centers, group homes, wilderness camps, ranches, farms, youth development centers, residential treatment centers, training or reform schools, and juvenile correctional institutions."

Every two years the OJJDP conducts a census of juvenile residential facilities around the country. As of April 2017, the most recent census was conducted in 2014. The results are presented by Hockenberry, Andrew Wachter, and Anthony Sladky in *Juvenile Residential Facility Census, 2014: Selected Findings* (September 2016, https://www.ojjdp.gov/pubs/250123.pdf). As shown in Table 10.6, there were 1,852 of these facilities in operation as of October 22, 2014. Just over half (1,008, or 54%) were public facilities, and 844 (or 46%) were private facilities. Overall, California (169) had the most facilities, followed by Pennsylvania (114) and New York (99). As of October 22, 2014, the nation's juvenile facilities held 50,821 youth. The largest numbers of youth in juvenile facilities were in California (7,019), Texas (4,324), and Pennsylvania (3,233).

TABLE 10.6

Juvenile offender facilities and youths, by state, as of October 22, 2014

State	Juvenile facilities			Justice-involved youth		
	Total	Public	Private	Total	Public	Private
U.S. total	1,852	1,008	844	50,821	36,110	14,711
Alabama	43	14	29	948	484	464
Alaska	17	8	9	199	159	40
Arizona	19	14	5	1,037	677	360
Arkansas	33	18	15	777	544	233
California	169	97	72	7,019	6,144	875
Colorado	35	15	20	1,107	851	256
Connecticut	5	—	—	213	—	—
Delaware	6	6	0	154	154	0
Dist. of Columbia	11	5	6	214	179	35
Florida	76	29	47	2,914	1,165	1,749
Georgia	29	25	4	1,390	1,281	109
Hawaii	4	—	—	55	—	—
Idaho	20	13	7	477	392	85
Illinois	31	26	5	1,704	1,585	119
Indiana	55	32	23	1,454	944	510
Iowa	53	10	43	977	280	697
Kansas	26	13	13	667	536	131
Kentucky	36	28	8	711	619	92
Louisiana	30	16	14	841	654	187
Maine	3	—	—	133	—	—
Maryland	29	15	14	685	471	214
Massachusetts	52	23	29	506	248	258
Michigan	58	30	28	1,868	980	888
Minnesota	50	18	32	930	545	385
Mississippi	14	14	0	195	195	0
Missouri	59	52	7	928	875	53
Montana	16	7	9	158	118	40
Nebraska	12	5	7	586	304	282
Nevada	20	12	8	597	518	79
New Hampshire	4	—	—	63	—	—
New Jersey	29	25	4	774	732	42
New Mexico	22	15	7	423	357	66
New York	99	22	77	1,524	585	939
North Carolina	27	21	6	463	394	69
North Dakota	10	4	6	115	90	25
Ohio	74	60	14	2,241	2,084	157
Oklahoma	30	18	12	528	393	135
Oregon	58	32	26	1,080	809	271
Pennsylvania	114	24	90	3,233	713	2,520
Rhode Island	7	2	5	188	127	61
South Carolina	19	8	11	670	394	276
South Dakota	16	7	9	313	169	144
Tennessee	26	18	8	691	502	189
Texas	90	69	21	4,324	3,691	633
Utah	30	17	13	579	371	208
Vermont	2	—	—	29	—	—
Virginia	45	—	—	1,484	—	—
Washington	36	31	5	958	908	50
West Virginia	41	10	31	637	261	376
Wisconsin	48	22	26	845	621	224
Wyoming	14	5	9	215	137	78

Notes: "State" is the state where the facility is located. Youth sent to out-of-state facilities are counted in the state where the facility is located, not the state where they committed their offense. Detail is not displayed in states with one or two private facilities to preserve the privacy of individual facilities.

SOURCE: Sarah Hockenberry, Andrew Wachter, and Anthony Sladky, "On October 22, 2014, 54% of juvenile facilities were publicly operated; they held 71% of justice-involved youth," in *Juvenile Residential Facility Census, 2014: Selected Findings,* U.S. Department of Justice, Office of Justice Programs, Office of Juvenile Justice and Delinquency Prevention, September 2016, https://www.ojjdp.gov/pubs/250123.pdf (accessed January 23, 2017)

The OJJDP also conducts the Census of Juveniles in Residential Placement, a one-day count of the juvenile offenders who are held nationwide. The data collected include juvenile offender demographics, such as gender, race, ethnicity, and most serious offense. As of April 2017, the most recent census of this type was conducted in 2013. The results are presented by Hockenberry in *Juveniles in Residential Placement, 2013* (May 2016, https://www.ojjdp.gov/pubs/249507.pdf). According to Hockenberry, 54,148 juvenile offenders were housed in public and private residential placement facilities around the country in 2013. (See Figure 10.3.) This was down considerably from 1997, when the number was 105,055. The gender split in 2013 was 86% male and 14% female. The racial and ethnic breakdown was as follows:

- African American—40% of the total
- White—32% of the total
- Hispanic—23% of the total
- Native American—2% of the total
- Asian American—1% of the total
- Other—2% of the total

Overall, 95% of the juveniles in residential placement were being held for delinquency including 33% for person offenses (homicide, sexual assault robbery,

FIGURE 10.3

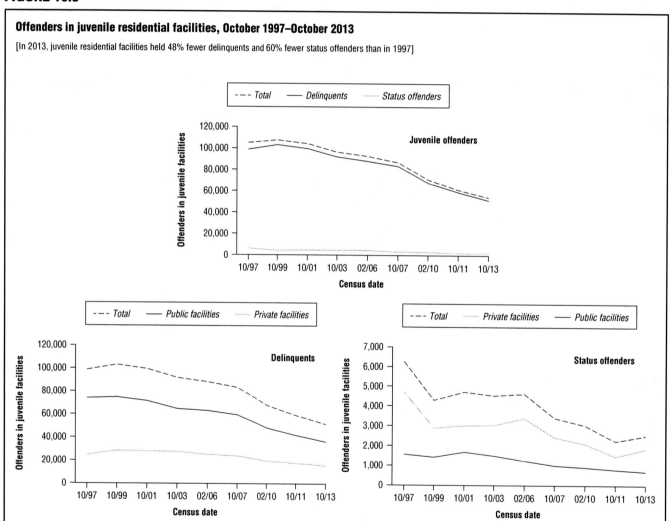

Offenders in juvenile residential facilities, October 1997–October 2013

[In 2013, juvenile residential facilities held 48% fewer delinquents and 60% fewer status offenders than in 1997]

Notes: The total number of juvenile offenders in residential placement facilities rose 2% from 1997 to 1999 and then decreased 50% from 1999 to 2013. The result was an overall decrease of 48% between 1997 and 2013.
The number of delinquents held in public facilities decreased 51% between 1997 and 2013, and the number held in private facilities decreased 38%.
Between 1997 and 1999, the number of status offenders held in juvenile residential facilities dropped sharply (31%). Between 1999 and 2006, the number of status offenders remained relatively unchanged, then decreased between 2006 and 2011 before increasing 13% in 2013. The result was an overall decrease of 60% between 1997 and 2013.
The number of status offenders held in public facilities peaked in 2001 and then decreased 59% by 2013. The number of status offenders held in private facilities increased 18% between the 1999 low and 2006, decreased 57% between 2006 and 2011, and then increased 26% in 2013.

SOURCE: Sarah Hockenberry, "In 2013, juvenile residential facilities held 48% fewer delinquents and 60% fewer status offenders than in 1997," in *Juveniles in Residential Placement, 2013*, U.S. Department of Justice, Office of Justice Programs, Office of Juvenile Justice and Delinquency Prevention, May 2016, https://www.ojjdp.gov/pubs/249507.pdf (accessed January 23, 2017)

aggravated assault, or simple assault). Other major categories within the delinquency category included technical violations (17%) and burglary (10%). At the time of the census in 2013, 5% of all juveniles in residential placement were being held for status offenses.

Sexual Victimization of Juvenile Inmates

As is noted in Chapter 8, the Prison Rape Elimination Act of 2003 requires the BJS to collect data on the incidence and prevalence of sexual assault within correctional facilities. Allen J. Beck et al. report on sexual victimization involving juvenile inmates in *Sexual Victimization in Juvenile Facilities Reported by Youth, 2012* (June 2013, https://www.bjs.gov/content/pub/pdf/svjfry12.pdf). The researchers note that the BJS conducted its second National Survey of Youth in Custody between February and September 2012. The survey covered 326 public and private juvenile facilities that held adjudicated juveniles for at least 90 days. National-level estimates of sexual victimization for all adjudicated juvenile inmates were developed based on the results of the survey. Overall, Beck et al. estimate that 9.5% of adjudicated juvenile inmates experienced sexual victimization by another youth or staff member within the previous 12 months or since their time of admission if admission occurred less than 12 months prior to the time of the survey. Any type of sexual activity involving staff was considered sexual victimization, and 7.7% of adjudicated juvenile inmates were estimated to have experienced such victimization.

JUVENILE DELINQUENCY PREVENTION

The criminal justice system also focuses resources on preventing juveniles from becoming delinquents in the first place and on helping delinquents to reform. For example, as of April 2017 the OJJDP (https://www.ojjdp.gov/) noted that it had programs devoted to preventing gang involvement, girls' delinquency, and underage drinking. In "Comprehensive Anti-gang Initiative" (2017, https://www.ojjdp.gov/programs/antigang/), the agency describes its role in developing, funding, and evaluating "community-based anti-gang programs that coordinate prevention, intervention, enforcement, and reentry strategies."

In accordance with the Juvenile Justice and Delinquency Prevention Act of 1974, as amended, the OJJDP provides funding for state programs that are devoted to delinquency prevention. These programs typically provide a variety of services to youths, such as mentoring, substance abuse education and treatment, and educational support. For example, the New York State Division of Criminal Justice Services (2017, http://www.criminaljustice.ny.gov/ofpa/juvdelprevfactsheet.htm) operates the state's Delinquency Prevention Grant Program with funding provided by the federal government. The program provides grants to local communities to fund delinquency prevention activities. The agency notes that "prevention

strategies succeed when they are positive in orientation and comprehensive in scope. Successful community strategies create opportunities for healthy physical, social, and mental development of juveniles. Programs consider the influence of family, peer group, school, and the community on a child's development." The North Carolina Department of Public Safety's Division of Juvenile Justice is also active in juvenile delinquency prevention and notes in "About Juvenile Justice" (2017, https://www.ncdps.gov/juvenile-justice) that it is "committed to the reduction and prevention of juvenile delinquency by effectively intervening, educating and treating youth in order to strengthen families and increase public safety."

Besides government resources, many private organizations devote themselves to juvenile delinquency prevention. For example, the Prevent Delinquency Project (2017, http://preventdelinquency.org) was founded in New York in 2003 and advocates "proactive parenting techniques." The organization's founder, Carl A. Bartol, is a former prosecutor and focuses on educating parents about the nature of juvenile crime and the measures they can take to help prevent their children from becoming juvenile delinquents.

JUVENILES IN THE ADULT JUSTICE SYSTEM

As shown in Figure 10.4, fewer than 6,000 juvenile cases were waived to adult criminal court in 2011. In "Delinquency Cases Waived to Criminal Court, 2011" (December 2014, https://www.ojjdp.gov/pubs/248410.pdf), Hockenberry and Puzzanchera of the OJJDP indicate that this number was down substantially from the 1990s, when more than 12,000 waivers were issued per year. They explain that this decline was driven by an overall drop in the juvenile violent crime rate as well as by more widespread use of nonjudicial transfer laws. These laws allow prosecutors to directly file charges against juveniles in adult criminal court, bypassing the juvenile justice system entirely.

According to E. Ann Carson and Elizabeth Anderson of the BJS, in *Prisoners in 2015* (September 30, 2014, https://www.bjs.gov/content/pub/pdf/p15.pdf), state prisons held 993 youths in 2015. Florida (131) had the most youth inmates in adult prisons, followed by New York (89) and Michigan (88). The federal prison system held no inmates aged 17 years or younger at yearend 2015. Carson notes in *Prisoners in 2013* (September 30, 2014, https://www.bjs.gov/content/pub/pdf/p13.pdf) that adult state and federal prisons held nearly 4,000 inmates aged 17 years or younger in 2000.

Until 2005 convicted criminals could be executed for crimes they committed as juveniles. Victor L. Streib of Ohio Northern University reports in *The Juvenile Death Penalty Today: Death Sentences and Executions for Juvenile Crimes, January 1, 1973–February 28, 2005*

FIGURE 10.4

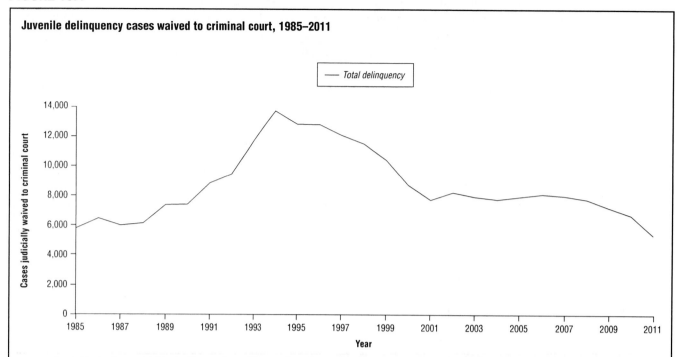

Juvenile delinquency cases waived to criminal court, 1985–2011

SOURCE: Sarah Hockenberry and Charles Puzzanchera, "The number of cases judicially waived to criminal court in 2011 was 61% less than in 1994, the peak year," in *Delinquency Cases Waived to Criminal Court, 2011*, U.S. Department of Justice, Office of Justice Programs, Office of Juvenile Justice and Delinquency Prevention, December 2014, https://www.ojjdp.gov/pubs/248410.pdf (accessed January 23, 2017)

(October 7, 2005, https://deathpenaltyinfo.org/documents/StreibJuvDP2005.pdf) that between 1973 and 2005, 22 offenders were executed for crimes they committed when they were younger than 18 years old.

In 2005 the U.S. Supreme Court, in *Roper v. Simmons* (543 U.S. 551), set aside the death sentence of Christopher Simmons, concluding that the "Eighth and Fourteenth Amendments forbid imposition of the death penalty on offenders who were under the age of 18 when their crimes were committed." Snyder and Sickmund note in *Juvenile Offenders and Victims: 2006 National Report* that few states applied death penalty provisions to juveniles at the time of the *Roper* decision, even though 20 states allowed juveniles to be sentenced to death under the law.

After the 2005 *Roper* ruling, the most severe punishment for juveniles convicted of committing serious crimes was a sentence of life in prison without the possibility of parole. This sentence, however, was also challenged on constitutional grounds. In May 2010 the Supreme Court ruled in *Graham v. Florida* (560 U.S. 48) that juveniles convicted of crimes in which nobody is killed cannot be sentenced to life in prison without the possibility of parole. The case involved Terrance Graham, a Florida juvenile who was convicted of several armed robberies when he was 16 and 17 years old. In 2005 Graham was sentenced to life in prison without the possibility of parole. Jeff Kunerth notes in "Life without Parole Becomes 25 Years for Terrance Graham, Subject of U.S. Supreme Court Case" (OrlandoSentinel.com, February 24, 2012) that in February 2012 Graham's sentence was converted to a 25-year term.

In June 2012 the U.S. Supreme Court ruled in *Miller v. Alabama* (No. 10-9646) and *Jackson v. Hobbs* (No. 10-9647) that juveniles cannot be subject to mandatory life sentences without the possibility of parole, even if they have committed murder. The subjects of both cases were 14 years old at the time their crimes were committed. Evan Miller was convicted of arson and murder for the 2003 death of a man in Alabama; Kuntrell Jackson of Arkansas was convicted for participating in a 1999 robbery in which an accomplice killed a store clerk. In giving the opinion of the court, Justice Elena Kagan (1960–) cited the precedents set in *Roper* and *Graham* and stated "mandatory life without parole for those under the age of 18 at the time of their crimes violates the Eighth Amendment's prohibition on 'cruel and unusual punishments.'"

IMPORTANT NAMES
AND ADDRESSES

American Bar Association
321 N. Clark St.
Chicago, IL 60654
(312) 988-5000
1-800-285-2221
URL: http://www.americanbar.org/aba.html

American Civil Liberties Union
125 Broad St., 18th Floor
New York, NY 10004
(212) 549-2500
URL: https://www.aclu.org/

American Correctional Association
206 N. Washington St., Ste. 200
Alexandria, VA 22314
(703) 224-0000
FAX: (703) 224-0179
URL: http://www.aca.org/

American Jail Association
1135 Professional Ct.
Hagerstown, MD 21740-5853
(301) 790-3930
FAX: (301) 790-2941
URL: http://www.americanjail.org/

Bureau of Alcohol, Tobacco, Firearms, and Explosives
99 New York Ave. NE
Washington, DC 20226
(202) 648-7080
URL: https://www.atf.gov/

Bureau of Engraving and Printing
U.S. Department of the Treasury
14th St. and C St. SW
Washington, DC 20228
(202) 874-4000
1-877-874-4114
E-mail: moneyfactory.info@bep.gov
URL: https://www.moneyfactory.gov/

Bureau of Justice Statistics
U.S. Department of Justice
810 Seventh St. NW
Washington, DC 20531
(202) 307-0765
E-mail: askbjs@usdoj.gov
URL: https://www.bjs.gov/

Congressional Research Service
Library of Congress
101 Independence Ave. SE
Washington, DC 20540
(202) 707-5000
URL: http://www.loc.gov/crsinfo/

Federal Bureau of Investigation
J. Edgar Hoover Bldg.
935 Pennsylvania Ave. NW
Washington, DC 20535-0001
(202) 324-3000
URL: https://www.fbi.gov/

Federal Bureau of Prisons
320 First St. NW
Washington, DC 20534
(202) 307-3198
URL: https://www.bop.gov/

Federal Trade Commission
600 Pennsylvania Ave. NW
Washington, DC 20580
(202) 326-2222
URL: https://www.ftc.gov/

National Center for Juvenile Justice
3700 S. Water St., Ste. 200
Pittsburgh, PA 15203
(412) 227-6950
FAX: (412) 227-6955
E-mail: ncjj@ncjfcj.org
URL: http://www.ncjj.org/

National Center for Victims of Crime
2000 M St. NW, Ste. 480
Washington, DC 20036
(202) 467-8700
FAX: (202) 467-8701
URL: http://www.victimsofcrime.org/

National Conference of State Legislatures
7700 E. First Place
Denver, CO 80230
(303) 364-7700
FAX: (303) 364-7800
URL: http://www.ncsl.org/

National Correctional Industries Association
800 N. Charles St., Ste. 550B
Baltimore, MD 21201
(410) 230-3972
FAX: (410) 230-3981
URL: http://www.nationalcia.org/

National Gang Center
Institute for Intergovernmental Research
PO Box 12729
Tallahassee, FL 32317
(850) 385-0600
1-800-446-0912
E-mail: information@nationalgang
center.gov
URL: https://www.nationalgangcenter.gov/

National Institute of Corrections
320 First St. NW
Washington, DC 20534
1-800-995-6423
URL: https://nicic.gov/

National Institute of Justice
810 Seventh St. NW
Washington, DC 20531
(202) 307-2942
URL: https://www.nij.gov/Pages/welcome
.aspx

National Organization for Victim Assistance
510 King St., Ste. 424
Alexandria, VA 22314
(703) 535-6682
1-800-879-6682 (victim assistance hotline)
FAX: (703) 535-5500
URL: http://www.trynova.org/

National White Collar Crime Center
10900 Nuckols Rd., Ste. 325
Glen Allen, VA 23060
(804) 273-6932
1-877-628-7674
FAX: (804) 273-1234
E-mail: onlinelearning@nw3c.org
URL: https://www.nw3c.org/

Office for Victims of Crime
U.S. Department of Justice
810 Seventh St. NW, Second Floor
Washington, DC 20531
(202) 307-5983
FAX: (202) 514-6383
URL: https://ojp.gov/ovc/

Office of Juvenile Justice and Delinquency Prevention
810 Seventh St. NW
Washington, DC 20531
(202) 307-5911
URL: https://www.ojjdp.gov/

Office of National Drug Control Policy
URL: https://www.whitehouse.gov/ondcp

Rape, Abuse, and Incest National Network
1220 L St. NW, Ste. 505
Washington, DC 20005
(202) 544-3064
1-800-656-4673
FAX: (202) 544-3556
URL: https://www.rainn.org/

Sentencing Project
1705 DeSales St. NW, Eighth Floor
Washington, DC 20036
(202) 628-0871
FAX: (202) 628-1091

E-mail: staff@sentencingproject.org
URL: http://www.sentencingproject.org/

Southern Poverty Law Center
400 Washington Ave.
Montgomery, AL 36104
(334) 956-8200
1-888-414-7752
URL: https://www.splcenter.org/

Substance Abuse and Mental Health Services Administration
5600 Fishers Ln.
Rockville, MD 20857
1-877-726-4727
URL: https://www.samhsa.gov/

Supreme Court of the United States
One First St. NE
Washington, DC 20543
(202) 479-3000
URL: https://www.supremecourt.gov/

UNICOR
Federal Prison Industries, Inc.
PO Box 13640
Lexington, KY 40583-3640
1-800-827-3168
FAX: (859) 254-9692
E-mail: UNICOR.CUSTOMER.SERVICE
@usdoj.gov
URL: https://www.unicor.gov/

Urban Institute
2100 M St. NW
Washington, DC 20037
(202) 833-7200
URL: http://www.urban.org/

U.S. Census Bureau
4600 Silver Hill Rd.
Washington, DC 20233

(301) 763-4636
1-800-923-8282
URL: https://www.census.gov/

U.S. Department of Justice
950 Pennsylvania Ave. NW
Washington, DC 20530-0001
(202) 514-2000
URL: https://www.justice.gov/

U.S. Drug Enforcement Administration
U.S. Department of Justice
8701 Morrissette Dr.
Springfield, VA 22152
(202) 307-1000
URL: https://www.dea.gov/index.shtml

U.S. Parole Commission
90 K St. NE, Third Floor
Washington, DC 20530
(202) 346-7000
E-mail: public.inquiries@usdoj.gov
URL: https://www.justice.gov/uspc

U.S. Securities and Exchange Commission
100 F St. NE
Washington, DC 20549
(202) 942-8088
E-mail: help@sec.gov
URL: https://www.sec.gov/

U.S. Sentencing Commission
Office of Public Affairs
One Columbus Circle NE, Ste. 2-500, South Lobby
Washington, DC 20002-8002
(202) 502-4500
E-mail: pubaffairs@ussc.gov
URL: http://www.ussc.gov/

RESOURCES

The various agencies of the U.S. Department of Justice (DOJ) are the major sources of crime and justice data in the United States. The Bureau of Justice Statistics (BJS) compiles statistics on virtually every area of crime and reports these data in a number of publications. The annual BJS National Crime Victimization Survey provides data for several studies, the most important of which is *Criminal Victimization*. The BJS also publishes data about the nation's corrections systems, including detailed counts and information about facilities and inmates, courts and sentencing, types of crime, the population of probationers and parolees, and justice system employment and expenditures.

The Federal Bureau of Investigation (FBI) collects crime data from state and local law enforcement agencies through its Uniform Crime Reporting Program. The FBI's annual *Crime in the United States* is the most important source of information on crime that is reported to law enforcement agencies. Major resources for white-collar crime information include the National White Collar Crime Center, the DOJ's Computer Crime and Intellectual Property Section, and the Federal Trade Commission's Consumer Sentinel Network and Identity Theft Clearinghouse.

The FBI's annual report *Hate Crime Statistics* provided valuable data about hate crimes, as did private organizations, such as the Southern Poverty Law Center.

The Office of Juvenile Justice and Delinquency Prevention within the DOJ publishes numerous helpful resources about juvenile crime and justice issues, particularly its annual series *Juvenile Arrests, Juvenile Court Statistics*, and *Juvenile Offenders and Victims*.

Other important government resources included the Office of National Drug Control Policy of the Executive Office of the President; the Substance Abuse and Mental Health Services Administration of the U.S. Department of Health and Human Services; the U.S. Drug Enforcement Administration; the Federal Interagency Forum on Child and Family Statistics; the U.S. Government Accountability Office; and the Congressional Research Service.

Key information was also acquired from polling results reported by Gallup, Inc., and the Pew Research Center.

INDEX